Jews: The Making of a Diaspora People

For Esther, my beautiful wife and best friend for over sixty years

Jews: The Making of a Diaspora People

Irving M. Zeitlin

For Betsy and
and Corey and
Their wonderful
daughter, Emma, with
great affection and
very best wishes —
Irv Zeitlin
Toronto, June 17, 2012

polity

First published in 2012 by Polity Press

Polity Press
65 Bridge Street
Cambridge CB2 1UR, UK

Polity Press
350 Main Street
Malden, MA 02148, USA

ISBN-13: 978-0-7456-6016-5
ISBN-13: 978-0-7456-6017-2(pb)

A catalogue record for this book is available from the British Library.

Typeset in 10.5 on 12pt Times
by Servis Filmsetting Ltd, Stockport, Cheshire
Printed and bound in Great Britain by MPG Books Group Limited, Bodmin, Cornwall

The publisher has used its best endeavours to ensure that the URLs for external websites referred to in this book are correct and active at the time of going to press. However, the publisher has no responsibility for the websites and can make no guarantee that a site will remain live or that the content is or will remain appropriate.

Every effort has been made to trace all copyright holders, but if any have been inadvertently overlooked the publisher will be pleased to include any necessary credits in any subsequent reprint or edition.

For further information on Polity, visit our website: www.politybooks.com

Contents

Acknowledgments   x
Preface   xi

1 "Diaspora": On the Genealogy of a Concept   1

The Relation of Theory to History and the Role of the Ideal
   Type   2
Global Diasporas by Robin Cohen   4
Diasporas by Stéphane Dufoix   9
Powers of Diaspora by Jonathan Boyarin and Daniel Boyarin   13
The Black Atlantic: Modernity and Double Consciousness by
   Paul Gilroy   18
Routes: Travel and Translation in the Late Twentieth Century
by James Clifford   26

**2 Varieties of Jewish Religious Experience (Resting, however, on
Unifying Jewish Religious Principles)**   29

Moshe Rosman's *Rethinking European Jewish History*   32
Cultures of the Jews   33
Syncretism in Jewish History   35
Polytheism and Monotheism   35
The Nature of Polytheism   36

3 Max Weber's Ancient Judaism   39

The Hebrew Prophets: The Setting   40
The Prophetic Ethic   45

4 The Babylonian Empire   50

The Revolt and the Destruction of the First Temple   53
The Emigration to Egypt   55

5   The Babylonian Exile and the Persian Supremacy (586–332 BCE)   57

The Diaspora in Babylon and Persia   61

6   Alexander the Great and the New Hegemony of the West   64

7   The World Diaspora   67

The Beginnings of the European Diaspora: Greece and Rome   70

8   The Diaspora in the First Century CE   72

Judaism's Proselytism   74

9   The Jews in the Roman Near East   78

10 The Jews Move to Poland   83

The Chmelnitzky Uprising of 1648–1649   86

11 Sabbatai Zevi   90

12 Gershom Scholem's Error   97

Dubnow on the Sabbatian Movement   100

13 The Rise of Hasidism and the Baal-Shem-Tob   104

Enter the Man, Israel, Who Became the Baal-Shem-Tob   105
The Fundamental Principles of the Besht's Teachings   107
The Growth of Tzaddikism   109
Hasidism, Rabbinism, and the Forerunners of the
   Enlightenment   112

14 The Jews of Spain   114

The Inquisition   117
The Jews, the Spanish, and the "*Conversos* Problem"   122
The Aftermath of the Pogroms   126
Jewish Mysticism: The Kabbalah in Spanish-Jewish Life   128

15 The Expulsion of the Jews from Spain   131

The Conquest of Granada   132

16   The Enlightenment and the Jews   136

The English Deists   138
Varieties of Enlightenment Views on Religion   141
Voltaire   143
Rousseau   146
Rousseau on Judaism and the Jews   148

17   The Germanies   152

The Emerging German National Mind   154
Luther   154
Luther's Attitude toward the Jews   158
Hegel   160
Hegel on Jews and Judaism   162

18   The Left Hegelians and the so-called "Jewish Question"   166

Bruno Bauer on the "Jewish Question"   168
Marx   172
Marx's Use of the Terms "Jew" and "Judaism"   174
Weber vs Sombart on the Spirit of Capitalism   176

19   From Religion to Race   179

Afro-American and Jewish Parallels   179
Arthur de Gobineau   181

20   From Gobineau and H. Stewart Chamberlain to Wagner   185

Nietzsche, the Jews, and Judaism   188
Nietzsche's Legacy   193

21   The Rise of Nazism   195

The Versailles Treaty   197
The Origins of the Nazi Party   199
After the Putsch   202

**22   The Early Nazi Regime and the Jews as Perceived by
       Non-Jewish Contemporaries**   206

23 World War I, the Collapse of the Old Regimes, and the Rise of Totalitarianism   212

More on Nazi Ideology, Internal Factions, and Foreign
  Policy Aims   214
The Turning Point: The Attack on Poland   216

24 Max Weber on Bureaucracy and its Relevance for an Analysis of the *Shoah* (Holocaust)   219
Bureaucracy   219
German Ideology and Bureaucracy   221
Weber's Serious Error   223

25 Charisma, Bureaucracy, and the "Final Solution"   226
Raul Hilberg's, *The Destruction of the European Jews*   226
The Administration of the Destructive Process   228
The Reich-Protektorat Area   230
The Creation of a Centralized Authority in Ghettoized Jewish
  Communities   230
The Polish Jews under the Nazis   232
The Jewish Councils (Judenräte)   234
Nazi Food Controls   237
Mobile Killing Operations   238
The Role of the Other Ethnic Groups   240
Definition of "Jew" Again, and Himmler   241
Ian Kershaw's Recent Re-examination of the Issues   243

26 Leon Poliakov's Complementary Analysis of the *Shoah* 246

Hitler's Euthanasia Program   247
Auschwitz   249
The "Death's Head" Formations (SS *Totenkopf*)   251
Back to the Question of a Distinctive German National
  Character   252
Significant Political Differences Between Eastern and Western
  Europe   254
The Role of the Christian Churches   255
Postscript   256

27 The Battle of the Warsaw Ghetto   258

A Reflection on Jewish Resistance   261

28 Zionism, Israel, and the Palestinians   263

Theodor Herzl   264
The Historical Jewish Presence in the Arab World   265
The Peace Conference of 1919   266
"The Unseen Question"   268
Arab Rebellion   273

Works Cited   276
Index   281

Acknowledgments

I owe many thanks to my wonderful daughter Ruth for enabling me to communicate frequently with my distinguished editor, John Thompson, by email. Without her assistance I would have had to employ the pre-industrial, handwritten-letter method on which I have relied since childhood.

I need, in addition, to thank the intellectually exciting scholar, Ato Quayson, for his gracious and generous response to my request for bibliographic suggestions concerning the concept of "diaspora." I have always found my conversations with him stimulating and illuminating.

Finally, I want to acknowledge the essential role my typist, Gloria Rowe, has played in transcribing, impeccably, my hardly legible handscript. She has typed all my booklength manuscripts for the past 35 years.

Preface

In Exodus 19:5 of the Hebrew Bible, we read: "Now therefore, if ye will hearken unto my voice indeed, and keep my covenant, then ye shall be mine own treasure from among all peoples; for all the earth is mine: and ye shall be unto me a kingdom of priests, and a holy nation." The Hebrew word *segula* does, in fact, imply "treasure."

The same Hebrew word appears in Deuteronomy 7:6: "For thou art a holy people unto the Lord thy God who hath chosen thee to be His own treasure, out of all peoples that are upon the face of the earth." In Deuteronomy 7:78, Moses explains why the Israelites were chosen:

> The Lord did not set His love upon you, nor choose you, because ye were more in number than any people – for ye were the fewest of all peoples – but because the Lord loved you, and because He would keep the oath which He swore unto your fathers, hath the Lord brought you out with a mighty hand, and redeemed you out of the house of bondage, from the hand of Pharaoh King of Egypt.

In the *King James Version*, Ex. 19:5 also reads: "if ye will obey my voice indeed, and keep my covenant, then ye shall be a peculiar treasure unto me above all peoples." In Deuteronomy 7:6, the parallel passage replaces "treasure" with "special." In the *Revised Standard Version*, the relevant passage in Ex. 19:5 reads: "if you will obey my voice and keep my covenant, you shall be my own possession among all peoples." Similarly, in Deut. 7:6 we read: "The Lord your God has chosen you to be a people for his own possession, out of all the peoples that are on the face of the earth."

Moses' explanation of God's choice is essential for an adequate understanding of the passage, for it illuminates the nature of the Deity. Why did he set his love upon the Israelites? As Moses stated, not because they were especially numerous. Nor because they were especially virtuous. Moses attributed no such quality to them. The reason for God's choice, then, is the conception of Him as an *ethical* deity who heard the cries of an oppressed people and decided to come to their aid. It was an act of grace, but a conditional one: If they will obey God's voice and keep his Covenant, then they will become a "peculiar treasure" to Him. The meaning of "peculiar" in this context is clear: all the nations of the world are God's, but Israelites or Jews are His in a *special manner*. All nations of the world are God's by reason of His power, *but the Jews are his by reason of their own consent and Covenant.*

The italicized passage is the animating principle and theological framework of the entire Hebrew Bible. The passage is also the key to the self-understanding of the Jewish people as they came under the influence of the Hebrew prophets of social justice. In tracing the process that led to exile, the central and most interesting question will be: How did this people survive despite the serious and recurrent challenges it faced? I was inspired to address this question by the work of Max Weber who has justifiably been described as the greatest social scientist of the twentieth century. Among his other contributions, it is his comparative studies of the world religions, East and West, which have earned him his reputation as a great scholar; and it is his *Ancient Judaism* in particular, which is, for our purposes, his most important work. For it is there that Weber fully grasps the characteristic uniqueness of the Jewish faith and the source of that uniqueness in the teachings of the Hebrew prophets of social justice. Indeed, the profound influence of the prophets will serve as the theoretical framework of the present study because I regard the prophetic legacy as the *sine qua non* of Jewish survival in the diaspora. However, before turning to Weber's profound analysis of the prophetic legacy, a full clarification of the concept of "diaspora" is advisable in light of the current application of the term to a wide range of ethnic groups.

1

"Diaspora": On the Genealogy of a Concept

With this book my primary aim is to provide a historical-sociological analysis of the process by which the Jews became a "diaspora people." I employ the concept of "diaspora" because I believe it effectively captures the characteristic uniqueness of the Jewish historical experience.

"Diaspora," as defined in the Oxford and other dictionaries, was originally applied *exclusively* to the early history of the Jews who, after the Babylonian exile, settled in scattered colonies outside Israel-Judea. By the fourth century BCE the diaspora population had increased to the point at which more Jews lived outside their ancestral homeland than inside.

It seems that one striking difference between Jews and most other ethnic groups is that, in the case of the latter, the *majority* remained in their lands of origin. The Jews appear to be exceptional not only in that regard but also because they constituted the most conspicuous ethnic-religious minority in the numerous societies in which they settled. This, as we shall see, was already true in antiquity; but it grew all the more striking and troublesome when the Jews became the most visible non-Christian hated and/or despised minority in Christendom. Hence, it appears to be a highly cogent proposition that the Jews may be regarded as the archetypal or prototypical diaspora people.

The cogency of this proposition carries with it no value or moral judgment. There is no intention here of attributing to the diasporic status of the Jews any special virtue that might be construed invidiously when compared with the status of other ethnic minorities. A group can be unique without implying invidiousness. Indeed, I believe that every ethnic group is unique. The role of concepts like "diaspora" impels me to return to Max Weber and to a key element of his historical-interpretive method.

The Relation of Theory to History and the Role of the Ideal Type

The "ideal type" or "pure type" is a concept that Weber regards as indispensable in any kind of analysis. He calls it a "Utopia," an intellectual construct arrived at by accentuating certain aspects of reality for heuristic purposes. Such constructs are analytical tools with which Weber himself approached the materials of world history in comparative analysis. Ideal types aid us to grasp the characteristic features of social and cultural phenomena, and their significant differences. How do we know that we have, in fact, constructed a good ideal-type conception of whatever it is we are interested in? The answer, for Weber, is that we never can know in advance of employing it and judging whether it actually enhances our understanding of a phenomenon. Weber's criterion for the assessment of the fruitfulness of a particular ideal type is pragmatic:

> there is only one criterion, namely, that of success in revealing concrete cultural phenomena in their interdependence, their causal conditions and their *significance*. The construction of ideal types recommends itself not as an end, but as a means.[1]

It is Weber's position that if we use such concepts, they ought to be well thought out and unambiguous. The greater the need for a clear and unambiguous delineation of a cultural phenomenon, the more imperative it is to construct the ideal type carefully. Weber did not, of course, invent the concept of an ideal-type construct. He is merely calling attention to the heuristic device historians, scholars, and social scientists have always employed, either deliberately or unconsciously. Ideal types are purely logical constructs, and have nothing to do with value judgments. As Weber remarked, "There are ideal types of brothels as well as of religions" (99). The goal of an effective ideal-type construct is to make clear and explicit *the unique individual character of a social phenomenon*.

In the pragmatic aspect of Weber's method, he converges intellectually with the great founders of the American pragmatic philosophical movement: Charles Sanders Peirce, William James, John Dewey, and George Herbert Mead. This school looked upon concepts as *analytic tools* and recognized that gaining knowledge requires an ongoing revision and reconstruction of our conceptual tools. The Pragmatists proposed that

---

[1] Max Weber, *The Methodology of the Social Sciences*, trans. and ed. Edward A. Shils and Henry A. Finch, Glencoe, IL: The Free Press, 1949, 92. Hereafter, all page references to this work will be cited in parentheses immediately following the quoted passage.

if a concept enables us to understand something better than we would have understood it without that concept – or better than we would have with an alternative concept – it is heuristically valuable because it yields definitely favorable results.

Weber converges methodologically with the Pragmatists in that regard as well. He, too, recognized the need for a

> perpetual reconstruction of those concepts through which we seek to comprehend reality. The history of the social sciences is and remains a continuous . . . attempt to order reality analytically through the construction of concepts – the dissolution of the analytical constructs so constructed, through the expansion and shift of the scientific horizon – and the reformulation anew of concepts on the foundations thus transformed. (105)

Although Weber regarded his epistemological approach as neo-Kantian, his grasp of the function of concepts is fully compatible with that of the Pragmatists. He writes:

> If one perceives the implications of the fundamental ideas of modern epistemology which ultimately derives from Kant, namely, that concepts are primarily *analytical instruments* for the intellectual mastery of empirical data and can only be that, the fact that precise genetic [i.e., historical] concepts are necessarily ideal types will not cause him to desist from constructing them. (106)

With this understanding of the role of concepts, perhaps it makes sense for our purposes to regard the Jews, owing to their distinctive historical experiences, as the ideal-typical diaspora people.

Are there other diasporas? Is there a need to distinguish diasporas from other forms of ethnic community? It is a historical fact that virtually all of the ethnic groups of Europe, Asia, and Africa have produced communities in countries other than those of their origin. This has prompted some scholars to raise the question whether those communities might also be characterized as "diasporas." Some of those scholars have proposed that a significant distinction may be made between "diasporas," on the one hand, and "transnational communities," on the other. The question, then, is by which criteria one would distinguish between the two categories.

My book is a historically specific analysis of the experiences of *one* people; it is not a comparative study, at least not explicitly. In light, however, of the immense and growing comparative literature concerned with the two categories, I feel an intellectual obligation to engage with it.

Global Diasporas[2] by Robin Cohen

Cohen opens by observing that until recently most characterizations of diasporas emphasized their catastrophic origins, as was the case in the original, forcible dispersion of the Jews. However, he correctly calls attention to the fact that although the word "Babylon" implies captivity and oppression, a careful reading of the narratives concerning the Babylonian period of exile can be shown to demonstrate the emergence of a new creative energy "in a challenging pluralistic context outside the natal homeland" (5–6). Beyond Babylon, moreover, Jewish communities flourished all over the Hellenistic world. In Alexandria, for example, under Ptolemy Philadelphus, the *Septuagint* was composed, and Jews served as administrators and army officers. Despite occasional expressions of anti-Jewishness, respect was the normal experience of the many Jewish communities scattered around the Greco-Roman world. So Cohen asks how we should account for the so-called "doleful" view of the Jewish diasporas.

To answer that question, Cohen proposes that we have to turn to the period of Roman domination. The Jewish war against Rome ended in the destruction of the Second Temple by the Roman general Vespasian and his son Titus in 70 CE. From the Christian ideological standpoint, this was interpreted as God's punishment. For what? For the Jews' rejection of Jesus as the Christ and for their alleged complicity in the execution of Jesus. There thus emerged the image of the "wandering Jew," condemned to eternal restlessness as a suitable punishment for these sins.

And yet, despite the strong anti-Jewish sentiment, the level of discrimination against the Jews was quite modest in the Roman world. However, things changed dramatically for the worse in the eleventh century with the Crusaders who, beginning in the summer of 1096, slaughtered or forcibly converted the Jews of the Rhine Valley. When the Crusaders finally arrived in Jerusalem in 1099, they gathered in a synagogue all the Jews they could find, and burned them alive.

Summarizing other well-known examples of Christian intolerance, persecution, and worse, Cohen cites several events, later discussed in my book. He also touches upon Jewish diasporas under Islam, where the experience was mostly positive until the Almohades had put an end to the fruitful interplay between Islam and Judaism. The center of Jewish

---

[2] Robin Cohen, *Global Diasporas: An Introduction* (Seattle, WA: University of Washington Press, 1997). Page references to this work will be cited in parentheses immediately following the quoted passage.

spiritual life then moved to the Ottoman Empire where Jewish experience varied hardly at all from that in earlier Muslim regimes.

Cohen next addresses the origin of the Ashkenazic Jews. Relying on the outstanding Jewish histories, he speaks of the conventional threefold classification: Jews of the Iberian Peninsula (*Sephardim*); Jews of the Muslim Middle East; and Jews of Northern Europe who came to be called (in the plural) *Ashkenazim*. *Ashkenaz* is the medieval rabbinical name for Germany. As the Jews migrated toward the Rhineland, and then further east, they became the large division of Jews comprising the Eastern European Yiddish-speaking Jews. Having originated in the Rhineland, Yiddish became a Germanic language in its syntax, grammar, and vocabulary, mixed, however, with Hebrew words and with words and phrases borrowed from the languages of the other peoples among whom the Jews lived.

In contrast to this sound historical explanation of the origin of the *Ashkenazim*, Arthur Koestler introduced the highly controversial theory that most of the Ashkenazim arose from the Khazars who, purportedly, had converted en masse to Judaism. When the Russians in 985 crushed the Khazarian domain, the Khazars migrated north, retaining their Jewish faith. Cohen recognizes that Koestler's once fashionable theory is no longer taken too seriously by scholars.

In the balance of Cohen's impressive work, he addresses the main sociological issue: what kind of inferences can be drawn from the Jewish diasporic tradition for the application of the concept to other ethnic groups? He notes that the term "diaspora" has come to be applied to a wide range of different categories of peoples. Relying on William Safran, Cohen mentions expatriates, expellees, political refugees, alien residents, immigrants, and ethnic and "racial" minorities. The term has also been applied to a vast array of different peoples: "Cubans and Mexicans in the USA, Pakistanis in Britain, Maghrebis (North Africans) in France, Turks in Germany, Chinese in Southeast Asia, Greeks, Poles, Palestinians, blacks in North America and the Caribbeans, Indians and Armenians in various countries, Corsicans in Marseilles and even French-speaking Belgians living in communal enclaves in Wallonia" (21–2). Cohen recognizes that generalizing the concept in this way tends to turn it into a vague and imprecise term that sheds little or no light. Cohen therefore implicitly follows Weber's admonition, demanding intellectual rigor and precision in the construction of our concepts.

If the Jews are taken as the prototype, Cohen argues, then, in order to qualify as a diaspora, a given group should have been dispersed to more than one land. Still relying on Safran, with some reservations, Cohen proposes that the concept of diaspora can be applied when members of an expatriate minority community share several of the following features:

- they or their ancestors have been dispersed from an original "center" to two or more regions;
- they have a collective memory or myth about their original homeland, its history and achievements;
- they doubt that they can be fully accepted in their "host" societies and, therefore, remain partly separate;
- their ancestral home is idealized to the extent that when conditions are favorable either they or their descendants should return;
- they believe that all or most members of the diaspora should commit themselves to the preservation or restoration of the original homeland, and to its security and well-being;
- they continue to relate to their homeland; and their ethnic consciousness and solidarity are, in a significant way, defined by such a relationship.

Cohen qualifies some of these features, amending, for example, the first one by adding that "dispersal from an original center is often accompanied by the memory of a single traumatic event that provides the folk memory of the great injustice that binds the group together" (23).

Cohen also adds three features:

1. Groups that scatter for aggressive or voluntary reasons. He calls this the most controversial departure from the Jewish diasporic tradition; but he thinks it "can be justified by reference to the ancient Greeks (who, after all, coined the word) and to the duality, voluntary *and* compelled, of the Jews' own migration patterns" (24).
2. Time has to pass before we can know whether any community that has migrated really is a diaspora.
3. There must be a pronounced recognition of the positive virtues prompting the retention of a diasporic ethnic identity.

In subsequent chapters of Cohen's thoughtful study, he discusses:

- victim diasporas: Africans and Armenians;
- labor and imperial diasporas: Indians and British;
- trade diasporas: Chinese and Lebanese;
- cultural diasporas: the Caribbean case.

Cohen acknowledges that in practice "migration scholars find it difficult to separate voluntary from involuntary migration. Nonetheless, there are, clearly, mass displacements that are occasioned by events wholly outside the individual's control – wars, 'ethnic cleansing,' natural disasters, pogroms and the like" (180).

So the question is whether a formal-technical definition of "diaspora," or checklists of criteria by which to distinguish diasporic from non-diasporic peoples, can be effective without implying invidiousness. Let us, then, employ Cohen's criteria to determine whether the distinction can be made in an objective, non-evaluative manner.

Ethnic immigration in the early eras of American history

In the modern period from, say, the seventeenth to the twentieth centuries, America was the chief "host" country for many millions of immigrants. In America, most ethnic minorities are the descendants of immigrants who freely left their lands of origin to settle in the United States. English, Scottish-Irish, Germans, Irish, Poles, Jews, Italians, Chinese, and Japanese are examples of such ethnic groups. There are, however, other minorities in the United States who, though they share a presumed common ethnic origin, must be placed in a different category. Afro-Americans are a case in point, for their ancestors, far from having been free immigrants, were brought to America in chains.

American Indians, on the other hand, are natives of America, a small remnant of a conquered and nearly annihilated people. Both blacks and Indians therefore have histories that distinguish them from all other American ethnic groups. Mexican Americans too, though descended from immigrants, are native to the American continent.

From 1820 to 1930 more than 37,000,000 immigrants, mostly Europeans, arrived in the United States. The major factor impelling that great mass of people to uproot themselves and to emigrate was poverty. The first of the impoverished Europeans to leave their homes in the nineteenth century were the Irish. The Poor Law, the enclosure of the land, and the potato famine of the late 1840s caused untold misery and starvation to millions. Alexis de Tocqueville, who visited Dublin in the 1830s, recorded the most appalling manifestations of poverty even before the Great Hunger caused by the potato blight. Between 1,800 and 2,000 paupers were received in the poorhouse each day. As he left the poorhouse, Tocqueville saw two paupers pushing a small closed wheelbarrow. They were on the way to the homes of the rich to collect their garbage and bring it to the poorhouse so that broth could be made of it.

To take only this dramatic example, one sees the difficulty in distinguishing voluntary from involuntary emigration. The emigration of the Irish was voluntary in the sense that they possessed enough consciousness and will to make significant choices and decisions. They were impelled to act by an economic disaster. But *they were not forcibly expelled from their homeland by a militarily stronger imperial power and dispersed.* For Cohen and other scholars, this is the chief criterion by which to discern the difference between voluntary and involuntary.

If I may be excused for stating the obvious, the case of black Americans best illustrates not only involuntary emigration, but much else that is relevant to the question of how to define "diaspora." The impoverished Irish immigrants to the United States suffered from extreme discrimination, as in employment opportunities where the signs read "Irish need not apply." But black Americans left their homeland chained two by two, left leg to right leg, which is also how they arrived to the American continent. Again stating the obvious, the African skin color became by the eighteenth century a badge of slavery and degradation. Chattel slavery had become firmly a part of American custom and law. And after emancipation, "Jim Crow" became a synonym for Negro. A high social barrier was erected between whites and blacks. Its purpose was to prevent interracial mixing of any kind, especially intermarriage. Separate drinking fountains, separate privies, separate schools, and so on became the order of the day. White nurses were forbidden to treat black men; white teachers were not allowed to teach black students. In Florida, even "negro" and "white" textbooks were segregated in warehouses. In Oklahoma, there were separate telephone booths; and in Atlanta courtrooms, Jim Crow Bibles were provided for black witnesses and regular Bibles for white. There is, of course, much more that needs to be said about those dark chapters in American history, with which most of us are quite familiar. For our purposes, however, it must suffice where its relevance to Cohen's thesis is concerned.

In his concluding remarks, Cohen again lists what he regards as the key features of a diaspora, including a "return" ideology: the parallel in black history to Zionism, the back-to-Africa movement of Marcus Garvey. What Negroes needed, he said, was an organization and a country. There was no hope of justice for a black man in America. Negroes must return to their motherland.

The features characterizing diaspora experience, Cohen avers, are analogous to Wittgenstein's fibers of meaning. In those terms, Cohen seems to intend his checklist of features to be interpreted in Wittgenstein's terms as "family resemblance" between Jewish experiences and those of other ethnic groups. This suggests, perhaps, that Cohen himself may have nagging doubts that checklists of features are the best way to go about our task.

That it is the wrong way is the stout argument Stéphane Dufoix makes in his superb, critical discussion of the issues.

Diasporas[3] by Stéphane Dufoix

Dufoix' slender, pithy, and superlative study is actually a history of the concept. Right at the outset he expresses his astonishment at how that ancient, simple word "underwent an amazing inflation that peaked in the 1990s, by which time it was being applied to most of the world's peoples."

In his highly illuminating genealogy of the concept, he points out that the modern usage of "diaspora" stems from a neologism in the translation of the Hebrew Bible into Greek. In the Septuagint Bible "diaspora" appears 12 times, but never referring either to the Babylonian exile or to any other historical event. Instead, "diaspora" always referred to the threat of dispersion if the Hebrews failed to obey God's will. The concept was applied almost exclusively to divine acts: it is God who will scatter the sinners and gather together the atoned in the future. To explain the growing popularity of the term "diaspora," Dufoix examines two cases that are both linked and opposed: the "Jewish diaspora" and the "black diaspora." As the substance of my book is devoted to the former, I will focus on what Dufoix has to say about the latter.

It is fully understandable why the descendants of Africans, living on other continents, would adopt the concept "diaspora" and apply it to themselves. For blacks, the biblical narrative of the Exodus, escaping slavery and reaching the Promised Land, resonated profoundly. Hence, the Zionist idea inspired the return-to-Africa cause. Earlier I mentioned Marcus Garvey, who advocated the founding of a black nation in Africa. His movement for black peoples' right to self-determination gained momentum for a while, but ran into serious financial difficulties which led to his downfall and the end of his "back-to-Africa" plans.

Dufoix shows that the special resonance the biblical narratives had for black thinkers goes back quite far. The concept of "diaspora" was often employed explicitly to draw analogies between Jewish history and black history. In his book *American Civilization and the Negro*, published in 1916, the African-American thinker and doctor, Charles Victor Roman, raised the question of the future of blacks in Africa and the American South:

> The Negro is not going to leave here for two reasons: in the first place *this is his home*, and in the second place *there is nowhere to go*. He is not going back to Africa any more than the white man is going back to Europe or the Jew is going back to Palestine. Palestine may be rehabilitated and Europe

---

[3] Translated by William Rodamor, with a foreword by Roger Waldinger, Berkeley, CA, and London: University of California Press, 2008.

be Americanized, but the Jew will not lose his worldwide citizenship, nor America fail of her geographical destination as the garden-spot of the world . . . The slave trade was the diaspora of the African, and the children of this alienation have become a permanent part of the citizenry of the American republic. (12)

It is truly remarkable that a year later, in 1917, the analogy was drawn on the Jewish side. The Yiddish newspaper, *The Jewish Daily Forward*, saw a parallel between the race riots that broke out in east St Louis on the second day of July, and the Kishinev pogroms of 1903, during which the Jewish victims counted 45 dead, over 500 wounded, and 1,500 houses and shops destroyed or looted. The Jewish editor wrote:

Kishinev and St. Louis – the same soil the same people. It is a distance of four and a half thousand miles between the two cities and yet they are so close and so similar to each other . . . Actually twin sisters, which could easily be mistaken for each other. Four and a half thousand miles apart, but the same events in both . . . The situation of Negroes in America is very comparable to the situation of the Jews in Russia. The Negro diaspora, the special laws, the decrees, the pogroms and also the Negro complaints, the Negro hopes, are very similar to those which we Jews . . . lived through. (12)

Dufoix observes that, until the 1950s, "diaspora" had mainly a religious meaning. And yet, much earlier, in the 1931 edition of the *American Encyclopedia of the Social Sciences*, it was the great Jewish historian, Simon Dubnov, who had argued that the term "diaspora" should *not* be limited to Jewish religious history. In his article on the concept of "diaspora" he wrote:

Diaspora is a Greek term for a nation or part of a nation separated from its own state or territory and dispersed among other nations but preserving its national culture. In a sense Magna Graecia constituted a Greek diaspora in the ancient Roman Empire, and a typical case of diaspora is presented by the Armenians, many of whom have voluntarily lived outside their small national territory for centuries. Generally, however, the term is used with reference to those parts of the Jewish people residing outside Palestine. (17)

Dubnov's text played a major role in diffusing the term "diaspora," in secularizing the concept, and in separating it from the historical experience of the Jewish people. Dufoix cites examples of how the concept was generalized. In 1949, an American sociologist, Rose Hum Lee, relying on Dubnov, proposed that "Chinatowns" might be regarded as "diasporas." And 10 years earlier, the distinguished sociologist Robert Park –

known for his theory of the "marginal man" and the phenomenon of the "stranger" brought to the fore by Georg Simmel – had reframed Dubnov to apply "diaspora" to Asians. Dufoix continues to document in this way the gradual shift of the concept from the specific historical situation of a people to a general term widely applied in the social sciences. In his research on the history of the concept "diaspora," Dufoix found that, except for the article by Simon Dubnov, the concept was almost absent from the social sciences before the 1960s. However, when the term began to emerge, no real attempt was made to define it.

Dufoix's primary aim in this critical and illuminating study is to address the question whether "diaspora," as the term has come to be widely applied, is anything more than an ambiguous cliché. Indeed, the term is increasingly being used, Dufoix notes, "without any definition in a scope that is both wide and loose." Dufoix attributes the broadening of the notion of diaspora to "postmodernism," "globalization," and "trans-nationalism." The growth in the number of phenomena and populations covered by "diaspora" has therefore attracted critics who argue that the word lacks theoretical or analytical power.

In his effort to clarify matters, Dufoix explores what he calls the "spaces of dispersion." Relying on the historian William McNeill, and on the research material of paleoanthropologists who were tracing the origins of the human species from the paleolithic period, Dufoix notes that, according to the "out of Africa" hypothesis, humans have a single origin in Africa, from which they progressively colonized the rest of the world. And Dufoix notes perceptively, "If this monogenetic (single origin) theory is correct, dispersion is written into humanity's very soul" (35).

In his illuminating sketch of the historic direction of migrations, Dufoix reviews the successive stages, from the original gathering-hunting stage to the relatively recent sedentary-agricultural period when the invention of boats made access to off-shore lands possible. Dufoix quotes Emmanuel Kant's amusing observation that a time eventually came when people covered the entire Earth's surface: "Because it is a globe, they cannot scatter to an infinite distance" (36). The result is that some 155,000,000 people now live far from the place where they were born.

In his continuing effort at clarification, Dufoix correctly observes that "diaspora," in its classic usage, applied to the peoples whose migrations over hundreds and, in some cases, thousands of years had not weakened significantly "a permanent collective conscience rooted in an enduring reference to history, a land or a religion" (38). Clearly, this describes the Jewish experience. The question for Dufoix, therefore, is: to what other peoples does the term apply? In his effort to answer that question adequately, Dufoix reviews the history of four migratory peoples: the Greeks, the Indians, the Chinese, and the Armenians.

It is the Armenian case, Dufoix convincingly argues, that bears some resemblance to that of the Jews. The historic homeland of the Armenians was located between the Black and Caspian Seas. They had been long-time traders between Asia and Europe since at least the fifth century BCE. The politically and economically powerful Armenian Empire dominated the entire Near East in the first century CE, until they were defeated by the Roman armies. Though the Armenians converted to Christianity in the fourth century, they maintained a form of Christianity distinct from the Roman and Orthodox Churches, and did so within the Roman Empire as more or less sovereign kingdoms. In 1045, after the Byzantine conquest of Armenia, many Armenians left the country, heading west to the Black Sea and Bulgaria, or northwest to Poland and the Ukraine. Many nobles and priests fled to Cilicia on modern Turkey's southeast coast, where they founded an independent state. It survived until 1375 and was the last Armenian state until the proclamation, in 1991, of the Republic of Armenia.

Parallel with the Jewish experience, the Armenians, even in the absence of a state, preserved a sense of ethnic community. The Armenian business ventures led to the establishment of commercial colonies in Europe, Persia, India, and the Far East. The Armenian Apostolic Church held the dispersed Armenians together until the idea of Armenian nationalism began to take hold in the eighteenth century.

Dufoix then reminds us of the fate of the Armenians in the Ottoman Empire. The fear, apparently, that Armenian nationalism was being supported by the Czarist Empire, led to the Ottoman pogroms of 1894–6 and 1909, in which hundreds of thousands of Armenians were killed, forcing survivors to emigrate mainly to the United States. In 1915–16, during World War I, the Ottoman regime forced the Armenians into the Syrian desert and "eliminated the Armenian elites in a genocide that killed three-quarters of the region's two million Armenians" (52).

Static thinking about dispersion

Continuing his effort to clarify the concept of "diaspora," Dufoix calls the word "slippery" and criticizes the use of it as a vehicle for static thinking that hides several illusions. In his complex and subtle argument, Dufoix calls the chief of the illusions the illusion of "essence," according to which naming something implies the real existence of a substance. Dufoix cites Ludwig Wittgenstein who had made the same point by saying "A substantive makes us look for a thing that corresponds to it" (55). For Dufoix, as for Wittgenstein, it is an illusory, scholastic enterprise to posit the ontological existence of a *real* diaspora that one can encounter in the form of archetypes, the best known of which is the Jewish diaspora. The illusory task then becomes a search for migratory phenomena that match the predefined criteria. The illusion and error lie in the reification of a concept, so that "only phenomena that are identical *in reality* can deserve the title of 'diaspora.'" Note the word "deserve," as if "diaspora" is an honorific term. The checklists of "features" that some scholars have constructed are examples of such scholastic and/or mechanistic enterprises in which, with checklists in hand, one goes in search of ethnic groups who embody the diasporic "essence."

How does one avoid what Dufoix calls "this epistemological impasse"? The answer lies, he says, in reversing our priorities. What he means is that instead of classifying migrant populations in accordance with pre-existing terms, we should first study the historically specific phenomena linked to the collective existence of groups outside a land, place of origin, or point of departure. Only in a second stage of analysis would we give the phenomena and processes a "name." Dufoix quotes Émile Durkheim's commonsensical methodological rule: "What matters is not to distinguish words; it is to succeed in distinguishing the things that are covered by the words" (58). First study the things, and then, if necessary, find the "new words" to designate the phenomena that resemble each other in Wittgenstein's sense. Dufoix goes farther, noting, as I had earlier, Max Weber's epistemologically pragmatic formulation of "ideal types" as instruments of analysis, not mere names or words.

In following Weber in this regard, we also avoid the danger of introducing into our analyses invidious distinctions and value judgments.

Powers of Diaspora[4] by Jonathan Boyarin and Daniel Boyarin

In the first of two essays in this volume, Jonathan Boyarin – whom I shall hereafter refer to merely as Jonathan – explores what he calls the "diasporic genius of Jewishness," by which he means the *cultural* power of the Jewish, diasporic experience.

Jonathan opens his Introduction by citing the rabbinic literature praising the "greatness" of Israel's humility – thus humorously calling attention to Israel's pious claims to humility by "loudly proclaiming how humble we are" (2). It is true, of course, that in contrast to most ancient peoples who boasted of their nobility, power, might, and the domination of other peoples, the Jews have always reminded themselves

---

[4] Minneapolis, MN: University of Minnesota Press, 2002.

of their original bondage: "We were slaves unto Pharaoh in Egypt!" In every generation the Jews are urged to look upon themselves as if they personally had escaped from Egyptian bondage. Moreover, according to the biblical tradition, the historic individual who led the Israelites and the "mixed multitude" out of Egypt, also exhibited the very opposite of hubris: "now the man Moses was very meek, above all the men that were on the face of the earth" (Num. 12:3). The Hebrew word *anav* connotes "meekness," "humility," and "much enduring."

Jonathan states that his co-authored book is "an argument *for* diaspora, and at the same time an attempt to identify and avoid at least some of the risks inherent in promoting 'diaspora' as a new catchword in the global theorization of diversity." He proposes that broadening the concept of diaspora "offers rich material for a reinvigoration of Jewish thought" (7).

When Jonathan employs the word "power," this word, it would seem, requires a good definition. For our purposes and for Jonathan's aim, it is Thomas Hobbes, I believe, who has provided the best and most fruitful definition. "Power," for Hobbes, refers to a "present means for the attainment of some future apparent good." As we are speaking of the diasporic experiences of the Jews, a historically stateless ethnic group, Hobbes's definition appears to be more appropriate than, say, Max Weber's, for whom "power refers to the ability to realize one's will against the resistance of others." In his discussion of the "state," Weber cites Trotsky's words at Brest-Litovsk: "Every state is founded on force." Weber goes on to say that a "state is a community that successfully claims the monopoly of the legitimate use of physical force within a given territory."[5] For the Jews, prior to the twentieth century, at least 2,000 years had elapsed from the time and place in which they could claim such a monopoly. Statelessness for the Jews meant that whatever power they had was certainly not founded on force. "Power" in Jewish diasporas was therefore exercised in the cultural sphere, in Jonathan's sense, and in accordance with Hobbes's definition. The aim of diasporic power for the Jews was the attainment, preservation, and further development of their apparent cultural goods, the nature of those goods having nothing to do with physical force. Indeed, those cultural goods were, in effect, a negation and repudiation of physical force and might.

Jonathan cites Nietzsche's famous characterization of the Jews as the people primarily responsible for the inversion of the noble-warrior values

---

[5] H. H. Gerth and C. Wright Mills, eds, *From Max Weber: Essays in Sociology*, London: Routledge & Kegan Paul Ltd., 1970, 78.

based on force and might. Nietzsche calls the Jews a priestly people par excellence, and describes in the most dramatic terms the historic role of the Jews in inverting the noble values:

> All that has been done on earth against "the noble," "the powerful," "the masters," "the rulers," is not even worth talking about when compared with what the *Jews* have done against them . . . With regard to the tremendous and immeasurably fateful initiative which the Jews have taken, through this most far-reaching of all declarations of war, I recall the proposition I arrived at on an earlier occasion (*Beyond Good and Evil*, 195) – that *the slave revolt in morality* begins with the Jews, a revolt which has a two-thousand-year history behind it and which is no longer so obvious because it has been victorious. (*On the Genealogy of Morals*, I, 7)

Historically, the political weakness and vulnerability of the diasporic Jews have meant that they could only engage in a spiritual revolt, what Nietzsche calls *ressentiment* or "spiritual revenge." Jewish resentment of oppression and persecution resulted in the inversion of the values of the high-and-mighty and a triumph over them. Nietzsche was therefore correct to recognize that "power" in the Jewish diasporic sense meant that the Jews possessed enough *spiritual* power to repudiate the "master morality" and to create a "slave morality" in the positive and creative meaning of that term. Indeed, one can go beyond Nietzsche to argue that this "slave revolt in morality" was rooted in ancient Israel's resentment of her Egyptian oppressors and in the subsequent ethical teachings of the Hebrew prophets of social justice. The "powers," then, that Jonathan Boyarin has in mind, where the Jewish diasporic experience is concerned, are those that have enabled the Jews to continue their cultural and spiritual creativity.

Basing himself on rabbinic texts, Jonathan discerns in them a tension on the issue of "accommodation versus resistance or tricksterism versus martyrdom" (67). Jonathan is proposing that in the history of Jewish diasporas, where they could not act in accordance with the noble-warrior values, they adopted the strategy rooted in the "slave morality." He cites the example of the Torah Jews of Eastern Europe who, by maintaining themselves as weak and passive, "were engaged in a more successful act of cultural resistance to the hegemony of Christian culture" (69). In effect, the rabbis gave positive sanction to a "slave-morality" strategy:

> Continue to live, continue to maintain Jewish practice, but do not behave in ways that draw attention or provoke the hostile intervention of the ruling powers. (70)

Jonathan, however, goes beyond Nietzsche in a direction that is, perhaps, problematic. He employs Freudian and Lacanian postmodern psychoanalytic concepts to set forth his thesis on the so-called "feminization" of Jewish diasporic tactics. Still on the basis of rabbinic texts, he proposes that the approved practice for diasporic Jews has been gendered feminine, while the oppressor's behavior has been gendered masculine. As a psychoanalytic corollary to the diasporic, "slave-morality" strategy, Jonathan explores the ways in which Jewish maleness was a form of resistance to Roman phallic masculinity. He cites approvingly the account by Kaja Silverman of the "dominant fiction," the myth of the equation of the penis to the phallus – the narrative defining maleness through ascribing to the male an "unimpaired bodily 'envelope' . . . fiercely protective of its coherence." And Jonathan comments: "the penis becomes phallus becomes then the very symbol of power and privilege as well as of completeness, coherence, univocity" (40). Silverman, in a later essay, argued that recent theory has benefited enormously from Lacan's distinction between the penis and the phallus. To this, Jonathan responds that

> the very myth of the phallus, is *never* politically productive. The issue is not whether we differentiate sharply or fuzzily [between the penis and the phallus] but whether we posit a phallus at all. It is the very transcendent immateriality of the phallus, and thus its separation from the penis, that constitutes its ability to project masculinity as the universal – as the Logos – and by doing so significantly enables both male and imperial projects of domination. A strong case can be made that this particular mode of idealization of the male body was instrumental, if not necessary, in the erection – pun intended – of empires, whether Roman or modern. (42–3)

Jonathan then adds: "such idealization of the phallic male role is typical of Zionist ideology" (45).

Jonathan's apparent aim, then, is more than merely proposing that gender is, of course, historically and sociologically constructed. He wants to argue that for men in the bottom layers of society, their being there is/was interpreted as "feminization" – but feminization trans-valued and thus receiving at least some positive significance. He writes:

> We claim that the absence of phallic power is not a lack. It need not be figured as a castration, as psychoanalysis figures the woman and the circumcised Jew, but as a gain, as a place from which a particular knowledge is generated . . .
>
> Both early rabbinic Jews and early Christians performed resistance to the Roman imperial power structure through "gender-bending," thereby making their own understanding that gender itself is implicated in the main-

tenance of political power. The various symbolic enactments of "femaleness" . . . were adopted variously by Christians or Jews as acts of resistance
against the Roman culture of masculinist power wielding. (78)

Jonathan thus wants to propose that Jewish diasporic men purportedly
inverted the dominant phallic-male image and created a quite different
conception of masculinity.

It needs to be said, however, that Jonathan's "feminization" thesis
is problematic in the extreme. Strength, courage, bravery, and heroism
are *human* virtues, not exclusively male virtues. It is, therefore, a false,
stereotypical, and sexist move on Jonathan's part to adopt the notion of
"feminization" to describe the stratagems Jewish men have employed,
historically, in diaspora. Furthermore, it is also doubtful that the
"feminization" thesis adds anything significant to the already brilliant
Nietzschean interpretation of the "slave morality" as an inversion of the
"master morality." Does the discussion of penis and phallus really shed
any new light, even if we ignore, for the moment, the invidiousness that
the "feminization" notion implies?

Still another problem with the "feminization" notion is that it ignores
the fact that even strong men in positions of power need to adopt stratagems. As we learn from Machiavelli, the prince "should learn from the
fox and the lion; because the lion is defenseless against traps and a fox
is defenseless against wolves. Therefore one must be a fox to recognize
traps, and a lion to frighten off wolves. Those who simply act as lions are
stupid" (*The Prince*, XVII, 99). Finally, as we shall see in due course, the
black male slaves in the antebellum South of the United States resorted,
as a matter of course, to the tactics of the fox – "tricks," dissembling,
and the like. Yet it is a near certainty that it never crossed the minds of
either the slave-owners or the slave-drivers to think of the black man as
"feminine."

The Socratic inversion of values

It is noteworthy that, from a Nietzschean standpoint, the inversion of the
noble-warrior values was neither an exclusively Jewish nor an exclusively
diasporic phenomenon. In his encounter with Callicles, Socrates' rebut-
tal contains elements of a "slave morality." Such elements are evident in
Socrates' inversion of Callicles' noble-warrior view that "might is right."
Socrates says:

I hold the view that it is *not* the most shameful of experiences to be wrongfully boxed on the ears, nor to have either my purse or my person cut,
but it is more disgraceful and, indeed, wicked, wrongfully to strike or cut

me; and furthermore, . . . any wrong done to me and mine is at once more shameful and worse for the wrongdoer than for me the sufferer. (*Gorgias*, 508D–509E)

Socrates goes quite far in inverting the "master morality." In the dialogue *Crito*, where a friend by that name tries to persuade Socrates to escape from prison to avoid execution, Socrates states that "there is no instance in which injuring others is good or honorable. In no circumstances must one do wrong, not even when one is wronged – which most people regard as the natural course . . .; it is never right to do a wrong or return a wrong or defend oneself against injury by retaliation" (*Crito*, 49A–E). Here anticipating certain attitudes attributed to Jesus the pious Jew, Socrates espouses a view that unequivocally repudiates "might is right."

Returning to Jonathan Boyarin's analysis, if we disregard what appears to be an invidious use of "masculine"–"feminine," he most likely stands on solid ground when he interprets the attitude of rabbinic Judaism toward force as subterfuge. He cites the legend concerning Yohanan ben Zakkai, who escaped besieged Jerusalem in a coffin – a form of trickery, "which the rabbis portray as the very antithesis of the military resistance of the Zealots who wanted to fight to the very last man and preserve their honor . . . The tenacity that is valorized by these [rabbinic] texts is the tenacity that enables continued Jewish existence, not the tenacity of defending sovereignty unto death" (102).

The Black Atlantic: Modernity and Double Consciousness[6] by Paul Gilroy

The quality of Gilroy's inquiry into the "double consciousness" of blacks under slavery and in the aftermath is superlative in all respects. His treatment of the black American experience, in particular, has touched me profoundly because of my own lifelong engagement with the condition of black Americans. Gilroy's skill in employing classical philosophical insights and applying them to black history and literature is truly extraordinary. A good example is his discussion of Hegel's explanation of consciousness.

In Hegel's *The Phenomenology of Spirit* (1807), in the section titled "Relations of Master and Servant," Hegel recognized that only by acknowledging an "other" is self-consciousness possible. But once the

---

[6] Cambridge, MA: Harvard University Press, 1993.

self-consciousness emerges in the self–other dialectic, it feels threatened and asserts its freedom by trying to dominate the other and force acknowledgment of its dominance. The ensuing struggle results in a master who dominates and a servant who is dominated. The master then forces the servant to produce material goods for the master's enjoyment. But at this point the master has become *dependent* upon the servant he has dominated. The master's self-consciousness as master is subject to his recognition as master by the servant. But while the master has been consuming what the servant produces, the servant has been learning to create – to act upon nature and bend it to his will, thereby establishing his own self-consciousness in relation to what he has created. Furthermore, the labor of the servant is essential for life, whereas the master's consumption depends upon the servant's production. Hence, by dominating the servant, the master, owing to his dependence on the servant, is also dominated. Hegel sees the solution to this contradiction in the mutual acknowledgment that neither master nor servant is free, and that freedom is not possible in relations of domination.[7]

Inspired by Hegel's allegory, Gilroy proposes that in Frederick Douglass's account of his bitter trial of strength with Edward Covey, the slave-breaker, Douglass can be read as if he is reworking the encounter between master and slave in a manner that inverts Hegel's scheme. In Douglass's account, it is the slave rather than the master who acquires a "consciousness that exists for itself," while his master becomes the representative of a repressed consciousness. Douglass's transformation of Hegel's self–other dialectic into one of emancipation, is all the more striking, says Gilroy, as it is also the occasion for an attempt to specify the difference between a spiritual mode of African thought, and Douglass's own African-American hybrid-outlook, "formed of the debilitating experience of slavery and tailored to the requirements of his abolitionism" (Gilroy, 60–1).

Douglass acknowledged that Covey had succeeded in breaking him in body, soul, and spirit, an experience that even led him to doubt all religion, especially after meeting Covey with his angelic smile on the Sabbath, who on Monday reverted to his usual brutality. This was the moment when Douglass resolved to stand up in his own defense. As Gilroy remarks, the Hegelian struggle ensued in which the two men were locked together while Douglass held Covey "so firmly by the throat that his blood flowed through my nails." A degree of mutual respect resulted when after two hours Covey gave up the contest and let Douglass go.

---

[7] This idea, of course, inspired Marx's concretization of it as applied to the capitalist system in which both the capitalist and the proletarian are alienated.

He was a changed man after the fight, "the turning-point" in his career as a slave. Gilroy observes that the physical struggle is also the occasion on which "a liberating definition of *masculinity* is produced" (63; italics added). Douglass wrote:

> I was nothing before. I was a man now. It [the fight] recalled to life my crushed self-respect and my self-confidence, and inspired me with a renewed determination to be a free man. A man without force is without the essential dignity of humanity . . . I was no longer a servile coward, trembling under the frown of a brother worm of the dust, but my long-cowed spirit was roused to an attitude of manly independence. I had reached a point at which I was not afraid to die. (Gilroy, 63)

In Hegel's allegory, which recognizes the centrality of slavery in "modernity," Gilroy observes that the servile combatant in the elemental struggle accepts his conqueror's version of reality, and prefers submission to death. For Douglass, however, the slave prefers "the possibility of death to the continuing condition of inhumanity on which the plantation system depends" (ibid.) Gilroy, quite perceptively, recognizes Douglass's preference for death, if necessary, as *agency* – the insurgent, human organism's active and creative resistance to domination and all that it entails. Douglass's rejection of his earlier pacifist stance reveals his new critical understanding of the brutality and hypocrisy of so-called "civilization." And it reveals, too, that the power structure of the plantation system "cannot be undone without recourse to the counter-violence of the oppressed." Douglass's account of his combat with Covey, Gilroy again observes, becomes a distinctively "masculinist" resolution of slavery's internal oppositions. For Douglass, however, "the idea of masculinity is largely defined against the experience of *infantilism* on which the institutions of plantation slavery rely rather than against women" (Gilroy, 64).

Years later, Du Bois also expressed a masculinist resolution of slavery's inner oppositions:

> This the American black man knows: his fight here is a fight to the finish. Either he dies or wins. If he wins it will be by no *subterfuge* or evasion or amalgamation. He will enter modern civilization here in America as a black man on terms of perfect and unlimited equality with any white man, or he will not enter at all. Either extermination root and branch, or absolute equality. There can be no compromise. This is the last great battle of the West. (Gilroy, 70; italics added)

I have italicized the word "subterfuge" for reasons that will soon become clear.

Every student of black American slavery knows about Nat Turner's insurgency, Denmark Vesey's conspiracy, and countless other assertions by individual black men of their masculinity. However, for the masses of slaves, being unarmed and facing the superior power of the white masters, insurgency was not an appealing option. Even if individuals contemplated insurgency, they soon recognized the virtual impossibility of communicating effectively with the slaves of other plantations with the aim of organizing resistance. Hence, "subterfuge" became relevant as a strategy for resistance, a strategy in which the slaves found countless ways to exasperate their masters. Although many slaves no doubt gained personal satisfaction in doing a piece of work well, others strove to resist or outwit the master by doing it badly or not at all. Slave-holders disagreed as to whether "smart" Negroes or "stupid" ones caused them the greater trouble. The bondsmen, it is clear, had good reason for encouraging their master to underrate their intelligence. Apparent ignorance or stupidity became a high virtue in a human chattel, and as it was the master's purpose to keep his bondsmen in this state of apparent incompetence, the slaves were shrewd enough to make him think he had succeeded. Visitors to the South often observed the furtive cessation of toil that invariably occurred when the overseer's eye was turned away from those who were working. Slaves effectively fixed their own work quotas, and masters had to adopt stern measures to persuade them that they were being unduly presumptuous. Every slave-holder learned that if a slave's regular hours of labor were increased, his movements became proportionally slower. Besides slowing down, many slaves bedeviled the master by doing careless work or damaging property.

Masters were also troubled by slaves who remained in their quarters, claiming illness or disability. Slave-women had great success with the stratagem of "shamming illness." Kenneth Stampp provides the example of one female who feigned a "protracted pseudo-pregnancy," during which she continued to gain increased rations as the reward for her expectation, until the truth was discovered and she received a flogging. Stampp writes:

> Almost every slaveholder discovered at one time or another that a bondsman had outwitted him by "playing possum" or by some ingenious *subterfuge*. One Negro spread powdered mustard on his tongue to give it a foul appearance before he was examined by a doctor. Another convinced his owner that he was totally disabled by rheumatism, until one day he was discovered vigorously rowing a boat. A master found two of his slaves "grunting" (a common term), one affecting a partial paralysis and the other declaring that he could not walk; but he soon learned that they "used their limbs very well when they chose to do so" . . .

In these and other ways a seemingly docile gang of slaves drove an inefficient manager well nigh to distraction. They probed for his weakness, matched their wits against his, and constantly contrived to disrupt the work routine. An efficient manager took cognizance of the fact that many of his bondsmen were "shrewd and cunning," ever ready to "disregard all reasonable restraints" and eager "to practice upon the old maxim, of give an inch and take an ell."[8]

Stampp's account of such subterfuges provokes gratifying, uproarious laughter as when he relates that, according to a certain Dr Cartright, there was another disease peculiar to Negroes which he called Drapetomania: the disease causing Negroes to run away. Fugitive slaves were numbered in the thousands every year, an important form of protest against bondage. Stampp even provides a rigorous proposition, explaining the extent of flight: the heavier the labor burdens, the higher the incidence of runaways in summer.

To conclude such examples of the role of subterfuge in the bondsmen's resistance and protest against their domination, we need to understand why strong, masculine men had to resort to shrewd and cunning stratagems. The answer lies in the explanation of why there was no conspiracy comparable to Denmark Vesey's and no rebellion comparable to Nat Turner's during the three decades before the Civil War. For Stampp, the various explanations that were given of this phenomenon

> do not sufficiently emphasize the impact which the Turner rebellion had on the slaves themselves. The speed with which it was crushed and the massacre that followed were facts soon known, doubtless, to every slave in Virginia and, before long, to almost every slave in the South. Among the Negroes everywhere, news generally spread so far and so fast as to amaze the whites. The Turner story was not likely to encourage slaves to make new attempts to win their freedom by fighting for it. They now realized that they would face a united white community, well armed and quite willing to annihilate as much of the black population as might seem necessary.
>
> In truth, no slave uprising [in the United States] ever had a chance of ultimate success, even though it might have cost the master class heavy casualties. The great majority of the disarmed and outnumbered slaves, knowing the futility of rebellion, refused to join in any of the numerous plots . . . The bondsmen themselves lacked the power to destroy the web

---

[8] Kenneth M. Stampp, *The Peculiar Institution*, New York: Vintage Books, 1956, 104–5.

of bondage. They would have to have the aid of free men inside or outside the South. (139–40)

This extended discussion of subterfuge prompts me to return to Jonathan Boyarin's "feminization" thesis in which he characterizes Jewish adaptation to diasporic experiences as "feminine," because the Jews (or especially Jewish males) employed trickery, slyness, cunning, and shrewdness. It should now be quite clear that in certain circumstances, as we noted earlier, even very strong men have to emulate the fox. No scholarly student of slavery in the antebellum South has ever employed the epithet "feminine" to describe the adaptation strategies of the black male slaves. Where the issues of gender are concerned, it is both men and women who will resort to subterfuge when necessary. In our context, recourse to foxy tactics is to be understood positively, as a means of preserving the lives and culture of diasporic peoples who face state-sponsored threats to their freedom or to their physical existence.

One more word about Jonathan Boyarin's thesis: he bases it not on historically known Jewish diasporas but on texts, rabbinic and others. He speaks of "femaleness" having been "adopted variously by Christians and Jews as acts of resistance against the Roman culture of masculinist power wielding" (78). But then he acknowledges that:

> It should be emphasized, of course, that (virtually) nothing can be learned about "real Romans" from this [rabbinic] literature. The "Romans," by the same or any other name, function here as the mirror over/against which the Rabbis formulate their own sense of identity and paradigms for human and especially male behavior. (79)

In effect, then, Boyarin admits that his "feminization" notion, based as it is on rabbinic texts, says little or nothing about "real," diasporic, Jewish male conduct. In any event, "feminization" aside, our review of the role of black men under slavery demonstrates that "subterfuge" certainly is not an exclusive characteristic of Jewish diasporas.

One more point is necessary: as we have just seen, strong men, like the black plantation slaves, might resort to subterfuge when the odds are against them. But it is also true, as the conduct of Frederick Douglass demonstrates, that standing up to one's oppressor at the risk of one's life illustrates a meaning of "masculinity" that is quite the opposite of the meaning Boyarin has assigned to the "phallus" as a symbol of domination.

Children of Israel or Children of the Pharaohs

Gilroy reminds his readers that the term "diaspora" entered black studies and pan-Africanist politics from Jewish thought. I would add that the term "ghetto" also was originally applied to Jewish diaspora communities. Gilroy acknowledges that Jewish scholarly discussions of the relationship between modernity and anti-Semitism, and other related issues, have been a rich source for him in "thinking about the problems of identity and difference in the black Atlantic diaspora."

Gilroy's work is informed by thinkers like Lukács and representatives of the so-called Frankfurt school: Adorno, Horkheimer, and Benjamin – and even by Kafka. He cites Fredric Jameson who, relying on those thinkers, speaks of the primary experience of human history itself, "namely that of fear and of vulnerability." The profound influence of Max Weber is also evident when Jameson speaks of the "scientific domination of nature and the self, which constitutes the infernal machine of Western civilization." Although he ascribes fear and vulnerability to human history itself – as had Hegel, centuries earlier, when he said that history is a slaughter-bench – Jameson recognizes the special vulnerability of Jews and blacks: "the helplessness of the village community before the perpetual and unpredictable imminence of the lynching or the pogrom, the race riot" (cited in Gilroy, 206).

I think Hobbes, when he said that we are all equal in the "state of nature," meant that we are all equally vulnerable in the "war of each against all," so characteristic of history. The human species is divided against itself in numerous, murderous ways – too numerous to enumerate. Owing to the slave experience of Jews and blacks, it is not surprising that the Exodus became a primary source in the elaboration of black-slave identity. We have already learned from Gilroy how influential political Zionism was in inspiring the back-to-Africa intellectual movement. Gilroy proceeds to draw ideological and other parallels between the two differently dispersed peoples: (1) the notion of a return to the point of origin; (2) the condition of exile, forced separation from the homeland; and (3) the "idea that the suffering of both blacks and Jews has a special redemptive power, not for themselves alone but for humanity as a whole" (208).

With respect to the first parallel, Gilroy cites Blyden who had a serious and sympathetic interest in the so-called Jewish Question, which he regarded as "the question of questions," and "that marvelous movement called Zionism" (209). Blyden believed that blacks and Jews were linked by a shared historical experience – servitude – and by a mission to act as "the spiritual saviors or regenerators of humanity" (211). Better known today is Du Bois who also played a key role in the twentieth-century formalization of pan-Africanism. He was a resident in Europe at the time of the Dreyfus trial and wrote about following its consequences as part of his own development. Gilroy also recognizes that in the present political moment the identification of blacks with the Palestinian struggle for justice and democracy frustrates any attempt to develop a dialogue about the significance of the convergences between Jews and blacks.

Black culture and ineffable terror

Under this heading, Gilroy opens his discussion with the statement: "It is important to emphasize that any correspondences that could be identified between the stories of blacks and Jews take on a radically different significance after the Holocaust" (213). Gilroy accepts arguments for its uniqueness. He does not, however, want the recognition of that uniqueness to stand in the way of a better understanding of the terror and mass killings that other peoples have experienced. It is in this regard that Gilroy sees black and Jewish writers as having missed untold opportunities to develop a critical dialogue. Mentioning Zygmunt Bauman as an example, Gilroy states that he appreciates Bauman's insights "into the complicity of rationality with racial terror and the advantages of marginality as a hermeneutic standpoint." But Gilroy criticizes Bauman for his failure even to mention the Americas in his discussion of racism and anti-Semitism, and hence practicing a Eurocentrism that detracts from the quality of his work. A similar criticism is leveled at Emmanuel Levinas's failure to come to grips with either slavery or colonial domination.

In contrast, Primo Levi is given credit for deepening our understanding of what racial slavery must have meant. "Levi speaks from a position," Gilroy avers, "that exemplifies the strengths of an understanding of the uniqueness of the Holocaust that is not prescriptive because it exists in a dialectical relationship with a sense of the ubiquity and normality of similar events" (215). Gilroy also makes the indisputable observation that anti-Semitism and racism in the nineteenth and twentieth centuries are closely associated by so-called "scientific" anthropology and other social sciences. This reality is well captured by black authors like Toni Morrison who, in her *Beloved*, introduces Schoolteacher, a slave-holder whose "rational" and "scientific" racism replaces the patriarchal and sentimental version of racial domination practiced at "Sweet Home" by his predecessors. What Gilroy sees so clearly is the destructive role of formal-technical rationality in the human condition – some of the consequences of which will be discussed in later chapters of this volume.

Routes: Travel and Translation in the Late Twentieth Century[9] by James Clifford

Under the heading of "Jewish Connections," Clifford provides a brief review of *Black Atlantic* and, in particular, Gilroy's concluding chapter where he rejects the idea of "Africa" as a kind of Holy Land, but retains the significant contribution that black history and culture have made to a counterculture of modernity. Gilroy's view in that regard parallels the thoughts about contemporary Jewish diasporism, with its criticism and even repudiation of Zionism. Clifford, like some of the other thinkers we have discussed, sees the ambivalence toward, or the outright rejection of the notion of "return" to, a point of origin as a valid expression of the historical experience of blacks and Jews. He "worries" about the extent to which diaspora, defined as dispersal, presupposes a "center," an actual "national territory" rather than a reinterpreted tradition, book, or "portable eschatology" (269). Clifford convincingly argues that the ideology of "origin and return" may seriously weaken the specific local interactions, both constructive and defensive, that are necessary for the maintenance of diasporic social forms. "The empowering paradox of diaspora," Clifford writes, "is that dwelling *here* assumes a solidarity and connection *there*. But *there* is not necessarily a single place or an exclusivist nation" (ibid.)

In a 1993 essay by the Boyarins, titled "Diaspora: Generation and the Ground of Jewish Identity," they argue against two alternatives to diasporism: (1) Pauline universalist humanism (we are all one in the spiritual body of Christ); and (2) autochthonous nationalism (we are all one in the place that belongs, from the beginning, to us alone). The former presumably attains a love for humanity at the price of imperialist inclusion conversion. The latter gains a feeling of rootedness at the expense of excluding others with old and new claims to the land. For the Boyarins, diaspora ideology requires a principled renunciation of both universalism and sovereignty, and the adoption of an attitude and conduct suited to the conditions of "diaspora," a social reality *sui generis*. The Boyarins assert forcefully that the Zionist solution to the so-called "problem" of diaspora – an exclusively negative conception of "exile" – is "the subversion of Jewish culture and not its culmination . . . capturing Judaism in a State" (cited in Clifford, 270).

The Boyarins thus want to bring to the fore the positive, creative dimensions of Jewish, diasporic history. Although that history was inspired, in some degree, by the messianic idea of "return," the Jewish historical

---

[9] Cambridge, MA: Harvard University Press, 1997.

diasporas, from the time of Babylon, have been creative cultures in their own right, which was made possible by the social and cultural *interaction* of the Jews with other peoples. "We Jews," Jonathan Boyarin writes, "should recognize the strength that comes from a diversity of communal arrangements and concentrations both among Jews and with our several others. We should recognize that the co-presence of those others is not a threat, but rather the condition of our lives" (ibid.).

The Boyarin conception of diaspora, Clifford correctly notes, is intended to serve as a model *of* (historical Jewish experience) and a model *for* (contemporary hybrid identities), an aim that is evident in the following passage:

> Diasporic cultural identity teaches us that cultures are not preserved by being protected from "mixing" but probably can only continue to exist as a product of mixing. While this is true of all cultures, diasporic Jewish culture lays it bare because of the impossibility of a *natural* association between this people and a particular land – thus the impossibility of seeing Jewish culture as a self-enclosed, bounded phenomenon . . . The production of an ideology of a pure Jewish cultural essence that has been debased by Diaspora seems neither historically nor ethically correct. "Diasporized," that is disaggregated, identity allows the early medieval scholar Rabbi Sa'adya to be an Egyptian Arab who happens to be Jewish and also a Jew who happens to be an Egyptian Arab. Both of these contradictory propositions must be held together. (Cited in Clifford, 271)

The Boyarins intend their theoretical and historical model of diaspora to replace national self-determination. They readily acknowledge, however, that their model "would be an idealized Diaspora generalized from those situations in Jewish history when the Jews were relatively free from persecution and yet constituted by strong identity – those situations, moreover, within which promethean Jewish creativity was not antithetical, indeed was synergistic with a general cultural activity" (273). Jewish life in Muslim Spain before the expulsions is an obvious example. And Clifford comments: "We enter, here, the whole 'Geniza world' of S. D. Goitein, the Mediterranean of the eleventh to the thirteenth centuries (and beyond) where Jews, Muslims and Christians lived, traded, borrowed, and conversed in the process of maintaining distinct communities" (273).

One cannot do justice to the superior qualities of Clifford's analysis without quoting him at length:

> There are no innocent periods of history, and the Geniza world had its share of intolerance. Without reducing these centuries to a romanticized

multiculturalism, one can recognize an extraordinary cosmopolitan network. As Goitein and his followers have shown, lines of identity were drawn differently, often less absolutely than in the modern era. For long periods and in many places, people of distinct religions, races, cultures, and languages coexisted. Difference was articulated through connection, not separation. (273–4)

Clifford also cites Max Weinreich's historical research showing that what the Ashkenazic Jews aimed at "was not isolation from Christians but insulation from Christianity" (275). For Weinreich, as Clifford correctly interprets his position, the "defining loyalty here is to an open text, a set of interpretable norms, not to a 'homeland' or even to an ancient tradition . . . The distinction of Jew or non-Jew is critical, but processual and nonessentialist" (275).

I fully appreciate the Boyarin, Weinreich, Clifford emphasis on the historically creative side of Jewish diasporic cultures. And I agree that ascribing eternal, immutable traits ("essentialism") to an ethnic or religious group is a serious error. But I also believe that one can grasp the characteristic uniqueness of a people's culture without committing that error. How? By recognizing that the varieties of Jewish social, cultural, and religious experience rest on a set of unifying principles.

2

Varieties of Jewish Religious Experience

(Resting, however, on Unifying Jewish Religious Principles)

What I have tried to accomplish in the subsequent chapters of this book is to provide a historical-sociological *overview* of the process by which the Jews became a diaspora people. In order to fulfill that task adequately, I have relied on the universally acknowledged, great Jewish and non-Jewish historians such as Graetz, Dubnov, Baron, Schürer, Y. Kaufmann, and others. Why is an "overview" in any intellectual field desirable and even necessary?

An overview is necessary if one wants to understand how a historical process began, how it developed, and how the consequences of that process came about. Over the last few decades, however, Jewish historians have shifted toward a very different approach to Jewish history, focusing on specific regions as the appropriate contexts. Trends in Jewish historiography have turned dramatically away from grand narratives toward local studies, cultural hybridism between Jews and their neighbors, and the rejection of "essential" characteristics that, purportedly, define Jews across time and space. This trend is evident, for example, in the publication and rapid adoption of David Biale's edited volumes, *Cultures of the Jews: A New History* (2002). But distinguished scholars such as Moshe Rosman have offered thoughtful and important criticisms of this trend in Jewish historiography.

In his highly illuminating discussion of the issues, Moshe Rosman begins by taking the great Jewish historians to task for ignoring what he calls "geography."[1] He states that, for Graetz, although "the details surely differed from place to place, the essential fate of the Jews – to create and to suffer – was the same everywhere." He continues: "Graetz's

---

[1] Jeremy Cohen and Moshe Rosman, eds, *Rethinking European Jewish History*, Portland, OR: Littman Library of Jewish Civilization, 2009. See also Moshe Rosman's *How Jewish is Jewish History?* Oxford and Portland, OR: Littman Library of Jewish Civilization, 2007.

perspective on Jewish history as unfolding on a *world-wide stage* was also adopted . . . by Simon Dubnov, who actually titled his classic multi-volume history 'The *World* History of the Jewish People'" (18). Rosman discerns the same "problem" in Salo W. Baron's monumental work. He too "discounted the geographical fragmentation of the Jews and affirmed their world-wide unity based on things they shared in common other than territory. Numerous passages in his work functioned to minimize the importance of local factors such as geography. The Jewish community and its religious, social and legal institutions '. . . were pliable enough to allow for infinite *local variations in detail, while maintaining unbroken continuity and unity in fundamentals*'" (19; italics added).

Rosman's criticism prompts us to ask this question: is it not historically true that, although one finds in the countless Jewish diasporas what we might properly call "varieties of Jewish religious experience," one also finds what amounts to "unifying Jewish religious principles"? Take, for example, the striking diversity that characterized first century Judaism. There were at least two major schools, Hillel and Shammai, and four known denominations: Pharisees, Sadducees, Zealots, and Essenes. This diversity, characteristic of Judea before the Roman destruction of the Second Temple, nevertheless presupposed unifying principles.

For purposes of clarifying the fundamental difference between "essentialism" and what I call "unifying principles" in first century Judaism, we need to turn to Josephus. A distinguished Josephus scholar, H. St John Thackeray, has described Josephus as "an egoist, a self-interested time-server and flatterer of his Roman patrons"; he was no Thucydides who recorded the "tragedy of his nation with strict and sober impartiality" (Zeitlin, 1988, chs 1 and 2). For all his criticisms, however, Thackeray acknowledges that "the narrative of our author [the Jewish war] in its main outlines must be accepted as trustworthy" (ibid.).

Josephus' work that is most relevant to the question of unifying principles is found in his *Against Apion*. Although Josephus, in this work, is explaining Judaism to polytheists, there is no good reason to doubt the accuracy of his explanation, for it is confirmed by two other major sources, the New Testament and the Mishna. Apion, a grammarian in Alexandria, who wrote harsh invective against the Jews, accused them of sedition. Why? Because there was no evidence among them of idols to the Roman emperors, or of any other idols for that matter: they must have been atheists as there were no images whatsoever of their deity. What Apion thus viewed negatively as atheism, Josephus affirmed positively: nothing had been found even in the Temple other than what was prescribed by the Torah. Apion also accused the Jews of infecting the populace with indolence by encouraging them to rest from their labors one day a week. The unifying principles of Judaism, Josephus thus avers, were to observe the Law (Torah) and pious practices, and to educate the children accordingly. This was true both in Judea and in the Diaspora. Apion himself attested to this when he took the Jews to task for *not* worshiping the same gods as the Alexandrians. Apion was especially astonished at the Jews' allegiance to their original religious laws even in a foreign country. Speaking to a sophisticated Hellenized audience, and tracing the Torah to Moses, Josephus informs them that whereas some peoples had entrusted the supreme political power to monarchies, others to oligarchies, and still others to the masses, Moses eschewed all these forms of polity and gave his political structure the form of a "theocracy" (a term he coined), placing all sovereignty and authority in the hands of God.

Moreover, Josephus continues, for our lawgiver, Moses, religion governs all our actions, occupations, and speech; none of these things did our lawgiver leave unexamined or indeterminate. There is incessant training in morals and the letter of the Law, which were to be followed in daily life: what foods we may or may not eat; how they should be prepared; how to clean utensils; with whom one should associate; which periods are to be devoted to labor and which to rest – all this and more is stipulated in the Law (including the twofold law).

Every week on the Sabbath and often on Thursday too, men desert their other occupations and assemble to listen to the Law, and to obtain a thorough and accurate knowledge of it. The "Law," the Canon, included the Pentateuch, the Prophets, the Psalms, the books of Samuel, and, most likely, the other components of the Hebrew Scriptures. Josephus insists that the Law is so methodically inculcated that it is internalized by Everyman. There was only one Temple for the one and only God; concern for the community takes precedence; there is to be no sexual liaison outside marriage; all children are to be brought up to learn and read about the words and deeds of their forefathers, and imitate them in their goodness. Honoring our parents is second only to honoring God.

The equitable treatment of aliens (*gerim*), Josephus continues, is one of our oldest laws and traditions. We welcome all those who elect to share the laws of Moses: proselytes are not only welcome but vigorously pursued. The Law enjoins us to show consideration even to declared enemies; it prohibits the spoiling of fallen combatants or outrage to prisoners of war, especially women. The Law also commands gentleness and humanity to beasts, and there are heavy penalties for the violation of those laws. But there is also the supreme reward for piety: the reward of future life. Here Josephus expresses a fundamental, Pharisaic, proto-rabbinic belief.

Josephus then endeavors to convey the characteristic uniqueness of the Judaism of his time by contrasting it with Greek and other polytheistic beliefs. Their gods are numerous and engendered in all manner of ways.

They reside in definite localities like animal species, some underground, others in the sea, and still others throughout nature. And all these deities are subordinate to an *impersonal, supradivine force* – in the Greek case called *moira* or Fate – and powerless before it. Josephus concludes his encomium on the Jewish Law by observing that it has stood the test of time and is widely imitated.

Josephus is, of course, writing after Titus' conquest of Judea. At the invitation of Vespasian, Josephus is writing in Rome where a Jewish diaspora had already existed; and although one might wish to view Josephus' encomium as, in some measure, an idealization, there is no reason to doubt its basic soundness. For as we reflect on subsequent, diasporic Jewish history, it is safe to say that the unifying principles prevailed despite the varieties of Jewish religious experience, and despite the definite social and cultural interaction with other peoples. I see no good reason, therefore, to regard the unifying principles as "essentialism."

Moshe Rosman's *Rethinking European Jewish History*

Rosman observes that even before the development of the multicultural conception of Jewish history, historians in the 1970s and 1980s were determined to become fully conversant with *specific* geopolitical entities (England, Spain, Poland, the Hapsburg empire, etc.) in which the Jewish community they were studying resided. The result was quite positive in producing well-researched, dense monographs on particular geographical contexts. Such narrowly focused studies certainly added not only a wealth of information but also fruitful interpretations. However, there was a drawback to this methodological approach of which these historians were apparently unaware. Rosman keenly observes:

> These new monographs were based on the unspoken, unexamined presumption that the fundamental organizing principle of Jewish history should be political geography . . . Granted the impressiveness of the monograph corpus, the question still needs to be asked. Virtually no one today would challenge the importance of contextualizing Jewish history. However, is the context demarcated by the political-geographical borders that a particular community happened to reside within the only relevant, or even always the most appropriate, one. (22–3)

Rosman then illustrates, from his own research, the disadvantages of the locally focused approach to the relationship between the Jews in the German states and those of the Polish-Lithuanian commonwealth. "The conceptualization of these as two separate communities," he writes, "has perhaps led to a lack of attention to the substantial relations between them in areas where boundaries determined by political realities were not dominant" (25). Rosman's examples in this regard are highly illuminating where the question of how to define a historical-cultural context is concerned:

- economically, Jews in Poland and Jews in the Germanies were a part of the same trade network;
- Poland and Germany were also in a close cultural relationship. Rabbis born in the German states were occasionally trained in Poland and then served in either place. Rabbis moved easily back and forth between the German and Polish communities. Many aspects of Jewish law and religious customs were also common to both regions.

In a word, Rosman's criticism is that "over the past fifty years scholars have . . . largely refrained from viewing Jewish communities as interconnected, irrespective of political borders" (25). Citing the work of Jonathan Israel, *European Jewry in the Age of Mercantilism*, Rosman writes:

> The term "European Jewry" in the title of the book, then, was not simply shorthand for the diverse collection of Jewish communities in various countries. It connoted the transnational, integral nature of Jews all over Europe; their belonging together more than to their places of residence . . . It was the Jews' *cultural* geography that mattered most, and this was "European," not determined by political divisions. (27; italics added)

For Rosman, then, the problem with the geopolitically localized studies is that they have not only neglected the trans-geographical aspect of Jewish history, they have, in effect, "abandoned it altogether . . . There is a cultural geography of Jewish history that transcends national political boundaries. It may not reveal a monolithic culture, but it will probably lend insight into one that resembles a rope with multi-colored strands all intertwined" (28).

Cultures of the Jews[2]

The point of the word "cultures" in the title is to address the question whether we can "speak of one Jewish culture across the ages or only

---

[2] In two volumes, ed. David Biale, New York: Schocken Books, 2002.

Jewish cultures in the plural, each unique to its time and place" (vol. I, xvi). In a sense, then, these volumes are concerned with some of the same issues discussed in Cohen and Rosman's *Rethinking European Jewish History*. Biale opens the preface to both volumes with a description of a small, silver casket fashioned by an Italian-Jewish craftsman some time in the fifteenth century. On the front panel of the casket there were three scenes of a Jewish wife fulfilling her cardinal religious duties: "separating the *challah* from the dough, lighting the Sabbath candles, and immersing herself in the ritual bath, which symbolized the separation of husband and wife during her menstrual period" (xv). Biale then proceeds to recount certain scholarly observations concerning the Bible, such as the Egyptian origin of the name "Moses," the Hebrew language alphabet borrowed from the Phoenicians, and the fact that the Bible is replete with intermarriages between Hebrews and others. Hence, earmarks, presumably, of "assimilation" are found in the Bible itself.

Biale's aim thus being to call attention to what appears to have been "acculturation," he invokes the *Mekhilta*, one of the oldest *midrashim*, the context of which was the Greco-Roman period. The texts show that Jews adopted Greek names and the Greek language. What Biale calls a "stunning example" of interaction between Jewish and Greek culture:

> was revealed in the excavations at Bet She'arim in the lower Galilee. An enormous 3rd Century C.E. Jewish burial chamber at the site contains many sarcophagi decorated with a variety of mythological motifs, such as Leda and the Swan, a favorite artistic theme from Greek mythology. Inscriptions in Greek are mixed with those in Hebrew. The Bet She'arim necropolis also contains the graves of rabbis contemporary with Judah the prince, the compiler of the Mishnah, demonstrating that the cultural *syncretism* [?] of the site was not alien to the rabbis themselves, despite the statements to the contrary in the *Mekhilta*. (xvi–xvii)

I have italicized the word "syncretism" because I believe it is misleading to apply it to the examples Biale has provided. In the first place, it should not be surprising that the Jews adopted the Greek *language* in the Greco-Roman world. Adopting the language – at least partially – of "host" societies was natural and unavoidable throughout the history of Jewish diasporas. But such adoption by the Jews says nothing about the nature of their religio-moral beliefs and practices in their respective diasporic contexts. Even the borrowing of sacral, cultural, economic, and other patterns does not necessarily inform us of the religious self-understanding of the Jews in a given time and place. We must distinguish between cultural "influence," on the one hand, and "syncretism," on the other. The latter term refers to the combination of distinct forms of belief and practice – the fusion, in effect, of two or more originally different forms. Biale asks whether the rabbis buried in the Bet She'arim necropolis "believed in some fashion in the Greek myths portrayed on their tombs" (xvii). The answer is that it is doubtful in the extreme that the rabbis believed any such thing. The most likely meaning of the Greek images and symbols is that they were purely ornamental, as Biale himself suggests.

Syncretism in Jewish History

The best-known example of this cultural and religious fusion occurred not in diaspora but in Jerusalem. The Maccabean revolt was largely provoked by the high priests who by their outrageous behavior had thoroughly discredited themselves in the eyes of the pious masses. This took place when Jason purchased for himself the high priesthood from Antiochus, the Hellenistic-Syrian king, and then had Onias III, the rightful incumbent, exiled. This flagrant violation of Pentateuchal law, far from having been foisted upon Jason by the foreign power, came about at his own initiative. An even greater outrage followed when Menelaus bought the high priesthood and, ousting Jason, went on to encourage sacrifices on the temple altar of swine's flesh to Zeus. The breach with the devout masses was now complete, and the door was thus opened for a new religious leadership consisting of the highly respected scribes, and Torah scholars and teachers. The syncretism had failed.[3]

Polytheism and Monotheism

Clearly, Jason's and Menelaus' attempt at syncretism, had it succeeded, would have meant the destruction of Jewish monotheism and its replacement by polytheism. But Biale is, somehow, not happy with the application of the concept of "monotheism" to Judaism. He cites the biblical period soon after the conquest and/or settlement of Canaan by the Hebrews. He states that "it is now generally accepted among scholars of the biblical period that ancient Israel's cult, especially in its popular manifestations, was bound up with Canaanite polytheism" (xviii).

We know, of course, that some of the people of that era practiced

---

[3] For a full discussion of this chain of events resulting in the "Pharisaic Revolution," see Irving M. Zeitlin, *Jesus and the Judaism of His Time*, Cambridge: Polity, 1988, chapter 2.

a form of idolatry that the prophets severely criticized. There were, apparently, other practices associated with the Asherah that smacked of polytheism. But the fundamental question in such cases is what *meaning* such practices had in the minds of the participants. Yehezkel Kaufmann has made the important point that the form of idolatry described in the Bible is a form of fetishism, not real polytheism. His argument deserves serious consideration:

> The Bible knows that the pagans worship national gods, certain of which are mentioned by name: Baal, Ashtoreth, Chemosh, Milcom, Bel, Nebo, Amon, etc. But it is remarkable that not a single biblical passage hints at the national or mythological qualities of these named gods. Had we only the Bible, we should know nothing of the real nature of the "gods of the nations." In a few isolated passages the pagans are said to worship spirits and demons, but these are anonymous, whereas what we know to have been mythological gods are, in the Bible, mere names . . .
>
> The Bible has a great deal to say about the image cult that was associated with the named gods. But if the god is not understood to be a living, natural power, or a mythological person who dwells in, or is symbolized by, the image, it is evident that the image worship is concieved to be nothing but fetishism.[4]

The concern with "polytheism" and "monotheism," and with the question of whether the latter can be appropriately applied to the early period in Canaan, brings us back to our discussion, in chapter 1, of concepts as analytical tools and, in particular, ideal-type constructs in Weber's sense. The issue is a significant one, as we shall see.

The Nature of Polytheism[5]

Polytheism entails a good deal more than worshiping many gods instead of only one. The most fundamental characteristic of polytheistic religions is that the gods do not reign supreme. Throughout, we find them dominated by a higher order, a supradivine, impersonal force to which they always remain subject. The superordinate power assumes diverse forms. However, it is best known to Western readers as "fate," the Greek *moira*,

---

[4] Yehezkel Kaufmann, *The Religion of Israel*, trans. and abridged by Moshe Greenberg, Chicago, IL: University of Chicago Press, 1969, 9.

[5] The aim of this discussion of "polytheism" and "monotheism" is to clarify their respective meanings. No value judgment is intended by either of the terms.

which not only predetermines the destiny of humans, but of gods as well. The inexorable power of *moira* over humans is most clearly expressed in Sophocles' *Oedipus Rex*. Oedipus kills his father in accordance with the oracle, and this despite the father's effort to foil the prophecy by abandoning Oedipus in his infancy. In the end, it is not known whether the oracle was fulfilled despite the precautions taken or because of them. Fate had its way.

No less inexorable is the power of *moira* over the gods. In Greek mythology Zeus is the supreme ruler. His power is greater than that of all the other gods combined. Yet he is neither omnipotent nor omniscient. Other gods can oppose and deceive him, and *fate* is so powerful that Zeus is helpless before it. He laments that he cannot save his own mortal son from the death that Fate has decreed. It is simply not within his or any other god's power to avoid the Fate that is ordained.

In the religions of the Far East, one may also discern a supradivine, impersonal force. In both Confucianism and Taoism it is this force that ensures the regularity and felicitous order of the world. Also, among the Hindus, there is the "notion of a supradivine and cosmic all-unity, superordinate to the gods and alone independent of the senseless change and transitoriness of the entire phenomenal world."[6]

Directly related to the supradivine are mythology and magic, two additional characteristics of polytheistic religion. The ancient Greeks, not atypical in this regard, "did not believe that the gods created the universe. It was the other way about: the universe created the gods. Before there were gods, heaven and earth had been formed."[7] From Hesiod's *Theogony* we learn of the origin of the gods, and from Homer's epics we learn about their own adventures and their relations with humans. In Greek as in other mythologies there are circumstances in which human beings gain the ability, by means of magic, to influence, control, or even coerce the gods. What makes this possible is the supradivine, impersonal force, the secret workings of which the magicians have learned to manipulate. Hence, the gods are not only subordinate to a superior force, and the creatures rather than the creators of the first forms of being; they may also be coerced and made to do the bidding of human magicians.

That is not all. The deities are literally dependent upon human beings in several fundamental respects, for they derive their nourishment from the offerings of the sacrificial cult. They are also dependent creatures in that they not only lust for one another, but for humans as well. Humans

---

[6] Max Weber, *Economy and Society*, New York: Bedminster Press, 1968, vol. II, 431 and 448.

[7] Edith Hamilton, *Mythology*, New York and Toronto: Mentor Books, 1940, 24.

may also achieve divine status (apotheosis), and short of that, they may become heroes and demigods. Finally, we learn from the mythologies of the world that gods war among themselves and that they ultimately represent two independent domains, such as good and evil, light and darkness, as in Zoroastrianism.

If, therefore, we review and list the chief elements characterizing polytheism, they are:

- the supradivine, impersonal force to which the gods are subordinate;
- the gods are creatures of rather than the creators of the universe;
- humans gain the ability, by means of magic, to influence, control and even coerce the gods;
- the gods are literally dependent on human beings, for they derive their nourishment from the sacrificial cult;
- humans may acquire divine status;
- and the gods war among themselves, ultimately representing two independent domains, good and evil.

This ideal-typical construction of the concept of polytheism, derived from a representative sample of the world's mythologies, but with a special focus on the mythologies of the ancient Near East, should make it easy, even for skeptics and hypercritics to grasp "monotheism" as the original, point-for-point negation and repudiation of polytheism, thus producing the first, unique Israelite conception of a formless, invisible, incorporeal, all-powerful, ethical deity who heard the cries of oppressed Semitic nobodies and came to their aid.

This is the inspired conception of the Israelite God who, in the self-understanding of the Jews, remained a profound historical presence throughout the many subsequent generations of the diasporic history of the Jews.

Biale explicitly and generously acknowledges – and all the participants do so implicitly – that for every major cultural formation discussed in the two edited volumes, many other approaches would be legitimate. I therefore trust that he and the participants will find my approach interesting and cogent.

3

Max Weber's Ancient Judaism

In contrast to the religions of the Far East, biblical Judaism conceived of the world as neither eternal nor unchangeable, but as having been created. The present condition of the world was the outcome of human actions and God's reaction to them, the criterion being whether they obeyed his commandments or strayed from them. "Hence," Weber explains, "the world was an historical product designed to give way again to a truly God-ordained order. The whole attitude toward life of ancient Jewry was determined by this conception of a future God-guided political and social revolution."[1] Weber's aim in this extraordinary work is to analyze the conditions in ancient Israel that gave rise to its "highly rational religious ethic of social conduct; it was free of magic and all forms of irrational quest for salvation; it was inwardly worlds apart from the paths of salvation offered by Asiatic religions" (4).

Weber begins with an analysis of the ancient Near East and the possible influences on the origins of the Israelite worldview. He recognizes that Egypt was an "essentially negative developmental stimulus." The Hebrews regarded the Egyptian *corvée* state and its fundamentally despotic nature as an abomination. They detested Egypt as a "house of bondage." Weber also recognized that the ancient Hebrews were not Bedouin. Ancient Israelite laws show no trace of Bedouin influence; and, besides, Israelite tradition maintains that the Amalek were the deadly enemies of Israel.

For Weber, the new Israelite worldview that aimed for a radical break with all forms of polytheism originated in the teachings of Moses and the prophets. The new monotheistic ethic rested on the distinctive relation of Israel to God, expressed and guaranteed in a unique historical event – the conclusion of a covenant with Yahweh. The prophets and the

---

[1] Weber, *Ancient Judaism*, trans. and ed. Hans H. Gerth and Don Martindale, New York: Free Press, 1952, 4. Hereafter, all page references to this work will be cited in parentheses immediately following the quoted passage.

devout Hebrews always hearkened back to that great, miraculous event in which God had kept his promise, intervened in history, and liberated the Hebrews from Egyptian bondage. That was proof not only of God's power but of the absolute dependability of his promises.

Israel, then, as the other party to the covenant mediated by Moses, owed a lasting debt of gratitude to serve and worship Yahweh, the Lord of the universe, and to follow his laws strictly. This rational relationship, unknown elsewhere, created an ethical obligation so binding that Jewish tradition regarded "defection from Yahweh as an especially fatal abomination" (119). The markedly rational nature of the relationship lay in the *worldly* character of God's promises to Israel. Promised was not some supernatural paradise, but "that they would have numerous descendants, so that the people should become numerous as the sand of the seashore, and that they should triumph over all enemies, enjoy rain, rich harvests, and secure possessions" (119). What God offered, writes Weber, was "salvation from Egyptian bondage, not from a senseless world out of joint. He promised not transcendent values, but dominion over Canaan, which one was out to conquer, and a good life" (126). If the nation or individuals suffered and God failed to help, that was a sign that some commandment had been violated. Which one?

> Irrational divination-means could not answer this question, only knowledge of the very commandments and soul-searching. Thus the idea of a *berith* [covenant] flourishing in the truly Yahwistic circles pushed all scrutiny of the divine will toward an at least relatively rational mode of raising and answering the question. Hence, the priestly exhortation under the influence of the intellectual strata turned with great sharpness against soothsayers, augurs, day-choosers, interpreters of signs, conjurors of the dead, defining their ways of consulting the Deity as characteristically pagan. (167)

In that way the devout Hebrews initiated the process of breaking magic's hold upon the world. Weber thus proposed that the new Israelite worldview served to negate and repudiate all forms of polytheism and to put in their place a rational ethic based on the covenant Israel had made with a formless presence that was felt and conceived as an Almighty, universal God who had heard the cries of the oppressed and had come to their rescue.

The Hebrew Prophets: The Setting

In the eighth century BCE, the northern kingdom of Ephraim, or Israel, and the southern kingdom of Judea found themselves in constant jeopardy, caught as they were between the superpowers of the time, Assyria on the one side and Egypt on the other. As Weber remarks, never before had the region witnessed warfare of such frightfulness and magnitude as that practiced by the Assyrian kings. The biblical writings of the time relate just how preoccupied the Israelites were with the fearful concern for their survival in the face of the merciless Assyrian conquerors. It was in this historical context that there emerged in Israel the great Hebrew prophets of social justice, Amos, Hosea, Isaiah, Micah – and later, in the face of the Babylonian menace, Jeremiah and Ezekiel.

These prophets functioned in one of their roles as "political demagogues." They were primarily *speakers* who conceived of the great powers of Assyria, Egypt, and Babylonia as rods of Yahweh's chastisement for Israel's disobedience to His commandments. Had it not been for the menace of these great powers, Weber avers, these prophets would not have emerged. They constituted an autonomous stratum that often confronted the Israelite kings and the wealthy and powerful, severely criticizing them for their oppression and exploitation of the poor. Occasionally, their admonitions became effective in lessening oppressive conditions.

Typically, the Hebrew prophet spoke on his own, to the public in the marketplace or to the elders at the city gate. The primary prophetic concern was the destiny of the state and the nation, a concern expressing itself in sharp criticism of the overlords. Weber uses the term "demagogue" to describe this prophetic role, but this epithet has to be properly understood. It is employed in its original Greek sense to refer to a speaker who champions the cause of the common people. The demagogue of Periclean democracy, for example, was a secular politician who strove to lead the demos through his personal influence. But the phenomenon of religious demagoguery in the manner of the Hebrew prophets appears to be historically unique. Formally, the prophet was a private citizen, so to speak, for he held no official office. And yet the political authorities paid close attention to the prophets' utterances and activities. Jeremiah's prophecies, for instance, were brought before the king because his message was considered an event of public significance.

Indeed, the political authorities faced the Hebrew "demagogue" with either fear, wrath, or indifference as the situation seemed to warrant. At times, the kings tried to draw a prophet into the royal circle, to co-opt him. At other times, the power holders took harsh action against the social critics. At still other times, members of the royal circle showed open contempt for their critics, as when King Joiakim threw the written prophetic warnings, sheet by sheet, into the fire. When Jeraboam II prohibited prophecy, Amos proclaimed God's wrath toward the northern kingdom for attempting to suppress prophecy. Amos' complaint, Weber remarks, is comparable to that of the modern political critic who demands freedom of speech and the press. But the prophets were more than "speakers." With Jeremiah and his scribe Baruch, the prophetic words were written down in the form of open letters to be read by both the king's circle and the public. Such letters and other prophetic writings constitute, for Weber, "the earliest known example of political pamphlet literature directly addressing itself to contemporary events." Typically, the prophet takes no pleasure from the fact that the catastrophe he anticipated has materialized. He shows neither jubilation nor despair, and alongside his lamentations he offers hope for God's grace and better times.

Although Weber refers to the prophets as political demagogues, he stresses that, to understand them as they understood themselves and were understood by their audiences, we must appreciate that their motives were strictly religious. When Isaiah, for example, in the face of the Assyrian siege of Jerusalem, prophesized that the city would not fall, that was not the result of any realistic assessment of the actual power relations of Assyria and Judea. It was, rather, the result of his assessment of Judea's moral conduct: the Judeans had, of course, sinned, but not so egregiously as to deserve the destruction of the city of David. About a hundred and some odd years later, Jeremiah, knowing of the advancing Babylonian menace toward Jerusalem, prophesized that the city *would* fall. His prophecy, too, was not the result of a realistic assessment of power relations. It was, rather, a matter of his believing that in the light of Judea's earlier sins – two cases of human sacrifice under the kings Manasseh and Ahaz – Judea cannot avoid God's severe punishment. The stench, Jeremiah proclaimed, had remained in God's nostrils. The prophets' stand with respect to foreign alliances, notably their unrelenting opposition to an alliance with Egypt, was also determined by religious motives.

Just as the prophets' views of foreign policy were based not primarily on realistic political considerations, neither were their attitudes toward domestic issues reflections of their social class background. Their concern for the oppressed, exploited, and poor certainly did not flow from a common, unprivileged background. Quite the contrary, they shared the same attitude despite their diverse social origins. Although they argued passionately in defense of the "little people," and excoriated the rich and powerful, the great prophets themselves were far from unprivileged. Isaiah was descended from a genteel family, he moved among distinguished priests, and had close relations with Hezekiah, as his councilor and physician. He was one of the eminent men of Jerusalem. Zephaniah had descended from David and was a great-grandson of Hezekiah. Ezekiel was a distinguished Jerusalem priest. All these men were therefore well-to-do Jerusalemites. Micah came from a small town, and Jeremiah from a village, but he stemmed from a landed clan of rural priests, and possessed sufficient resources for the purchase of land. And even Amos – who was a small stockbreeder and called himself a shepherd who lived on sycamore fruit, the food of the poor – was a highly educated man. Weber thus shows that the social class background of the prophets was certainly not the determinant of their attitudes. That they were not ideologues is also clear from the fact that they were as critical of the common people for failing in their religious duties as they were of the noble landowners for forcibly appropriating and enclosing the land of the poor. In a word, the meaning and motives of the prophets' words and actions were not political in the Greek sense. No Hebrew prophet was a champion of "democratic" ideals, deliberately serving as an ideological spokesman for the impoverished peasants or proletarians.

To the extent that the prophets derived "community" from any source, it was not from the demos. On the contrary, if they received any personal, material support at all, it was from the distinguished, pious families of Judea, where there were sympathetic supporters among the *Zekenim*, the elders, who as guardians of the pious traditions held the prophets in high regard. Weber notes that although most prophets spoke out against debt slavery, the pawning of clothes, and the violation of the charity commandments that benefited the poor, the prophets never received support from the peasants.

As for the kings, they, too, never supported the prophets, who were the chief critics of the politically necessary concessions the kings had made in allowing foreign shrines for the wives of their diplomatic marriages. From the time of Solomon and his *corvée* state, the prophets despised the royal adoption of practices that emanated from Egyptian despotism. Consequently, Solomon had no positive significance for any of the prophets, and it was David who was regarded as the pious ruler. Hosea viewed the kings of the northern kingdom as illegitimate because they had usurped the throne without the will of Yahweh, but no prophet denied the legitimacy of David's descendants. In their reaction to prophetic censure, the kings tolerated the prophets only when they had to, but when the kings felt sure of themselves, as did Manasseh, who ruled as an Assyrian puppet for 50 years, they resorted to bloody persecution.

Again and again, the prophets spoke out against reliance on pagan, military technology – horses and chariots – and against political alliances. Dealings with Egypt were especially loathed for religious reasons. Egypt was described as a weak reed that would break and pierce the hand that leaned upon it. The ground of prophetic opposition was again religious, not simply because of the dangerous influence of foreign cults on Judean soil, but especially because Judea's primary reliance should be on the *berith* (covenant) with Yahweh. Trust in foreign alliances and in advanced military technology indicated a lack of trust in God. As Jeremiah viewed the covenantal relationship with Yahweh, he had ordained as Israel's punishment Nebuchadnezzar's conquest of Judea, and one had to accept the fact that no alliance of any kind could change Israel's God-ordained destiny. "Clearly," writes Weber, "the whole [prophetic] attitude toward internal as well as foreign affairs was purely religious in motivation; nothing bespeaks of political expediencies" (282).

Biblical criticism in Weber's time had introduced the notion of a fundamental dichotomy and even antipathy between the priests and prophets of Israel. Weber, however, regarded that notion as misleading, for the prophets "were by no means always antagonistic to the priests. Isaiah had close relations with the priests of Jerusalem, and Ezekiel was thoroughly priestly in outlook" (282). Weber makes the important point that although Hosea had said of God, "For I desire mercy (*hesed*), and not sacrifice, and the knowledge of God rather than burnt offerings" (6:6), neither he nor any other prophet had repudiated the sacrificial cult per se or attacked the Temple proper. Another example requiring clarification is Jeremiah's having been charged with a capital crime for prophesying that the Temple would share the fate of the shrine in Shiloh, which the Philistines had once destroyed. The authentic meaning of his statement is clarified in Jer. 7: 4f. and 11f.: the Temple in itself is useless and will suffer the fate of Shiloh if you do not resolve to change your conduct. The meaning of Jeremiah's critique was not a repudiation of priests in general or of the priestly office. It was a critique of certain priests insofar as they were failing to heed the divine imperatives that the prophet had proclaimed as directly inspired by Yahweh.

Moreover, Weber stresses, before we entertain the notion of a basic antagonism between the prophets and priests of Israel, we have to remember that Jeremiah himself came from a priestly family and that he repudiated those whom he called "false prophets" with a passion at least equal to that with which he admonished certain priests. For Jeremiah, Yahweh's actions were contingent upon the nation's *moral* conduct, so the Temple was no automatic guarantee of the deliverance of Jerusalem. The confidence of certain prophets, notably Hananiah, in the absoluteness of Yahweh's commitment to Israel, Jeremiah branded as false. That is why he accuses Hananiah of making the people "trust in a lie" (28:15). Jeremiah proclaimed that "circumcision of the heart" (9:24) is more important than circumcision of the flesh. Thus the prophetic criticism of the cult is not an outright rejection of the sacrificial ritual, but a strong devaluation of all ritual that individuals believe can somehow replace right ethical conduct or compensate for the lack of it.

As observed earlier, the prophets were all literate and well informed concerning world events, and they showed no signs of attempting to flee from the world in the Hindu sense. Even the faintest hint of a *unio mystica* is absent from the prophetic literature. The prophets conceived of themselves as neither more nor less than individuals directly inspired by Yahweh, even interpreting the divine message as they understood it in light of the world-historical events transpiring at the time. The form of the inspiration, being always *auditory*, was entirely congruent with the conception of Yahweh as formless and invisible. The content of the prophetic message, strongly demanding ethically right conduct and social justice, was also entirely congruent with the conception of Yahweh as an almighty, universal, and *ethical* deity. Universal and almighty because his Almighty presence had been felt in Egypt, in the Exodus, in the wilderness, in the conquest and settlement in Canaan, in the victories over the Philistines, and in numerous subsequent events in which Yahweh was felt to have intervened on Israel's behalf. From the prophetic standpoint, the effects of God's will and presence were unmistakable in determining Israel's destiny in the face of the empires, Assyria and Babylonia. The prophets, in a word, heard the voice of the divine presence, attained clarity of the message's meaning, and communicated with equal clarity what Yahweh had commanded them to proclaim.

The Prophetic Ethic

The Hebrew prophets made no claim that they were conveying Yahweh's message verbatim. They had to interpret Yahweh's intention in the light of foreign and domestic events. Weber underscores repeatedly that the "wonders" attributed to the prophets were always effected by the spoken or written word, invoking the will of God, but never by any sort of sympathetic or other magical manipulation. The prophets sometimes acted as if they had the ability to influence Yahweh. Abraham and Moses had served as intercessors, and Amos, the first of the eighth century prophets of social justice, occasionally appears as an intercessor. But no prophet had ever reckoned with the possibility of influencing Yahweh by means of magic. Nor had any prophet ever claimed the right to be worshiped or even venerated, or to be free of sin. The prophets never judged themselves to be in possession of holiness. They conceived of themselves as nothing more than a means of communicating Yahweh's imperatives. For Weber, this "emissary type" of prophecy had never before been so highly developed.

The Hebrew prophets concerned themselves primarily with ethics, the ethic enjoined upon Israel through the covenant. They were, therefore, proclaiming no new conception of God, no new means of grace, no new commandments. It is presupposed that God and his will are known to all concerned: "He has shown thee, O man, what is good" (Micah 6:8), "to abide," in Weber's words, "by those commandments of God which are known from the *Torah*. Isaiah also called the Torah of God his own prophecy" (30:9) (300). Hence, from the prophetic standpoint, the Torah provided the ethical principles with which to approach the threats to national sovereignty posed by Assur, Babel, and Egypt. Panic, rage, and fear of devastation and enslavement naturally agitated the people and determined the content and urgency of the prophetic messages. There was, however, no doubt in the prophetic mind that the only correct answer to the question of why a misfortune had befallen the nation was that Yahweh had willed it so: "Shall there be evil in a city, and the Lord hath not done it?" (Amos 3:6).

Opinions had differed, among the Israelites, as to whether the zealous God of the confederacy or the sublime world monarch stood more in the foreground. Yahweh had in the past, Weber observes, "repeatedly visited military disaster on the enemy and rescued Israel; often, however, this was only after having let his people suffer . . . [frightful] misfortune for quite a time. Therefore, and for this reason alone, the prophets became politicians" (301). They were "politicians" in that they urgently concerned themselves with the current political crisis facing the nation; but their political approach to the crisis was determined by the belief that the crisis was willed by God as punishment for the nation's sins. This meant that the nation had failed, above all, to abide by God's *ethical* commandments. That was the view commonly held by Amos, Hosea, Isaiah, Micah, and Jeremiah. The ethical commandments implicit in their criticisms and demands were, in substance, identical with the commandments of the Torah.

It is misleading, Weber demonstrates, to speak of the Hebrew prophets as "prophets of doom." No prophet absolutely opposed the hope of better times returning after the disaster, nor could he have done so and still exert any influence on his audience. The whole point of the prophetic understanding of the covenantal relationship was that it always held out hope if the offenders would change their ways. Jeremiah, for example, "considered a true prophet only one who lashed the sins of the people and – in connection therewith – prophesied disaster. But misfortune must be not absolute and definitive, but conditional through sin" (306).

The inner-worldly or this-worldly orientation of the Hebrew prophets and their world-political concerns, domestic and international, meant that it never would have occurred to them to ask a metaphysical question, such as "what is the meaning of the world and life?" Nor did the prophets, out of a need for salvation, seek the perfection of the "soul" as against the imperfect world, as did the holy men of India. Indeed, the idea of the soul as a spiritual entity that survives the death of the body, and lives on to eternity, is absent from the Hebrew Bible. Such an idea first appeared in post-biblical Judaism and early Christianity under Hellenistic and other influences.

The *this-worldliness* of the prophets meant, therefore, that Yahweh's motives were understandable and justifiable, and world events were rational in character, that is, determined neither by blind chance nor by magical forces. What Yahweh demanded in his ethical commandments every child could understand; and though Yahweh was formless and transcendent, this was never transformed into a philosophical problem by the prophets. Insofar as the prophets engaged in careful reflection, this was focused on the human condition. Thus Ezekiel (chs 14 and 18), for example, first posed the question of why the righteous suffered with the wicked; and Jeremiah (31:29) offered hope for a future in which every individual will suffer only for his own misdeeds, and one would no longer say, "the fathers have eaten sour grapes and the children's teeth are set on edge."

In the prophetic view, then, evil in the human condition resulted from actions carried out in opposition to God's commandments. There was no anti-god principle, force, or domain in biblical Judaism, and hence no problems requiring a theodicy. In Weber's words:

> The prophetic horizon remained . . . completely this-worldly in contrast [not only to the Far Eastern religions, but also] to the Hellenic mysteries of the Orphic religion which operated throughout with promises of the beyond . . . Yahweh's commandments like his ancient promises were quite concrete and positive and purely this-worldly . . . Conduct according to the commandment of God, not knowledge of the meaning of the world behoved man. (317)

The religion of Israel, as represented by the prophets, required "good works," as is evident from their admonitions and demands. However, the prophets also demanded a certain kind of "faith":

> The faith which the Jewish prophets demanded, was not that internal behavior which Luther and the reformers intended. In truth it [the faith of the prophets] signified only the unconditional trust in Yahweh's omnipotence and the sincerity of his word and conviction of its fulfillment despite all external probabilities to the contrary . . . Obedience and particularly humility were the ensuing virtues and both were especially appreciated by Yahweh, especially humility, the strict avoidance not only of *hubris* in the Hellenic sense, but in the last analysis of all trust in one's own abilities and all self-renown. This representation was of great consequence for the development of later Jewish piety. (318)

And although the prophets judged the conduct of the people and, in particular, some of their foolish practices, such as venerating the shapes of wood and stone which they had fashioned with their own hands, it was the conduct of the ruling strata of Israel that was decisive in determining the nation's destiny. For Weber, then, there could be no doubt that it was the tremendous influence of the prophets that reinforced and rendered authoritative the conception of Yahweh as the Almighty ethical God of the universe:

> The entire inner construction of the Old Testament [Weber writes] is inconceivable without its orientation in terms of the oracles of the prophets. These giants cast their shadows through the millennia into the present, since this holy book of the Jews became a holy book of the Christians too, and since the entire interpretation of the mission of the Nazarene was primarily determined by the old promises to Israel. (334)

The question of how the Jews came to constitute a pariah community, Weber shows, must be viewed as the result of both prophecy and the special ritual requirements of Judaism, which the Jews took with them into exile and held to stubbornly and tenaciously.

With the destruction of the First Temple in 586 BCE, and the exile of the Jews, sacrifice, permissible only in Jerusalem, became impossible. The question therefore first arose among the Babylonian exiles of how to preserve the faith based upon the Torah and the prophetic tradition. The answer, as it took shape over time, was to establish a "temporary" house of study and worship, where the Torah texts could be read and pondered, and where the congregants could pray to God and worship Him.

It was a "temporary" house of worship because, given the general Jewish acceptance of the prophetic eschatology, the Jews of the diaspora lived in the hope that God would, in due course, restore them to their homeland. It was in this context that the proto-synagogue was invented to serve the religious needs of the people until the time of their return and the reconstruction of the Temple. In exile, preserving the faith based on the Torah and the prophets meant not only following the ethical commandments but also remaining ritually pure by guarding against any and all polytheistic influences. Slowly, there emerged a distinctive, religious community organization with new institutions peculiar to the exile.

The destruction of the Temple and the resulting exile were, of course, interpreted by the Jews as God's punishment for offences against his commandments. And since the prophets had taught that after the chastisement of the nation and its repentance the commonwealth would be restored, the exilic community became especially zealous in its efforts to insulate itself against the influence of polytheism. Weber therefore proposes that "toward the outside world Jewry increasingly assumed the type of a ritualistically segregated guest-people (pariah people). And indeed Jewry did this voluntarily and not under pressure of external rejections" (417).

In the earliest period of the diaspora, the Jews had ritually segregated themselves out of fear of ritual "pollution" and their antipathy toward the pagan beliefs and practices of the "host" peoples. But the resistance to breaking bread with the host people and intermarrying with them engendered a reciprocal antipathy.

When the Babylonians were defeated by the Persians, the Jews were eventually allowed, in the fifth century BCE, to return to Judea and to rebuild Jerusalem and the Temple. There the religion based on the Torah and the prophets was rejuvenated and the sacrificial cult was restored. By that time, however, the religious institution that had originated in exile – a house of worship and study, which in the Hellenistic era was called a "synagogue" – had become so firmly a part of Jewish cultural life that it was successfully transplanted in Judea. With the expansion of the Roman Empire into the Near East, Judea became subject to Roman rule. The Jewish revolt against Roman rule that broke out in 66 CE was finally put down by the Roman legions under Vespasian and Titus in 70 CE. The result was the destruction of the second Temple and Jerusalem, and much of Judea. Once again, a large portion of the Jewish populace was forced into exile. The Romans, vengeful over the protracted Jewish war against their domination, and resolving that the land of Israel – Judea – should be erased from memory, gave the land the new name of Palestine, a name derived from the Philistines whom the Israelites under David had conquered many centuries earlier. The Romans also tried, unsuccessfully, to change the name of Jerusalem to Aelia Capitolina.

It was, therefore, under Roman imperial rule that the Jews now lived in exile. As they refused to venerate the Roman, pagan deities whose "guest-rights" they enjoyed, and as the Jewish God was invisible, the hosts often regarded the Jews as godless. Owing, then, to the self-segregation of the Jews and to the anti-Jewish feelings of the host-people, the Jews acquired the status of what Weber called a "pariah people." This status, as the Jewish exiles eventually sojourned in Europe, soon had definite implications for the economic role the Jews played in the Christian societies of their hosts.

4

The Babylonian Empire

The final collapse of the Assyrian Empire occurred during the early years of the reign of the Judean king Jehoiachim. The Medes and the Babylonians laid waste the renowned Assyrian capital at Nineveh after a three-year siege (606 BCE). Thus, the empire that had destroyed the northern kingdom of Israel, and had seriously threatened the southern kingdom of Judah, perished.

The conquerors had divided among themselves the Assyrian Empire so that the Medes ruled in the northern and some of the southern districts, while the Babylonians ruled in southern Mesopotamia. The new Babylonia regarded itself as the legitimate ruler of Syria, which had just been conquered by Egypt, and war between the two powers became unavoidable. Nabupolassar, King of Babylonia, died at this time and was succeeded by his son, Nabukudrussur II, or Nebuchadnezzar, as he is called by the Hebrew prophets. He led his army against the Pharaoh Nechoh, who was moving from Syria toward the Tigris River. A decisive battle took place between the Babylonians and the Egyptians at the city of Carchemish, on the upper reaches of the Euphrates. The Egyptians were defeated and forced to relinquish their control of Syria to the new rulers (604 BCE). Along with Syria, Judah, as a part of the Syro-Palestine province, was also forced to recognize the supremacy of the Babylonian king.[1] In Jerusalem, there arose a militant party calling for active resistance to the new conqueror. Counting on Egypt's assistance, the royal court, too, favored an armed struggle.

When Isaiah, in the face of the Assyrian siege, prophesied that Jerusalem would not fall, his proclamation could hardly have been based on a realistic assessment of the relation of forces between the besieger

---

[1] The present discussion is based on the Book of Jeremiah and on Simon Dubnov's *History of the Jews: From the Beginning to Early Christianity*, vol. I, transl. from the Russian by Moshe Spiegel, New York: Thomas Yoseloff, 1967.

and the besieged. Similarly, it appears that the great prophet Jeremiah's prophecies were based more on his assessment of Judah's sinfulness, and less, if at all, on the comparative military strength of Babylonia and Judah. If, therefore, the degree of sinfulness was the criterion for the respective proclamations of these two great prophets, it explains why Isaiah said that Jerusalem would not fall, and why Jeremiah, as we shall see, prophesied a different fate for the city and its Temple.

After his conquest of Syria, Nebuchadnezzar advanced westward toward Judah. The agitation in Jerusalem grew from day to day. As disaster loomed, a day of fasting and worship in the Temple was proclaimed. Jeremiah took this opportunity to act. He authorized his disciple, Baruch, to transcribe all the prophetic speeches that he, Jeremiah, had delivered over the course of 23 years, from the time of King Josiah down to the present, and to read them publicly in the Temple on the day of the fast. When Baruch appeared before those assembled and read aloud Jeremiah's most recent utterances, asserting the inevitability of Babylonian hegemony, the reading produced a disturbing reaction in the assembled multitude.

The courtiers then demanded of Baruch that he read the manuscript before them once more. Surrounded by his attendants, King Jehoiakim sat impassively listening and warming himself by a brazier beside him. And as each section of the scroll had been read, he threw it into the fire, so that by the end of the reading the entire manuscript was consumed. After having shown his disdain for the views of the prophet, he ordered that Jeremiah and Baruch be taken into custody. Their friends and supporters, however, prevented the arrest by hiding them from the king's servants.

As the Babylonian forces approached Jerusalem, the war party recognized the city's vulnerability and the futility of relying on Egypt. Jehoiakim therefore yielded to Nebuchadnezzar (602 BCE), paying him tribute for three years, and then refusing to continue. Anticipating, mistakenly, a general uprising against the Babylonian ruler, the Judean king's refusal produced far worse consequences. Nebuchadnezzar conquered the neighboring tribes of Moab and Ammon and then sent them to devastate the border areas of Judah, intending to proceed to Jerusalem with his own forces soon afterward. Jehoiakim died during this tumultuous time, and the Jerusalemites then crowned his 18-year-old son, Jehoiachin (597 BCE). But the new government lasted only three months, for Nebuchadnezzar had by this time invaded Judah with his huge army, captured several cities, and reached Jerusalem. As soon as the siege of the city began, it was generally recognized by the inhabitants of Jerusalem that they could not withstand the overwhelming power of the Babylonian forces. Jehoiachin, together with his mother and retinue, left Jerusalem, and they made their way to the enemy camp, hoping to soften the wrath of Nebuchadnezzar by expressing submission personally. But the conqueror, unrelenting, ordered the Judean king and his mother taken into captivity. Along with them, Nebuchadnezzar carried away many thousands of captives, including the leading citizens and the most skilled and educated. The prophet Ezekiel, son of a well-known priestly family, was among the captives. By way of tribute, Nebuchadnezzar plundered the Temple and the royal palace, and appropriated a large quantity of gold and silver. Jerusalem thus lost a substantial part of its populace and wealth. The conqueror then appointed as king the uncle of the exiled ruler, Zedekiah, who swore allegiance to Babylon.

The trauma the Judeans had just suffered served to intensify the hatred of Babylon, strengthening the advocates of rebellion and sharpening the strife between them and Jeremiah's peace party. And as one might expect in such agonizingly complex situations, King Zedekiah continually wavered between the war and peace parties, between the policies of resistance or submission. He had great respect for Jeremiah, who continually exhorted the people to bear the yoke of Babylon patiently, lest they experience a greater misfortune.

During the early years of Zedekiah's reign, a rebellious movement arose among the several peoples of Syria-Palestine. In c.594 BCE, representatives of Moab, Ammon, Tyre, and Sidon arrived in Jerusalem, proposing to Zedekiah that he form with them a military alliance for war against Babylon, their common enemy. Jeremiah, however, in vehement opposition to the proposed alliance, appeared before the Temple with chains and a wooden yoke hanging about his neck. Displaying this dramaturgical device before the foreign delegates as a token of slavery, he declared that Nebuchadnezzar would impose just such a yoke and chains on whoever would rise up against him. The prophet then turned toward Zedekiah and his officials and asserted that the Judeans should submit to Babylonian hegemony rather than defy the conqueror and risk total annihilation. But the war party also had supporters among the prophets. One of them, Hananiah, proclaimed in the Temple in the name of God, that the power of Babylon would be broken within two years, and that the deposed King Jehoiachin, together with the rest of the exiled Judeans, would return from captivity to a Judah that would once again be free. Hananiah, also seeking dramatic effect, removed the yoke from Jeremiah's neck in full view of the assembled, and declared: "Thus saith the Lord: Even so will I break the yoke of Nebuchadnezzar king of Babylon from off the neck of all nations." But Jeremiah was quick to reply: "Thus saith the Lord: thou has broken the bars of wood; but thou shalt make in their place bars of iron . . . I have put a yoke of iron upon the neck of all these nations, that they may serve Nebuchadnezzar."

Jeremiah's warnings prevailed temporarily, and the coalition against Babylon failed to materialize. But the political unrest in Jerusalem continued. The hatred of the Babylonian king who had led thousands of Judeans into captivity was especially hot among the families and friends of the captives. The exiles longed for home and sent secret messages to Jerusalem, urging an uprising. The young exiled prophet Ezekiel, a follower of Jeremiah, warned his fellow exiles to bear the yoke of exile patiently. He not only dashed *their* hopes for an early return, but went further, proclaiming that many who were still living in their own land would soon also be led into captivity, and that Yahweh would show compassion for his people only when they had purified themselves through suffering and greater obedience to God's commandments. When Jeremiah learned of the exiles' restlessness, he wrote a letter exhorting them to stay peacefully in the place Yahweh had determined: "After seventy years are accomplished for Babylon, I [Yahweh] will remember you, and perform My good word toward you, in causing you to return to this place" (Jeremiah, 29).

The letter disappointed the exiles. Indeed, the leaders of the exiled Judeans, looking upon Jeremiah as a "scoundrel who prophesies," demanded from the priest Zephaniah and the other Jerusalem leaders that Jeremiah be punished and prohibited from making his traitorous utterances, either orally or in written form.

The Revolt and the Destruction of the First Temple

In the year 588 BCE, the war party in Jerusalem decided to act, seeing a favorable opportunity in the new Egyptian pharaoh's campaign to wrest Syria from Nebuchadnezzar. As the Babylonian king was at the time engaged in a war with Tyre and Sidon, in which the Phoenicians were putting up fierce resistance, the peoples of Palestine began once again to plan rebellion against the Babylonian ruler. The rebellious spirit mounted also in Judah where negotiations for a coalition were taking place with Egypt, whose support had been promised. In this situation Zedekiah, after nine years of loyal subjection, proclaimed the independence of Judah by ceasing to send tribute to Nebuchadnezzar. In response, the Babylonian king, encamped at the time in central Syria, dispatched a large force toward Judah, with an order to devastate the rebel country. The Babylonian forces invaded Judah, occupying and plundering several cities, and taking the people captive. Many Judeans fled to Jerusalem, adding to its already swollen population, and hoping that because of the city's strategic site and its strong fortifications, they would be safe in the impregnable city of David.

In the winter of 587 BCE, Nebuchadnezzar laid siege to Jerusalem, whereupon the entire population took up arms, determined to defend themselves to the last drop of their blood. The wealthy even released their bonded compatriots with the intention of mobilizing the freed slaves for military service. The pharaoh kept his promise and advanced with a large force against Nebuchadnezzar, causing him to make a hasty retreat from Jerusalem. The Jerusalemites, imagining the Babylonian withdrawal to be a sign of defeat, were jubilant – so jubilant that the slave-holders enslaved their fellow Judeans once again. For Jeremiah, this action taken against the Hebrew slaves was an unforgivable outrage that he sharply denounced, proclaiming that the Babylonians would soon return – thus making for himself new enemies.

The prophet resolved to leave Jerusalem for his native village, but as he approached the city gates he was arrested on the suspicion that he intended to join the enemy; he was then beaten and incarcerated in an improvised jail. Zedekiah, hoping the prophet would have an encouraging message, summoned him secretly and asked, "Is there any [new] word from the Lord?" "There is," Jeremiah tersely replied. "Thou shalt be delivered into the hand of the king of Babylon." The king then ordered that Jeremiah remain under a sort of honorary arrest.

By this time, the Babylonian forces, in a counter-attack, had succeeded in overwhelming the Egyptians and renewed their siege of Jerusalem. As the enemy assault intensified, the Judean defenders became increasingly dispirited. For, in addition to their military setbacks, Jeremiah declared that those who remained in the city would die by the sword, by famine, and by pestilence. Those, however, who went forth to the Chaldeans, should live. The prophet thus foresaw an impending catastrophe and strove to lessen the consequences of it by counseling submission. He was branded a traitor, however, and the general indignation and hostility toward him was such that the city officials called for his death.

In overcrowded Jerusalem, the supply of grain was soon exhausted and famine spread. Warriors, struck by enemy arrows, fell from the ramparts. Men and women wandered through the streets, begging for bread. In June of the year 586, the Babylonians breached the wall and entered the city. A massacre ensued as the enemy killed everyone in sight, sparing no one. Zedekiah, under cover of darkness, fled with some of his courtiers toward Jordan. Soon overtaken near Jericho, however, the king and his sons were taken to Riblah, the military headquarters of Nebuchadnezzar. The conqueror, showing no mercy, ordered Zedekiah's sons killed in his presence, and then had Zedekiah blinded and taken in chains to Babylon.

Soon afterward, the conqueror's captain, Nebuzaradan, was sent to Jerusalem with orders to destroy the city, during which all the treasury of precious vessels and ornaments of the Temple were confiscated and sent as spoils to Babylon. Nebuzaradan then set fire to the royal palace and to the magnificent Temple that had stood there since the time of Solomon. The high officials of the now desolate Jerusalem were sent to Riblah, where all were killed in Nebuchadnezzar's presence. And all that remained in the war-impoverished suburbs were a few vine-growers.

The Emigration to Egypt

With the destruction of Jerusalem, Nebuchadnezzar had taken as captives to Babylon primarily the upper strata – the skilled, educated, wealthy, and prominent – leaving only the small farmers and vine-dressers. Gedaliah, the high official who had once rescued Jeremiah from his enemies, was appointed ruler of the laboring populace of Judea. Gedaliah had become reconciled to Babylonian domination as preordained, which is why the Babylonian conqueror designated him as his deputy in Judah. To Jeremiah, Nebuchadnezzar offered the choice of going to Babylon, where he would be under royal protection, or remaining in Judah as Gedaliah's counselor. Jeremiah chose the latter.

Since Jerusalem lay in ruins, Gedaliah selected Mizpah, north of Jerusalem, as his headquarters. There, in his role as a satrap of sorts, he intended to establish a new religious and administrative center for the remnant of the nation. And it appears that under his administration the ravaged land began to recover, as the former inhabitants who had fled before the invading enemy returned to their villages and began once again to till the soil. Some of these returnees were Judean warriors who had hidden in the mountains to avoid submission to the enemy. However, not all the warriors who returned to Mizpah were reconciled to Gedaliah's administration, and to his deputy status. One of these military officers was a prince, a descendant of the Davidic dynasty by the name of Ishmael ben Nataniah, who, either out of personal jealousy or resentment at Gedaliah's being not of the dynasty, resolved to murder him and succeeded. Ishmael and his fellow conspirators then forced the Judean residents of Mizpah to leave the city and flee with them to Jordan. But a friend of the murdered Gedaliah, Johanan ben Kareah, with his own men, pursued Ishmael's band, overtaking them at Gideon. Johanan succeeded in freeing the Judeans that Ishmael had taken captive, but he and a few of his followers escaped into Ammon.

Fearing that when Nebuchadnezzar learned his deputy was murdered he would once again ravage the country, Johanan and his fellow officers decided to flee to Egypt and place themselves under the protection of Judah's recent ally, the Pharaoh Hophrah (Apris). However, before taking this step, they consulted Jeremiah who opposed the move, fearing that with the departure of Johanan's men Judah would lose the only group competent to administer the territory. If they left, the demoralization of the people tilling the soil would surely follow. But Johanan and his men, ignoring the prophet's counsel, forced Jeremiah and Baruch and many Judean families from Mizpah and its environs to move to Egypt.

The pharaoh allotted to these Judean emigrants the city of Taphnis, or Daphna, not far from the caravan route leading from Egypt to Palestine and Syria. But it is an important fact that there were already in Memphis and in other Egyptian cities Judeans who had fled there during the wars with Assyria and Babylon. They lived in the hope that Egypt would destroy Nebuchadnezzar's control of Palestine, so they could return to their homeland. However, it appears that some of these Judean emigrants had picked up Egyptian customs and rituals, including the veneration of Isis, the "queen of heaven," the local equivalent of the Assyrian cult of Ashtar, which had been prevalent in Jerusalem, especially among women in aristocratic circles. They were, of course, severely rebuked by Jeremiah who never ceased to exhort them to change their ways so that the Lord would have compassion for the dispersed and lead them back to their own land. But the prophet failed to see what he had hoped for and died in Egypt.

In Judah, conditions continually worsened. After the assassination of Gedaliah, Nebuchadnezzar again ordered his commander, Nebuzaradan, to Judah where he captured several hundred more Judean families and sent them to Babylon. As a consequence of emigration and exile, Judah lost nearly all of its population in many areas. Some districts were totally devastated, and the desolation of Jerusalem was the grimmest sight of all.

What prompted Jeremiah, in contrast to Isaiah, to prophesy that Jerusalem would fall? The most cogent answer is the nature of the sins committed by Ahaz and Manasseh: two cases of human sacrifice to the Assyrian gods, the stench of which, Jeremiah averred, remained in Yahweh's nostrils.

5

The Babylonian Exile and the Persian Supremacy (586–332 BCE)

The downfall of the kingdom of Judah under the Babylonian assault brought to an end the long period that had begun with the Israelites' entry into Canaan. Doubtless, Yahweh had meant well when he promised the Hebrews a land flowing with milk and honey. But they soon learned that life in the land of Canaan meant an unending series of trying experiences that threatened to undermine both their moral commitment to the covenant and their very existence as a people. It seems quite clear that it was the Hebrew prophets of social justice who strove unrelentingly to maintain that commitment, thereby shaping the soul of biblical Judaism so that it could preserve and refine itself in exile. From the moment of their arrival in the Promised Land, the Israelites were forced to engage in serious military encounters with the internal peoples – Canaanites, Ammonites, Moabites, Edomites, and Philistines; and not too long after that with the superpowers of the region.

First Assyria had devoured the northern kingdom of Israel. A century and a half later Babylon, Assyria's heir, devastated the southern kingdom of Judah, leading thousands of Judeans into captivity – all their princes, military officers, craftsmen, and smiths. It appeared that history had come full circle. The descendants of Abraham and Moses who had left the shores of the Euphrates and Nile, had returned to those same shores, some as captives and exiles, and the rest as immigrants. This was the moment at which the Jewish diaspora had come into being.

The first test of the people's soul came in the 50-year Babylonian captivity (586–537 BCE). Would the exiles continue to adhere to the religious and ethical principles inculcated by the prophets and Torah-teachers? "Israel," or Ephraim, of the kingdom of Samaria had earlier faced the same test in the eighth century, and had, for the most part, failed. A large portion of those exiles had been simply assimilated in the Assyrian torrent. But the Judean captives weathered the crisis by holding on to their religious-national identity even in exile. Political conditions accounted for the different adaptations of the Assyrian and Babylonian exiles. Sargon's policy was a twofold colonization, in which he transferred the inhabitants of Samaria to the far provinces of his empire, and the peoples of the provinces to Samaria. Nebuchadnezzar, in contrast, simply banished the populace of Jerusalem to Babylon, but without colonizing Judah's territory with foreign, ethnic groups. The Assyrian policy was more of a threat to the Judean national identity than the simple exile policy of Nebuchadnezzar.

The Babylonian policy was, therefore, an objective factor that contributed to the spiritual consolidation of the Judeans in exile. But, as Weber recognized, the chief source of the exiles' spiritual strength lay in their internalization of the profound doctrine of their prophets. In exile, the spiritual solidarity of the Judeans was derived from the covenantal principles, and not from concerns of armed might, kingship, and territory. The historical evidence suggests that the Judeans on the banks of the Euphrates lived like a closely knit community, refusing to merge religiously with the surrounding peoples, and clinging zealously to their own unique cultural ways.

Moreover, the continuing spiritual development of those whom we may now call Jews seems to have deepened in exile. Ezekiel reflects the sadness of the first generation of exiles, but also their strong belief in the promise of return; and "second Isaiah" comforts them, calling for the rebuilding of the homeland. Indeed, the rebirth of Judah was made historically possible by the downfall of the Babylonian Empire and the emergence of Persian hegemony in the East under the great Cyrus. Judah was now drawn into the Persian sphere of influence, which the Jews regarded as their good fortune, for Persian domination was quite different from that of her two imperial predecessors. The Persians were liberators, not oppressors of the Jews. Cyrus inherited from Babylon a devastated Judah that had been forcibly deprived of the skilled, educated, and leading members of the populace. Hence, in response to the entreaty of his Judean subjects, the gracious Cyrus granted them the privilege of returning to their land and establishing it as an autonomous, Persian province.

Some of the exiles availed themselves of the privilege immediately; others, who remained in Babylon and Persia, maintained relations with Judah, sending support and colonists from time to time. Although the Judeans now enjoyed something less than full political independence, they gained an advantage temporarily in that Persian power in the region freed them from the burden of defending themselves against external enemies. Thus, freed of the military regime formerly required for self-defense, the Judeans' energy could be directed toward cultural aims.

During the first century of Persia's supremacy, desolate Jerusalem and its environs were repopulated by the Judeans, the Temple and other structures were rebuilt, and new foundations were laid for self-government.[1] This first phase of restoration lasted about 20 years, from 537– 516. Half a century later, efforts continued to widen and fortify Jerusalem and the adjacent areas, but also to purify the faith, projects associated with Ezra and Nehemiah (458–420). And, during the second and final century of Persian domination (420–332), a form of theocracy emerged in Judah.

In the Persian period, another notable phenomenon appeared: *the Jewish diaspora*. Along with the governmental center in Judah, there emerged a network of Judean colonies, beyond the borders of Palestine. The first such colony was in Babylon, mother of the Jewish diaspora. Vital relations were established between the Babylonian Jews and Jerusalem. Much less populous and vitally related to Jerusalem was the Judean colony in Egypt, established, as we have seen, around the time of the destruction of Jerusalem, by emigrants and fugitives, and headed by the prophet Jeremiah. Thus began the prolonged, historical dialogue between Judah and the diaspora.

In this period, under the influence of the prophetic legacy, a concerted effort was made to purify the religious-moral outlook of the people by purging it of polytheistic elements. The 50-year separation of the Judean exiles from their native soil tended to sever any previous ties they might have had with the pagan or pagan-appearing elements of Canaan. In Israel and Judah a form of quasi-monotheism had prevailed: a veneration of Yahweh together with fetishistic idolatry. This now gave way in exile to a strict and absolute monotheism, which recognized Yahweh as the sole God, and the Jewish people as His chosen instrument. However, before enlightening others, it was necessary for the Jews themselves, both in Judea and in the diaspora, to strive for a spiritual and moral purity. Such striving had necessarily imposed limits on the kind of mingling they may or may not engage in with pagan peoples. Hence, there emerged among the Jews religiously prescribed limits on what Weber has called commensalism and connubium. The policies of Ezra and Nehemiah were designed to create a strict social discipline that would prevent Judaism from dissolving itself in the heterogeneous cultures of the East. The Torah was to become the Constitution of the Jews wherever they happened to dwell.

---

[1] This historical sketch is based on Heinrich Graetz, *History of the Jews*, Philadelphia, PA: Jewish Publication Society of America, 1939, vol. I, 341–88; and Simon Dubnov, *History of the Jews*, transl. from the Russian by Moshe Spiegel, revsd edn, vols. I and II, New York: Thomas Yoseloff, 1967, 331–405.

In striving, therefore, to maintain spiritual purity, the Judean captives in Babylon felt the need to keep aloof from the pagan indigenous groups. The deportees settled themselves in accordance with their former communities of residence in Judea – e.g., Jericho, Ramah, Anatoth, and so forth. These communities were joined by some of the descendants from the northern kingdom of Israel, who had been exiled by the Assyrians in the eighth century. Most of the Israelites had merged with the other peoples of the Assyrian Empire. But many of them had managed to preserve something of the religio-moral legacy during the 130 years before the arrival of the Judean exiles in Babylon. The remnants of the Assyrian exile now joined the Judean captives. "Israel" and "Judah," which had been divided in their own land, drew closer as captives and former exiles eventually merged. Ezekiel perceived in this phenomenon the beginning of the restoration of the dispersed nation and envisioned a political union of the "house of Israel" and the "lineage of Judah" in the near future (Ezekiel 16:53f; 37:16).

The religious organization of these exiles had to adapt to the new circumstances. In exile on foreign soil it never crossed their minds, apparently, to offer sacrifices to Yahweh. And the three chief annual festivals, rooted as they were in the agriculture of Judah, lost their significance beyond its borders. Prayer replaced sacrificial offerings and the meaning of the yearly festivals became purely historical: anniversaries of momentous events such as the exodus from Egypt and the sojourn in the wilderness. The Sabbath acquired a new significance, becoming the holiest of days (Ezek. 20:12f). The religious assemblies on the Sabbath were devoted to prayer while facing Jerusalem. Such religious gatherings served, of course, to unite the members of each community socially and spiritually. These gatherings may be described as the prototypes of the synagogue, which after the restoration became a firmly established institution first in Judea, and later throughout Palestine.

For Ezekiel, the great prophet of the Babylonian exile, the regeneration of the nation was to be achieved through the righteousness of individuals. He stressed the foundational importance of the religion of the heart, thus saving personal religion after the destruction of the Temple. When the prophet heard cries of despair, comparing the dismembered nation to a scattered heap of dry bones, he provided a consoling vision: the bones were drawn together, taking on flesh and becoming filled with the breath of life and standing on their feet. Then the prophet hearkened to the Lord's voice:

Son of man, these bones are the whole house of Israel . . . Behold, I will open your graves, O my people; and I will bring you into the land of Israel . . . And I will put My spirit into You, and ye shall live, and I will place

You in your own land; and Ye shall know that I the Lord have spoken and performed it, saith the Lord. (ch. 37).

This vision, together with the much later one of Daniel, became the basis for the concept of bodily resurrection in the post-biblical Judaism of the Pharisees and in early Christianity.

The Diaspora in Babylon and Persia

After the sixth century BCE, the Judeans became a people, large numbers of which lived outside the border of their homeland. From the time of the Babylonian exile and the subsequent restoration, the Judeans or Jews had created substantial communities in Babylon, Persia, Syria, Asia Minor, and Egypt. Although Jerusalem remained the spiritual center of the Jewish diaspora, some of its components exerted a reciprocal influence upon that center. The most influential part of this diaspora was the Babylonian Jewish community, which regularly sent contributions for the maintenance of the Temple; and the community's more God-fearing members made frequent pilgrimages to Jerusalem to participate in Temple services during the annual festivals. The unexpected prosperity of the Babylonian captives seems to have been a pleasant surprise, which prompted many of them to remain in Babylon. And, since so many of these exiles had kinsmen and friends among the tens of thousands of their fellow Judeans who had returned to Judah in the times of Zerubabel and Ezra, there was bound to be a continuing cultural and economic relationship between the Babylonian and Jerusalem communities.

There were Jewish communities in Persia itself, descendants of the Judean exiles. Nehemiah twice came from Susa or Shushan, the capital of Persia proper. The Persian Empire, having incorporated the entire Near East, could not but influence the economic life of Judah. The biblical literature of the period provides clues to the role of Judah in trade and handicraft. The Judeans went to sea in merchant vessels (Proverbs 31:14; Psalms 107:23), and manufactured textiles (Prov. 31:24) for sale to the Canaanites (i.e., the Phoenicians), the chief traders in commodities for export. As for the Judean domestic economy and the Jerusalem market, Nehemiah stated that Judean vintners produced wine even on the Sabbath, bringing grapes and other fruits to Jerusalem on the backs of donkeys. The Tyrians brought fish and other goods there (Nehemiah 10:32, 13:7). Nehemiah also mentions merchandise stalls (*bet harochlim*) in the city (3:31–2).

One of the salient consequences of international trade in the context of the Persian Empire was the emergence of Aramaic (or Syriac) as the prevalent language of the time. This language, cognate to Hebrew, spread in Judah with remarkable speed. The biblical form of ancient Hebrew was retained in literature and in the religious liturgy, but was supplanted as the vernacular and as the language of commerce. As part of the vast Persian Empire, Judah had to adopt Aramaic as the language of legal, commercial, and financial transactions. It is noteworthy that in the Book of Ezra, official Acts are quoted in the Aramaic original. In time, the Judean populace Hebraized the new international language they had adopted, producing thereby an Aramaic-Hebrew dialect that gradually became a second national language. The new, synthetic dialect penetrated even the synagogues: in the reading of the Torah the ancient Hebrew text had to be translated into Aramaic (*Targum*) for the benefit of those who by that time had lost the ability to read and understand the ancient Hebrew script.

The diffusion of Aramaic among the Jews brought with it the transformation of the ancient Hebrew characters. The ancient Canaanite or Phoenician alphabet, employed in writings of the ninth and eighth centuries BCE, consisted of complex, hooked characters, hard to decipher. Hence, Aramaic or Syrian script, simple and lucid in form, replaced the ancient script. The new, simple characters of the Aramaic type were continually perfected until they became the Hebrew print we are familiar with today.

With the popularization of the religious literature both in Judah and in the diaspora, the functional importance of the "house of assembly," or "synagogue" as it was later called in the Hellenistic period, rose considerably. In Judah, this meant a corresponding decline in the control of education by the Temple priests in Jerusalem. The proto-synagogue emerged in the small religious gatherings of the Judean exiles in Babylonia. But even after the restoration of the Temple at Jerusalem, the need for communal, religious gatherings was great, especially among the people of the provinces, who could attend the Temple only during the major annual festivals. Moreover, the religious needs of the people intensified their desire for a warmer and more intimate kind of worship than was possible at the great Temple. The proto-synagogue served as an "assembly of the saints" (*kahal hasidim*), mentioned in Psalm 149. As houses of worship and study, where chapters of the Torah were read regularly, followed by excerpts from the prophets, all elements of the populace welcomed an institution enabling them to fulfill their spiritual and social needs at one and the same time.

The synagogue as an institution gave rise to what might be termed a non-sacerdotal clergy of scribes and Torah-teachers (proto-rabbis), parallel to the positions occupied by the official clergy (priests and

Levites) in the Temple. Unlike the priests, who often felt superior and set themselves apart from the people, the scribes and/or Torah-teachers strove to educate every social layer of the nation. The synagogue thus became a school and a house of prayer, and a fundamental component of the culture of the Jewish people wherever they happened to reside.

6

Alexander the Great and the New Hegemony of the West[1]

As one reflects on the experiences of the Hebrew or Israelite-Judean people during the first millennium of their history, one sees that they were associated exclusively with the other peoples and cultures of the near East – Egypt, Assyria, Babylonia, Persia – either yielding to some of their cultural influences or rejecting them until they, the Hebrews, developed as a distinct ethno-religious group.

However, in the course of the second millennium of their history, the Hebrew people found themselves in a quite different international context. Conquerors from the West were establishing their imperial regimes over the peoples of Asia Minor and Africa with whom the Hebrews lived in proximity. First, Judea and the diaspora came under the domination of Alexander's successors, the Ptolemies and the Seleucids, who had founded their imperial regimes on the ruins of the Persian Empire. Then, not long afterwards, the Jews became subjects under the Roman Empire, during its rule of three continents of the Old World. The new, Western hegemony over the East, beginning with the destruction of the Persian Empire by Alexander of Macedon (332 BCE) continued until the disintegration of the Roman Empire in the fifth century CE. Under Alexander's successors, the Greeks spread their colonies over the whole extent of Asia Minor and North Africa. As the Hellenic culture diffused through the East and in its turn adopted certain regional ways and ideas, what is known as the Hellenistic culture emerged. This term is employed to indicate the blending of Eastern with Hellenic culture after the conquest of the East by Alexander the Great and the founding of Hellenized governments. Hellenization of the original denizens of the

---

[1] The following discussion is based on Josephus, *The Jewish War*, Books I–III, transl. H. St J. Thackeray, Cambridge, MA: Harvard University Press, 1976; and Simon Dubnov, *History of the Jews*, transl. from the Russian Fourth Definitive, revised edition in 2 volumes, by Moshe Spiegel, New York: Thomas Yoseloff, 1967. See vol. II, *From the Macedonian Conquest to the Rise of Christianity*.

regions was the master trend of the time. This trend manifested itself in varying degrees in Judea and in the diaspora, the latter having expanded throughout the entire territory under Greek domination.

The cultural fusion was especially notable under the Ptolemies in Egypt, where a Hebrew colony had sprung up in Hellenized Alexandria. These Hebrews adopted Greek as their spoken language in place of Aramaic. Educated individuals were fascinated by the works of Greek literature. And it was at this time that the Torah, translated into Greek (the Septuagint), opened to the Hellenized the treasures of the biblical literature. In the diaspora the Greeks, as successors to the Phoenicians, became prominent in trade, as did the Hebrews. International trade encouraged cosmopolitanism, and an attractive Hellenized culture emerged into which many Hebrews were drawn, fascinated by the free life of the Greeks, their cult of beauty and athletic contest. Assimilation, as a clear and present danger, came to be felt acutely in Judea, which around 200 BCE, after a century of domination by the Egyptian Ptolemies, came under the Greco-Syrian sway of the Seleucid rulers of Asia. A strong party of Hellenists, partisans of assimilation, emerged in Jerusalem. The strength of the party grew to the point of placing at the head of the people the Hellenized high priests, Jason and Menelaus, who had allied themselves with the Syrian despot Antiochus Epiphanus, with the aim of forcibly Hellenizing Judea.

The Jewish Hellenizers, as the admirers of Greek culture were called, began by adopting Greek games and entertainments and, in accordance with Greek custom, competing in the nude in public games. Becoming ashamed of everything distinctively Jewish, including circumcision, they went so far as to undergo surgery to hide the results of the ancient Jewish rite. These Hellenized Jews were drawn primarily from the upper social layers of Jerusalem, those whom Max Weber called urban patricians who strove to transform Jerusalem into a polis. Naturally, the Hellenizers thus provoked a reaction from the most populous party, the Hasideans, or "pious," who bolstered religious discipline in order to curb the enthusiasm for the alien culture. The Hasideans, following the policy of Ezra and the scribes, initiated a process intended to prevent the populace from succumbing to the pressures of assimilation. Close contact with the Hellenizers was forbidden, as was, of course, participation in their gatherings, especially in their public games and festivities. A more rigorous regime was introduced, requiring a strict observance of the Sabbath and religious holidays, rites, and customs.

Given the popular support for the Hasideans, the Hellenist minority resorted to requesting support from the Syrian ruler who recognized the material gains to be had from the prospect of Hellenizing the Jews. Antiochus IV (175–164 BCE) returned from Rome, where he had been a hostage for 15 years. From the time of Julius Caesar, if not earlier, the Romans had taken hostages from the families of their subject rulers to ensure submission and to minimize the likelihood of rebellion. This despot, Antiochus, had a characteristic predilection for luxury, outward splendor, and violent subjection of the people. In Syrian cities he erected shrines, grandiose public buildings, and monuments after the Athenian model, and in Antioch he emulated the Roman rulers by introducing gladiatorial contests. His official nickname was Epiphanus ("Divine"), but the name assigned to him by the people was Epinanes ("violent, insane"). The initiative of the Jerusalem Hellenizers was the opportunity for the Syrian despot to intervene in the internal affairs of Judea and to try to impose on Jerusalem Greek cultural and religious practices.

The conflict between the Hellenistic and Hasidean parties expressed itself saliently in the family of the high priest, the presumed head of the Jewish people. A member of this family, named Joshua, who had joined the Jerusalem party of Hellenists, became so enamored of their religious and political ideology that he changed his name to Jason, and did his utmost to impose a Greek way of life and education on his homeland. But upon encountering the opposition of the Hasidean-led populace, he became so embittered as to repudiate the authority of his brother, Onias III, with the aim of supplanting him with the aid of Antiochus. Doubtless, personal ambition also played a role here, prompting Jason to commit treason, offering Antiochus a huge sum – either in the form of a single tribute or an increase in Judea's annual tax assessment – on condition that Jason should be appointed high priest instead of Onias. Jason promised, in addition, to open in Jerusalem a *gymnasium* for athletic contests, and an *ephebeum*, a military school like the one at Athens, for the training of the Jewish youth. Finally, Jason requested that Jerusalem's inhabitants be granted the title of "citizens of Antioch," an honor that bestowed certain privileges upon the ruling elite. As these proposals corresponded with Antiochus' ambitions and interests, he granted everything Jason requested, banishing Onias to Antioch and placing Jason in the office of high priest. Upon assuming authority, Jason proceeded to build a gymnasium not far from the Judean holy of holies.

7

The World Diaspora

From the time of Pompey's invasion of Judea in c. 60 BCE, Rome's domination and Herod's regime prompted an increased emigration of Jews to other countries.[1] A contemporary of Herod, the Greek geographer Strabon, had observed that Jews were present in all the city-states and that it was hard to find a place where this people had not established communities. Under Rome's power, which extended over the former Seleucid and Ptolemaic domains, the diaspora grew socially closer to Judea and it became culturally and religiously more unified. When the Ptolemaic kingdom, which had existed for three centuries, first came under Roman sovereignty in the time of Julius Caesar and Mark Antony, the well-populated Jewish community in Egypt found itself between two forces: the Greek, or Hellenized, non-Jewish population and the Roman administration. Rome first supported Jewish congregational autonomy and civil rights for the Jews. Julius Caesar and Augustus protected the Jews because of their more accommodating attitude than that of the Egyptians and the Hellenized populace who resented the Roman invaders.

In Alexandria, an enormous residential area was assigned to the Jews who enjoyed political autonomy under an ethnarch, appointed by them, who held magisterial powers. The Alexandrian Jewish philosopher, Philo, avers that in the first decades of the Christian era there lived in Egypt "up to the Ethiopian border," a "hundred myriads" – perhaps as many as a million Jews, in a population of seven or eight million. The Jewish ethnarch in Alexandria headed an advisory board of elders or *Gerusia*, which, from the time of the Ptolemies, had managed the affairs of the Jewish community.

The Jews of Egypt had, however, to fight continually to maintain their

---

[1] In the present discussion I rely on Simon Dubnov, *History of the Jews*, transl. from the Russian Fourth Definitive revised edition in 2 volumes, New York: Thomas Yoseloff, 1967, vol. II, part 3, ch. 5.

civil rights and autonomy. Their Hellenized neighbors were unfriendly and even hostile – the source of the hostility being both political and economic. The conquered Hellenized populace had never quite accepted their status as Roman subjects, and they considered the Jews, who had adapted to Roman power, as political enemies. Indeed, the Egyptian populace, both the Hellenized and non-Hellenized, resented the copper pillar in central Alexandria on which was inscribed the decree of Julius Caesar granting to the Jews full citizenship. Doubtless, it thus appeared to the Alexandrians that the Jews had been granted by the Roman power a special status of privileges and protection. An additional source of tension between the two groups was the commercial rivalry in the mercantile trade and shipping on the Nile, and in other financial operations.

Furthermore, in the religious life of the Egyptian Jews, it was the Temple in Jerusalem, not the Temple of Onias at Leontopolis, which had real significance for them. It was to the Jerusalem Temple that they sent their donations and to which they made pilgrimages during the major festivals. In Alexandria itself, it was in the many synagogues of the Jewish quarters that religious worship took place. According to Philo, the galleries in the yards of the synagogues displayed protective shields and golden laurels with inscriptions honoring the emperor.

The synagogues themselves were nothing more than houses for worship and schools for study. The ancient national tongue of Hebrew and its surrogate, Aramaic, had disappeared among the Alexandrian Jews and was replaced by Greek, which had long been in everyday use both orally and in script. The Greek translation of the Hebrew Bible – the translation that had been made under Ptolemy Philadelphus, the so-called *Septuagint* – replaced the original Hebrew scriptures, and even prayers and other religious texts were written in Greek. The mature Jewish community in Egypt had extensions in the bordering North African countries, notably in Lybia and in Cyrenaica (Tripoli). As regards the diaspora in Asia Minor, Syria, and Mesopotamia, it seems that there, too, as in Egypt, it was only after the Seleucid reign, and only when Rome had taken control, that the Jewish struggle for cultural autonomy and civil rights met with some success.

We can now see rather clearly the cogency of Max Weber's thesis in which he proposes how the diaspora Jews acquired a "pariah" status. On the positive, religiously determined side, the Jews led their lives so as to preserve their monotheism in accordance with the strict ethical and ceremonial principles of the Torah. They worshiped a formless, invisible, incorporeal God and did their utmost to insulate themselves from the influences of their idolatrous neighbors. But it was precisely this insulation – including often their religiously determined refusal of commensalism and connubium – that accounted for the hostility toward them of their non-Jewish neighbors. Of course, even this "negative" consequence of the diaspora Jews' clinging to their faith was not the whole story.

The powerful elite in Rome, since the time of Julius Caesar, had banned political associations for everyone, it appears, except the Jews. The Jewish communities of Asia Minor had received from Caesar special privileges, such as full freedom of worship and the right to live by their own statutes, which the later Roman consuls and proconsuls continued to reaffirm. When, for example, the municipal power on the Isle of Paras attempted to restrict or abolish Jewish autonomy, Rome addressed the city government, to demand that the edict against the Jews, "our friends and confederates," be rescinded (c.46 BCE). As Dubnov observed, it was more than once that the heirs of Caesar confirmed the rights and liberties of the Jewish communities in Asia Minor and Syria. In Marc Antony's time, the Jews of Ephesus and other cities of Asia Minor were exempt from military service in the Roman legions because it would conflict with their Sabbath observance and their dietary laws. Later, Augustus confirmed, among other privileges, the right of the Jews in Asia Minor and Cyrenaica to collect funds for religious, congregational needs. The historical evidence thus suggests strongly that the Jews of the diaspora stubbornly defended their social and spiritual autonomy, which they considered the chief or perhaps even the sole means by which to preserve their characteristic uniqueness as a religious-ethnic entity. Of course, the neighboring and surrounding non-Jewish groups resented, despised, or hated the Jews for their isolationist or self-segregating solidarity.

Second to Alexandria, in the size of the Jewish population, was Syria, in the two main cities of Antioch and Damascus. There, too, relations between the Jews and the Hellenized populace were strained and antagonistic for the same reasons as elsewhere in the diaspora. In Syria the Jews had rather successfully spread the ideas of Judaism, thereby lessening in some measure the socio-economic antagonism. However, the religious leaders of the polytheistic faiths were enraged by the successful Jewish proselytizing.

Of all the remains of the old Seleucid Empire, only one region had remained outside the circle of Roman power, and that was Babylon where, from ancient times, Jewish communities continued to exist. This region remained under the Parthian monarch, Arsakid, who supported the last Hasmonean king Antigonus in his struggle against Roman domination. In Babylon, Hellenization had proceeded far less than in the diasporas of Egypt, Syria, and Asia Minor. The distinctive religious elements of Judaism were, therefore, preserved there with greater ease. Hillel, one of the great creators of intertestamental Judaism, may be regarded as the prototypical representative of Babylonian Jewish culture, just as Philo may serve as a prototype of the linguistically syncretic Jewish culture of Alexandria.

The Beginnings of the European Diaspora: Greece and Rome

The dates of Jewish settlements in Greece can be determined by the inscriptions preserved from the second century BCE, where mention is made of Jewish slaves who, most likely, had been taken captive in the Hasmonean Wars (170–140 BCE). Other Greek-speaking Jews of the Eastern diaspora settled and adapted rather easily in European Greece owing to their knowledge of the language. By the first century CE, we know from Paul's letters and other sources of synagogues in Athens, Corinth, Thessalonica, Phillipi, and other cities. Jewish communities emerged also in Italy, not later and perhaps earlier than the first century BCE. When Pompey conquered Jerusalem in 63 BCE, he took many prisoners and sold them into slavery. Their strict observance of the Sabbath and other Jewish customs made them undesirable slaves, and some were ransomed by relatives in Judea. Hence, many of the freed Jewish slaves remained in Rome, in a separate quarter of the city near the Tiber River where they developed their distinctive cultural community.

There is evidence to suggest that these Jews had already acquired political influence in Rome even under Pompey. The Roman proconsul of Asia, Valerius Flaccus, had committed misdemeanors and felonies while in office, and had confiscated a large sum of money intended for the Jerusalem Temple. Charged and brought to trial, he was defended by Cicero who served as consul when Pompey invaded Jerusalem. At the trial were many Roman Jews with a definite interest in the proceedings (59 BCE). Cicero, who strongly disliked the Jews and wished to give those in the audience no pretext for loud critical outbursts, deliberately spoke quietly so only the judge could hear him. From that event we learn two significant facts: (1) that the Jewish inhabitants of Rome enjoyed the right to participate in political gatherings; and (2) that even before Pompey had conquered Jerusalem, the Jews of Italy were already sending to the Judean capital the Temple tax (Dubnov, 712f). These were the concluding words of Cicero's remarks: "How far the immortal gods detest this people [the Jews] can be seen by the fact that it is vanquished, under heavy tribute and enslaved" (quoted in Dubnov, 713).

In these words we hear the Roman contempt for the defeated. In another of his speeches, Cicero mentions Syrians and Jews as "people who were born for slavery." Superiority in war is Cicero's Roman criterion for religious and moral superiority. In terms, then, that tend to confirm Nietzsche's *Genealogy of Morals*, the "good" for the Romans were the powerful and warlike, those who conducted themselves in accordance with the "master morality." This view was the antithesis, as Nietzsche recognized, of the already partially formed and developing "slave morality" of the Jews. From the time of their enslavement by the pharaoh and the full grasp of its significance by the Hebrew prophets of social justice, the Jews had repudiated the right of might and had taught that the weak, poor, and humble must be protected against the strong.

Dubnov avers that Cicero was undoubtedly influenced by his Greek teacher, Apollonius Molon of Rodos, who had written a work replete with hatred of the Jews. Although that work is no longer extant, Josephus polemicized against it in his *Against Apion*. Apollonius reproached the Jews for godlessness, owing to the absence of any iconic representation of their formless, incorporeal God. Cicero's orations thus reveal an idolator's hatred for the Judaic conception of the ethical God of the universe. We need to note again that Cicero's attitude was foreign to his contemporary, Julius Caesar, who defended the rights and liberties of the Jewish community in Rome with the same determination he had first displayed in defending the Jews of Asia Minor. There is a certain irony in the fact that Caesar, the mighty patrician warrior and military genius, showed more respect for the vanquished Jews and their religious autonomy than did Cicero, the sophistic specialist in rhetoric. The Roman Jewish community appreciated Caesar's friendly attitude and mourned him deeply following his violent death. Augustus maintained Caesar's policy where the Jews were concerned, enabling the Roman-Jewish community to establish definite relations with Judea's capital, and to play an active role in the battle between the political parties in Judea. And, judging from the Roman writers of the "golden era" (Horace, Ovid), the Jews of Rome rigorously obeyed their religious laws, the Sabbath rest, in particular (Dubnov, 714).

8

The Diaspora in the First Century CE

From his *Delegation to Gaius* (Caligula), by Philo Judaeus of Alexandria, we gain a sense of the vast scope of the Jewish diaspora in the first century CE. He wrote:

> Jerusalem is the capital not only of Judea, but also [of the Jewish population of] many other countries, because of the colonies it established in neighboring lands – Egypt, Phoenicia, Syria, Coele-Syria, as well as in the more remote lands of Amphilia, Cilicia, districts of Asia Minor to Vitinia, in the distant frontier areas of Pontus and also in Europe – Thesalia, Boethia, Macedonia, Etolia, Attica, Argos, Corinth, and parts of Peloponnesia. And it is not only the mainland that is covered with Jewish communities, but also the well-known islands: Aibea, Cyprus, Crete. I am not speaking of the countries on the other side of the Euphrates; for all of them, with the exception of a small part of the city of Babylon and the adjoining fertile districts, have Jewish inhabitants. (Dubnov, II, 810–11[1])

The Book of Acts in the New Testament tends to confirm Philo's statement, for it speaks of Jewish pilgrims who came to Jerusalem from Parthia, Mesopotamia, Asia Minor, Egypt, Lybia (Cyrenaica), and Rome. And the Apostle Paul found Jewish synagogues in many cities of Asia Minor and Greece, where between 40 and 60 CE he preached in the name of Jesus. From its communities in Asia, the Jewish diaspora extended more and more into Europe. Very early, splinters of the diaspora reached the northern shores of the Black Sea and the Crimean Peninsula.

But, as we observed earlier, in some of the colonies the relations

---

[1] In the following discussion I rely on Simon Dubnov, *History of the Jews*, transl. from the Russian Fourth Definitive revised edition in 2 volumes by Moshe Spiegel, New York: Thomas Yoseloff, 1967, vol. II, chs 5 and 6, 800–59.

between the Jews and "Greeks" (Hellenized non-Jews) often assumed the form of bloody encounters, prompting Claudius, at the behest of Agrippa I, to issue a decree that the Jews should be allowed to observe the customs of their ancestors. He did, however, add "on condition that they remain calm and orderly, *and should not despise the beliefs of other peoples.*" The italics I have added to Claudius' statement suggest, unfortunately, that the strict, self-segregation of the Jewish communities may very well have appeared to their neighbors as disdain for their beliefs.

Despite the decree and its communication to the Roman administrations of all cities, the anti-Jewish agitation did not cease in large diasporas such as the one in Alexandria. A leading representative of Alexandrian hatred for the Jews was the "grammarian" Apion, as we learn from Josephus' famous book, *Against Apion.* Among all the opponents of the Jews, this Apion stands out for the depth of his hatred and for the lengths to which he went in fabricating falsehoods concerning the Jewish faith. His many falsehoods included the allegation that the Jews were atheists because they worship no iconic representation of their God, claiming that he is formless, invisible, and incorporeal. They repudiate the "Caesar cult" and foster indolence by teaching the populace to rest on one day of the week, which they call the Sabbath. Apion had intended his writings to incite violence against the Jews, and his intention materialized in the Alexandrian pogrom of 38 CE.

The Jewish war against Rome made it easier for the purveyors of anti-Jewish propaganda to influence elements of the populace that had cause, imaginary or real, to resent the Jews. It is noteworthy, however, that even after the Jewish rebellion the anti-Jewish propaganda had less effect on Roman notables, such as Titus, than on the heathen populace. In Antioch, for example, after failing to organize a pogrom against the Jews, the Jew-haters turned their efforts toward a legal means of injuring or expelling the Jews. When Titus launched his triumphal campaign across Syria after conquering Jerusalem, the leaders of Antioch's Greeks prepared an enthusiastic reception for him. They took what appeared to be a favorable opportunity to urge the Roman general to expel the Jewish "enemies of Rome" from Antioch. Titus did not respond immediately, but when the city council came to him with the same request, he stated it would be impossible to drive out the Jews, if for no other reason than that they had nowhere to go, since their country had been destroyed. More, Titus also spurned the Antiochians' request to destroy the copper tablets engraved with the rights and privileges of the Jews in Antioch.

Judaism's Proselytism

It is something of a paradox that as the anti-Jewish hostility of the diaspora polytheists was on the rise, so too was their conversion to Judaism. Much of the Judean *national* culture was quite alien to Greco-Roman society. I have italicized the term "national" because the Jews had already possessed a national consciousness. They constituted themselves as a national group, and were perceived as such by the other peoples among whom the Jews lived. The self-segregation of the Jews irritated the other peoples who, of course, took pride in their own culture. They found offensive the Jewish contempt for any iconic representation of divinity. From the standpoint of the polytheistic peoples, their cult, derived from the Greeks and Romans, was rich in symbolic and aesthetic meaning. Hence, religion without visual images seemed hideous and devoid of beauty to the same extent that the Jews found pagan mythology repulsive or silly.

The revulsion felt against Greco-Roman polytheism, even by Jews educated in that culture, can be gathered from the caustic criticisms to which Josephus, in his *Against Apion*, subjects Greek mythology with its representations of Zeus and the other gods and goddesses, and what must have appeared from the Jewish perspective as the deities' dissoluteness and base passions.

Typical polytheists who viewed their idols as representing their deities must have looked upon the Jews at prayer as a bizarre phenomenon. Jews at prayer made the impression of men either talking to themselves or with heaven, hence the Roman expression *coelicolae*: those who pray to heaven. In a word, the strict observance of the customs and rites of the Jews, together with the deliberate insulation of themselves from the pagan religious culture, evoked resentment and hostility. And yet it is a historical fact that Greeks and Romans who had become acquainted with the teachings of Judaism, either through conversations with Jews or through the Greek translation of the Bible or the works of the Judeo-Hellenistic literature, were often impressed by the monotheistic conception of an ethical, almighty, formless God of the universe. The Jews not only defended their faith; they also propagated it. Matthew's Gospel may have exaggerated when it stated that the scribes and Pharisees "compass sea and land to make one proselyte" (Matt. 23:15), but it is highly likely that it was not merely scholars who propagated Judaism among those of other faiths. It was every man and woman, with all those they had dealings with in everyday life, who did so.

The result was the considerable dissemination of the Jewish monotheistic concept among the pagan peoples of the diaspora – Syria, Asia

Minor, Greece, and Italy. Josephus, again, states that from the time of Moses:

> our lives have not only stood the test of our own use, but they have to an ever increasing extent excited the emulation of the world at large . . . But that is not all. The masses have long since shown a keen desire to adopt our religious observances; and there is not one city, Greek or barbarian, not a single nation, to which our custom of abstaining from work on the seventh day has not spread, and where the fasts and lighting of lamps and many of our prohibitions in the matter of food are not observed. (*Against Apion*, II, 282–3)

Women were particularly attracted to Judaism, their formal conversion being easier without the rite of circumcision. In Damascus, women who professed Judaism restrained their husbands, who had remained pagan, from participating in the massacres of the Jews in 66 and 67 CE. Circumcision, doubtless, was the major obstacle – as Paul understood – to the conversion of pagan men to Judaism. A significant number therefore became "God-fearers," Jews in all respects except for being uncircumcised, who promised to circumcise their sons.

Simon Dubnov reminds us (vol. II, 817f.) that the ferment of Judaism in the ranks of Roman society is evident from the works of Roman writers such as Horace, a poet of Augustus' time, who noted ironically in his satires the success of Judean propaganda in Rome. He was fond of jeering at the circumcised Judeans, while his friend, the writer Fuscius, confessed that he "as one of many" was sympathetic to Judaism and observed the Day of Rest. The poet Ovid also mentions the observance of the Sabbath three times in his *Art of Love*. But among some cultured Romans the spiritual life of the Jew and its influence caused irritation, as can be seen in the words of the Stoic philosopher Seneca, an administrator under Claudius and Nero. Seneca sharply criticized the Jewish institution of the Day of Rest, which he considered harmful, promoting idleness and the loss of a seventh of one's life. "The customs of this criminal nation," he wrote, "have acquired such force that by now they already have followers in all lands, and thus the conquered have given their laws to the conquerors" (Dubnov, II, 823).

However, in the third quarter of the first century, when Jewry was engrossed in its struggle with Rome, and especially after the fall of Jerusalem, the shattered nation could not even think of propagating its faith among others. Indeed, it was at this time that the religious leaders decided to call a halt, at least temporarily, to proselytism, now viewed as perhaps weakening rather than strengthening the nation in its time of crisis.

From the time of the Hebrew prophets of social justice, the Jewish religion offered a universal vision of hope for a God-ordained revolution that would usher in a new era radically different from the past. The Jewish religion was in these terms universal, but only potentially so. For in practice, as we have seen, the Jewish people had constituted themselves as a national entity from the necessity of adapting themselves to the reality of living among other peoples and coping with the sequence of imperial powers that dominated, assaulted, or conquered them. Such experiences taught the Jews and their spiritual leaders that their *political* kingdom was too frail a framework for the nation. It was soon recognized that to preserve the nation and its distinctive ethical core, a strict religious discipline was required (Dubnov, vol. II, 383ff).

From the time of Ezra to the Pharisaic Revolution, it came to be understood that ethical discipline alone was inadequate. What was needed, in addition, were ordinances and ritual. The Pharisees sought consistently to put into practice the ideal of living in conformity with the Torah, which for them meant the twofold law or what the New Testament refers to as "the tradition of the elders." The Pharisees thus forged an iron armor of legal regulations that would be impenetrable to the arrows of Greco-Roman culture. Though some might have felt this armor as a heavy yoke, it was tolerated because the political and spiritual pressures from the surrounding pagan world were great.

When the Jews had thus isolated themselves from the outer world, the pagans reciprocated with resentment and hostility. This self-insulation against pagan influences meant that the Jews drifted away from realizing the prophetic ideal of universal Judaism. The only way left to the Jews for the realization of that ideal was proselytization, which, as we have seen from Matthew's Gospel and other sources, was actively pursued by the Pharisees in the intertestamental period. But proselytization became increasingly difficult as the Jews faced an apparently hopeless dilemma: to preserve the Jewish nation, it was necessary to prevent merging with other peoples; but to make Judaism universal it was imperative for the Jews to merge with others, but only on the condition that the merging would preserve the distinctive ethical, monotheistic core of Judaism.

A chief element of the pharisaic outlook was the belief in a Messiah, a human messenger of God, sent to rescue "God's people" and usher in a kingdom of Heaven on earth. Roman domination, and the struggle against it, suggested that human powers alone could not liberate Judea. A political and/or spiritual redeemer was necessary. The pro-Zealotic Pharisees believed that active resistance against the Roman oppressor was a means of clearing the way for the Messiah. But others among the Pharisees and the populace, who recognized the fundamental inequality of power between Rome and Judea, yearned for a spiritual Messiah who would redeem the individual. This "school" questioned whether so costly a struggle for political freedom was necessary. They argued that in the continual struggle for the political freedom of the nation, the needs of the individual had been forgotten. Faith and ethics, it was argued, were not at all contingent on a larger or smaller degree of political freedoms and national unity. Religion was given to the individual, not the nation. The "kingdom of Heaven" was approaching, and soon the Messiah would appear to save not the nation, but the individual soul. This emphasis by Dubnov on the individual may be too one-sided. The redemption of Israel as a whole was an essential element of the messianic vision.

9

The Jews in the Roman Near East

Jesus of Nazareth never lived to witness, or experience, the consequences of the Jewish revolt against Rome, having died some 40 years before it began. As our main aim is to illuminate the process by which the Jews became a diaspora people, and since the Christianity that emerged with Paul and the Church Fathers developed after the Jewish war, it is necessary to return to Rome of the ancient Near East because it is directly relevant to the making of a diaspora people.

In an important recent study,[1] Fergus Millar addressed the question of whether and to what extent the various Near Eastern populations had experienced a continuous ethnic or proto-national identity; and, if so, what that identity implied for the relation of a given population to the imperial power.

Millar rightly underscores the enormous significance of the great revolt against Roman power that broke out in Judea in 66 CE and ended with the mass suicide of the defenders of Masada in 74. Not generally known is a fact that Millar brings into relief: it is in Josephus' *Jewish War* that we find the fullest available account of any event in the entire Roman Empire in the first century. We learn from that account that after some fighting in the outskirts of Jerusalem, Gallus decided to withdraw his army, and that its retreat was forced into headlong flight with the loss of the equivalent of an entire infantry legion and the equivalent of a whole cavalry *ala* as well. And Millar observes: "There is no other example of a comparable defeat of Roman regular forces by the population of an established province" (71).

The defeat led to Nero's appointment of Vespasian and to a very substantial increase of Roman forces in the Near East. It was at Caesarea

---

[1] See Fergus Millar, *The Roman Near East, 31BC–AD337*, Cambridge, MA, and London: Harvard University Press, 1993. Hereafter, all page references to this work will be cited in parentheses immediately following the quoted passage.

in Judea that Vespasian in person was first hailed as emperor by his troops; and Vespasian's coup marks, for Millar, an important phase in the political integration of the Near East in the empire. As for the siege of Jerusalem, it required one seventh of the entire Imperial army and five months in 70 CE to capture the city. "Nothing," writes Millar, "could have served to emphasize more clearly the degree to which the coherence of the Empire depended on at least passive acquiescence of the provincial populations, or at the very least the absence of any coherent local or regional nationalisms which might offer a challenge to Rome" (76).

But the fact that the Jewish revolt was at no point supported by the non-Jewish populations of the surrounding area raises a significant question: were the Jews unique in the Near East where intense and powerful religio-national feeling is concerned? A document of 139 CE shows that, in the aftermath of the second Jewish revolt of 132, there were at least three cavalry *alae* and 12 *cohortes* stationed in Judea. No other province, not situated on a frontier, had so large a garrison. And, indeed, the Romans were doubtless fully aware of the *national* significance of the name "Iudea," for they soon replaced it with "Syria Palaestina."

Both the first Jewish revolt of 66 and the second of 132 leave no doubt that they were intensely nationalist in nature, giving rise to regimes which sought the realization of religio-national traditions in political independence from Rome. And from Millar's careful survey of the evidence concerning the other populations of the Near East, it does appear that none of the others possessed anything like the heightened national identity of the Jews. None of the others had the equivalent of the Bible as a *national history*, and not merely as a source of theological beliefs and ethical conduct; and none of the others seem to have produced writings like those of Josephus, embodying the conception of their history and experience as a continuity, from the Creation to their own time.

Among all the groups in the Roman Near East who spoke a Semitic language, the Jews alone possessed a sacred text and national history in that language. The Jews were conspicuously different in that they worshiped a formless God and observed a day of rest, and dietary and other ordinances. The resulting communal hostilities between the Jews and the others were unparalleled elsewhere, as were the major conflicts between the Jews and the Roman state. The scale, duration, and intensity of the Jewish revolts brought about significant changes in the structure of the Roman Empire as a whole and offer a contrast to the comparatively easy suppression of other dependent kingdoms, which in the case of Nabataea or Osrhoene appears to have involved no military encounters at all. At one level, then, the conflict between Rome and Jerusalem was a conflict between paganism and Judaism, and at another level between empire and a claim to liberty (352–3).

There is, however, another factor that needs to be taken into account in exploring the social causes of the intercommunal conflict between the Jews and others in the Roman Near East. In his new book, *Rome and Jerusalem*,[2] Martin Goodman attempts to illuminate the causes in that period of the ceaseless tension between the Jews and non-Jews. He subtitles his book "the clash of ancient civilizations," suggesting thereby that Rome and Jerusalem had symbolized a chief antinomy in the eyes of Jews and Romans. But it appears that his analysis has overlooked a key factor.

In an extraordinarily insightful review, Clifford Ando[3] reminds us that it was Tertullian who first framed a question in three parts: "What has Athens to do with Jerusalem, the academy with the Church, the heretic with the Christian?" This was an attempt to define the boundaries of the Christian community, and to separate it from the philosophical and intellectual traditions of Classical culture. Hence, it was Athens and Jerusalem that became the chief polarity in Western thought. Goodman, however, seeks to endow the conflict between Romans and Jews and, therefore, "Rome" and "Jerusalem" with a similar historic importance. But, as Ando rightly comments, "it is by no means clear that Romans or Jews, before or after the destruction of the Temple, understood opposition to the other as constitutive of themselves" (6).

One of Goodman's aims is to suggest that European anti-Semitism is rooted in Roman politics and, in particular, in the way the Roman emperors suppressed the revolt of 66–70: (1) prohibiting the reconstruction of the Temple; (2) imposing upon the Jews a special tax: the tithe formerly sent to Jerusalem was now to be directed to Rome for the temple of Jupiter; and (3) after the second revolt in 132–135, when the Romans had run out of patience with Jewish insurgency, they hoped to erase Judea from memory by renaming it "Syria Palaestina." Goodman interprets these punishments as unique. Ando, however, states correctly that all but the tax

> had precedents in Roman action against special enemies in earlier centuries, whether those, like Carthage in the Punic Wars, who through power and persistence drew Roman blood for generations, or others, like Fregellae in Italy, or Corinth in Greece, whom the Romans understood as treasonable – as having revolted in contravention of legal treaty and religious sanction.

Ando adds that though the Romans practiced genocide against small and localized populations, they never applied such policies to the Jews.

---

[2] See Martin Goodman, *Rome and Jerusalem*, New York: Alfred A. Knopf, 2007.
[3] *Times Literary Supplement*, April 6, 2007, No. 5427.

But Ando's main contribution to our understanding is consistent with an aspect of the thesis we have been defending from the beginning: under Rome, the Jews, as we have seen, became conspicuous both in Judea and especially in the diaspora in winning from the empire unique, legal privileges, an insight one fails to gain from "Goodman's otherwise exemplary volume," as Ando remarks. Ando now proceeds to make the strongest case for the unique status of the Jews in the empire:

> If there is a connection to be drawn between Roman policy and anti-Semitism, it lies not in the governance of Judea but in the Diaspora, and is located in the history not of punishment, but of privilege.

The Jews seem

> nearly universally to have obtained the right to maintain their ancestral customs – their religion – even when these conflicted with local and imperial law. The Jews of the Diaspora were thus bracketed from the communities in which they were embedded, not simply ethnically or culturally, by descent, or practice, or both, but also in their political and legal identities, and this through the power of Rome.

As a result, there was a long history of violent eruptions in the diaspora – not between Romans and Jews, but between Jews and their neighbors. And if, as in the century and a quarter before the revolt, violence had greatly declined, it was due to the protection that Rome had extended to the Jews of the diaspora. After the revolt in 66, and even after the second revolt of 131, "the privileges of the diaspora Jews were not compromised in any significant way. In fact, in 70 CE some cities petitioned the emperor to rescind the privileges of the Jews but were refused" – as we saw earlier when Titus himself, fresh from the war and a triumphal march, turned down such requests from the non-Jewish citizens of Antioch. The privileging of the Jews continued in the second century: when the emperor Hadrian outlawed circumcision, the Jews were exempted from the law. Finally, addressing the chapter of Goodman's that is devoted to the relations between Christians and Jews, Ando argues quite convincingly that Goodman's

> emphasis on the importance of the Jews' ongoing punishment, in the form of the tax and loss of the Temple, does not allow the full force of Christian identification with Rome as against Jerusalem, as it were, to emerge. For unlike the Jews, the Christians were legally if sporadically persecuted; and had they identified themselves as Jews – as Jesus of the house of David, and Paul of Tarsus, a Hebrew of Hebrews, had done – their fate under

the Empire, and the later history of anti-Semitism, might have proceeded far differently. As it happens, Christians rejected the identification with the religion of their eponym, and in so doing chose death rather than life before the law. Such was the hostility Christians felt toward their erstwhile co-religionists. (Clifford Ando, *TLS*, 7)

10

The Jews Move to Poland

As conditions worsened for the Jews of Western Europe, they sought
refuge in the East, in the hospitable regions of Poland and Lithuania. In
the agrarian economy of Poland, whose population consisted of nobles
and serfs, with no middle classes to speak of, the Jews soon assumed
the chief role in all activities relating to commerce.[1] And it is a near
certainty that at first they lived on good terms with the Christians. The
Polish people of the thirteenth century had yet to be indoctrinated with
the Christian, anti-Jewish prejudices; and the pre-capitalist nature of the
economy opened for the Jews a domain in which they faced no competition. In 1264, King Boleslav V granted the Jews a Charter, the terms
of which were quite similar to those granted by the German princes in
earlier centuries. Then, 100 years later (1364), the Charter of Casimir the
Great equated the Jews with the nobility where injury and murder were
concerned, imposing identical punishment upon the guilty. But in time,
of course, this preferential treatment provoked the resentment and vehement protests of the clergy. Soon, the Polish ecclesiastical authorities
began to legislate against the Jews just as actively as had the authorities
of Western Europe. In 1279, they attempted, unsuccessfully, to impose
upon the Jews the wearing of distinctive insignia. But in the next century
we hear for the first time in Poland accusations of profanation of the Host
and of ritual murder. In 1454, yielding to the Church powers, the king
(Casimir IV) abrogated some of the Jewish privileges. Three decades later
the Jews were expelled from Warsaw and from Cracow, expulsions that
were soon followed by an attempt to expel them entirely from Lithuania.

As Poliakov remarks, history appeared to be repeating itself, the Jews

---

[1] In the present discussion I rely heavily on Leon Poliakov, *The History of
Anti-Semitism*, vol. I, trans. Richard Howard, Philadelphia, PA: University of
Pennsylvania Press, 1975, chs 11 and 12. Hereafter, all page references to this work
will be cited in parentheses immediately following the quoted passage.

now encountering in the East the same hostility they had met with in the West. But in Poland the Jews had so thoroughly entrenched themselves in the economic foundations of the country, that it was impossible, for the time being, to oust them. In Poland, moreover, and in the East generally, "the existence of a Jewish social class culminated in the emergence of a nation in a class by itself" (248). The influx of Jews fleeing from the persecutions of the West increased after the Black Plague. Apparently, the Polish Jews suffered much less from the scourge, and constituted by the eighteenth century about 10 percent of the country's population. This substantial demographic base enabled them to organize themselves as a state within a state, so to speak, in which to practice all trades and monopolize several and, in a word, to prosper – in sharp contrast to their previous tribulations.

The Jews lived not in ghettos, but in streets and neighborhoods of their choice. The range of their occupations was broad and included all types of commerce and trade, administrative posts, the development of salt mines and forests, and even agriculture. This meant that a significant proportion of the Jewish populace lived in the countryside, some becoming bankers to the nobles and even landowners on their own account. Others, among the better-off Jews, became important merchants, importers, and, above all, exporters of wood, wheat, skins, and furs. But the vast majority of the Polish Jews were artisans and small tradesmen who now had to compete with the rising Polish bourgeoisie. In the countryside, the Jews made a living as innkeepers, retail dealers, and even simple farmers. Becoming in that way a notable middle class in Polish society, the Polish Jews continued to speak a German dialect that became Yiddish. This special feature, together with their religious and social-class distinctiveness, was bound to raise a barrier between the Jews and their Polish Christian neighbors.

It therefore seemed natural for the Jews to create a form of self-government at both the local and the national levels. The form may be described as a community or *kahal* in Hebrew, corresponding to a geographic unit that included the Jews of a city as well as those who lived in its environs. The oligarchic government of the *kahal* consisted of the wealthiest and most influential members of the community, who made all important administrative and economic decisions and who also appointed the rabbi, a personage of considerable importance since his moral authority was reinforced by his powers in judicial matters. The *kahal* form of organization was acceptable to the Polish rulers who found it convenient for the collection of taxes en bloc.

Eventually, the Polish rulers decided it would be even more convenient to impose a total annual payment upon all the Jews in the country and to charge the Jewish leadership with allocating the tax burden among the various communities. The meetings of the *kahal* representatives, at first irregular and sporadic, became in the second half of the sixteenth century semi-annual conferences that determined tax-quotas, settled conflicts between *kahals*, enacted new laws, and addressed questions concerning Polish Judaism. The Jewish federal institution thus improvised, a Jewish parliament of sorts with about 30 members, received the name "Council of the Four Nations" – in Hebrew, "Vaad Arba Aratzoth." The "four nations" were: Greater Poland (Posnan), Lesser Poland (Cracow), Red Russia or Ruthenia (Lvov), and Lithuania. Subsequently, Volhynia was added, while in 1623 the Jews of Lithuania seceded and formed their own council. Soon it became known throughout the diaspora how privileged, in comparative terms, the Polish Jews were in that period.

It is, therefore, not surprising that a form of anti-Jewish animus set in and developed within the Polish populace. This animus, however, was different from the anti-Semitism the Jews had experienced in the West. In Poland, though the earliest manifestations of hostility toward the Jews may have been caused by the religious differences between the two peoples, the Jewish group had become so numerous, and its economic role so indispensable, that the nature of the conflict was altered. In Poland the Jews had become an integral element of the social body. Every Pole, whether nobleman or laborer, peasant or city-dweller, turned to the Jew to buy or sell, to borrow or to pay taxes, to travel or to patronize a tavern. It followed that although the Jews' rejection of Christ made it easy to hate or despise them, the essential economic role of the Jews meant that the consequences of that hate or contempt varied with the social-class position of the Poles.

The Polish nobles, for example, as the chief beneficiaries of Jewish enterprise, tended to protect the Jews. The nobles treated them with greater disdain than that reserved for other classes of society, but without much malice in doing so. When the custom of defaming the Jews in print came to Poland as it had everywhere else, no defamatory text of that kind came from the pen of a noble. Such works were written or sponsored by the Christian, urban bourgeoisie that was in a permanent, competitive conflict with the Jews. The aim of the hate literature was to oust the Jews from trade or prevent them from becoming artisans. Poliakov cites the fact that a special commission from the elected magistrates of Cracow prompted Sebastian Miczynski to write in 1618 his *Mirror of the Polish Crown* in which "the wealth of the Jews, as well as their commercial techniques, were described at length for the first time. Religious accusations are of minor importance in this work" (255; italics added).

The clergy, in contrast, specialized in religious charges. The leader at the end of the sixteenth century was the well-known Jesuit, Peter Skarga, perhaps the most illustrious Polish preacher of all time, and author of the

Lives of the Saints (1579), which for centuries served as bedside reading for the Polish people. The pupils of the Jesuits were the chief purveyors of slander, resulting in riots that degenerated into pogroms. The Jews resorted to paying an annual fee in the hope of preventing molestation and massacres. But Poland soon faced what is known in Polish history as the Deluge, marking at one and the same time the decline of Poland as a state and the end of the golden age of the Polish Jews.

The Chmelnitzky Uprising of 1648–1649[2]

In 1648, Poland was assaulted by a vicious storm in the shape of a bloody uprising by its Ukrainian peasants against the Polish overlords, an event with catastrophic consequences for the Jews. The Poles were predominantly Catholic. But in the southeastern border provinces of Poland, the so-called Ukraina – meaning "border" or "frontier" – the native population was Russian by nationality and Greek Orthodox in its religion. The entire vast region of those provinces was subject to the political and economic power of the Polish kings and magnates. Enormous estates, comprising numerous villages populated by Russian peasants, were controlled by wealthy Polish landlords who enjoyed all the privileges of feudal masters. The peasant-serfs or *khlops*, as they were contemptuously referred to by the Polish nobles, were foreign to their masters religiously and nationally. And, in the eyes of the Polish-Catholic clergy, the Greek Orthodox faith of those serfs was quite objectionable. The Poles looked down upon this Russian populace as an inferior race, more Asian than European.

Apart from the oppressive agricultural labor, or *corvée*, to which the serfs were subjected, they were burdened with numerous imposts and taxes levied on pastures, mills, hives, and other sources of subsistence. Moreover, the Polish lords lived, as a rule, far from their Ukrainian properties, leaving the managements of them to stewards; and those stewards included a number of Jews who allowed themselves to become conspicuously complicit in the exploitation of the serfs. Naturally, the South Russian *Muzhik* hated the Polish Pan as a landlord and Catholic. No less and perhaps even more intensely did he hate the Jewish steward with whom he came in daily contact, and whom he regarded as a despi-

---

[2] The following discussion is based on Leon Poliakov, *The History of Anti-Semitism*, vol. 1, 356f, and on Simon Dubnow (Dubnov), *History of the Jews in Poland and Russia*, trans. from the Russian by I. Friedlaender, Philadelphia, PA: Jewish Publication Society of America, 1918. Hereafter, page and author references to these works will be cited in parentheses immediately following the quoted passage.

cable tool of the Pan – and on top of that an "infidel" who practiced a strange religion. Thus, the Jew of the Ukraine found himself between the Pan and the *khlop*, between the Catholic and the Greek Orthodox, between the Pole and the Russian, never realizing, apparently, the potentially catastrophic role he was playing for himself and his co-religionists.

These South Russian peasants were far from submitting themselves to their harsh conditions passively and patiently. Indeed, they possessed a warlike spirit fostered by the proximity of the Russian steppes and the Khanate of the Crimea, out of which the Tatars had often burst forth and descended upon the eastern provinces of Poland, compelling the Ukrainians to organize themselves in military units – Cossacks – to fight off the invaders. In that way, a quasi-military caste, Ukrainian Cossackdom, emerged as an autonomous organization. Apart from these Ukrainian Cossacks, were the so-called Zaporozhian Cossacks, from beyond the falls of the Dnieper in the steppes, who engaged in ceaseless battles with the Tatars of the Crimea. The two Cossack groups were often in touch with one another and even collaborated occasionally. The Ukrainian populace looked upon them with pride, hoping that the Cossacks would sooner or later liberate them from the Poles and the Jews. The Polish government failed to recognize the magnitude of the Cossack threat to the Polish republic, and the Jews failed to foresee that the formidable forces threatening the Polish lords would soon be directed at themselves.

The first sign of trouble occurred in 1637, when the Cossack leader, Pavluk, suddenly appeared in the province of Poltava, inciting the peasants to rise up against the Pans and the Jews. Responding to Pavluk's call, the angry peasants demolished several synagogues in the town of Lubny and its environs, killing about 200 Jews. But the real beginning of the mutinous groundswell dates from 1648, when the popular Cossack leader, Bogdan Chmelnitzky from the province of Kiev, called for armed resistance on the part of the Ukrainian Cossacks. Elected leader, he was empowered to enlist the aid of the Zaporozhian Cossacks and also to conclude an alliance with the Khan of the Crimea, who agreed to send Tatar fighting units in support of the uprising.

In April, 1648, the combined forces of the Cossacks and Tatars moved to the borders of the Ukraine and, confronted by the Polish armed forces, inflicted upon them a decisive defeat which served as a signal for the whole region on the eastern banks of the Dnieper to rise in rebellion. The Ukrainian populace organized itself in bands and proceeded to devastate the estates of the Pans, slaying them and their Jewish stewards. Even where the Jews played no role as stewards, as in the towns of Pereyaslav, Piryatin, Lokhvitz, and Lubny, thousands were killed and their property destroyed or pillaged. Only those who were willing to embrace the Greek

Orthodox faith were allowed to remain alive. Some of the Jews who managed to escape from the Cossacks into the Tatar camp gave themselves up as prisoners of war, knowing that, as a rule, the Tatars refrained from killing the Jews and preferred to hold them captive with the aim of having them ransomed by their Turkish co-religionists. Dubnov cites Russian and Jewish sources describing the process by which the Cossack forces began to murder Poles and Jews, but with the greatest cruelty shown toward the Jews. The Cossacks, not content with merely murdering men, women, and children, deliberately refrained from finishing off their victims, so as to subject them to a wide range of frightful tortures.

In September 1648, Chmelnitzky himself, accompanied by his Tatar allies, approached the walls of Lemberg and besieged the capital of Red Russia or Galicia. They succeeded in pillaging the suburbs, but failed to penetrate the fortified center of the town. Chmelnitzky offered to raise the siege if all the Jews and their property were handed over to him. The magistrates responded that the Jews were under the jurisdiction of the king, and that the town magistrates had no authority to hand over the Jews. Chmelnitzky then offered to withdraw for a ransom and kept his promise when the Jews took the initiative in mobilizing from the town residents an enormous sum, the bulk of which the Jews themselves contributed.

Heading for Warsaw, Chmelnitzky was informed that the new king, John Casimir, offered to enter into peace negotiations with him. But the talks were soon broken off, owing to what the king regarded as excessive demands. The war resumed and many more Jewish communities were devastated. In the continuing battles, the Polish forces were defeated, and Casimir consented to a peace treaty, the terms of which precluded the residence of Jews in the portion of the Ukraine controlled by the Cossacks. The war continued, however, and the Polish government called up the national militia, which included a Jewish detachment of 1,000 men. This time the Poles got the upper hand and a new Treaty favorable to them was concluded in 1651. The terms of the new Treaty restored the right of the Jews to live in the Ukraine.

In the course of the final decade of 1648–58, the losses inflicted upon the Jews of Poland were appalling. The number of Jewish victims varies between 100,000 and 500,000. But even the lower figure far exceeds the number of Jewish victims of the Crusades in Western Europe. Some 700 Jewish communities had endured massacre and pillage. In the Ukrainian cities on the left banks of the Dnieper, controlled by the Cossacks, Jewish communities disappeared almost completely. Even in the Polish part of the Ukraine, where the Cossacks had made inroads, only one tenth of the Jewish population survived. Some of the Jews who remained alive were the ones carried off by the Tatars to Turkey. Others had escaped to Lithuania, to the central provinces of Poland, or to certain areas of

Western Europe. "All over Europe and Asia," writes Dubnow (also spelled Dubnov):

> Jewish refugees or prisoners of war could be met with, who had fled from Poland, or had been carried off by the Tatars, and ransomed by their brethren. Everywhere the wanderers told a terrible tale of the woes of their compatriots and of the *martyrdom of hundreds of Jewish communities*. (Dubnow, 75; italics added)

I have deliberately italicized this phrase because it speaks directly to the historical event we are about to discuss: the Sabbatai-Zevi messianic movement and the social and cultural conditions that gave rise to it. Gershom Scholem, the famous scholar of Jewish mysticism and the author of the most detailed study of this false messiah, has claimed that all treatments of the Sabbatian movement that preceded his own had assigned to the Chmelnitzky massacres a causal priority in stimulating the Sabbatian movement into existence. All such treatments, Scholem argued, are misleading and/or simply wrong. The rationale for Scholem's study was, therefore, to offer an alternative interpretation of the social causes of the messianic movement of the seventeenth century. As this is clearly an important historical issue, deserving of careful consideration, we shall return to Scholem's view after a brief outline of the rise and spread of the Sabbatian movement.

11

Sabbatai Zevi

In the seventeenth century, Jews almost everywhere in Europe lived spiritually within the religious framework of the Talmud, the rabbinical teachings rooted in the principles of the Pharisaic Revolution. The four fundamental elements of the Pharisaic-Rabbinical movement were the twofold law (written and oral), prooftexting, the belief in resurrection, and faith in the coming of a Messiah, an extraordinary human individual who would usher in the kingdom of God on earth, a condition of redemption from the travails and suffering of the past.

But parallel to this ideological framework there emerged a form of Jewish mysticism that has been termed "Kabbalistic." "Kabbalah" means literally "tradition," embodying ideas and tendencies that have been going on since Talmudic times if not earlier. The tradition is based on a secret doctrine treating the most deeply hidden and profound matters of human existence; secret, too, because as in all mysticisms, the doctrine is the property of a small elite chosen to impart the esoteric knowledge to their disciples.

The earliest of such Jewish mystics about whom we know something were active in the Spanish town of Gerona in Catalonia in the first half of the thirteenth century. They were the first who succeeded in familiarizing influential circles of Spanish Jewry with Kabbalistic thought. But following the expulsion of the Jews from Spain in 1492 – which will be discussed in a later chapter – Kabbalism began to undergo a total change, becoming spiritually more and more influential in Judaism and transforming itself from an esoteric to a popular doctrine. The expulsion was a traumatic catastrophe that set in motion the process that gradually fused the messianic and apocalyptic elements of Judaism with the elements of Kabbalism. By the time of Isaac Luria's teachings in the sixteenth century, the mystical movement had in fact become popular among the dispersed Jewish masses. In Luria's new doctrine we hear the concept of *tikkun*, which appeared after the *Zohar* (*The Book of Splendor*), and refers to the human task in the world of restoring the unity of God, a precondition for restoring the unity of the people of Israel.

In Scholem's interpretation of the Lurianic message, it is the human being who

> completes the enthronement of God, the King and mystical Creator of all things, in His own Kingdom of Heaven . . . The historical process and its innermost soul, the religious act of the Jew, prepare the way for the final restitution of all the scattered and exiled lights and sparks. The Jew who is in close contact with the divine life through the Torah, the fulfillment of the commandments, and through prayer, has it in his power to accelerate or to hinder this process. Every act of man is related to this final task which God has set for His creatures.
>
> It follows from this that for Luria the appearance of the Messiah is nothing but the consummation of the continuous process of Restoration, of *Tikkun*.[1]

The symbolism is clear: in an age in which the historical exile of the people is a terrible and basic reality, the exile of the *Shekhinah*, the Divine Presence, gained greater importance than ever before. The unity of God can be restored only by *Tikkun*, by repairing the "broken" state of things here on earth. *Tikkun* in the realm of divine potentialities is contingent upon the religious acts of the Jew.

All this is essential background for an understanding of how the messianic pretensions of Sabbatai Zevi (1626–76) could have created an almost irresistible appeal. He was born in Smyrna where his father, Mordecai, descended from a Spanish family and formerly residing in Morea, acted as a broker to an English mercantile firm. It is likely that father and son had heard from those merchants that in Christian millenarian circles the year 1666 was to be the year of grace in which the Jews would be restored to Palestine. But in Jewish Kabbalistic circles, 1648 was the date for the messianic redemption. Although Sabbatai had received the conventional Talmudic education, he was already in his youth more attracted by the study of the Zohar, along the lines of Luria's exposition. He became an ascetic, mortifying his body and bathing frequently in the sea, day and night, in winter as in summer. Though he married early to a not-unattractive girl, there is doubt that the marriage was ever consummated, and he, soon after marriage, agreed to a divorce. He then repeated the process with another girl. Then he somehow attracted to himself a

---

[1] Gershom G. Scholem, *Major Trends in Jewish Mysticism*, New York: Schocken Books, 1941, 273–4.

circle of disciples, to whom he introduced the mysteries of the Kabbalah. At age 20, he became master of the small group, and impressed all who knew him with his seriousness. Tall and engaging, he also had a pleasant voice as he sang Luria's verses of his own composition in Aramaic, the language of the Zohar, and in Spanish as well.

In 1648, Sabbatai broke the age-old tradition by pronouncing the *name* of God – Yahweh. He thus presumed to declare that the Godhead, impaired by human sin and the consequent dispersion of the Jewish people, has been restored and unified, and that the perfect order of the messianic era has begun. Sabbatai's act did not go unchallenged, and the rabbis excommunicated him. But the community was divided, and though certain highly placed members believed in him, he was persecuted and forced to leave his native city with means of livelihood furnished by his family.

In Salonika, a Kabbalistic center, Sabbatai married the Torah, in the mystic union of the Anointed King with the Heavenly Daughter. This act shocked the religious conscience of the rabbis who banished Sabbatai from this city as well. Wandering about, but finding the Jews unreceptive, he came to Cairo where he was more successful. There he met other Kabbalists with whom he engaged in discourse and even dropped hints as to his pretensions. He had convinced himself that he was the Messiah. From Cairo it was natural for him to go to Jerusalem where, if anywhere, he might hope for a miraculous sign of intervention. He won respect in the Holy City by fasting much, praying devoutly, weeping and chanting psalms through the night.

The Jerusalem community was at that moment in dire circumstances since pious donations had ceased to flow from Poland due to the Chmelnitzky massacres. Moreover, the extortionate Pasha was demanding the compulsory tribute. Sabbatai, while in Cairo, had met Raphael Joseph Chelebi, a fellow Kabbalist who, as a wealthy tax-farmer, was master of the Egyptian mint. Sabbatai thus left Jerusalem as a successful messenger in the quest for charity, for Chelebi had readily responded to the urgent needs of the Jerusalem community. It was then that Sabbatai first heard of the girl Sarah seeking to meet the self-proclaimed Messiah and become his mate. The reputation she had for her free manner was not only no deterrent, but was a desirable part of the Kabbalistic, messianic program. For did not the prophet Hosea, at the apparent request of God, marry an unchaste woman? (It is more likely that Hosea did no such thing, and that the biblical passage in question was simply a bit of prophetic dramaturgy in which he dramatized what he regarded as the unchaste conduct of Israel at the time.) In any event, she was sent for, the couple was wedded in the home of Chelebi who, placing his fortune at the disposal of Sabbatai, became his first influential supporter.

In Gaza, on his return journey, Sabbatai found another ally, Nathan, a youth of 20, who announced himself to be the prophet Elijah come down to earth to pave the way for the Messiah. He spoke of a message having come down to him that within a year and a few months the Messiah would manifest himself in his glory and establish his kingdom by a peaceful conquest of Turkey. The common folk in Jerusalem are said to have greeted this news with joy. Nathan, with his heavenly message, elevated Gaza to the status of a holy city.

Sabbatai then left Jerusalem and was received with triumph in Aleppo. From there he proceeded to Smyrna, his native city, and was received with a greater ovation when he arrived there in the company of the Jerusalemite, Samuel Primo, his secretary, in the autumn of 1665. Sabbatai now proclaimed himself publicly in the synagogue, amid the blowing of trumpets, as the expected Messiah, the worshipers shouting exultantly, "Long live our king, our Anointed one!" Frenzy prevailed as the crowds, in the language of the Zohar, acclaimed Sabbatai as the true Savior. Men prepared themselves for the exodus to the Holy Land, abandoning their worldly affairs. In honor of the Messiah, the people alternated between ascetic and hedonistic exercises. All discipline broke down in the tumultuous jubilation. The aged rabbi Aaron Lapapa, an opponent of Sabbatai, was speedily deposed and replaced by Hayim Benveniste, an eminent Talmudist whose adherence to the Sabbatians was greeted with delight by the believers. All opposition was overcome – by force when necessary. Sabbatai became the undisputed master of the Smyrna community. His supporters bribed the Turkish authorities to back him against the rabbis, among whom Lapapa was the most inimical.

The events in Smyrna were repeated elsewhere. Samuel Primo from Smyrna and Nathan of Gaza flooded the Jewish communities of the world with propaganda announcing the appearance of the Messiah and his wonderful doings. The Christian agents of Dutch and English firms spread the news to European capitals. Jews everywhere greeted the news with joy, and even Christians lent credence to the story. At Venice, Moses Zacuto, a student of Spinoza, conveyed the message to the all-too-credulous Jews; in Leghorn, Sabbatai's early adherent, Moses Pinheiro, acted with no less zeal. Even Spinoza himself was not altogether skeptical about the truth of the propaganda. The only man who stood out in resisting and opposing the general intoxication was Jacob Sasportas. In London, Jews wagered a hundred pounds against ten that within two years Sabbatai would be anointed king of Jerusalem.

Soon Sabbatai's devotees began to speak of him in divine terms. Samuel Primo issued a proclamation in the name of the Messiah bidding the Jews throughout the world to turn the fast-day of the Tenth of Tebeth into a festival. The rabbis were outraged but helpless to stem the tide. Solomon Algazi, of the Smyrna rabbinical academy, barely escaped death at the hands of the believers, and fled the city. Next, Sabbatai set sail for Constantinople, expecting that the sultan would honor him as the greatest of the kings on earth. When the storm-tossed ship put off its passengers on the coast of the Dardenelles, Sabbatai was arrested and taken in chains to Constantinople where he was imprisoned. As Turkey was at war at that moment, the grand vizier decided it was impolitic to provoke the Jews by harsh measures against the man they so adored; nor was it wise to leave him in the capital as an object of their adoration. So Sabbatai was transferred to the fortress of Abydos where political prisoners were incarcerated.

At Abydos, the detention was rather mild. His friends and followers had visitors' privileges, and far from losing faith in him, looked upon his imprisonment as a temporary and necessary step toward the triumph of their cause. The Abydos fortress was Kabbalistically construed as the "Tower of Strength." And the prisoner continued to conduct himself as the Messiah. On the eve of Passover he had a paschal lamb killed for himself and his companions, and he consumed it with the suet in disregard of Talmudic law. In effect, then, he acted as if he were abrogating the law of Moses together with the teachings of the rabbis. "Blessed be God," he proclaimed, "who looseth (permits) that which is bound (forbidden)."

Thanks to the rich gifts he received from pilgrims near and far, he lived in regal splendor. Seeing himself as a sovereign above tradition and the Law, he did away with the fast day of the Seventeenth of Tamuz because on that day he became aware for the first time of his messianic role. Then on the seventh day thereafter – a Monday – he ordered the Great Sabbath to be kept. Finally, the ninth of the month of Ab, the fast-day in commemoration of the destruction of the Temple, and also the anniversary of his birth, he ordained as a festival. All his orders were obeyed by multitudes throughout the diaspora.

In due course, however, Sabbatai's career reached a turning point. Two Lemberg Jews, Isaiah, the son of the highly respected David ha-Levi, and his stepbrother, paid a visit to the pretender. They informed him that in Poland a prophet named Nehemiah Cohen was predicting the proximity of the messianic kingdom, but not with Sabbatai in that role. In response, Sabbatai sent by their hand a letter to the Jews of Poland promising them redemption for the sufferings they had endured and, in effect, ordering Nehemiah to appear before him. The prophet came, confronted Sabbatai, and called him a mere pretender. Some of the believers, offended by Nehemiah's repudiation of Sabbatai's claims, conspired to kill Nehemiah. But he managed to escape to Adrianople, where, after embracing Islam, he informed the authorities that Sabbatai was plotting to overthrow Ottoman rule, and that the constable at Abydus had found the huge influx of Jews so good for business that he had decided to do nothing about the plot.

This information was conveyed to the sultan (Muhammad IV, 1648–87), and a state council was promptly convened. At the advice of the mufti, a Jewish convert to Islam who was also personal physician to the sultan was sent to persuade Sabbatai, who had meantime been transferred to Adrianople, to embrace Islam. And Sabbatai agreed! His motive was apparently either a failure of courage or a fear that if he persisted in pursuing his messianic claim a catastrophe would befall the Jews. On September 16, 1666, he was brought before the sultan where he immediately cast off his headgear and donned the white Turkish turban. The so-called "Jewish Messiah" thus became Mehmet Effendi, a pensioner of the regime. It was rumored that the sultan, even after Sabbatai's conversion, contemplated destroying the Jewish followers of the pretender, but that the sultan's mother countered the proposal on the ground that the followers had been misled and deceived. The Turkish authorities were persuaded that bloodshed was unnecessary, and that the Sabbatian movement would collapse of itself.

Sabbatai, however, not yet through with his pretense, informed the circle about him that he had turned Muslim in obedience to God's command. And as his staunch supporters recovered from their first shock, they consoled themselves with diverse fantasies: It was not Sabbatai who had become a Turkish Muslim, but a phantom who took on his appearance. The "Messiah" himself had gone up to heaven, from where he would soon return in glory to accomplish the redemption. Indeed, Nathan, the prophet of Gaza, clinging to the notion that the chain of events was an unfathomable Kabbalistic mystery, traversed Asia Minor, Turkey, the Greek Islands, and Italy, urging believers not to lose faith in Sabbatai's messianic mission. But most of the diaspora Jews would not accept Nathan's Kabbalistic rationale, branding him a false prophet. Though he was excommunicated, and expelled from the cities he visited, he stubbornly retained his faith to the very end, dying in Turkey in 1680.

But the movement as a whole did not die. Despite the disillusionment in the Jewish communities of Europe, Asia, and Africa, segments of the populace still held on to their original beliefs. Another prophet of the movement, Sabbatai Raphael, was welcomed in many a city as he wandered through Germany, Holland, and Poland. In Leghorn, Moses Pinheiro had drawn into the Kabbalistic lore Abraham Michael Cardoso, a Portuguese convert to Christianity who had returned to Judaism. He became an enthusiastic propagandist of Sabbatai's messianic status, thereby preventing many from abandoning the movement as a lost cause.

As for Sabbatai himself, he appears to have lived a dual life, maintaining the appearance of being a devout Muslim while chanting psalms and expounding the Zohar to a small gathering of Jewish followers with whom he was permitted to meet on the pretext of striving to win them over to Islam. Eventually caught, however, in the act of psalm-singing, he was banished to Dulcigno, a small town in Albania, where he died in 1676.

12

Gershom Scholem's Error

In his monumental study (1,000 pages) of Sabbatai Zevi and the movement that arose in his name, Gershom Scholem begins by raising this fundamental, social-historical question: "what exactly were the decisive factors that brought about the messianic outbreak?"[1] He then states, rather condescendingly, that

> the usual, somewhat simplistic explanation posits a direct historical connection between the Sabbatian movement and certain other events of the same period. According to this view, the messianic outbreak was a direct consequence of the terrible catastrophe that had overtaken Polish Jewry in 1648–49, and had shaken the very foundation of the great Jewish community in Poland. The destruction had, in fact, surpassed anything known of earlier persecutions in other countries. This explanation was plausible enough as long as it could be maintained – as, indeed, it has been until now – that Sabbatianism as a popular movement started as far back as 1648, when Sabbatai Sevi came forward for the first time with messianic claims. It was supposed that Sabbatai's followers conducted a propaganda campaign converting more and more believers until the movement reached its climax in 1666. (1–2)

Scholem then makes the point that all earlier messianic movements in Jewish history from the time of Bar Kokhba were limited to a certain area; whereas the Sabbatian movement swept the whole House of Israel. It followed for Scholem that

---

[1] Gershom Scholem, *Sabbatai Sevi: The Mystical Messiah*, transl. R. J. Zwi Werblowski, Princeton, NJ: Princeton University Press, Bollingen Series XCIII, 1973, 1. Hereafter all page references to this work will be cited in parentheses immediately following the quoted passage.

It would seem unwise to try and explain this wide extension [of the move-ment] by factors that were operative in one area only, whatever their weight and significance there. Our caution will increase when we consider the fact that the Sabbatian movement did not originate in Poland, but in Palestine. *If the massacres of 1648 were in any sense the principal cause, why did the messiah not arise within Polish Jewry?* (2; italics added)

Thus proceeding to develop his argument, Scholem observes that the Sabbatian movement had spread wherever Jews lived – "from the Yemen, Persia, and Kurdistan to Poland, Holland, Italy, and Morocco. There is no reason for assuming that Moroccan Jewry was particularly affected by the massacres of 1648, of which they had heard very little anyway" (2). Questioning, in this way, the earlier interpretations, Scholem argues that although the 1648 massacres no doubt contributed their share, "we must look for other factors of wider and more fundamental validity" (3). The movement manifested no less momentum in Jewish centers that enjoyed peace and prosperity. Nor did the movement show signs of having been an eruption of social or class tensions within Jewry; the Jewries of Constantinople, Salonika, Leghorn, Amsterdam, and Hamburg, whose conditions had been in the ascendant, were in the vanguard of Sabbatian enthusiasm.

Where the "class" factor is concerned, Scholem acknowledges, on the one hand, that the opposition to Sabbatai Zevi included rich mer-chants, lay leaders, and rabbis, that is, members of the ruling class. At the same time, says Scholem, "All later statements notwithstanding, the majority of the ruling class was in the camp of the believers, and the prominent and active part played by many of them is attested in all reli-able documents" (5). But soon Scholem begins to make observations that tend to contradict the lighter causal weight he wants to assign to Poland:

In the period under discussion, the spectacular rise to economic prosperity of certain Jewish groups was matched by the pauperization of the Jewish masses in such important centers as Poland. The net result of these devel-opments was a perpetuation of the Jews' sense of instability. The feeling of uncertainty had become general and deep-seated, and in this respect at least, there was no difference between the experience of the rich and the poor. (67)

What Scholem is acknowledging, then, is the fact of no class distinction at the time as far as the general, Jewish feeling of insecurity was concerned, strongly suggesting a pan-Jewish hope for messianic redemption.

Scholem continues to lighten the specific causal weight of Poland and

1648, because he wants to posit a *general* factor underlying the existence of the Sabbatian movement wherever Jews lived. If there was one such general factor, Scholem writes:

> Then this factor was essentially religious in character and as such obeyed its own autonomous laws . . . It was this religious factor that set up the peculiar spiritual tension out of which Sabbatian messianism could be born, manifesting itself as an historical force throughout Israel, and not merely in one of the many branches of the Diaspora . . . Impinging on the social situation, the religious factor caused the various groups, the leading classes in particular, to join the messianic movement. As it happens, we are in a position to identify and name the religious factor. It was none other than Lurianic Kabbalism, that is, that form of Kabbalah which had developed at Safed, in the Galilee, during the 16th Century and which dominated Jewish religiosity in the 17th Century. (7)

But if we reflect carefully on this thesis of Scholem's, we will see that his emphasis on the religious factor need not contradict the causal priority of the Chmelnitzky massacres in triggering the fast spread of the bad news throughout world Jewry, and thus awakening or reawakening the messianic idea that such a catastrophe must mean the Messiah is on his way or has come.

Scholem's "general religious factor" is cogent in the sense that Jewry everywhere – in every diaspora community in the seventeenth century – continued to live within the ideological framework of Talmudic or rabbinic Judaism; which included the eschatological hope and expectation of the coming of the Messiah, and the radical break with the vale of tears of the past that messianic redemption promised. Scholem may also be right that the Jewish ideological framework of the seventeenth century contained, as a central element, the Lurianic Kabbalism that had developed in the sixteenth century. But that proposition, too, would not necessarily contradict the fundamental role of the 1648 massacres in prompting the extraordinarily rapid diffusion of the bad news throughout the diaspora.

Scholem tends to question the possibility of relatively rapid communication in the technically primitive conditions of 1648. But as we shall soon see, he overlooks a key historical fact concerning the Chmelnitzky events, which indisputably demonstrates that the bad news of the terrible experiences of 1648 had in fact traveled with extraordinary speed from Poland and the Ukraine to Turkey and the Near East.

Dubnow on the Sabbatian Movement

The first point that needs to be made is that Graetz and Dubnow were fully aware of the Kabbalistic influence on the Jews of Poland. Itinerant and local preachers had long sought to convey to the Polish Jews the notions of the "practical Kabbalah," according to which Kabbalistic practices could influence the course of nature. Furthermore, the secret writings of *Ari* (the initials of *A*shkenazi *R*abbi *I*saac Luria who died in Safed, Palestine, in 1572) and his school circulated in Poland in manuscript copies, going continually from hand to hand. Indeed, Jewish mystical tendencies were very much in vogue among the masses of Polish Jewry. Dubnow now proposes as a historical fact that the messianic movement that originated with Sabbatai Zevi, in 1648, spread like wildfire throughout the entire Jewish world. This speaks directly to Scholem's questioning of how a catastrophic event that occurred in Poland in 1648 could have been relevant to the emergence of a messianic pretender at Smyrna in the same year.

For Dubnow, it was more than a mere coincidence that in one and the same year, 1648, there occurred the wholesale murder of the Jews of the Ukraine and the first public appearance of Sabbatai in Smyrna. Dubnow now calls attention to an essential historical fact that, to the best of my knowledge, Scholem nowhere even mentions in his voluminous study of Sabbatai Zevi. Dubnow writes:

> The thousands of Jewish captives who in the summer of that terrible year had been carried to Turkey by the Tatar allies of Khmelnitzki and ransomed there by their coreligionists, conveyed to the minds of the Oriental Jews an appalling impression of the destruction of the great Jewish center in Poland. There can be no doubt that the descriptions of this catastrophe deeply affected the impressionable mind of Sabbatai, and prepared the soil for the success of the propaganda he carried on during his wanderings in *Turkey*, Palestine, and Egypt. (*History of the Jews in Russia and Poland*, 99; italics added)

I have read Scholem's study rather carefully, and it is a near certainty that in the body of the text itself he nowhere discusses the significance of the Tatars' carrying off thousands of Jewish captives to Turkey, and the ransoming of them by their fellow Jews. This error of omission is a serious one, both substantively and methodologically: he claimed to have corrected and superseded the analyses of his predecessors, but ignored an essential historical fact. For Scholem's great predecessors, the role of the Tatars was a central and salient one for several reasons. Graetz, for example, recognized that:

Fortunate were those [Jews] who fell into captivity with the Tartars; they [the Jews] were transported to the Crimea, and ransomed by Turkish Jews. Four Jewish communities (Porobischa and others) of about 3,000 souls resolved to escape massacre by surrendering to the Tartars with all their property. They were well treated, and sold into Turkey, where they were ransomed in a brotherly manner by those of their own race [sic]. The Constantinople community sent a deputy to Holland to collect money from the rich communities for the ransom of captives. (Graetz, vol. V, 8)

Leon Poliakov also cites the fact that Chmelnitzky "was able to unite the anarchic Cossack groups and form an alliance with the Crimean Tartars" (vol. I, 257). Collections were taken everywhere to feed those who had fled by the thousands into Hungary and Romania, and "especially to ransom the Jews sold into slavery, who were concentrated in great numbers in Constantinople" (I, 261). Here, there are three aspects we need to consider: (1) the fugitives scattered rapidly to the four corners of Europe, spreading the dreadful news; (2) the role of the Tatars and the ransoming by Turkish Jews of the Jewish captives "who were concentrated in great numbers in Constantinople;" and (3) alms-collectors began urgently combing Europe for donations. With an awareness of these facts there should be no difficulty in recognizing that it took no time at all, so to speak, for everyone in the Jewish world, wherever they happened to live, to have heard of the catastrophe and even to have given it an eschatological, messianic significance. Hence, when Scholem asks how a catastrophic event that occurred in Poland and the Ukraine could account for the rise of the Sabbatian movement in Turkey and the Near East, we now see that there is a clear and cogent answer to his question. Moreover, if Scholem himself had given at least brief attention to the Tatars and the Jewish captives, and the wider ramifications of that event, he might have recognized that his question was not as significant as he had supposed. He intended the question to serve as a refutation of the views of his great predecessors, Graetz and Dubnow; but the historical evidence supports them, not him.

It is interesting that when dealing with other related aspects of the Sabbatian movement, Scholem himself acknowledges the speed with which news traveled in pre-industrial Europe. In his discussion of the appearance of the prophet in Gaza and the "anointing" of the messianic pretender, Scholem writes:

the news generally traveled via Italy to Germany, Holland, England, and the rest of the Continent. *To Poland there was an additional route from Turkey via the Balkans.* Information reaching what today are Bulgaria and Yugoslavia was *immediately* relayed further north. Certain cities were

centers for the transmission of news, for example, Vienna and especially
Amsterdam. Italy and Holland, on the one hand, and Turkey, on the other,
were connected not only by close commercial ties, but also by many family
relations. In fact, it was to the family relations that the intense trade was
largely due. Those expelled from Spain, and the descendants of escaping
marranos in particular, were dispersed in many countries. Even members of
the same family would be scattered, some settling in Holland or Hamburg,
others in Italy or Turkey. Practically every Sephardic family in Europe had
relatives in Smyrna or Salonika, who would keep them posted of the great
awakening. Ashkenazic Jews too had family relations, albeit to a much
lesser extent, in the Orient and especially in the Holy Land. (Scholem,
Sabbatai Sevi, 469–70)

And here is another passage in which Scholem nullifies, in effect, the
significance of his question:

> It was *soon* known in Poland that Sabbatai had declared the massacres of
> 1648 to have been the beginning of the era of redemption . . . *It had been
> the news of the great massacres which had probably inspired Sabbatai's first
> messianic fantasies.* Now it was the turn of Polish Jewry to hear the message
> of comfort and hope, coming to them in their distress and affliction. (591–2;
> italics added)

The Chmelnitzky revolt meant that between 1648 and 1658 there was
virtually no Jewish community in Poland that went completely unharmed.
There was no longer a single Jew on the left bank of the Dnieper, since
those who had escaped were sold as slaves to the Turks. And, of course,
the economic foundations of Polish-Jewish life had collapsed. The Jews
who survived were no longer the country's chief bankers, since that role
had passed to Christian capitalists, especially to churches and monasteries whose wealth, consisting chiefly of lands, had remained intact despite
Chmelnitzky's onslaught and the demotion of Poland from her former
great power status. Impoverishment spread little by little until the Jewish
"social-economic class" was ultimately liquidated. The Polish Diet eventually suppressed the Council of the four nations, thus putting to an end
Jewish semi-state autonomy. Given the traditional, religious-ideological
outlook, the Jews did penance, seeing their misfortune as retribution for
their sins, and seeking to expiate them with a greater piety and austerity.
    Long before the massacres of 1648, that date had already had a special
meaning for many Jews, since the Kabbalists had declared that would be
the year of the coming of the Messiah, according to the *Zohar*. And in
the tragedy of Poland's Jews the Kabbalists saw a striking confirmation
of the prophecy. Deliverance, they believed, must be at hand, and the

tragedy must be the labor pains of its birth. At such a time Sabbatai Zevi entered and, in 1666, after many adventures and having failed to prove his superhuman status in response to the sultan's challenge, ended his days as the apostate Mehmet Effendi.

Thus the Sabbatian movement became a sectarian heresy. In contrast to events in the West, where the downfall of the false Messiah had quickly put an end to the earlier euphoria, the Sabbatian movement had set down deeper roots in Poland, where the resurrection of Sabbatai was expected from year to year. The proximity to Turkey and the city of Saloniki, the headquarters of the Sabbatian sect, imparted a special intensity to the sectarian movement in Poland, the main center of which came to be Podolia, part of which had been annexed by Turkey, after the Polish–Turkish War of 1672.

The collapse of the Sabbatian movement may be regarded as a watershed event in Jewish history, for it weakened considerably the belief in messianic redemption. But before the minds of many European Jews became receptive to the secular ideas of the Enlightenment, a new and powerful religious movement emerged that offered a different kind of answer to popular Jewish hopes. This movement, called Hasidism, strove to give a new religious meaning to the lives of the poverty-stricken masses scattered throughout Eastern Europe.

13

The Rise of Hasidism and the Baal-Shem-Tob

The apostasy of Sabbatai Zevi and the widespread shock and disappointment it caused, had not yet brought a decisive end to the Sabbatian movement. The former mass movement had become a mere sect – but a dangerous and heretical one from the standpoint of rabbinic Judaism. These "secret Sabbatians" continued to regard many of the ordinances and fasts as having been abrogated by the "Messiah." They therefore engaged in practices containing elements both of asceticism and libertinism. And although these secret Sabbatians no longer constituted a mass movement, their cult did spread in Poland – in Galicia and Podolia, in particular.[1]

Alarmed by the growth of this heresy, leading rabbis assembled in Lemberg in the summer of 1772 and proclaimed a *herem* (excommunication) against all Sabbatians who would refuse to renounce their errors. Only following a renunciation and a return to orthodoxy would they be allowed to remain in the community. In most cases the sectarians clung stubbornly to their beliefs and practices, so that in 1725 the rabbis proclaimed a second *herem* against them. But this second measure – requiring every orthodox Jew to report to the rabbis all secret Sabbatians known to him – was no more effective than the first. It failed to wipe out the heresy, which degenerated further into the form of "Frankism."

When Jacob Frank died in 1791, his sect began to disintegrate, and his successor, Eve, heavily in debt for her failed attempts to attract new recruits, died in 1816. The Frankists who had remained in Poland stayed loyal to the "Holy Lord" to the day of his death, but soon afterward lost the character of a sect as they merged with the Catholic population.

---

[1] The following discussion is based on Simon M. Dubnow, *History of the Jews in Poland and Russia*, transl. from the Russian by I. Friedlaender, Philadelphia, PA: Jewish Publication Society of America, 1918, ch. VI. Hereafter, all page references to this work will be cited in parentheses immediately following the quoted passage.

Frankism proved to be the effective gravedigger of Sabbatianism. But the grossly negative, materialistic nature of the movement left in its wake a spiritual vacuum in the Judaism of Eastern Europe. The urgent need arose for a positive religious movement that would resonate with the sentiments of the Jewish masses and harmonize, at the same time, with the traditional religious and ethical principles of Judaism from the time of the prophets.

We learn from Dubnow that there existed in Polish Jewry a significant cultural difference between the Jews of the northwestern and southwestern regions of Poland. In the northwest – Lithuania and White Russia – rabbinic, Talmudic scholasticism reigned supreme. The Talmudist had the first claim on all honorary posts in the community. Things were quite different, however, in Podolia, Galicia, Volhynia, and in the entire southwestern region. There the Jewish masses were remote from the sources of rabbinic learning, and from the influence of the Talmudic scholar. While in northwestern Poland book-learning was the criterion of a godly life, in Podolia and Volhynia Talmudic learning and discourse had failed increasingly to speak to the religious cravings of the common man.

Enter the Man, Israel, Who Became the Baal-Shem-Tob

Israel was born in 1700 on the border between Podolia and Wallachia, into an impoverished family. Orphaned in early childhood, he came under the care of charitable townsmen who sent him to *heder*, the typical, one-room; elementary Jewish school of the time, to study the Talmud. But the subject matter held no special attraction for the boy, who absented himself frequently, and who was more than once seen in the neighboring forest, lost in thought. For his truancy, he was expelled from school at the age of 12, and earned his meager living first as a teaching assistant and later as a synagogue beadle. He was looked upon as eccentric because he was found often in the synagogue at night, praying fervently or reading Kabbalistic texts such as the manuscripts of "Ari" (the initials of Ashkenazi Rabbi Isaac [Luria] who died at Safed, Palestine, in 1572), which were circulated from hand to hand. Under Kabbalistic influence, he taught himself the art of healing by means of incantations.

At age 20, Israel settled in Brody in Galicia, and married the sister of a well-known rabbi and Kabbalist, Gershon Kutover, who tried to interest his brother-in-law in Talmudic studies. But as all such attempts proved futile, the rabbi urged him to leave Brody to avoid further embarrassment stemming from Israel's growing reputation as an ignoramus where Jewish learning was concerned. At the rabbi's advice, Israel and his wife moved to a village in the neighboring Carpathian Mountains, where in strict solitude he habitually fasted, prayed, and lost himself in his thoughts. He eked out an existence by digging clay, which his wife carried or carted off to the city market.

At the age of 36, Israel resolved – inspired from above, as his followers eventually came to believe – to reveal himself to the world. He began to practice as a *Baal-Shem*, literally "master of the name." Such "masters of the name" belonged to a category of itinerant healers who wandered from one village to another, seeking patients and barely making a living thereby. This was a common phenomenon among Polish Jews at the time. These itinerant shamans or "doctors," steeped in Kabbalistic or quasi-Kabbalistic lore, claimed they could heal and cure by means of secret incantations, amulets, and medicinal herbs. The attitude of most village Jews toward these traveling shamans was mixed. Sometimes, as when there were serious illnesses or injuries, especially of children, the general mood of the village was one of desperation and the shamans were welcomed. But because they were generally unkempt, their hygiene poor, and their attire and appearance weird – not to mention their strange uttering – children, in particular, feared and detested them. Hence, when children heard that a Baal-Shem was coming to town, their impulse was to flee.

But Israel soon proved himself to be a famous exception. As he traveled from village to village and from town to town, curing successfully not only Jews but also Polish peasants and even nobles, he earned the reputation of being a miracle worker and gained the nickname, the "good master of the name" (Heb. the *Baal-Shem-Tob*, abbreviated "the Besht"). In the eyes of the impoverished Jewish multitude to whom he administered his cures and care, he was no ordinary "master of the name," but rather an extraordinary, charismatic, righteous, and saintly individual. As his reputation went before him, children now awaited his visit with excitement and glee.

The "Besht" – an acronym of endearment – became more than a healer of bodies. He became a teacher of new religious ideas, challenging the conventional view that Talmudic learning can lead, somehow, to salvation, and proposing, instead, that it is a whole-hearted devotion to God in faith and in fervent prayer that brings us closer to deliverance. When he encountered the learned, he defended the validity of his view with arguments from the Kabbalah – but not arguments enjoining asceticism. On the contrary, what he taught came from those elements of Jewish mysticism that urged the striving for an intimate communion between humans and God; and the means to be employed for the achievement of the desired nearness to God might be any means that cheered the human soul by belief in God's goodness, and by obedience to his ethical commandments.

In *c.*1740, the Besht made the town of Medzhibozh his permanent residence, and became the teacher of a large circle of disciples and followers. His teaching took the form of pithy sayings and parables, in sharp contrast to the Talmudists' formal exposition of texts. And it was the parabolic form of his teachings that so appealed to the multitude of plain people who were relatively uneducated where texts were concerned. Indeed, the Besht himself left nothing in writing, and we rely entirely on his disciples for the writings that have preserved his utterances.

The Fundamental Principles of the Besht's Teachings[2]

The first principle, derived from the Kabbalah, is that between the divine world and the human world there is only a superficial difference, for actually the two worlds are intimately tied to one another and perpetually acting upon one another. This world exists owing to emanations of the Divine, consisting of both materiality and spirituality – divine sparks. The Creator is always present in his creation, and nature is only the outward attire in which the Divine hides from human eyes. And it is the aim of the devout believer to discover the spirituality immanent in nature.

Humans must understand that God is with them always and everywhere; that his presence is poured out throughout the universe. When humans perceive things material, they actually behold the Divine Countenance. Bearing this in mind, humans can serve God at all times, even in the trifles of everyday life. The second principle – of intimate and perpetual interaction between the divine and human world – means not only that God influences human conduct, but also that human conduct influences the Deity. This principle of reciprocity is, of course, rooted in the biblical conception of the Covenant.

It follows from the Besht's teachings that communion with God ought to be the chief endeavor of every genuinely religious individual. The highest form of this communion is attained by feeling God's presence in all life's events. This is achieved in the emotions, not the intellect. The warmer and more intense the emotions, the nearer is the human being to the Divine. Hence, prayer is the essential medium by which humans can commune with God. To render communion pleasing to God, prayer must be ecstatic and fervent, so that the praying individuals throw off or transcend their materiality, as it were. To attain the ecstatic state, the Besht

---

2 From Simon Dubnow's Hebrew text, *Toledot Ha-Hasidut, the History of Hasidism*, on the basis of primary sources, handwritten and printed, copyright by the Devir Publishing Company Ltd, Tel Aviv, Israel, 1966.

taught that singing, dancing, clapping in rhythm, or shouting are not only permitted, but much more pleasing to God than ascetic exercises. The study of Jewish laws and texts retains importance for the Besht, but its role in communion with God is effective only when it arouses the exalted, effervescent religious state.

Moreover, what is essential in communion with the Divine is one's state of mind, one's *intentions*, which are more pleasing to God than excessive minuteness in religious observance. The pious individual or Hasid (hence Hasidism, the name of the mass movement that emerged in the Besht's name) ought to serve God not only by observing holidays and festivals, but also and especially in his everyday thoughts and actions. By means of such perpetual communion with God, humans may receive the divine gifts of clairvoyance, prophecy, and miracle-working. The Hasid is not only pious but also righteous. The Tzaddik or Righteous Individual lives up to the precepts of Hasidism to the highest degree possible, and is on that account nearest to God. The role of the Tzaddik is to serve as mediator between God and the plain people, assisting them to achieve purity of soul and heavenly and earthly blessings.

Clearly, then, the Besht's message contrasted sharply with the traditional rabbinic, scholastic emphasis in Judaism, and contrasted, too, with the ascetic elements of the Kabbalah. Moreover, it seems to be historically true that it was the personality of the Besht, as the first Tzaddik, that impressed the people more than his teachings. In thus acquiring, inadvertently, a powerful charisma in their eyes, the Besht had set in motion the process by which Hasidism became a mass movement. The Besht's original charisma meant that Hasidim (Heb. plural of hasid) in later generations would bestow on their leaders a similar charisma that raised the Tzaddik to the status of a miracle-worker, revered as if he were more than human.

The Besht himself had in *c.*1750 a miraculous revelation in which – as he reported it – on the day of the Jewish New Year his soul ascended to heaven where he beheld the Messiah and many souls of the dead. Addressing the Messiah, the Besht asked: "my master, when wilt thou appear on earth?" In reply, the Messiah averred:

> This shall be a sign unto thee: when the doctrine shall become known, and the fountains of thy wisdom shall be poured forth, when all other men shall have the power of performing the same mysterious feats as thyself, then shall disappear all the hosts of impurity, and the time of great favor and salvation shall arrive. (Dubnow, 110)

It is a general characteristic of mysticism, apparently, that the founder – through his followers' belief that he has achieved some form of *unio mystica* – acquired a superhuman status of sorts. Something similar soon occurred to the Besht. The idea spread that he was in touch with the prophet Elijah, and that the Besht's teacher was the biblical seer Ahijah of Shilo. It was the common people's love for the Besht that turned him into an extraordinary miracle-worker far above the all-too-human. When we speak of the "common people" in the Jewish context of the time, we mean all those men and women who worked with their hands in the full range of productive and menial occupations, who struggled to subsist, and who were largely unlearned where Hebrew and Aramaic religious texts were concerned. Even those who had acquired enough elementary education to enable them to read the Hebrew prayer books rarely understood even the literal meaning of the Hebrew words. That is why the learned often expressed contempt for the illiterate or semi-literate; and that is why the vast majority of the poor and comparatively uneducated Jews constituted such fertile soil for the Besht's message, which soon gave rise to the mass movement called Hasidism.

What the common people loved most about the Besht as a religious teacher was that he made no invidious distinction between the educated and the uneducated Jew. Indeed, he taught both audiences that book knowledge in itself, or the study of sacred texts, does not necessarily bring one closer to God. The Besht's message and personal example taught the common people that, far from being lesser Jews for the want of book knowledge, they were equal to the learned and perhaps even closer to God, owing to the enthusiasm and inspiration (Heb. *Hitlahavut*) with which they communed with God, and the intimacy they felt in their relation with Him.

The Growth of Tzaddikism

When the Besht died in 1760, his first successor was the preacher Baer of Mezherich, the town that became the headquarters of Hasidism in Volhynia, just as Medzibozh had been in Podolia. Baer, more learned than the Besht, was able to convey the Hasidic message successfully to the scholar class. In the course of 12 years (1760–72), Baer won over a large circle of prominent Talmudists by bringing into relief the centrality of Tzaddikism. He trained disciples who became Tzaddikim (plural of Tzaddik), the founders of dynasties in Poland and Lithuania. The dynastic principle became an integral feature of Tzaddikism, as the people increasingly put their faith in these new religious leaders, venerating them and their male descendants as the chief exponents of religious truths.

Another disciple of the Besht was Jacob Joseph Cohen who was the first to reduce the Hasidic teachings and parables to writing. In 1780, he published *Toledot yaakob yoseph* (*History of Jacob Joseph*, an allusion to the Hebrew text of Genesis 37:2), a collection of sayings he had learned from the Besht. He, too, makes salient the role of the Tzaddikim as intercessors on behalf of the common people; assailing at the same time the Talmudists who were Hasidism's main adversaries and who persisted in their arrogant contempt for the people. However, despite the Talmudic opposition and the contemptuous attitude, Hasidism continued to spread among the Jewish masses, even in the former strongholds of the Talmudists. By the last decade of the eighteenth century, Hasidic congregations and their separate synagogues had become increasingly common, even in Lithuania. The services of these new Hasidic congregations distinguished themselves by their ecstatic, effervescent character, by their loud singing and shouting, and even by merry drinking to create the right cheerful, emotional mood for prayer and communion with God.

The Tzaddik phenomenon may have been a chief factor accounting for the extraordinary speed with which Hasidism diffused throughout Poland and other areas of Eastern Europe. As Dubnow observes, the most characteristic trait of the Hasidim was their boundless veneration of the "holy" Tzaddikim. Though historically the product of Hasidism, Tzaddikism in practice was in many cases its antecedent, since the appearance of some miracle-working Tzaddik in a given neighborhood frequently resulted in wholesale conversions to Hasidism. In those terms, it is plausible that some earlier, traditional "masters of the name" (Heb. *Baalei shem*), who had remained relatively obscure, gained importance and recognition as Hasidism became a mass movement. For by embracing Hasidic theory and practice, and by continuing their medical-therapeutic "trade" and their Kabbalistically inspired "wonder-workings," these former itinerant shamans could now lay claim to a Tzaddik's status and role. This "trade" was most likely handed down from father to son, contributing thereby to the emergence and development of the dynastic principle. By adopting Hasidism, such individuals acquired a legitimacy, and perhaps even a charismatic aura, which they had never possessed before.

Once Tzaddikism became a firmly established Hasidic institution, a fairly typical scene was one in which the Tzaddik's home was overrun by crowds who in their credulity hoped to obtain a cure, remedy, blessing, "prophecy," or even practical advice. Anthropologists tell us that the relative success of shamanism in "primitive" societies – primitive from a scientific-technological standpoint – is explained by the high probability in normal times that most people will recover naturally and not die from their first illnesses. The typical shaman is "sophisticated" enough to recognize, in any specific case, whether a patient is likely to recover, and acts accordingly. As applied to the Tzaddikim, when they succeeded in helping, curing, or predicting, their fame spread as "miracle-workers," and the populace of the locality was won over to Hasidism. As Dubnow observes, Hasidism grew as a movement in direct proportion to the increase in the number of Tzaddikim, and a great number of these were practicing in the last two decades of the eighteenth century.

Already at that time, however, the reverence for the Tzaddik had become extreme, almost idolatrous. Preachers indoctrinated the people that the first duty of a Hasid is to revere the Tzaddik, a mediator between Israel and God. It is through his intercession, the people were told, that God bestows upon the faithful all earthly blessings – "life, children, and sustenance," an allusion to a well-known Talmudic dictum. The preachers went so far as to assert that if the Tzaddik wills otherwise, the flow of blessings would cease. Blind faith was demanded of the Hasid – to look upon the Tzaddik as his principal benefactor who therefore deserves to be supported by donations in cash and kind, so that he may devote himself fully to his role as intercessor. The Tzaddik's calling thus became profitable and, hence, hereditary, passing from father to son to grandson, and soon gave rise to petty rival "dynasties," multiplying rapidly and striving to wrest supremacy from one another. The cult of the Righteous taught by the Besht had now assumed a gross materialistic form; but there were notable exceptions, Tzaddikim who were selfless and genuinely devoted to the material and spiritual well-being of the people.

Dubnow calls our attention to Hasidism's diverse paths of development: whereas in the South, Hasidism captured entire communities rather easily, in the North – in Lithuania and White Russia – it met with the strong resistance of Rabbinism as represented by the *kahal* (community) organization. Moreover, the Besht's disciples who carried Hasidism to the North – Baer of Mezerich, Aaron of Karlin, Mendel of Vitepsk, Zalman of Ladi – absorbed several elements of the dominant doctrine of the rabbis. The principal exponent of the new teaching in the North, Zalman Shneorsohn (or simply Shneor Zalman), succeeded in imparting to Hasidism a measure of rationality, summed up in three key concepts: "wisdom, understanding, and knowledge" (Heb. *Hokhma, Binah, Daat*, abbreviated *HaBaD*), from which the Northern Hasidim received the nickname "Habadniks."

Zalman injected into the Besht's method a degree of religious and philosophical investigation or speculation, which, he proposed, was not only permissible but obligatory. He demanded of the Tzaddik that he be more of a religious teacher and less of a "miracle-worker." Zalman – perhaps under the influence of the emerging Enlightenment of the eighteenth century – purged Hasidism of its numerous superstitions, adapting it to the comparatively high intellectual level of the Jewish populace of the northwest.

Hasidism, Rabbinism, and the Forerunners of the Enlightenment

It is understandable why the rabbis had sensed a new, dangerous, heretical enemy in Hasidism, it having emerged and become popular so soon after the false-Messiah movements of Sabbatai Zevi and Jacob Frank. Moreover, the Besht's doctrine that the human being is saved by faith and not by religious knowledge was fundamentally antithetical to the central dogma of Rabbinism that measured religious virtue by the extent of biblical and Talmudic learning. The rabbis looked upon the Tzaddik as a new type of popular but fraudulent priest who not only fed on, but fostered and perpetuated the superstition of the masses.

In the latter part of the eighteenth century, the leader of the Lithuanian rabbis was the renowned Elijah of Vilna (1720–97), who had earned the old honorific title of *Gaon* (Genius). Elijah, already as a child, had impressed everyone with his erudition, which included not only his grasp of the Talmudic and Kabbalistic texts, but also mathematics, astronomy, and physics. But he understood the plain people as little as they understood him. There was an inherent elitism in some forms of Rabbinism, and the Gaon, as an intellectual aristocrat, was bound to condemn the "plebeian" notions of Hasidism. As early as 1772, when the first Hasidic groups had organized themselves secretly in Vilna, the rabbinical court, with the approval of the Gaon, pronounced a *Herem* (a ban) against the "godless sect." All orthodox Jews were called upon to shun all contact and intermarriage with them. The opponents of those following Hasidism (Heb. *mitnagdim*) regarded them as dangerous schismatics and treated them accordingly.

We need to remind ourselves that this is the eighteenth century we are discussing, the time of the Enlightenment movement of Western Europe, the ideas of which penetrated certain circles of Eastern Europe. Hence, Rabbinism and Hasidism, despite the war between them, soon found common cause in combating the new Enlightenment philosophy proceeding from the Moses Mendelssohn circle in Berlin. The rabbis actively opposed secular knowledge for the moral relativism it implied; and the Tzaddikim were even more hostile toward secular learning, recognizing that their mystical outlook and healing methods would find themselves increasingly powerless against the new rational sciences. The rabbis with their scholasticism and the Tzaddikim with their mysticism succeeded temporarily in closing Poland's Jews to the Enlightenment ideas. The few Jewish individuals who found those ideas fascinating and exciting, and wished to study them, had to go abroad, primarily to Berlin.

There is, in Max Weber's sense, an ancient, rational aspect in biblical Judaism, in the Covenant, the this-worldly nature of God's promises, and in the classical prophets of social justice. And, in the post-biblical period, elements of Hellenistic logical reasoning were absorbed and employed by the Pharisees and proto-Rabbis – in prooftexting, for example – despite their opposition to Hellenization. And in the Spanish Middle Ages, as we shall see, we again witness strong rationalism in Maimonides, under the profound influence of Greek philosophy. Given, then, the diffusion in the eighteenth century of the rational, empirical Newtonian scientific outlook, it should not be surprising that the Jews, too, became intoxicated with modern, rational philosophy.

Dubnow provides an example of one Polish Jew's movement in that direction, the well-known case of Solomon Maimon (1754–1800). Born in Lithuania and endowed with an exceptionally sharp and searching mind, he made his way from the Talmud to the Kabbalah, and from there he made a sudden leap into the religious philosophy of Maimonides and other medieval Jewish rationalists. In 1777, he left home and headed for Germany in his quest for secular culture. In Berlin he made contact with Mendelssohn and his circle, and rapidly acquired a good knowledge of German literature, the science of the time, and philosophy, especially Kant's system.

But his experience with rational-secular "Critical Philosophy" had upon him the very effect that the rabbis anticipated: he challenged his own previous religious beliefs, denying any transcendent foundations to religion and morality. On his path to what amounted to moral relativism or nihilism, he published several books on metaphysics, logic, and transcendental philosophy, and went much farther than Kant, who nevertheless acknowledged that none of his critical opponents had grasped the essence of his system as profoundly as Solomon Maimon. But his encounter with rational, secular thought meant that he spent the last years of his life, until his death in 1800, pretty much estranged from Judaism.

We have surveyed Sabbatianism and Hasidism, the last mass movements inspired by the religious framework based on the Talmud and the Kabbalah. Millions of Jews continued, of course, to lead their lives within the framework of orthodox Judaism, in a variety of its forms. But Jews in Western and Eastern Europe alike soon faced a formidable challenge to that framework: the Enlightenment movement of the late eighteenth and early nineteenth centuries. Before we discuss that movement, however, and its implications for the Jews, we need to backtrack and consider the history and destiny of the Jews in Spain.

14

The Jews of Spain

There was a golden age in Spain in which the symbiotic relationship between Jews and Muslims had produced a thriving economy and an extraordinarily high culture. Not too long after the death of Muhammad, the Jews accepted the challenge of Muslim society, which opened to them the doors of its mosques, schools, bazaars, markets, and civil service. The doors were open for education, social assimilation, and full participation in society's civic and political life. The Jews generally prospered by taking full advantage of all the intellectual and spiritual resources offered by the dominant Muslim elite – without disappearing or suffering the fate of a marginalized, persecuted minority. In effect, the Jews had joined the Muslim *Ummah* as sustaining members.

For 700 years the destiny of the Spanish Jews was bound up with that of the Muslims. As Ellis Rivkin has remarked in his *The Shaping of Jewish History*, "Every phase of Islamic growth was accompanied by a positive and creative reaction among Jews. Every phase of Muslim breakdown was accompanied by a [Jewish] disintegration: a golden age when [Muslim] Spain's wealth grew; humiliation and exile when it dwindled" (138). And in the same vein, Joel Carmichael, in his *The Shaping of the Arabs*, considered it "very strange that while Christianity was gradually to disappear in most parts of the Muslim empire, Jewish communities survived and flourished – in Bukhara, formerly a great Christian center; in Yemen, once a Christian bishopric; and in North Africa, the home of St. Augustine" (54). And a distinguished Muslim scholar, Barakat Ahmad, remarks: "It would not look strange if the restricted nature and the limits of the Muslim–Jewish conflict were seen in their proper perspective."[1]

---

[1] Barakat Ahmad, *Muhammad and the Jews: A Re-examination*, New Delhi: Vikas, 1979, 125. The passages from Rivkin and Carmichael are cited in Ahmad's work.

While Jewish life in Muslim Spain was reaching its peak in material and cultural development, the foundations of new Jewish communities were being laid in the Christian territory to the north. A Jewish community had already existed in Barcelona in the late Carolingian period, and it had a continuing religious-cultural contact with the Babylonian center. The Jews could obtain land only by purchasing or leasing it, and they cultivated their fields and vineyards themselves, as was also the case in France and Germany. Land was the basis of the economy and the social position of the Jews. In the urban life of Barcelona at about this time, the Jews became visible as an integral part of it. Jewish shops and stalls existed during the twelfth century in the marketplace outside the city. Even before that date, the sources mention the variety of Jewish occupations: tailors, shoemakers, and gold- and silversmiths. There were, as well, a few wealthy Jews engaged in money-lending activities, extending loans to the notables of Barcelona. But the status and condition of the Jews was contingent upon the privileges granted by the nobles. In Catalonia, for example, the relation of the Jews to the local count was one of near servitude. It was only on sufferance that the Jews resided in any Christian domain, their limited rights set forth in Charters granted by the noble or the Crown.

It is noteworthy, then, that land was everywhere the basis of the Jewish economy, with only modest beginnings of commerce. Even before the Reconquest we see scattered settlements of Jews in the north of Spain. Agriculture was their principal source of livelihood, with a few urban handicraft trades, and even fewer commercial occupations. They lived in a territory dotted with numerous Benedictine monasteries, amid a warlike Christian population of peasants and knights. The Jews were dependent for protection on the kings and lords, and when that source of safety failed they were exposed to attack from all quarters.

Increasingly, the struggle on Spanish soil of the two faiths, Islam and Christianity, became fateful for the Jews. The more the small Muslim states weakened each other through internecine warfare, the greater grew the zeal for reconquest among the Christian rulers. Until the middle of the eleventh century, the Christian princes took advantage of the fraternal strife that had afflicted the Muslims by attacking and plundering the Arab territories or exacting tribute from their rulers. But from about 1060 on, the Christians descended upon the Muslim south with the aim of permanent conquest, and were halted only twice by counter-attacks of Muslim tribes. The Christian warriors of the Spanish Reconquest were fired up by the same zeal that animated the Crusaders. The French Knights who came to the aid of the Spaniards were quite experienced in anti-Jewish violence, and as early as 1066 had to be warned by Pope Alexander II to refrain from acts of violence against the Jews. But the treatment of the Jews soon came to be dictated by practical, political interests. As Yitzhak Baer observes:

> The Jews were during this period an important element in the founding of new cities throughout Europe. This is a known fact in the rise of cities in Germany; and the economic importance of Jews in Spain was even greater. The political situation which confronted the Christian kings in the reconquered territories compelled them to employ Jews in important positions in the state organization. The Jewish population of Muslim Spain was the largest in Europe.[2]

At this time the burgher class among the Christians was quite small, while the Jews, already living in cities, were skilled in commerce and handicraft. The Christian kings needed functionaries proficient in Arabic and familiar with Muslim culture. Moreover, the Christian conquerors had before them the precedent of the Muslim rulers who had from earliest times employed Jews as government officials, advisers, and scientists.

In the course of the thirteenth century, the political structure of Spain underwent marked changes that affected the well-being of the Jewish communities. At the beginning of the century, the peninsula still bore a predominantly feudal character. The barons and the knights, preoccupied with the war against the infidel, tolerated the status of the Jews. By the end of the century, however, much of the Iberian Peninsula had been unified into several large states. A professional state bureaucracy was now being trained, and, in addition, the Jews now came up against the competition of the Christian burghers in the economic sphere. The Spanish rulers now began to bring their treatment of the Jews in line with the prevailing nationalist and religious policies of Christian Europe. Hence, both in Castile and Aragon the official policy aimed at assimilating and absorbing the Jews into Christian society through conversion or, failing that, expulsion from the land.

In the reform laws enacted by the king in 1348, one law forbade the Jews from lending money at interest. The propaganda of the Church had borne its fruit, and King Alfonso XI copied the laws introduced in England shortly before the Jews were expelled from that country. But in Spain, at that moment, such a law was hardly relevant, since the vast majority of Spanish Jews depended for their livelihood not on money-

---

[2] Yitzhak Baer, *A History of the Jews in Christian Spain*, vol. I, transl. from the Hebrew by Louis Schoffman, Philadelphia, PA: Jewish Publication Society of America, 1961, 47. Hereafter, all page references to this work will be cited in parentheses immediately following the quoted passage.

lending, but on petty trade, handicrafts, and the sale of produce from their fields and vineyards. The law therefore affected only a small group of well-to-do Jews engaged in granting the state credit and in collecting state taxes.

The Inquisition[3]

Soon after consolidating their conquest, Ferdinand and Isabella decided to solve the *conversos* problem – the Jews who had converted to Christianity – along the lines proposed by the Dominicans and others, namely, to extirpate heresy and to take harsh measures against the Jews to forestall their influence on the Christian populace. On September 27, 1480, the king and queen appointed two Dominican friars as the inquisitors for the entire realm. The inquisitors issued orders to the nobles and to the municipalities, requiring them to deliver up the *conversos* who had fled persecution and taken refuge with them.

Who were the *conversos*? They were the new Christians, converts from Judaism, who numbered in the thousands throughout the kingdoms of Aragon and Castile. They had become thorns in the monks' flesh because many of them held high state offices, and wielded considerable influence. Furthermore, owing to their high rate of intermarriage with the Spanish nobility, there were few aristocratic families who had no Jewish blood, so to speak, in their veins. Moreover, some or many – we cannot be sure which it was – had never truly turned their backs on Judaism, and continued to observe Jewish rites and customs. The suspicious Catholic clergy looked upon these *conversos* as Judaizing Christians or as outright heretics. And, of course, the inquisitors took no account of the method by which the Jews had been converted – by fire and sword. The Jews had been *forcibly* baptized, which nevertheless meant for the inquisitors that the baptized Jews and their descendants were obliged to remain in the Catholic faith, however repugnant that might have been to them.

Although at first Ferdinand was by no means zealous for the faith, nor fond of persecution, he eventually assented to the inquisitorial scheme when he saw that his coffers would be filled with the plunder of the accused. The queen, too, had hesitated, so they appealed to the Pope for advice. In 1478, Sixtus IV issued a bull empowering the temporal sovereigns to appoint inquisitors from among the clergy, with full authority to sit in judgment on all heretics, apostates, and their patrons, to sentence

---

[3] In the following discussion, I continue to rely heavily on Yitzhak Baer's *A History of the Jews in Christian Spain*.

them and – most important of all – to confiscate their goods. Isabella, more scrupulous and favorably inclined toward the new Christians, resisted applying harsh measures. But when a new Christian took it upon himself to publish a short work characterizing the Church's form of worship as idolatrous, the queen was won over and the tribunal of the Holy Inquisition was appointed on September 17, 1480.

The mayor and other officials of Seville were so uncooperative with the inquisitors that it was necessary to issue a second decree on December 27, 1480. The nobles, close to the converted Jews either through blood or friendship, stood by them and sought by every means to protect them against the new tribunal. As the news of the establishment of the Inquisition spread, the *conversos* held a meeting to consider how to prevent the blow aimed at them. Some of the leading men of Seville, Carmona, and Utrera, among them Abulafia, the financial agent of the royal couple, prepared to resist their persecutors by force if necessary. They distributed money and weapons among the people for armed self-defense. But the inquisitors, with their threats of excommunication, confiscation of property, and expulsion from office so inspired terror among those who would disobey them that even the nobles succumbed, imprisoning those to whom they had promised protection. Only four days after the installation of the tribunal, six *conversos* who had either reaffirmed their Judaism or had made false confession on the rack, were condemned and burnt alive. The tribunal had selected for its functions a castle in Triana, a suburb of Seville, where the city authorities created a special site as an execution ground, which became the infamous Quemadero, the place of burning.

The inquisitors adopted a stratagem by which they ensnared as many victims as possible. They gave the new Christians guilty of a relapse into Judaism a certain length of time in which to declare their remorse; and, if they did so, to retain their property. The more naively credulous obeyed the summons, contritely confessing and hoping thereby to be left in peace. But then the inquisitors imposed a new condition, that the *conversos* provide the names and particulars of all their acquaintances whom they know to be apostates. Thus terrorized, and assured that the betrayed would never learn the names of the informers, the more faint-hearted loosened their tongues and the tribunal soon acquired a long list of victims.

The Inquisition defined heresy and apostasy with the following criteria: if baptized Jews still cherished hopes of a Messiah; if they held Moses and his laws to be as efficacious as Jesus for salvation; if they observed the Jewish Sabbath or holidays; if they had their sons circumcised; if they observed the Jewish dietary laws; if they wore cleaner or better garments on the Sabbath; or laid tablecloths or lit no fire on that day; if they went

barefoot or in stocking feet on the Day of Atonement, or asked pardon
of one another on that day; if a father in blessing his children placed
his hands upon their heads without making the sign of the cross; if one
prayed facing East toward Jerusalem; if one uttered a blessing over the
wine cup; if a *converso* recited a psalm without adding the Gloria; if a
woman failed to appear in church 40 days after her lying-in; if parents
gave their children Jewish names. There was, then, more than enough
opportunity for denunciations, enabling the tribunal to accuse even the
most authentic proselytes.

The dungeons of the Inquisition soon swelled with "Jewish heretics" –
15,000 were thrown into prison at the outset. Then on January 6, 1481,
the priests and monks inaugurated the first *auto-da-fé*, the burning of the
condemned, which was carried out innumerable times during the following 300 years. Adding to the horror was the hypocritical mockery that the
death sentence was handed down not by the tribunal but by a temporal
authority, as the Church was supposed not to desire the death of a sinner.
The Jewish victims were given to the flames immediately after the verdict,
or, if they showed remorse, were first strangled. Up to November of the
same year, 298 burnt offerings to Christ gasped out their lives in the single
district of Seville. In the archbishopric of Cadiz, no fewer than 2,000 *conversos* were burned alive in the course of that year, their property going,
of course, to the royal exchequer.

But even death was not the end of the ordeal, since the corpses of those
who had died in the flames were dug out of their graves, and the meager
possessions left to the heirs were confiscated. When it proved difficult to
convict a wealthy heir, the tribunal manufactured "proofs" of a relapse
to Judaism, and the property was divided between the Crown and the
Holy Inquisition. Some of the potential victims fled to the neighboring
kingdom of Granada or to Portugal, Africa, Provence, or Italy. Those
who reached Rome brought their bitter grievances to the papal court
where, after providing the court with a handsome gift, the fugitives
obtained a hearing; on January 29, 1482, the Pope addressed a letter to
Ferdinand and Isabella, censuring the conduct of the Inquisition. But the
wily Ferdinand, fully aware of the avarice of the papal Cabinet, made it
worth their while to issue a new bull dated February 11, 1482, in which
Sixtus appointed six monks and clerics as chief inquisitors, among them
Thomas de Torquemada, the general of the Dominicans of Avilo, a monk
who had already distinguished himself as a bloodthirsty fanatic.

In the kingdom of Aragon, however, where the nobility and the middle
classes carried weight in political matters, the condemnation of the *conversos* without a formal trial raised such strong opposition that Cardinal
Borgia, who became the infamous Alexander VII, and the king himself,
petitioned the Pope for a change in the practices of the tribunal. Sixtus, in

response, excused himself from making changes, owing to the absence of the cardinals who had fled Rome in fear of the plague. He did, however, order that accuser and witnesses should be confronted by the accused, and that the trial be conducted in public.

Often, *conversos* condemned by the tribunal succeeded in escaping to Rome where they could purchase absolution from the papal throne. The Spanish sovereigns naturally disliked this means by which their appetite for the *conversos'* confiscated goods was thwarted. The Spanish court therefore insisted that the Pope appoint a judge of appeals in Spain itself, so that the rulings of the Inquisition might not be reversed in foreign countries. The Pope, who for material reasons very much desired good relations with the Spanish court, issued another bull decreeing that no bishop, vicar, or member of the higher clergy descended from a Jewish family should sit as a judge in any court for the trial of heretics. From this prohibition it was only one small step to the condemnation of clergy of "Jewish blood" to the stake.

Anyone familiar with the history of the corruption and depravity of the papacy in the fifteenth and sixteenth centuries will know that one could hardly have expected different conduct from Sixtus IV who appointed boys that he himself had abused to bishoprics and cardinal dignity, and who bestowed no clerical office without payment. In response to urgent appeals from Spanish Catholics and *conversos*, Sixtus did finally issue another bull exhorting the king and queen "by the bowels of Jesus Christ," to remember that in mercy and kindness alone may men resemble God. Although Sixtus concluded the bull by assuring all concerned that it was entirely his own decision and not due to any external influence, it was well known in high circles that it was bought with new-Christian gold. But the bull had no effect on the Spanish rulers whose appetite for the confiscated property of the victims had no bounds.

As terrible as the work of the tribunal had so far been in its three short years of existence – during which many thousands had been cast into flames, left to rot in dungeons, driven from their country, or reduced to pauperism – it fell short of the death and destruction soon to follow. For until now the Inquisition had been confined to southern Spain, to the districts of Seville and Cadiz, and the Christian province of Andalusia. In the other provinces of Spain it had failed to get a foothold due to the opposition of the provincial courts and the populace. But the avaricious royal couple persuaded the Pope to appoint an inquisitor-general to supervise and control the provincial courts. The Pope assented and, in May 1483, appointed the cold-blooded Dominican Torquemada (until then prior of a monastery) as Inquisitor-General of Spain. The Holy Inquisition was now extended to all the large towns of Spain. More than ever before, Spain now was the scene of ubiquitous flames in which Jews, innocent of any crimes, were burned to death – and this after having been converted by force into a faith, the falseness of which was demonstrated by every action of the servants of the Church. Throughout Spain, the closed and secret nature of the tribunal's proceedings meant that if in spite of the so-called evidence laid against an individual he denied he had ever relapsed into Judaism, he was condemned to the flames as impenitent.

Under Torquemada, new and improved methods of eliciting confessions of guilt were introduced. When "proof" of relapse in the accusations brought against a *converso* were inconclusive, he was stretched on the rack; if he confessed under torture, he was subjected to a second trial. If he then adhered to what he had confessed under torture, he was condemned to death; if he denied it, he was tortured again.

One should not suppose, however, that the inquisitorial terror engendered no resistance. In Aragon and Valencia the towns had, from the first, registered their disapproval of the tribunal. Ruled less despotically than the subjects of Castile, the Aragonese cherished their freedom. They valued, above all, the strong tradition – which had the force of law – against the confiscation of their property even in cases of offenses. So now that Torquemada was invested with unlimited power over life and property, the new-Christians of Aragon, many of whom were politically influential, sought to direct the general, anti-tribunal sentiment in a politically effective direction. As soon as the first victims fell to the Inquisition in Saragossa, the *conversos* and their allies pressured the courts to register strong protest, both to the king and the Pope, against the introduction of the tribunal into Aragon. Commissions were dispatched to the royal and papal courts to bring about the repeal of the ordinances permitting the intrusion of the inquisitorial regime. They expected success in Rome, where everything could be had for money. But the king was, predictably, immovable, given his insatiable appetite for the property of the tribunal's victims.

News of the failure of the commissions' efforts gave rise to an Aragonese plot to remove Pedro Arbues, chief inquisitor for Aragon, by violent means, in the hope of crippling the Inquisition and forcing the king to give way. In order to achieve near-unanimous support for the conspiracy, the *conversos* agreed to cover the expenses entailed in hiring the assassins. Arbues was, in fact, assassinated and the killers escaped. But news of the event spread quickly in Saragossa, producing a violent reaction. The Spanish Christians gathered in crowds, shouting, "to the flames with the Jew-Christians! They have murdered the chief inquisitor!" The *conversos* present barely escaped massacre, and only survived thanks to the youthful Arab-bishop Alfonso of Aragon who, mounted on his horse, restrained the crowds by the threat of armed force. King Ferdinand made good use of the entire affair by proceeding with the establishment of the Inquisition in Aragon.

Although certain towns of northern Spain continued to resist the introduction of the tribunal, their resistance ultimately failed due to the greed of Ferdinand, the bloodthirstiness of Torquemada, and the avarice of the corrupt papal court being too strong to overcome. The number of victims continued to grow. On February 12, 1486, an *auto-da-fé* was celebrated in Toledo with 750 burnt offerings; on April 2, there were 900 victims, and on May 7, 750. On August 16, 25 "Jewish heretics" were burned alive in Toledo, and on December 10, 950 were condemned to shameful public penance. In the following year the Inquisition was established in Barcelona and on the island of Majorca, and 200 *conversos* were burned alive in these two places alone. It is estimated that one third of the *conversos* perished in the flames, another third escaped, but became homeless wanderers, and the remainder lived in perpetual terror of the tribunal.[4]

As we seek the motivating factors behind the Inquisition and the subsequent expulsion of the Jews from Spain, clear thinking compels us to recognize that the motives were envy and jealousy, taking the form of "racial hatred" in the guise of religious fanaticism. The Jews had lived and worked in Spain for hundreds of years, constituting themselves as a religious-cultural minority. Some became conspicuously successful economically and politically. This fact alone certainly aroused resentment in at least two classes of the Spanish populace: (1) the economic rivals of the Jews; and (2) the disadvantaged Spaniards who had suffered exploitation or indignities in situations in which Jews were either directly responsible or visible accomplices. If we add to that the Church's traditional indoctrination of the populace, characterizing the Jews as "Christ-killers," it should not be surprising that there existed in Spain an intense hatred of the Jews.

The Jews, the Spanish, and the "*Conversos* Problem"

A good place to begin is with the chain of circumstances that led to the massacre of Spanish Jews in 1391, and the mass conversions of the Jews to Catholicism that followed.[5] In 1378 the archdeacon of Ecija, Ferrant Martinez, began to deliver public harangues in Seville against the Jews. He demanded that their 23 magnificent synagogues be razed to the ground, and that the Jews be confined to their own quarter to prevent

---

[4] See Heinrich Graetz, *History of the Jews*, Philadephia, PA: Jewish Publication Society of America, 1939, vol. IV, ch. X.

[5] See Yitzhak Baer, *A History of the Jews in Christian Spain*, vol. II.

social intercourse with Christians. He also enjoined the rural population of Andalusia to prohibit Jews from living in their midst. With the death of the archbishop in 1390, Martinez became the administrator of the diocese, and called upon the Christians to demolish all synagogues in their district. He then baptized all servants of the Jews, and summoned Jewish tax-farmers to appear before the ecclesiastical court. His remarks were permeated with vulgar Jew-hatred, with hints in his sermons to the people that the king and queen would not punish those who attacked the Jews physically. The Jews appealed to the royal court and even brought suit publicly against Martinez, to no avail. Martinez announced that he would not fail in his Christian duty, and would continue to preach as he had.

But the royal government's attitude was typically medieval: the Jews had become essential elements of the economic order and had, therefore, to be protected out of material considerations; law and order had to be maintained, and the prestige of the Crown upheld. But the incited, popular movement was growing. When King John I of Castile died in 1390, the Crown prince was still a minor, and the government in support of the boy-king was too weak to hold the rebellious forces in check. On June 4, 1391, the massacres began in Seville, many Jews were slaughtered, the synagogues were converted into churches, and the Jewish quarter was taken over and settled by Christians.

The pattern was repeated in all the other communities of Andalusia, and in New and Old Castile. *In all cases the forced conversion of the Jews to Christianity followed.* The famous synagogues of Toledo fell into Christian hands, and others were simply destroyed. In Madrid most of the Jews were killed or baptized. The municipal authorities placed all the blame on the "little people" (*pueblo menudo*), who continued to loot for a whole year. In other cities like Cuenco, it was the heads of the municipality who were responsible for the destruction of the Jewish community. The municipal councilors forced the Jews to convert; officials and notables assembled to the ringing of the church bells, with the aim of looting and destroying the Jewish quarter.

The Crown then sent out announcements to several cities in Castile, stating that in Seville and Cordona Jews had been murdered, despoiled, and forced to change their religion because the archdeacon of Ecija had incited the "little people" who lacked understanding, were unconcerned with the harm done to the king's interests, had no respect for the king's justice, and had no fear of God in their hearts. The government's communication added that it would not tolerate such shameful actions because the kings had always protected the Jews, such being the command of the Catholic Church itself. But the weak government's pronouncements were ignored and the killing and looting continued. In Burgos, for example, rioters from the lowest strata of society attacked the Jewish quarter only days after the government's proclamations. The Jews fled and sought refuge in the homes of the Christians.

Many Jews of Burgos were baptized by force and soon a whole quarter inhabited by *conversos* sprang up. The other Jews in Burgos, who remained loyal to their faith, requested and received from the national government a written guarantee of protection. But the number of these faithful families was now quite small. When the disorders ended, the government imposed fines on the municipalities for the losses to the royal revenues caused by the riots. However, it was all but impossible to seize and punish the rioters, for in every locality noble families had been as involved in the crimes as had the priests.

The riots had spread from Castile to Aragon. The Crown declared that attacks upon the Jews would not be tolerated, as the Jews were the king's "treasure," and it was his official duty to protect them. The killing and baptism by force nevertheless continued and spread. Similar attempts were made on Muslim quarters, but fear of reprisals from Muslims living in the many villages of Valencia made the rioters desist. When the king received reports of the "explosion" in Valencia, he expressed his outrage in such strong terms that Baer remarks: "Never before, probably, had a non-Jewish king written so resentfully about crimes committed against the Jews." Baer then adds: "But no action was taken. And, indeed, how could anything be done? The aristocratic families of the knights, and the citizens whose members had participated in the atrocities, were powerful enough to prevent the holding of any legal inquiries" (Baer, vol. II, 101).

The governing authorities had a definite interest in putting an end to the disorders, because the riots affected not only the Jews. The wide discontent among the peasants was such that it was likely to develop into a general revolt. In response to peasants' demands, decrees were issued, some of which affected the Jews adversely. Peasant debts to Jews and *conversos* were cancelled. *Conversos* were forbidden to bear arms or to sail to Muslim lands. The peasants' main demand was simple: Jews must choose between death and conversion.

As tension increased in Catalonia and the Jews of Tarragona fled to the local fortresses, the king tried to place them under the protection of the archbishop and the royal and municipal officers. The king, in his directive, spoke not only of defense but also the restoration of the Jewish community. But despite all such efforts on the part of the government, the Jewish communities of Valencia and Barcelona were destroyed. Indeed, all the Jewish communities of Catalonia, urban and rural, were either destroyed or despoiled.

The massacres spread from Castile to Aragon together with the more general strife. In the cities the artisans were in revolt against the oligarchic regime of the patricians, and outside the city the peasants also pressed against the city walls. This general struggle developed in the fifteenth century into a full civil war threatening the entire political structures of the state. The general civil strife was not the key factor in the "holy war" against the Jews, but it certainly was a factor. Baer proposes that religious hostility was the determining motive behind the widespread pogroms of 1391, religious fanaticism having by then permeated all classes of Spanish society. But this proposition needs to be supplemented with another. Yes, the Jews were a unique object of hate; but the haters had both a material reason and incentive for hating and attacking them. For as we shall see, the *conversos*, the Jews who had converted to Catholicism, continued to be hated, and now, most probably, more than ever before. Why? Because the privileged and influential Jewish-Christians had not only retained their higher economic and political status, but they had done so with the Christian imprimatur of having been baptized. These Jewish Christians thus acquired, in the eyes of all classes of Spanish society, a legitimacy they did not deserve. This legitimacy had to be nullified so that the hatred would be directed not at Christians but at Jews.

In the pogroms of 1391, the vast majority of Jewish converts were baptized by force. Some sought baptism voluntarily in the aftermath of the pogroms, hoping thereby to cease being vulnerable objects of hatred and violence. But there were some Jews for whom the conversion had been an authentic act, making it possible, in due course, for them to attain even the highest positions in the Catholic hierarchy. However, in the Inquisition that emerged almost a century later, no real distinction was made between authentic proselytes and those who secretly remained Jews.[6]

Both the perpetrators and the king had material motives in the pogroms of 1391, the former for the plunder of the victims and the latter for their property. In September of that year, the king instructed royal officials throughout Catalonia and Valencia to gather information concerning the communal property of the *aljamas* (Jewish communities) before the pogroms, and also concerning the property of the murdered Jews, especially those who had left no heirs or who had taken their lives to avoid forced conversion. The king, who had been helpless to prevent the destruction of the Jewish communities, now proposed to salvage from the upheaval what was, in his judgment, owed to the state. He therefore

---

[6] For a fuller discussion of the Spanish Jews, see Americo Castro, *The Structure of Spanish History*, transl. Edmund L. King, Princeton, NJ: Princeton University Press, 1954, chs 13 and 14. This outstanding Spanish historian speaks of the "Supremacy of the Despised," and describes both the negative consequences and positive, creative products of that status.

proceeded to deprive the kindred of the Jews who had committed suicide of their just rights of inheritance. More, he denied communal property to the few Jewish survivors. This included synagogues, other public buildings, ornaments of Torah scrolls, and the like; all such property and articles were confiscated for the benefit of the royal treasury. Appropriated as well, were libraries of Jewish books, some of which were presented to Catholic theologians.

A king, according to medieval conceptions of monarchy, was supposed to guarantee that law and justice would be maintained. Suppression of public disturbances and civil strife was held to be the state's duty not only for material reasons and fear of damage to its treasury, but also because the prestige and very existence of the state required that order be quickly restored. Spain was, in fact, in a condition of insurrection, no less threatening than the contemporary agrarian movements in France and England, or the revolts that broke out in Catalonia and Germany at a later date. Baer writes:

> The outcome of all these revolutionary movements shows that the monarchs of Europe had the power and ability to suppress them. But these same monarchs were never able [or willing] to put down anti-Jewish riots at their height . . . When the disorders broke out, the rulers usually lacked not only energy and determination, but a consistent and uniform policy. Many of the letters written by King John and his wife during the fateful weeks were filled with agitation and anxiety at the sight of disturbances that were likely to cause the utter annihilation of Spanish Jewry. Yet, at the same time, they cold-bloodedly furthered the royal treasury at the expense of the victims of the catastrophe. King John had often objected to compulsory baptism. But when the fanatics kept up their pressure, the king felt obliged to approve actions that were clearly coercive. (Baer, II, 111–12)

The Aftermath of the Pogroms

How did the Jews of Spain fare after the massacres of 1391? The large communities, like those of Seville, Toledo, and Burgos, had been effectively destroyed. Efforts toward the rehabilitation of Spanish Jewry originated chiefly in Saragossa. John I expressed the intention, in various decrees, to re-establish the *aljamas*. But his government's intentions were violently opposed by the urban Christians, and very few Jews were willing to return to Barcelona because of that opposition. In Majorca, a few Jews had remained even after the pogroms, and a small number of those who had fled to Algiers returned. Early in 1394, about 150 Jews came from Portugal to settle in Majorca. In 1395, King John pledged to protect all

Jews who had fled abroad and now wished to return. But nothing came of his pronouncements.

Together with such meager and on the whole fruitless efforts to restore ruined Jewish communities, there was an opposite trend. Some devout Christians regarded forced baptism as unpleasing in the sight of God; but, once baptized, the converts were to be considered as Christians under canon law. Those who reverted to their former religion and those who encouraged them to do so were, therefore, heretics. The devout Christians sought to strengthen the new faith of the *conversos* by instruction and argument, and by organizing them into *converso* fraternities. In 1393, John I issued regulations designed to isolate the new converts from their former co-religionists by forbidding them to live or even eat together. With that aim, the king revived the older ordinances requiring Jews – but not *conversos* – to dress differently from the Christians. Furthermore, the *conversos* were placed under the supervision of the bishops. The "public," whether Christian by birth or by conversion, voluntarily maintained a close watch on the behavior of the new Christians; and the king instructed secular officials to conduct criminal investigations of *conversos* suspected of trying to flee the country with the intention of returning to Judaism. The secret practice of Jewish rites by *conversos* was also to be regarded as a crime.

Reliable evidence shows that some Spanish Jews killed their wives, their children, and themselves to prevent forced conversion. But they were far outnumbered by those who readily acknowledged the Christian Messiah "who came to them by force." Most of the proselytes came from the wealthy classes; and the devoutly religious Jews, seeing the cause of apostasy among the wealthy, pointed their finger at the non-Jewish philosophical views of the converts – in contrast to the common people whose strong faith had stood the dreadful test.

What the devout Jewish critics perceived as the non-Jewish philosophical outlooks of the converts was the rationalism inspired by Maimonides and Averroes. From the twelfth and thirteenth centuries, the views of these thinkers, rooted in Plato and primarily in Aristotle, exercised a marked influence on the Jewish aristocrats and courtiers. It was their descendants, the devout Jews believed, who betrayed both their faith and their people during the great ordeal that began in 1391. Under Greek philosophical influences, the culturally assimilated courtiers looked upon the Jewish *halachot*, or ordinances, as mere customs or hygienic measures. Even the ethical commandments became a subject for philosophical speculation. Indeed, from the standpoint of the devout Jews, philosophy itself was an attempt to rationalize the aristocrats' indulgence in sensual pleasures at the expense of others. As Baer observes, such criticisms by the devout Jews were intended to expose the religious and moral nihilism which was gnawing away at the conscience of the courtier group, the practical men of the world. These Jews who, utilizing the opportunities opened up to them during the 12th and 13th centuries, attained political power and high office in the administration of the reconquered territories, resorted to the type of political ruthlessness which had become prevalent in the cities of southern Europe. Casting all restraint to the winds they did not wince at violence, plunder and even murder. Having succumbed – in thought – to convictions so completely antithetical to the faith and traditions of their people, they did not hesitate to trample upon the vital interests of their coreligionists. (Baer, I, 241–2)

It was with very good reason, Baer concludes, that the Jewish community rose up ideologically and otherwise against these presumptuously domineering courtiers and their oppressive measures. The courtier policies had introduced into the Jewish communities of Spain a serious social divisiveness, which made it easier for the violent enemies of the Jews to attack and destroy them. And from the standpoint of the devout and humble Jews who constituted the vast majority of the community's members, it was the Greek rationalism of Maimonides and Averroes that provided the Jewish courtiers with a false ideology with which to rationalize their high-handed and oppressive practices.

Jewish Mysticism: The Kabbalah in Spanish-Jewish Life

Jewish mysticism in Spain had both social and religious roots in that it was a reaction against the rationalist ideology of the Jewish courtier class. The Kabbalists contributed decisively to the shaping of Spanish-Jewish history, for they strove to raise the level of religious and moral life by delivering a vigorous assault upon the dominant courtier class. In Spain, Kabbalism became a movement for *social* reform. Recent arrivals from northern France and Germany exercised considerable influence upon this movement. In Spain we see a definite social dimension to their preaching, since they gained the sympathetic attention primarily of artisans, and of the poorer classes in the towns and hamlets. Castile was the birthplace of the Kabbalah in the form in which later generations accepted it as authoritative. The canon of the Kabbalah, the *Zohar* (*Book of Splendor*), was most likely composed in Castile.

The attack on rationalism in the name of faith is typical of all Kabbalistic works produced in this period. It is most evident in Nachmanides' commentary on the Pentateuch, and his unrelenting opposition to allegorical interpretations of the Torah. His aim was to refute and repudiate the opinions of Abraham Ibn Ezra and Maimonides, on whom the rationalists leaned for support. Nachmanides denies that the universe operates according to fixed laws, and that the so-called wise individual who knows those laws can base conduct upon them. All creation is a miracle. It is God who created and guides the world. All the phenomena to which we are subject are works of the Divine – not caused by natural law. The Jewish mystics appealed to the common people: the divine law and the destiny of the Jews were represented symbolically as emanations from the world above. They are also channels by which the individual might exert influence upon the higher spheres. The antitheses between polytheistic idolatry and monotheism were formulated as manifestations of the struggle of Satan against God. The people singled out for suffering on earth and for ultimate redemption became, in a metaphysical sense, the preferred seed, "the holy root, the truth-bearing stock," thus creating a new, mystical ethnic concept (Baer I, 245–6). The conflict between Israel and Edom (all enemies of Israel) is conceived as a struggle between the world of light and the realm of Satan. To stray from the faith, to act against the people's interest, to compromise with the *outlook* of the non-Jewish world or with rationalist philosophy, *even to accept service in the princely courts, is to surrender to Satan.*[7]

The *Galut* (exile, dispersion) is conceived not only in its historical aspects, but also in a metaphysical sense: the Divine Presence is in exile along with Israel. The Kabbalists believed in the imminence of revolutionary changes in the entire order of society and nature. By thus reviving the messianic eschatology they bolstered the popular faith in redemption. The chief social-moral principle was never to perpetrate injustice by depriving fellow humans of their fields, vineyards, or any other possessions. Clearly, this was directed against the Jewish owners of large estates in Spain who had annexed the smallholdings of their neighbors. The Kabbalists castigated those in high places who lorded it over their people and confined debtors in chains when they were destitute and unable to pay. What the ethical element of the Kabbalists' teachings strove to inculcate is that a sense of mutual responsibility for the entire community is the precondition for salvation. Every individual is duty-bound to seek the well-being of the community and to correct unethical conduct, defined as the failure to obey the commandments of social justice. These teachings of the Kabbalists were directed against the Jewish grandees and their much-resented practices. The people, as moral agents, must wage a relentless campaign for social reform against the exploitative courtiers.

---

[7] The Kabbalists opposed the *outlook* of the non-Jewish world, but not the human beings of that world. The Kabbalists opposed the "collection of interest for a loan, even from Gentiles" (Baer I, 371f).

For all their efforts, however, the Kabbalist reformers failed to effect an elevation in the moral conduct of the courtier aristocracy. If, as Gershom Scholem has proposed, the *Zohar*, the most authoritative work of the Kabbalah, was composed by Moses de Leon between the years 1280 and 1286, we can say that the author's primary concern was the social ills that had afflicted Spanish-Jewish society and his earnest commitment to eliminate those ills. Manifest often in the *Zohar* is Rabbi Moses de Leon's hatred of the wealthy, selfish aristocracy that held the destiny of Spanish Jewry in their hands. And it is the Averroist outlook of this group that is blamed for its moral corruption. The author of the *Zohar* is fully aware of the social conflicts and injustices that characterized the Jewish communities in this period, and his heart was with the poor and lowly. But, as Baer regretfully notes, the valuable lesson that the Kabbalists attempted to teach was practically ignored by the wealthy Jewish aristocracy of Spain, "who had directed the internal affairs of their communities during the flourishing period of Judeo-Arabic culture. The social problem engendered by this partial blindness cropped up again in Jewish life at a later date. The scene was now Christian Spain" (Baer, I, 266).

In Christian Spain, the courtiers continued the pattern of habitually looking down on the simple Jewish masses and treating them accordingly. It was these masses who scrupulously observed the commandments to the fullest of their ability, and feared not to maintain their faith even when faced with apostasy or death. When the courtiers, in contrast, faced the same test, they lacked the spiritual fortitude to resist apostasy. Just as earlier they had denied the authority of the biblical law, they now "accepted the rites and ceremonies of an alien religion" (Baer II, 138). The Jewish aristocracy, in the years between 1391 and 1492, continued to fail in its responsibility of providing effective leadership in a national and religious emergency.

15

The Expulsion of the Jews from Spain

It seems indisputable that the wrath the Inquisition had poured out against the *conversos* or new Christians was actually aimed at the Jews. As we have suggested several times, there was a definite social dimension to the Spanish people's resentment of the Spanish Jews. Despite the historical fact that it was a minuscule minority of the Spanish Jews – the aristocratic courtiers – who occupied advantageous and influential positions in the economy and in the state apparatus, the Spanish people's resentment was directed not toward that class in particular, but at the Jewish populace as a whole. Once those despised agents of the state, such as tax-farmers, for example, were identified as Jews, the already existing anti-Jewish animus rooted in the Gospels and in Church doctrine came into play, creating an especially virulent form of hatred that was, at one and the same time, religious, social, and "racial."

It seems, therefore, inevitable in hindsight that the Inquisition would stretch its deadly tentacles over the *conversos* as Jews, and then over the Jews themselves. For it was evident to observers that the relations of the Jews to the *conversos*, especially those who were baptized by force, was close and intimate, bound as they were to one another by ethnic ties. Feeling compassion for their brethren who so unwillingly posed as Christians, the Jews strove to keep them close to the Jewish community. They instructed the Christian-born *conversos* in the essentials of Judaism, held secret meetings with them for prayer, supplied them with religious books and writings, kept them informed of the fasts and festivals, provided them at Easter (which coincided roughly with Passover on the calendar) with unleavened bread, and, throughout the year, with meat prepared in accordance with Jewish dietary laws. Finally, the Jews saw to the circumcision of the *conversos'* newborn sons.

In Seville and in the whole of Andalusia, there were countless new Christians who were baptized by force at the time of the assault upon the Jews by Ferdinand Martinez, and later during the terrible events of 1391. There were, then, plenty of candidates for the work of the Jews who were determined to bring the *conversos* back to Judaism. When the king and queen agreed to establish the Inquisition in Andalusia, the first step was to separate the Jews from the new Christians, to sever every connecting link between them. The Cortes of Toledo enjoined the strict enforcement of the law of separation, which soon became operative throughout the kingdom. This entailed the creation of special living quarters for Jews (and Moors). However, despite all such measures, the Jews and the *conversos* succeeded in maintaining their close association, but more secretly and circumspectly. Given the need for such secrecy and the danger of discovery by the priestly spies, Baer surmises that the meetings between Jews and new Christians and Jews and Moors bore an aspect of gratifying excitement.

When Torquemada became Chief Inquisitor he made every effort to prevent all such meetings and to sever all such ties. He issued a command ordering the *conversos* to present themselves for confession. According to the same command, the rabbis of Toledo were to convene and swear an oath that they would inform against new Christians who observed Jewish rites, and would excommunicate Jews who refused to become informers. The rabbis, threatened with heavy punishment if they refused to take the oath, were forced into a tragic predicament. They were asked to become accomplices in handing over their faithful co-religionists to the stake, and, naturally, they refused and faced the punishment. Judah Ibn Verga, for example, ordered by the inquisitors to turn over pseudo-Christians who secretly clung to Judaism, left his native Seville and fled to Lisbon where he eventually met a martyr's death. It soon became clear to the inquisitors that they could not attain their ends by enlisting the cooperation of the Jews, so the king and queen were exhorted to issue a decree for the partial expulsion of the Jews from Andalusia, especially from Seville.

The Conquest of Granada

The general expulsion of the Jews from Spain was postponed from year to year. The Reconquista had originally defined the peculiar status of the Christian states of the Iberian Peninsula; and with the unification of Spain under Christian rule, the political structure of the Spanish-Jewish community was effectively undermined. In a bitter and protracted war, which raged from 1481 to early 1492, the Spaniards conquered the last remaining Muslim strongholds on their soil. The Jews of the conquered Muslim areas became prisoners of war and their exorbitant ransom had to be raised by all the Jewish communities of Spain. The coerced new Christians who had fled to Granada, and there reverted to Judaism, were ordered by their conquerors to choose – within a short, specific time –

either to live completely Christian lives or to leave the country. Expulsion of the Jews from the entire conquered area was proposed, but not as yet adopted. But with the entry of the Catholic monarchs into the city of Granada on January 2, 1492, the fate of Spanish Jewry was sealed not merely in the conquered territory, but throughout Aragon and Castile as well.

Remarkably, as late as 1491, the government of Castile renewed its contracts with the Jewish tax-farmers for four years. Similar new contracts were signed early in 1492. As Baer stresses, however, this "does not mean that Expulsion was not already being considered as a practical proposition at the time" (Baer, II, 433). These contracts by the Catholic monarchs on the eve of expulsion reveal their intention to convert several of their most competent and useful men, and thus to retain them in the service of the state even after the expulsion. In December 1491, the sovereigns enacted new laws for the reorganization of the tax-farming system, to prepare the way for eliminating the Jews from the body-politic without upsetting the state's internal administration.

On March 31, 1492, in the city of Granada, the royal couple signed the edict for the expulsion of the Jews from all the territories of Castile and Aragon. The reason given for the expulsion was to prevent further harm to the Christian religion. Enumerated in the Edict were the steps taken during the preceding years to end Jewish influence on the *conversos* and to purify the Christian faith: segregation of the Jews in separate quarters; strengthening the powers of the Inquisition; expulsion of the Jews from Andalusia. As all these measures had failed in their aim, the Crown had no choice – according to the text of the Edict – but to resort to the drastic step of expelling the Jews from the country once and for all. The substance and style of the Edict make it clear that it had been drafted by the Inquisition. The Jews were commanded to leave the country "by order of the King and Queen, our sovereigns, and of the Reverend Prior of Santa Cruz, inquisitor general in all the kingdoms and dominions of their majesties" (Baer, II, 434).

The Expulsion began in May, the authorities intending the evacuation of the Jews to be carried out in a peaceful and orderly manner. The state placed the Jewish quarters under its protection. Instructions were issued to all localities to pay the Jews all that were owed them; to enable the Jews to pay their own debts and to dispose of their possessions on fair and equitable terms. Nevertheless, extortion and chicanery prevailed. The Jews were prohibited from taking away gold, silver, or precious stones. Synagogues, cemeteries, and the property of the *aljamas'* public institutions were confiscated and appropriated by the royal treasury. Some synagogues were immediately converted into churches. When certain Christian municipalities had promised, for monetary consideration, to protect ancestral graves from desecration, such agreements were nullified by the royal authorities. And the *aljamas,* or Jewish communities, were compelled to pay their regular taxes several years in advance, so that the royal treasury would lose less than it would have without that stipulation.

In Saragossa and other cities of Aragon, it was the inquisitors, not the civil officials, who took over the sale and liquidation of Jewish property. Through a new regulation of their own making, the inquisitors ruled that Jewish property fell into the same category as that of heretics or persons associated with heretics. Jews were ordered to have their property appraised, and to report its value to the commissioners of the Inquisition. Cheaters would be liable to the punishment meted out to heretics who had been pardoned their recalcitrance and who then relapsed.

As Baer remarks, we have in the Expulsion policy a curious mixture of motives: racial, religious, and material. For no sooner had the expulsion Edict been published than the clergy launched a widespread campaign for the conversion of the Jews. On the very day of the Edict, the rabbi of Teruel was confined to his home so that the Franciscan monks could proceed with their proselytizing without hindrance. Almost 100 persons – men, women, and children – were baptized in a single morning. The municipal councilors themselves went from door to door, urging the Jews to accept baptism so that they would be permitted to remain in Teruel; for in the absence of the Jews, the city would be ruined altogether. Just as this was occurring, another distinguished rabbi, who had been banished from his own city for preaching against the acceptance of conversion, arrived in Teruel with the same message and was expelled from there as well. His sermons were effective, however. Conversions ceased and the Jews prepared for departure.

All municipal records, Baer informs us, contain lists of the names of Jews who were converted during those months, "and the Jewish religious leaders made no attempt to conceal the fact that apostasy was on the increase again, especially amid the wealthy and educated among whom secular culture had wrought much havoc" (II, 436).

By the time of the expulsion of the Jews from Spain in 1492, Jews had already been banished from England, France, and some of the Germanies. But the expulsion from Spain was unique in that it was an expulsion of an entire, demographically huge community. This meant that the policy could be implemented only if the bordering countries would allow the exiles to enter their territories. The French frontier in the north was almost entirely closed to Jews, except for *conversos* requesting admission as Christians. From Jewish and Christian sources, Baer estimates that the majority of exiles, numbering between 100,000 and 120,000, moved into Portugal. But since the Inquisition was an active institution in that country as well, Jews were allowed to remain there for a limited period only. In Portugal, the Jews were regarded as illegal immigrants, forced either to leave the country or to embrace Christianity. The rest of the expelled, numbering about 50,000, sailed from southern ports (Almeria) for North Africa or from eastern ports (Valencia and Barcelona) for Italy and the East. Turkey was the only powerful state to receive the exiles with no reservations or restrictions; state authorities having recognized, most likely, that the Jews would contribute significantly to the strength of the Turkish economy. But those Jews were the fortunate ones, compared to the impecunious exiles who could not pay the passage money ship owners demanded, or who were turned away from places where they had hoped to find refuge. From the date of the Edict of Expulsion, the Jews were given three months within which they had to leave Spain. Under the protection of government officials, the Jews left on foot and in carriages for the frontier and then in boats for the seaports. Baer notes that the priest Bernaldez, who resented the "hopeless obduracy of the Jews" where conversion to Christianity was concerned, could "hardly restrain his admiration for the manner of the exodus: with hymns on their lips, each man helping and encouraging his fellow, and firm in their naïve belief that the sea would divide for them as it had divided for their forefathers when they departed from Egypt" (II, 439). On July 31, 1492, the last Jew left Spain, except for the few who had managed, somehow, to hide, but who were soon rounded up and either baptized by force or expelled if they rejected conversion.

16

The Enlightenment and the Jews

In the eighteenth century, as we have seen, the vast majority of European Jews remained steeped in traditional Judaism, the theological framework of which consisted of three component elements: the Hebrew Bible or so-called Old Testament; the Talmud; and the Kabbalah. The ideological weight of the respective elements varied, of course, in the religious movements that emerged and developed in the seventeenth and early eighteenth centuries. The framework included the messianic eschatology rooted in the visions of the classical prophets of social justice, though the belief in the coming of the Messiah had been severely weakened by the profoundly disappointing denouement of the Sabbatian movement. Moreover, the Hasidic movement inspired by the Baal-Shem-Tov, embodying significant elements of Kabbalistic teachings, had spread with dramatic rapidity among the poorest strata of East European Jewry. Little wonder, then, that Hasidism soon engendered a counter-movement called Mitnagdim ("opponents"), viewing the followers of the Baal-Shem-Tov with suspicion and the fear that they now face another false-Messiah movement, and so soon after the earlier one. At about the same time that the minds of European Jews were dominated by traditional religious ideas, an intellectual movement arose in Western Europe that challenged all forms of religion in the name of Reason.

The term "Enlightenment" refers to the intellectual movement that unfolded within the 100-year span beginning with the English Revolution and culminating in the French Revolution. Montesquieu was born in 1689 and Baron d'Holbach died in 1789. The movement's leading representatives were religious skeptics, political reformers, cultural critics, historians, and social theorists who exercised considerable influence from Edinburgh to Naples, Paris to Berlin, and Boston to Philadelphia. Although these thinkers claimed to be committed to the rational pursuit of truth, they also had their philosophical and political differences. In spite of the merciless criticism leveled against Christian dogma and myth, a few of these thinkers held to the vestiges of their formerly religious beliefs. Others embraced materialism and atheism. Some, a distinct minority, remained loyal to the dynastic authority, while radicals proposed democratic ideas. The British thinkers were relatively content with their social and political institutions. The Germans were almost entirely apolitical. But, in sharp contrast to the British and Germans, it was the French *philosophes* who most vehemently criticized Church and state, campaigning unrelentingly for freedom from arbitrary power, freedom of speech, freedom of trade, and freedom to realize one's talents. It was in eighteenth-century France that the conflict of the Enlightenment became the most intense. Typically, the French *philosophe* was most uncompromising in his opposition to the old regime. There is a sense in which he tore it down intellectually, thus paving the way for its actual destruction by the Revolution of 1789.

The Enlightenment naturally had its pre-history, its roots in the past. Several centuries earlier, a secular mode of thought had slowly been developing. In the 400 years between 1300 and 1700, social forces first weakened and then shattered whatever unity Western Christendom had possessed. Those social forces may be summarized in the catch-phrase, "Protestantism, science, and capitalism." It must, however, be remembered that medieval science was teleological: its purpose was to attain knowledge for the sake of God. The aim of science was to discover God's intentions for his creation. Even the most rational of medieval thinkers conceded that there were sacred areas into which they must not venture, spheres in which revelation, faith, tradition, and ecclesiastical authority offered the answers – and issued the orders. Scientific curiosity as applied to those spheres was an unwelcome intrusion into holy ground. It was this inviolable domain of the *sacred* that distinguished the Middle Ages at its most scientific and skeptical from the later ages of criticism. The medieval mind was dominated by the Church, literally, emotionally, and intellectually.

In contrast to the medieval era, most thinkers of the Enlightenment regarded *all* aspects of human life and works as subject to critical examination – the various sciences, religious beliefs, metaphysics, aesthetics, education, and so on. Self-examination, a scrutiny of one's own actions and one's own society, was an essential function of thought. By gaining an understanding of the main forces and tendencies of their epoch, human beings, it was believed, could determine their direction and control their consequences. Through reason and science, humanity could attain ever-greater degrees of freedom and, hence, ever-greater degrees of improvement and perfection. Intellectual progress would serve to further humanity's general progress.

The *philosophes* waged an unceasing war against superstition, bigotry, and intolerance; they fought against censorship and demanded freedom of thought. They attacked the privileges of the feudal classes and their restraints upon the commercial and industrial classes. It was the Enlightenment faith in science and education that provided so powerful an impetus to their work, making them humanitarian, optimistic, and confident. Philosophy was no longer a matter of abstract thinking. It now acquired the practical-political function of asking critical questions about existing institutions, and demanding that the unreasonable and oppressive ones, be changed. All social obstacles to human perfectibility were to be progressively eliminated.

Unlike the rationalists of the seventeenth century (Descartes, Leibniz, Spinoza), for whom explanation was a matter of strict deduction, the *philosophes* constructed their ideal of explanation on the model of the contemporary natural sciences. They turned primarily not to Descartes, but to Newton, whose investigations rested not only on mathematical theory, but also on the data of experience and observation. Employing Galileo's discovery that falling bodies accelerate at a constant rate, and Kepler's observation of a fixed relationship between the distance of a planet from the sun and the speed of its revolution, Newton arrived at the law that the sun attracted planets to itself at a rate directly proportional to their mass and inversely proportional to the square of the distance between them. Eventually, he was able to demonstrate that all bodies of the universe took their positions and movements through the force of gravitation: that the force that held the planets in their orbits also made objects fall to the ground. This law was operative throughout the universe, which had become an apparently infinite machine moving by its own power and mechanisms. External causation accounted for its operation, which was seemingly devoid of purpose and meaning. Space, time, mass, motion, and force were the essential elements of this mechanical universe that could be comprehended in its entirety by applying the laws of science and mathematics. Newton's theory had an incalculable impact on the intellectuals of the Enlightenment, giving rise, in due course, to a discussion of the theory's implications for religion.

The English Deists

English thought in the seventeenth and eighteenth centuries gave rise slowly and hesitantly to new and comparatively bold ideas advocating a "natural religion," stressing the centrality in it of morality and denying the interference of the Creator with the laws of the universe. Newton had considered that the main value of his discoveries lay in demonstrating the existence of a God, for the force of gravity implied a "Great Clockmaker." Influenced by this conception of things, English intellectuals were attracted by the idea of a religion consistent with the moral message of the Gospel and yet compatible with the new scientific spirit: a religion that would be both rational and natural. Originally, the early Deists suggested, humanity practiced a form of "natural religion," but it was, in time, corrupted by the Church. Newton himself had proposed that the beginnings of such a systematic adulteration of "natural religion" could be found in some corruptions of the biblical text, which he attributed to St Jerome.

But it was John Toland, the "first free thinker in Western history," who regarded the Church Fathers as corrupters of true Christianity. He never ceased preaching a "reasonable" Christianity freed of its mystical accretions and, therefore, faithful to the teachings of Jesus. For Toland, this was the Christianity of the Ebionites, whom he described as Nazarenes or more simply as Jews. In fact, Toland proposed that:

> The true Christianity of the Jews was over-born and destroyed by the more numerous Gentiles, who, not enduring the reasonableness and simplicity of the same, brought into it by degrees the peculiar expressions and mysteries of Heathenism, the abstruse doctrines and distinctions of their philosophers, an insupportable pontifical Hierarchy, and even the altars, offerings, the sacred rites and ceremonies of their priests, tho they wou'd not so much as tolerate those of the Jews, and yet owning them to be divinely instituted . . . and so this very Tradition is alleg'd by others to warrant the invocation of Saints, prayers for the dead, the worship of images, with the whole train of Greek and Roman superstitions, whereof the least footstep appears not in the Bible.[1]

Toland urged his contemporaries to return to the purity of the Two Testaments, which enjoined the Jews to remain good Jews, and the Gentiles to become good Christians:

> It follows indeed that the *Jews*, whether becoming Christians or not, are forever bound to the Law of Moses, as now limited; and he that thinks they were absolv'd from the observation of it by Jesus, or that tis a fault in them still to adhere to it, does err not knowing the Scriptures; as did most of the converts from the Gentiles, who gave their bare names to Christ, but reserv'd their idolatrous hearts for their native superstitions. These

---

[1] Leon Poliakov, *The History of Anti-Semitism,* trans. Miriam Kochan, Philadelphia, PA: University of Pennsylvania Press, 1975, volume III, 60–1. Hereafter, all page references to Poliakov's work will be cited in parentheses immediately following the quoted passage.

did almost wholly subvert the True Christianity . . . So inveterate was their
hatred for the Jews (tho indebted to them for the Gospel) that their observing of anything, however reasonable or necessary, was a sufficient motive
for these Gentile converts to reject it. (Ibid., 61).

Toland moves from a defense of the Jews of the past to a vindication
of his Jewish contemporaries. In 1714 he published his *Reasons for
Naturalizing the Jews in Great Britain and Ireland*, advocating collective
immigration into the British Isles of Jews from the continent.

Toland was, however, an exception, since the main phalanx of Deists
who denounced the corruption of Christianity tended to blame the Jews.
If the Roman Church viewed the debasement of the chosen people as
proof of the truth of Christianity, these Deists often also based their
arguments on such a debasement. Poliakov gives these thinkers some
attention to illustrate the evident Judeophobia in their writings and the
identification of the Jew with a twister. There was, for example, William
Whiston, who succeeded Newton in his Cambridge Chair. Like Newton,
he engaged in countless calculations with the aim of coordinating biblical chronology with astronomic time. When the calculations failed
to produce the results he was after, he attributed the discrepancy to a
disturbance of the delicate machinery of the universe by a comet at the
time of the Flood. Hence, for Whiston, mathematical inconsistencies
were the result of human wickedness in Noah's generation. Whiston
attributed other errors to the malice of Jewish scribes. In his *Essay
Towards Restoring the True Text of the Old Testament* (1722), he wrote
that the Jews "about the beginning of the second century of the Gospel,
greatly alter'd and corrupted their Hebrew and Greek copies of the Old
Testament; and that, in many places, on purpose; out of opposition to
Christianity" (Poliakov III, 64). And yet, Poliakov surmises, Whiston
must have had the reputation of being a friend of the Jews, since it was he
who was entrusted by an anonymous gentleman with a hundred pounds
sterling to be distributed among them after a fire ravaged the Jewish
district of London in 1736.

Poliakov cites several other writers who had set forth "arguments"
which might strike us as bizarre or preposterous, but which were
advanced with the greatest seriousness. William Warburton tried to
demonstrate that God's choice of the "coarsest and vilest" of peoples
was the best proof of the truth of the Revelation. More venomous was
the famous pastor Woolsten, who was charged with blasphemy and was
said to have died in prison. Many thousands of copies of his burlesque
publications, which influenced Voltaire, were in circulation. His practice
was to ridicule traditional methods of biblical exegesis, while pretending
to defend them and making the "noisy stinking" Jews a favorite object of

his wit. In sum, the Jews were used as writers saw fit, to prove either the falsity or truth of Christianity.

The representatives of Deist opinions cited by Poliakov rarely devote a great deal of space to the Jews; nor do they seem to be obsessed with them. They do, however, seem to remain imprisoned in the traditional Christian world of ideas when they deal with the subject of the Jews, whether past or contemporary. Only John Toland broke out of that prison, as is shown by his call for the emancipation of the Jews and by his belief in the perfectibility of humanity through education.

Varieties of Enlightenment Views on Religion

In their attitude toward religion as toward other institutions, there was diversity among the French, British, and American participants in the Enlightenment. Some were ostensibly agnostic. Montesquieu argued that, if there is a God, he must necessarily be just. For Montesquieu, a "law," whether in nature as in the Newtonian sense, or in society, referred to "the necessary relations deriving from the nature of things." It followed for Montesquieu that "justice is a true relation between two things: the relation is always the same, no matter who examines it, whether it be God, or an angel, or lastly man himself." Aiming thus to secularize ethics and morality, Montesquieu continues:

> Thus if there were no God, we would still be obliged to venerate justice, that is, we should do everything possible to resemble that being of whom we have such an exalted notion and who, if he exists, would necessarily be just. Free though we might be from the yoke of religion, we should never be free from the bonds of equity.[2]

Other thinkers were thoroughgoing materialists and atheists. Baron d'Holbach contended that the unavoidable verdict of common sense upon religious views is that they have no foundation; "that all religion is an edifice in the air; that theology is only the ignorance of natural causes reduced to a system; that it is a long tissue of chimeras and contradictions" (ibid). For Holbach, there is only one criterion by which to assess a system of morals, and that is whether it conforms to human nature and needs. If it conforms, it is good; if it fails to conform, it should be rejected

---

[2] See Isaac Kramnick, ed., *The Portable Enlightenment Reader* (New York: Penguin Books, 1995, 106). Hereafter, all page references to this work will be cited in parentheses immediately following the quoted passage.

as contrary to the well-being of our species. For Holbach, there is no reason an atheist cannot have a moral conscience.

La Mettrie, another materialist, published a book titled *Man a Machine*. "The human body," he proposed, "is a machine which winds itself up" (ibid). Employing this mechanistic metaphor, La Mettrie held that all talk about a soul separate from the body is nonsense. Without food, the soul pines away and dies together with the body. But there were also prominent Enlightenment thinkers who retained a religious outlook. In a letter to Ezra Stiles, president of Yale College and a fellow member of the American Philosophical Society, Ben Franklin conveyed his own personal creed:

> I believe in one God, Creator of the universe. That he governs it by his providence. That he ought to be worshipped. That the most acceptable service we render to him is doing good to his other children. That the soul of man is immortal, and will be treated with justice in another life respecting its conduct in this. (Ibid., X)

Thomas Paine also retained a personal religious creed, the essentials of which he stated in his *The Age of Reason*.

As we remarked earlier, it was in France more than elsewhere that the struggle between the *philosophes* and the old regime became especially intense. The issues were not only social and political but also religious. Indeed, often the religious issues were the most salient. In mid-eighteenth-century France two bitterly opposed camps fought one another. On the one side stood the authoritarian and intolerant Catholic Church; on the other stood the predominantly irreligious *philosophes*. And there were also agnostics, as we have seen. It will, therefore, be interesting to hear how some of them viewed Jews and Judaism.

In Book XXX of his *The Spirit of the Laws*, where Montesquieu continues his discussion of the relation of religion to civil matters, he follows Locke in advocating religious toleration. Montesquieu makes the important distinction between tolerating a religion and approving of it, a distinction that neither the ecclesiastical nor the civil authorities of the old regime wished to recognize. If several different religions are present in a state, then the laws of the state "must oblige them to tolerate one another. It is a principle that every religion that is repressed becomes repressive itself. For as soon as it throws off oppression, by some chance, it attacks the religion that repressed it, not as a religion, but as a tyranny" (Montesquieu, XXX, 9).

Montesquieu now takes up the question of whether the Jewish religion ought to be tolerated, and what status Jews should have in an enlightened civil state. Entitled *"Très humble remonstrance aux inquisiteurs d'Espagne et de Portugal*" ("Very Humble Remonstrance to the Inquisitors of Spain and Portugal"), chapter 13 of Book XXX is in the tradition of the French *Conte Philosophique*, a philosophical tale designed to convey an ideal as effectively as possible. What prompted the tale was the Catholic Inquisition in the Iberian Peninsula and the comparative religious freedom, as we have seen, in non-Christian Turkey. Montesquieu, reacting to the burning at the stake of an eighteen-year-old Jewish girl, places these bitingly ironic words into the mouth of the imaginary Jewish author of a long soliloquy:

> You complain, he said to the Inquisitors, that the Emperor of Japan is having all the Christians in his domain burnt on a slow fire; but he could answer you: "We treat you, who do not believe as we do, as you treat those who do not believe as you do" . . . But it must be stated that you are far more cruel than this emperor . . . we follow a religion which you yourselves know was once beloved by God . . . You think that he no longer loves it; and because you think this you torture with steel and fire those who cling to this pardonable error of believing that God still loves that which he once loved . . . If you do not want to be Christians, at least be human: treat us as you would if you had neither a religion to guide nor a revelation to enlighten you and had to act only on the basis of the weak intimations of justice with which nature endows us . . . We must warn you of one thing: in future ages if someone will dare say that in the century in which we live the peoples of Europe were civilized, you will be cited as the evidence that they were barbarous; and your image will be such that it will dishonor your age and make your contemporaries the object of hatred. (*Oeuvres Complètes*, II; cited in Herzberg, 746–9)

Voltaire

On the positive side, we hear from this *philosophe* continuing criticisms of the Inquisition in which he denounces the persecutions of the Jews as evidence of the unworthiness of the Church. In the *Sermon du Rabbin Akib*, he places in the mouth of the rabbi an indictment of the Inquisition quite similar to the one we heard from Montesquieu. Voltaire, in that passage, even goes so far as to absolve the Jews of responsibility for the execution of Jesus. Where tolerance was concerned, Voltaire was direct and eloquent. Let Christians, he demanded, "stop persecuting and exterminating the Jews, who as men are their brothers and who as Jews are their fathers. Let each man serve God in the religion in which he is born . . . Let each man serve his king and his country, without ever using obedience to God as an excuse for disobeying the [moral] law" (*Oeuvres Complètes*, XXIV; cited in Herzberg, 284).

But Voltaire also hurled dark and unsavory epithets at the Jews. Scholars have for the most part either ignored this side of Voltaire or have attempted to explain it away. How? By suggesting he attacked the Bible to get at Christianity. But a survey of Voltaire's writings on Judaism and Jews suggests that in order for the Jews to be able to enter his new heaven, they had to purge themselves of their despicable traditions and history. They had to abandon their particularism and become "enlightened." But the evidence of his letters, in which he is most candid and frank, indicates something more than demanding that the Jews give up their particularism. Responding to his correspondent's favorable comments about the Spanish-Portuguese Jews in the British colonies – who had been expelled from the Iberian Peninsula – Voltaire wrote:

> I know that there are some Jews in the English colonies. These Marranos [*conversos*] go wherever there is money to be made . . . But that these circumcised Jews who sell old clothes to the savages claim that they are of the tribe of Naphtali or Issachar is not of the slightest importance. They are, nonetheless, the greatest scoundrels who have ever sullied the face of the globe. (*Correspondence*, LXXXVI, 166; cited in Herzberg, 285)

Both Arthur Herzberg and Leon Poliakov propose that the view expressed in Voltaire's correspondence is an early form of secular anti-Semitism. The essence, after all, of the Enlightenment message is that humans are not bad by nature, and that they can be improved and perfected through freedom and education. As a general proposition that applies to all humans, it ought to include the Jews. But from Voltaire we hear something else: that the Jewish character has not changed from ancient times to the present. It is an eternal trait. The issue for Voltaire is not the theological quarrel between Christians and Jews. It is, rather, the clash between Greco-Roman Western culture and those who infected it with Oriental ideas.

In 1771, Voltaire adopted one of his favorite poses, that of a classic Roman, and wrote *Lettres de Memmius à Ciceron*, placing in the mouth of Memmius a description of Syria in which the Jews were singled out as the worst of men, hating all others and in turn hated by them: "The Persians and Scythians are a thousand times more reasonable . . ." Voltaire then goes on to praise Cicero for his anti-Jewish oration *Pro Flacco*, the climax of which reads: "They [the Jews] are, all of them, born with raging fanaticism in their hearts, just as the Bretons and the Germans are born with blond hair. I would not be in the least bit surprised if these people would not some day become deadly to the human race" (*Oeuvres Complètes*, XXVIII, 439–40; cited in Herzberg, 300). And Herzberg comments: "Voltaire had thus, being an ex-Christian, abandoned entirely the religious attack on the Jews as Christ-killers or Christ-rejectors. He proposed a new principle on which to base his hatred of them, their *innate character*" (Herzberg, 300; italics added). Herzberg then goes on to aver that this "racist" remark by Voltaire is no accident as is shown by what he wrote the following year in his *Il faut prendre une partie*. It consisted of speeches by the adherents of various religions, each speech designed to make the particular religion appear ridiculous. At the end, a "theist," Voltaire, reviews the speeches and addresses the Jews:

> You seem to me to be the maddest of the lot. The Kaffirs, the Hottentots, and the Negroes of Guinea are much more reasonable and more honest people than your ancestors, the Jews. You have surpassed all nations in impertinent fables, in bad conduct, and in barbarism. You deserve to be punished, for this is your destiny. (*Oeuvres Complètes*, XXVIII; cited in Herzberg, 549)

But Voltaire's new form of Jew-hatred is in continuity with the old: he blames the Jews for their expulsion from Spain – they brought it on themselves because they allegedly controlled all the money and commerce in the country. Why are the Jews hated?

> It is the inevitable result of their laws; they either had to conquer everybody or be hated by the whole human race. They kept all their customs, which are exactly the opposite of all proper social customs; they were therefore rightly treated as a people opposed to all others; . . . they made usury a sacred duty. And these are our fathers. (*Oeuvres Complètes*, XII, 159–63; cited in Herzberg, 302–3)

Voltaire's utterances soon take on the character of silliness as well as venom: the Jews borrowed everything in their culture from others. He goes so far as to assert that the Jewish religion was borrowed from the Greek. How did they manage to do so? By identifying Lot's wife with Eurydice and Samson with Hercules. The Jews, for Voltaire, were inveterate plagiarizers and there is not a single page of the Jewish books that was not stolen, mostly from Homer. The gist, then, of Voltaire's view of the Jews is this: there is a cultural, philosophical, and ethnic tradition of Europe that was handed down, from the values taught by the Greeks, and then carried to all reaches of the European world by the Romans. This was the normative culture of which Voltaire approved. But the Jews, he asserts, are a different family, and their religion is rooted in their character. It is possible to redeem Europe by bringing it back to its pre-Christian values. But the Jews are radically different: being born a Jew and the obnoxiousness of the Jewish outlook are indissoluble; it is, therefore, most improbable that even the "enlightened" can escape their innate character. "The Jews," as Herzberg sums up Voltaire's position, "are subversive of the European tradition by their very presence, for they are the radically other, the hopeless alien. Cure them of their religion, and their inborn character remains" (304). Thus, it seems that Voltaire, by providing a new, secular anti-Jewish rhetoric in the name of European culture, rather than in the name of religion, planted the seeds for a quasi-racial or racist conception of the Jews. However, before we trace the subsequent development of those seeds, we should hear the views of a more healthy-minded *philosophe* who held more firmly to the Enlightenment's principle of perfectibility through education.

Rousseau

As noted earlier, many of Rousseau's friends among the *philosophes* were materialists or atheists who denied the existence of a supreme Deity and teacher, but who nevertheless accepted the moral principles that originated in the belief in such a Deity. Rousseau, however, discerned certain disturbing implications in the materialist views: do not such views carry with them the dangerous inference of moral relativism or nihilism? What disturbed Rousseau can best be stated in the question of a later thinker: "If God is dead, is everything permitted?" This is, of course, the question Dostoevsky addressed in the proto-Nietzschean characters of his great philosophical novels. Similarly, Rousseau sought to formulate his own religious outlook in opposition to the materialist views of his own time.

Rousseau's writings on religion deserve special attention for another reason. Although he shared certain Enlightenment principles, he also departed from them by anticipating several key ideas of the Romantic-Conservative reaction to the Enlightenment and the French Revolution. The Romantic-Conservative thinkers turned away from what they regarded as the mechanistic rationalism of the eighteenth century. They did so not only by recognizing the irrational factors in human conduct, but also by assigning to them a positive value. Tradition, imagination, feeling, and the religious experience were now regarded as natural and positive. In every area of culture – literature, art, music, philosophy, and religion – the aim was to free the emotions and the imagination from the austere rules and conventions imposed in the eighteenth century. In religion the importance of *inner* experience was restored.

Rousseau is justly famous not only for his political theory but also for his ideas on education, found primarily in his *Émile* (1762), the most important text the Enlightenment had produced on the education of children. Rousseau called this text *"mon traité d'education"*. It is an imaginative work in which Rousseau plays the role of tutor, bringing up Émile from infancy to manhood. At the age of 16, under the guidance of his tutor and with the expansion of Émile's sympathetic imagination, he begins to see himself in his fellow creatures and to be touched by their signs of pain. Émile is beginning to put himself in the place of those who can claim his pity. It dawns on him that the fate of miserable and wretched individuals may one day be his own. He recognizes that he, like others, stands on the edge of an abyss into which he might be plunged at any moment by unexpected and unavoidable misfortunes. Émile is learning to put no lasting trust in his good health and fortune, because it may be entirely temporary. He is gaining a sensitive conscience and trying to relate to others as he would have them relate to him.

His tutor has until now spoken not a word to him of religion as such. But now that Émile is learning to think for himself, the time has come, his tutor believes, to help him understand what it means to be a truly religious human being. Hence, in Book IV of *Émile*, we encounter a section called "The Creed of a Savoyard Priest." Although Rousseau claimed, in the text, that he had received this "profession of faith" 30 years earlier, he eventually acknowledged it as his own; and that it was his aim to set down the basic religious-moral principles with which to guide his conduct throughout his life.

Basically, Rousseau's creed affirms the reality of human consciousness, will, and autonomy. His cognitive ability tells him that matter has no power of action in itself. Even Newton had to add a projectile force to account for the elliptical course of celestial bodies. Matter in motion points to a will; and matter in motion in accordance with fixed laws points to an *intelligence*. Hence, to appreciate fully what Rousseau is trying to accomplish we have to understand that he strives to make his case not by means of reason or science alone. He is urging his readers to go beyond cold reasoning and to listen to the *inner voice of feeling*; for if one listens to the inner voice, one cannot fail to hear that the visible order of the universe proclaims a Supreme Intelligence. Although this being hides himself from our senses, we feel not only his presence, but our dependence upon him. Rousseau feels God everywhere in his works and within himself.

We now arrive at a paramount element in Rousseau's religious outlook, inspired, no doubt, by the covenantal idea of the Hebrew Bible and perfectly compatible with it. Humans are active and free: they act of their own accord. What humans do freely, therefore, is no part of a system determined by providence, and cannot be imputed to a determinative system. Rousseau's point is that God is no puppeteer and we are not marionettes. Providence does not will the evil that humans perpetrate when they ignore or disobey the ethical commandments of God, and abuse the freedom granted them. Nor does providence intervene in human affairs to prevent evil. For what would be the point of granting humans freedom if providence were to intervene everywhere and every time evil is done? Providence has made humans free so that they might choose the good and refuse evil. The misuse of human freedom cannot undermine the general cosmic order, but the evil that humans do reacts upon themselves – upon the species as a whole. To complain that God does not prevent evil is to complain that he has given us freedom – together with the understanding of what is right and what is wrong. "Man!" Rousseau therefore declares: "Seek no farther for the author of evil; the author is you, yourself. There is no evil other than the evil you do or the evil you suffer and both come from you."[3] Does God nevertheless owe something to his human creatures? Yes, says Rousseau. God gave us the idea of good and made us feel the need for it. That is tantamount to promising humanity the good *if* we obey his ethical commandments.

Rousseau on Judaism and the Jews

In contrast to Voltaire, Rousseau looked upon the children of Israel favorably. In his *Creed of the Savoyard Priest*, of which we have just provided a brief exposition, he compares the Church triumphant with the muffled synagogue:

> Do you know many Christians who have taken the trouble to inquire what the Jews allege against them? If anyone knows anything at all about it, it is from the writings of Christians. What a way of ascertaining the argument of our adversaries! But what is to be done? If anyone dared to publish in our day books which were openly in favor of the Jewish religion, we would punish the author, publisher and bookseller. This regulation is a sure and certain plan for always being in the right. It is easy to refute those who dare not venture to speak.
>
> Those among us who have the opportunity of talking with Jews are little better off. These unhappy people feel that they are in our power; the tyranny they have suffered makes them timid. They know that Christian charity thinks nothing of injustice and cruelty; will they dare to run the risk of an outcry against blasphemy? Our greed inspires us with zeal, and they are so rich that they must be in the wrong. The more learned, the more enlightened they are, the more cautious. You may convert some poor wretch whom you have paid, to slander his religion; you get some wretched old-clothesman to speak, and he says what you want; you may triumph over their ignorance

---

[3] Jean-Jacques Rousseau, *Émile*, Paris: Gallimard, 1969, 424.

and cowardice, while all the time their men of learning are laughing at your stupidity. But do you think you would get off so easily in any place where they knew they were safe? At the Sorbonne, it is plain that the messianic prophecies refer to Jesus Christ. Among the rabbis of Amsterdam it is just as clear that they [the prophecies] have nothing to do with him. I do not think that I have ever heard the arguments about the Jews as to why they should not have a free state, schools and universities, where they can speak and argue without danger. Then alone can we know what they have to say. (cited in Poliakov III, 100–1)

And Poliakov remarks, "note the *avant la lettre* Zionist argument at the end" (ibid., 101).

Rousseau was, however, a "child of his time," declaring his horror of the cruel Hebrew God of battle, and describing the ancient Jews in the conventional, unsavory terms. On balance, however, as Poliakov recognized, the love for the God of Sinai prevailed over whatever hatred he might have had in his mind. Moreover, he found more truth in Moses and his teachings than in anything else, and explained at length why he admired him. Indeed, the long passage I am about to quote could have been cited in the Introduction to the present author's work; it so clearly conveys the historical beginnings of the formation of God's "special people." Rousseau wrote in his *Considerations sur le government de pologne . . .*:

Moses planned and carried out the astonishing undertaking of setting up into a national body a swarm of wretched fugitives, without arts, without weapons, without talents, without virtues, without courage and who, not having a single inch of ground in its own right, made a strange troop on the face of the earth. Moses dared to make this wandering and servile troop into a political body, a free people, and, while it wandered in the deserts without a stone on which to rest its head, he gave it institutional form which has stood the test of time, of fortune and of conquerors, which five thousand years have not been able to destroy or even alter and which still continues to exist today in full force even when the national body no longer exists.

To prevent his people from fusing with foreign peoples, he gave it customs and practices which are incompatible with those of other nations; he over-loaded it with ritual, specific ceremonies; he encumbered it in thousands of ways to keep it incessantly in good shape and to render it always a foreigner amongst other men; and all the bonds of fraternity that he placed between the members of his republic were so many barriers that kept it separate from its neighbors and prevented it from mingling with them. It is in this way that this strange nation, so often subjugated, so often apparently dispersed and destroyed, but always passionately attached to its code, has still been preserved up to the present day scattered amongst the others without mixing with them, and that its customs, its laws, its ritual continue to exist and will last as long as the world, despite the hatred and persecution of the rest of the human race. (cited in Poliakov, vol. III, 103)

In the same vein, Rousseau avers that "the Jews provide us with an astonishing spectacle: the laws of Numa, Lycurgus, Solon are dead; the very much older laws of Moses are still alive. Athens, Sparta, Rome have perished and no longer have children left on earth; Zion destroyed, has not lost its children (cited in Poliakov, III, 104).

On the character of Jews and Judaism, there are, then, significant differences between Montesquieu and Rousseau on the one side and, say, Voltaire, Diderot, and Holbach on the other. Among the latter, the anti-Jewish rhetoric was more marked, tending in Voltaire's writings to border on a secular, quasi-racial interpretation of the tenacity with which the Jews have held on to their religious particularisms. But, as we reflect on the Enlightenment movement as a whole, the positive, political consequences of it for the Jews is clear.

Where popular influence is concerned, the Enlightenment was much more significant than the Renaissance. The ideas of the *Aufklärung* did not remain the possession of a small aristocratic circle. On the contrary, the ideas filtered downward to the middle classes and, with the growth of popular education in the nineteenth century, affected the outlook of the lower social strata as well. In France, Britain, and America – the peculiarities of the German case will soon be addressed – the conception of the universe as a law-ordered cosmos, the opposition to ecclesiastical domination, the belief in religious toleration, the importance of civil rights and liberties, all came to be regarded as the essential liberal-democratic principles of a good society. In these terms, the Enlightenment thinkers deserve credit for some of the lasting, positive accomplishments of the French Revolution – despite the human costs of the guillotine, terror, and the Napoleonic Wars. The revolution had put an end to royal absolutism and the privileges of the nobility. It converted the Church into a department of state, and expropriated its expansive landholdings. The rationale for these changes is found in the Declaration of the Rights of Man, the Charter embodying the basic political and social tenets of the Enlightenment, which was employed by the Constituent Assembly as a guide for its work of reconstruction.

It seems to be historically true, then, that Jewish emancipation in Europe was achieved first in France – but certainly not with the ease with which Jews could take their freedoms for granted on the other side of the ocean. In France, the Declaration of the Rights of Man and of Citizens established the principle of religious freedom; but as the logical and favorable consequences for the Jews did not immediately follow, a struggle was necessary. The Jews of southern France, determined to advance their interests, presented a petition signed by 215 heads of families in Bordeaux, which was favorably reported on by Bishop Talleyrand. The Portuguese Jews and those of Avignon, previously under the Holy See but now preparing to be joined to France, were declared full citizens (January 28, 1790). Young Parisian Jews, members of the National Guard, among them the learned Polish Jew Zalkind Hourwitz, an ardent supporter of the revolution, appealed to the Paris Commune. The advocate Godard supported their appeal and, as a result, 53 out of 60 districts voted in favor of the enfranchisement of all French Jews. Abbé Merlot presented the resolution of the Commune to the National Assembly. The opponents of the Jews caused another delay, but the opposition was soon overcome. On September 28, 1791, on the motion of Duport, a decree was promulgated granting all the Jews of France full civic rights on a par with other citizens.[4]

But those achievements in France were just the beginning of Jewish struggles for emancipation in the rest of Western Europe, aided only temporarily by Napoleon's conquests. Following the Napoleonic penetration of the Germanies, the medieval treatment of the Jews was swept away and they were permitted to dwell on German soil – but not as citizens. With the decisive defeat of Napoleon, however, the Congress of Vienna restored the old regimes in Germany, and the Jewish struggle for citizenship continued.

---

[4] Max L. Margolis and Alexander Marx, *A History of the Jewish People*, Philadelphia, PA: Jewish Publication Society of America, 1941, 609–10.

17

The Germanies

The effect of French hegemony upon the Germans was far-reaching. In 1792 Germany consisted of about 350 independent states. By 1806 Napoleon's policy had reduced the number of such states to 39. This momentous consolidation was the result of treaties with Prussia and Austria, which gained some territory during the first stages of the reorganization. A Prussian-Austrian deputation, largely responsive to the will of the French, ratified the transfer of 97 states on the west bank of the Rhine to France. On the east side of the Rhine, 112 states were apportioned among Prussia, Austria, Bavaria, and the smaller South German states. Only one of the ecclesiastical states and six of the city-states remained independent.

These territorial changes were accompanied by political reforms that benefited the remaining German princes. The lands and the revenues of the Church became subject to the control of the various German regimes. In Catholic territories the extensive holdings of the clergy made these appropriations extraordinarily profitable for the princes; the Bavarian king alone, for example, appropriated 66 monasteries. Throughout, the Church thus became increasingly subservient to the native princes. The defeat of the Austrians at Austerlitz and the destruction of the Prussian military power at Jena-Auerstadt enabled Napoleon to create the Confederation of the Rhine (1806). This organization, with the emperor himself in the role of protector, was composed of Bavaria, Würtemburg, Westphalia, Baden, and several of the lesser principalities. Only Austria and Prussia among the larger German powers remained independent. The ancient, decrepit Holy Roman Empire now disappeared. Imperial France had bound their German vassals by means of offensive and defensive alliances, obligating them to hold in readiness an army of 63,000 men. Reforms characteristic of post-revolutionary, Napoleonic France were introduced; and the Napoleonic partial consolidation of the German states paved the way for the unification movement of the nineteenth century.

The French defeat of the German states revived and intensified German nationalism. The humiliating defeat of the Prussian army in 1806, and the rather onerous terms imposed by Napoleon in 1807, forced the Prussian leaders into a desperate self-appraisal. It had become painfully obvious that it would require substantial political and military changes before the French could be driven back across the Rhine. Moreover, Bavaria, Würtemburg, Saxony, and Baden had become allies of Napoleon, while Austria seemed helpless after the defeat at Wagram in 1809. Furthermore, the Germanies were traditionally particularist and cosmopolitan, many Germans viewing the French emperor both as hero and as invincible. It followed that the only hope lay in a reformed and strengthened Prussia on the one hand, and an aroused and invigorated German nationalism on the other.

It was Baron vom Stein who led the reform movement in Prussia. He attempted to gain the support of the peasants by an Edict of Emancipation (1808) that abolished serfdom. However, the feudal system was still so strongly entrenched that servile dues remained in effect even after the Edict, and the Prussian peasants, constituting two thirds of the population, failed to attain the position of the French peasants before the revolution. But the gains made by the German peasants were sufficient, apparently, to awaken their sense of identity with the "German nation," a new and increasingly propagated catchword.

Although municipal government gained a measure of autonomy, the king reserved the right to appoint the mayor and control the police. The entire bureaucratic system was reconstructed with the aim of centralizing power in the state. Provincial privileges were abrogated, cumbersome political divisions were simplified, superfluous ministries were eliminated; and, most importantly, the military machine was refashioned on the French model. All these reforms, imposed from above by the ruling classes to secure greater efficiency within the old regime, were also designed to arouse the patriotic feelings of the populace. The *Tagenbund*, a secret society organized to inflame national feeling, had a widespread influence. The philosopher Fichte made lofty appeals to the people, urging German unity in opposition to foreign control.[1] "No man, no God, and no possible event can save or help us; we must help ourselves!" he proclaimed. When a Nuremberg bookseller was executed for the alleged violations of the Napoleonic censorship laws, it raised the indignation of the German peoples to a very high pitch; and when the French armies were retreating across Germany after the disastrous

---

[1] See William J. Bossenbrook, *Development of Contemporary Civilization*, Boston, MA: D.C. Heath and Company, 1940, chapter V.

Russian campaign of 1812, the Prussians became mentally and militarily ready for their war of liberation.

The Emerging German National Mind

In Germany of the eighteenth century the middle classes were politically insignificant. The German Enlightenment therefore assumed a peculiar form, owing to the fragmented nature of the country and its economic and social backwardness when compared with England, the Netherlands, and France. It is noteworthy that the Lutheran Church was open to the enlightening spirit of the time, and that German Protestant pastors were among the first to propagate the new ideas of science and rationality, and to instill them primarily in their middle-class flocks. The pastors were revising their theology and introducing "higher criticism" of the Bible. But, in contrast to the revolutionary force with which the English and French middle classes had translated Enlightenment ideas, German intellectual development proceeded with caution, remaining duly under the control of the regime. Radical tendencies were practically non-existent, and only princes dared flirt with philosophical materialism. The peasant masses, virtually untouched by the new ideas, remained steeped in Lutheran Christianity.

Luther

This brings us to another factor that helps explain the distinctive character of German social, political, and cultural development: the Lutheran legacy or the spirit of Lutheranism, which made unconditional obedience to Caesar – to the temporal authorities – the chief national virtue. Luther's doctrine, in that regard, can be traced to the peasants' war of the sixteenth century. As Roland Bainton explains, the peasant uprisings "did not arise out of any immediate connection with the religious issues of the 16th Century because agrarian unrest had been brewing for fully a century."[2] Uprisings had taken place throughout Europe, especially in south Germany, where feudal anarchy was being superseded by the centralization of power. In Spain, England, and France this had occurred on a national scale, but in the Germanies only on a territorial basis, in each

---

[2] See Roland Bainton, *Here I Stand: A Life of Martin Luther*, Nashville, TN: Abingdon Press, 1950, 268. Hereafter, all page references to this work will be cited in parentheses immediately following the quoted passage.

principality. As the princes strove to integrate administration by means of a bureaucracy of salaried, court officials, the expenses were met by increased levies on the land, on the peasants. Law was being unified by replacing the diverse local codes with Roman law, which again caused peasant suffering, since Roman law dealt only with private property and therefore imperiled the commons, which according to the old Germanic tradition gave the peasant community free access to the woods, streams, and meadows.

Moreover, the revival of urban commerce after the Crusades led to the increasing substitution of exchange in coin for exchange in kind. The growing demand for precious metals raised their value, and the peasants at first benefited from paying a fixed monetary sum instead of a percentage in kind. But soon, owing to the lords' intensified squeezing of the peasants, deflation set in; and the peasants who could not meet their impost obligations sank from freeholders to renters, and from renters to serfs. The peasants began with modest demands: free woods, waters, and meadows as in former days, the reduction of the imposts, and the reinstatement of the ancient Germanic law and local custom. To express their grievances, the peasants gathered in thousands rather spontaneously, and presented their petitions to the princes who occasionally made concessions and eased peasant burdens somewhat, but not enough to forestall growing discontent. Bainton's analysis suggests that the initiative for the redress of grievances came not from the poorest and most exploited, but from the better-off peasant strata. As the movement spread north it included peasants who were also artisans and townsmen, who called for more democracy in the town councils, less restrictive membership in the guilds, the subjection of the clergy to civil tax burdens, and full rights for citizens to engage in brewing.

Prior to the peasants' war of 1525, the mass movement was called the *Bundschuh*. This name came from the typical leather shoe of the peasant, containing a long thong with which it was laced, called a *Bund*. The term carried a double meaning because a *Bund* was also an association or a covenant. This movement was often anti-clerical but not anti-Catholic. Bishops and abbots were resented as exploiters, but "Down with the bishop" did not mean "Down with the Pope" or "Down with the Church." The banners of the *Bundschuh* often carried, besides the shoe, some religious symbol such as a portrait of Mary or a crucifix. As Bainton remarks, a "movement so religiously minded could not but be affected by the Reformation. Luther's freedom of the Christian man was purely religious *but could very readily be given a social turn*" (270; italics added).

Luther's sturdy peasant nature asserted itself in the stormiest fashion in the first period of his activities. Against the Roman churchmen, if they continued in their ways, he urged that they be punished with arms, not with words. Since we punish thieves with the halter, murderers with the sword, and heretics with fire, why do we not turn on all those evil teachers of perdition, those popes, cardinals and bishops, and the entire swarm of the Roman Sodom with arms in hand, and wash our hands in their blood?[3]

But this ardor was short lived as Luther's message struck home, with the entire German people being set in motion. On the one hand, peasants and plebeians saw the signal to revolt in his appeals against the clergy and in his sermon on Christian freedom; and, on the other, moderate burghers and a large segment of the lower nobility, and even princes, were drawn into the movement. The day had come, the people believed, to throw off all their oppressors; while the nobles and princes saw an opportunity to break the power of the clergy, the dependence on Rome and the Catholic hierarchy, and to enrich themselves with the confiscated Church property. But the princes and the people, despite their distinct aims, viewed Luther as their spokesman. As Frederick Engels observed: "Luther had to choose between them. He, the protégé of the Elector of Saxony, the revered professor of Wittenberg who had become powerful and famous overnight . . . did not hesitate a single moment. He dropped the popular elements of the movement, and took the side of the burghers, the nobility and the princes" (ibid., 63).

The most popular of the peasants' manifestos, *The Twelve Articles*, opened with phrases reminiscent of Luther himself: "To the Christian reader, peace and grace of God through Christ . . . The gospel is not a cause of rebellion and disturbance." It is those who refuse reasonable demands who are the disturbers. "If it be the will of God to hear the peasants, who will resist His majesty? Did he not hear the children of Israel and deliver them out of the hand of pharaoh?" Their demands did seem to reflect Luther's message: the congregation should have the right to appoint and remove its own minister; the tithe on cattle should be abolished; the common fields, forests, and waters should be guaranteed; the farmer should be free to hunt, fish, and protect his lands against game; death-dues, which impoverished the widow and orphan by requisitioning the best cloak or the best cow, should be abolished; rents should be in accord with the productivity of the soil; common lands should not pass into private hands. Bainton notes that the only Article that exceeded the earlier demands was the one calling for the total abolition of serfdom. Land, the Articles continued, should be available for lease with stipu-

---

[3] Cited in Frederick Engels, *The Peasant War in Germany*, Moscow: Foreign Languages Publishing House, 1956, 62–3.

lated conditions. If a lord exacts any labor in excess of the agreement, he should pay for it in the form of wages. *The Twelve Articles* conceded in advance that any demand not consonant with the word of God should be null. Bainton avers that the peasant demands were conservative, in line with the customs and traditions of the old feudal economy, and that any sort of attack on government was notably absent.

How did Luther respond? The evangelical ring of the Articles pleased him, but he disparaged and rejected their demands nevertheless. The right of the congregation to choose its own minister depends on whether they pay him. "The abolition of tithes is highway robbery, and the abrogation of serfdom is making Christian liberty a thing of the flesh." After thus criticizing the Articles, Luther turned to the means of trying to realize the program. "Under no circumstances must the common man seize the sword on his own behalf." Bainton proposes, in Luther's defense, that his response

was not intended to justify the unspeakable wrongs perpetrated by the rulers. To the princes Luther addressed an appeal in which he justified many more of the peasant demands than he had done when speaking to them . . . The demands of the peasants for redress of their grievances were fair and just. The princes had none but themselves to thank for these disorders, since they had done nothing but disport themselves in grandeur while robbing and flaying their subjects. The true solution was the old way of arbitration.

But that way neither side was disposed to take, and the prediction of Luther was all too abundantly fulfilled, that nothing would ensue but murder and bloodshed. Luther had long since declared that he would never support the private citizen in arms, however just the cause, since such means inevitably entailed wrong to the innocent. He could not envisage an orderly revolution. (274)

It was, then, the experience of the peasant war, together with his religious outlook, that produced Luther's political attitude. He was a "minister" or "teacher" without any magisterial powers with which to arbitrate the conflict successfully. He recognized the justice of the peasants' demands, and the injustice of the princes' recalcitrance, but he nevertheless taught that obedience and submission to the temporal authorities was a cardinal virtue in all circumstances. It is from the time of Luther, then, that obedience and submission became a German, *national* virtue. As Kant remarked, "The German, of all civilized peoples, adapts himself most easily and constantly to the government under which he lives, and is the most remote from the quest for innovation and oppo-sition to the established order" (Poliakov, III, 159). And Madame de Staël, though favorably disposed to Germans, viewed them as "energetic flatterers and vigorously submissive . . . [They] utilize philosophical arguments to explain what is least philosophical in the world: the respect for strength and the softening power of fear which changes that respect into admiration" (ibid.). And as submission of the masses and adulation of the leader will become especially relevant in a later discussion of the twentieth century, it is of interest to listen to the well-known, democratic socialist, Robert Michels:

> The German people in especial exhibits to an extreme degree the need for someone to point out the way and to issue orders. This peculiarity, common to all classes not excepting the proletariat, furnishes a psychological soil upon which a powerful directive hegemony can flourish luxuriantly. There exist among the Germans all the preconditions necessary for such a development: a psychological pre-disposition to subordination, a profound instinct for discipline, in a word, the whole still persistent inheritance of the influence of the Prussian drill sergeant, with all its advantages and disadvantages; in addition, a trust in authority which verges on the complete absence of a critical faculty.[4]

Michels notes further that Marx was quite aware of the "risks to the democratic spirit" of this national character, and that "he thought it necessary to warn the German workers against entertaining too rigid a conception of organization." Marx insisted that in Germany, "where the workers are bureaucratically controlled from birth upward, and for this reason have a blind faith in constituted authority, it is above all necessary to teach them to walk by themselves" (ibid., 55). As for the German leaders, on the other hand: "Engels," wrote Michels, "regarded it as deplorable that [they] could not accustom themselves to the idea that the mere fact of being installed in office did not give them the right to be treated with more respect than any other comrade" (ibid., 222). The leaders of the German Social Democratic Party thought and acted in a manner reminiscent of the Sun King: each was inclined to think of himself: *Le parti c'est moi* – in Michels' phrase.

Luther's Attitude toward the Jews

Luther had early accepted the view of the Jews as a "stiff-necked" people, and especially for having rejected Christ. But how could his contempo-

---

[4] Robert Michels, *Political Parties*, New York: Dover Publications, 1959, 53. Hereafter, page references to this work will be cited in parentheses immediately following the quoted passage.

rary Jews be blamed for the sins of their fathers? And given his excoriation of the papacy for its corruption, the Jews might readily be excused for their rejection of Christianity. "If I were a Jew," he said,

> I would suffer the rack ten times before I would go over to the pope.
>
> The papists have so demeaned themselves that a good Christian would rather be a Jew than one of them, and a Jew would rather be a sow than a Christian.
>
> What good can we do the Jews when we constrain them, malign them, and hate them as dogs? When we deny them work and force them to usury, how can that help? We should use toward the Jews not the pope's but Christ's law of love. If some are still stiff-necked, what does that matter? We are not all good Christians. (Bainton, 379)

Luther was confident that by eliminating the abuses of the papacy he would win the Jews over to his reformed Christianity. But only a few were won over, and not always permanently. And when he tried to convert some rabbis, they endeavored, in return, to make a Jew of him. A rumor emerged, somehow, that the papists had hired a Jew to murder him, which he received with less than complete incredulity. In Luther's latter days, when he was often nervous and irate, news came from Moravia that Christians were effectively Judaizing. Then, as Bainton remarked, Luther "came out with a vulgar blast in which he recommended that all the Jews be deported to Palestine. Failing that, they should be forbidden to practice usury, should be compelled to earn their living on the land, their synagogues should be burned, and their books, including the Bible, should be taken away from them" (379). Bainton, great and gracious scholar that he is, remarks "one would wish that Luther had died before ever this tract was written."

As Bainton cogently argues, clarity about what Luther was recommending, and why, requires the understanding that his position was entirely religious and in no sense racial. For him, the greatest sin was the persistent rejection of the fundamental doctrinal principle of Christianity: God's revelation of himself in Christ. Jewish suffering over the centuries was itself a sign of divine displeasure. In effect, Luther was proposing a program of enforced Zionism: the diaspora people should be returned to their biblical homeland. But if that turned out to be impracticable, then the Jews should be compelled to live from the soil. From Bainton's remarks that follow, we hear confirmation of the historical fact that the Jews' finding themselves in occupations other than agriculture and crafts was certainly no free choice, but rather forced upon them. Bainton writes:

Luther was unwittingly proposing a return to the condition of the early Middle Ages, when the Jews had been in agriculture. Forced off the land, they had gone into commerce and, having been expelled from commerce, into money lending. Luther wished to reverse the process and thereby inadvertently would accord the Jews a more secure position than they enjoyed in his day. The [proposed] burning of the synagogues and the confiscation of the books was, however, a revival of the worst features of Pfefferkorn's program. One other word must be added: if similar tracts did not appear in England, France, and Spain in Luther's day, it was because the Jews had already been expelled from these countries. Germany, disorganized in this as in so many other respects, expelled the Jews from certain localities and tolerated them in others, such as Frankfurt and Worms. The irony of the situation was that Luther justified himself by appealing to the ire of Jehovah against those awhoring after other gods. Luther would not have listened to any impugning of the validity of this picture of God, but he might have recalled that scripture itself discountenances human imitation of the divine vengeance. (380)

Hegel

The Enlightenment posited the eventual triumph of reason over unreason. In eighteenth-century Germany, however, although the leading philosophical idealists were somewhat influenced by the secular orientation of the French *philosophes*, the main trend was to return to the earlier spiritualist tradition. *Geist* (spirit) was the central concept of this tradition, the aim of which was the "revaluation" of the inner, creative forces of originality and spontaneity, expressing themselves in higher forms of literature, art, and religion. In opposition to the mechanistic outlook and concepts of the Enlightenment (the spring-and-wire universe, the social contract theory of the origin of society, the human body as a machine), German philosophers advanced a view of society as an organism developing from below by means of institutions such as family and community. Renewed attention was paid to the "natural" or "organic" as the source of creative spontaneity, rooted in the national, cultural soil. Such ideas found dramatic expression in the movement known as Sturm und Drang (storm and stress), chiefly a literary movement of young authors like Herder, Schiller, and Goethe. They represented a highly emotional revolt against what was perceived as the cold rationalism of the *philosophes*, in which everything spoke to the intellect, but nothing to the feelings and convictions derived from them.

Rousseau, we will recall, proposed that humans could rise to a higher level if they used reason to recognize the limits of reason. In his *social contract* he argued that human beings might, in the right circumstances, widen the boundaries of freedom by democratically imposing upon themselves government and laws of their own choosing. In France, Rousseau became the prophet of popular sovereignty; in the Germanies, however, he became the symbol of inner freedom. At first, German intellectuals greeted the events of 1789 as opening a new and liberating era in human development. But as the revolution entered its more violent phase, beginning with the massacres of 1792 and culminating in the reign of guillotine terror of 1793–4, attitudes changed. Under the influence of Edmund Burke, a second phase in the Idealist and Romantic movement was initiated, a phase that turned to the "nation" as the means of restoring the organic continuity with the historic past after the revolution and Napoleon had, as it were, severed the German people from their ancient roots.

It was in the course of this phase that *Geist* and *Staat* (spirit and state) became embodied in the concept of *Volk* (people or nation). And it was Hegel who contributed much toward bringing *Volk* and *Staat* together in a new synthesis that would have a decisive influence on German thinking during the remaining years of the nineteenth century. For Hegel, Reason or Spirit was a synonym for divine providence, immanent in history and guiding its progressive development from lower to higher stages of rational self-consciousness and freedom, *achieving its highest stage in the Prussian state*. The process by which Reason manifests itself in history is through the struggle of opposites, operating in historical development as it does in dialogue.

Hegel encapsulated the dialectical character of his philosophy in his celebrated aphorism: "what is real is rational and what is rational is real." This utterance contained a fundamental ambiguity that his conservative and radical followers interpreted to suit their respective ideological purposes. Emphasizing the real – the existing state – appealed to the conservatives concerned with justifying the status quo. Stressing the other half of the aphorism – that the "rational is real," that the rational is a revolutionary process accounting for history's ascent to higher and higher forms of human association – impressed the radicals. The Prussian conservatives embraced the first part of Hegel's formula, including his apotheosis of the Prussian state, which included or implied the Lutheran doctrine of strict obedience and submission to the temporal authorities. The most radical thinker of the time who appropriated the second half of the formula was Karl Marx – to whom we shall return in due course (chapter 18).

Hegel on Jews and Judaism

Hegel's criticisms of Judaism are directed against its so-called "oriental," "national" exclusiveness, criticisms that were first heard in pre-Christian antiquity and then again in the writings of the Church Fathers. Hegel found offensive, for example, the solemnity and "idleness" of the Sabbath:

> the three great yearly festivals, celebrated for the most part with feasts and dances, are the most human element in Moses' policy; but the solemnity of every seventh day is very characteristic. To slaves, this rest from work must be welcome, a day of idleness after six days full of labor. But for living men, otherwise free, to keep one day in a complete vacuum[?], in an inactive unity of spirits, to make the time dedicated to god an empty [?] time, and to let this vacuity return every so often – this could only occur to the legislator of a people for whom the melancholy, unfelt unity is the supreme reality. (Poliakov, III, 183)

Is it possible, Poliakov asks, that this serious philosopher failed to understand that the Jewish Sabbath is not a day in a "complete vacuum," an "empty time"? Did he fail to understand that the Sabbath was a day devoted to Spirit rather than Matter; devoted to worship of the Divine and to a study of the Lord's commandments, and how best to observe them in changing and diverse circumstances? Ironically, it is this failed understanding of Hegel's that prompts him to accuse Judaism of failing to recognize a Spirit:

> Spirit alone recognizes spirit. They [the Jews] saw in Jesus only the man, the Nazarene, the carpenter's son whose brothers and kinfolk lived among them; so much he was, and more he could not be, for he was only like themselves, and they felt themselves to be nothing. The Jewish multitude was bound to wreck his attempt to give them the consciousness of something divine, for faith in something divine, something great, cannot make its home in a dunghill. The lion has no room in a nest, the infinite spirit none in the prison of a Jewish soul. (Ibid., 184)

"They saw in Jesus only the man!" Did the erudite Hegel not know that in the messianic Idea of Israel the Messiah is a human being – an extraordinary human, but nevertheless human? And did he himself – at least in his youth in the Berne and other essays – not reject the Christian doctrine of Incarnation, signifying that God became man?

Hegel was a student of the world religions, East and West. In his *Philosophy of History*, he surveyed the cultures and religions of China, India, Persia, the Assyrians, Babylonians and Medes, as well as Syria,

Semitic Western Asia, Judea, Egypt, and, finally, the Greek, Roman, and Germanic worlds. In his analyses of these cultures, he asserted that they were too "sense-bound." They represented themselves in a "primitively sensual fashion" and therefore had inadequately fulfilled the needs of the human spirit. These world religions had failed to ripen and mature so as to include what Hegel considered to be essential, namely, *rational thought.* Hegel's assertion raises an unavoidable question: how can he feel justified in characterizing biblical Judaism as "sense-bound" and "primitively sensual," when the biblical and, indeed, the post-biblical conception of God is of a *formless, invisible, incorporeal,* almighty, ethical presence? And if "rational thought" is Hegel's essential criterion for fulfilling the needs of the human spirit, what could be more rational, as Max Weber observed, than the covenantal relationship between God and humanity and the this-worldly nature of God's promises?

Hegel, like many nineteenth-century thinkers, subscribed to a theory of *social* evolutionism and progress, a theory that cultures have evolved from the beginning of history, from lower to higher stages. It is quite clear, however, that from a moral standpoint such theories can find no support in historical evidence. The human species is murderously divided against itself no less today than it ever has been. To "test" Hegel's theory and recognize its fallaciousness, it is enough to ask in what sense the genocidal twentieth century was an advance over the nineteenth century. Hegel explicitly applies the notion of social evolution and progress to the world religions. But it is doubtful in the extreme that such theories are anything but subjective and arbitrary. As applied to Judaism and Christianity, a Hegelian evolutionist theory implies a form of "super-sessionism": the daughter is an advance over the mother. Indeed, for Hegel, Christianity is the highest form of religious consciousness. And yet the young Hegel's most striking criticism of Christian doctrine was the contradiction between Reason's teaching that a life of virtue and justice is its own reward, and Christianity's freedom-denying doctrine that original sin precludes our being good. For the young Hegel, the other objectionable element of the Christian doctrine is that happiness, if it is to be found at all, can be achieved only in an afterlife, where it is dispensed by the grace of the Deity. Finally, for the young Hegel, even the doctrine of the historical actuality of Christ, made into an article of faith and a condition of salvation, offends reason and common sense because of its "esoteric, authoritarian and exclusionary character."[5] It appears, however, that the older Hegel had repudiated his early views.

---

[5] See G. W. F. Hegel, *Three Essays, 1793–1795,* ed. and transl. with an Introduction and notes by Peter Fuss and John Dobbins, Notre Dame, IN.: University of Notre Dame Press, 1984, Introduction.

It is indisputable that for Hegel the "Oriental" cultures were the most primitively sensual and the least developed where reason, freedom, and universality were concerned. He thus describes biblical Judaism as possessing

> a "servile consciousness" resting obstinately on its particularity, so that God is the exclusive Lord and God of the Jewish people. It need not surprise us that an Oriental people should limit religion to itself, and that this religion should appear as absolutely connected with its nationality, for we see this in Eastern countries in general . . . Still this exclusiveness is rightly regarded as more striking in the case of the Jewish people, for such strong attachment to nationality is in complete contradiction with the idea that God is to be conceived of only in universal thought, and not in one particular characterization. (Poliakov, III, 513)

Hegel knew, however, that he could not stop there without acknowledging that

> It is true that amongst the Jewish people, too, consciousness rises to the thought of universality, and this thought is given expression to in several places . . . So now this limitation is explained for us from the nature of the *servile consciousness*; and we see, too, now, how this particularity arises from the subjective side. (Ibid.)

In the italicized phrase "servile consciousness" I call attention to Hegel's deprecation of that consciousness, thus failing, apparently, to recognize that the slavery of the Israelites in Egypt was precisely the archetypal experience that gave rise to the foundational, ethical principles of Hebrew monotheism; principles raised to the highest level and accentuated by the Hebrew prophets of social justice.

Hence, when Hegel asserts in the quoted passage that, in biblical Judaism, "universality . . . was given expression in several places," his polemical aim of putting down Judaism prevails over his purportedly moral commitment to his calling as a philosopher dedicated to the pursuit of truth. Any reader of the Hebrew prophets from Amos to Jeremiah will readily recognize in their messages the centrality of universalism. One example should suffice. Isaiah of Jerusalem, writing in the eighth century BCE, states "that the mountain of the Lord's house shall be established in the top of the mountains, and shall be exalted above the hills; and *all nations shall flow unto it*" (Isaiah 2:2).

One more word is in order concerning Hegel's characterization of biblical Judaism's "Oriental," particularistic consciousness in which its religion appeared intimately connected with its nationality. That there is no contradiction in such a connection should have been clear to Hegel as a student of the *histories* of religion. In the concrete historical circumstances of the biblical and post-biblical epochs, the struggles of the Hebrews with the neighboring peoples and with the imperial powers such as Assyria and Babylonia – and later with Rome – gave rise naturally to the Judean's group-feeling as a nationality.

Finally, was Hegel unaware of how "absolutely connected" were religion and nationality in his own religious-philosophical outlook? "Reason" or "Spirit" was for him a synonym for the immanent, divine providence guiding history onward and upward until it achieved the highest stage of rational self-consciousness and freedom. And where, for Hegel, did it attain its highest stage? In the Prussian state!

18

The Left Hegelians and the so-called "Jewish Question"

The 20 years between 1830 and 1850 in Europe, and especially in France, began and ended with revolution. In Germany, the chief impulse to political agitation came from France. Stimulated by the revolutionary events in that country, associations and clubs of young students emerged in Germany during the 1830s and 1840s in opposition to the monarchy, the nobility, and the Church. Among these clubs was a group of young intellectuals who earlier had been profoundly influenced by Hegel's philosophy, but who now found Hegel too conservative. The group came to be called the Left Hegelians because they retained certain elements of Hegel's dialectical philosophy but rejected his philosophical idealism and the political conservatism of his mature writings.

As we look back on those writings, it would be hard to deny that Hegel's outlook had taken a conservative turn. In 1806, Hegel left Jena after Napoleon's victory over the Prussians. Most Hegel scholars are inclined to agree that Hegel's attitude toward life was thereafter shaped by the events that followed the defeat of Prussia, and that his thinking increasingly reflected the transition from the revolutionary to the reactionary era in the political history of Europe.

If, for instance, we take Hegel's view of the state and, in particular, the Prussian state as the embodiment of the highest form of Reason, it seems clear, as Richard Kroner has observed, that Hegel's "belief in civil liberty was limited by his belief in the superior prerogative of the nation at large. He therefore defines the state as the perfect totality of the nation." From Hegel's conception of history shaped by providence, Kroner continues,

a certain quietism resulted, satisfaction with actual conditions. It cannot be denied that in this acquiescent attitude a danger is involved. What we call "historicism" – a belief in the absolute determination of the historical process against which the will of man is powerless – is certainly a symptom of weariness and pessimism. Though Hegel was not a historicist in that sense, he opened the door to this unbalanced philosophy.[1]

Moreover, like other close students of Hegel, Kroner avers that "a presentiment of weariness and decay does seem to have haunted Hegel at the height of his maturity, as it haunted Goethe and other contemporaries." Kroner cites a famous passage from Hegel's preface to his *Philosophy of Right*:

> When philosophy paints gray in gray, a form of life has become old, and this gray in gray cannot be rejuvenated, only understand it. The owl of Minerva begins its flight [or spreads its wings] with the falling of dusk. (65–6)

And Kroner comments:

> This is a melancholy consideration, after a life devoted to the discovery of truth and the advocacy of freedom and right. We may lament this resignation. But the author of these words may well have had a foreboding of what was in store for Germany and the whole continent. (Ibid.)

The Left Hegelians, as we have said, reacted against the conservative side of Hegel's thought and against his philosophical idealism. The most prominent members of the group were Ludwig Feuerbach, Bruno Bauer, Max Stirner, David Friedrich Strauss, Karl Marx, and Søren Kierkegaard. Their assault upon the religious premises of the existing order had far-reaching effects on the development of a radical secularism and existentialism. All of these men, with the exception of Kierkegaard, were thoroughgoing materialists who paid a personal price for their radicalism. Feuerbach, Bauer, and Stirner were dismissed from their teaching positions, and Marx and Kierkegaard were reduced to the direst of circumstances. Marx was driven into exile, living often in jeopardy of the police. Probably the loneliest figure among them was Kierkegaard, a Dane, who first had been an admirer of Hegel's and who then turned against him, seeking God in solitude.

The significant writings of this group were concentrated in the 1840s. Their general point of departure was the second half of Hegel's formula, that the "rational is the real." From a dialectical standpoint, this meant

---

[1] G. W. F. Hegel, *Early Theological Writings*, transl. T. M. Knox, with an introduction and fragments transl. by Richard Kroner, Chicago, IL: University of Chicago Press, 1948, 65. Hereafter, page references to this work will be cited in parentheses immediately following the quoted passage.

that all institutions, religions, and philosophies, as expressions of the onward march of reason, have no special sanctity in themselves; they are transitory, marking only the transition to Reason's next creations. Like all social forms, Christianity, capitalism, and the state will be transcended by superior forms. For every positive historical form, its negation can be projected.

The assault on existing values and institutions was directed first against religion as the source of the sanctity of existing political and social forms. In Germany from the time of Luther, as we have seen, religion had provided legitimization formulae for temporal authority and the state; and now Hegel sought to cement the union of religion with the state by making universal reason culminate in Protestant Christianity and the Prussian state. In their repudiation of this conclusion of Hegel's, the Left Hegelians employed Hegel's own dialectical logic to refute the identity of Reason and actuality, and in so doing contributed substantially to the undermining of faith in traditional Christianity. They went even farther, by exposing what they regarded as religious and philosophical illusions in general.

In a sense Hegel himself had provided these opponents with the weapons they employed against him: he had made reason the paramount means by which to know the divine spirit and its manifestations in history. For, although Hegel believed that revelation is the ultimate source of our knowledge of right and wrong, he tended in the end, in such works as *The Phenomenology of Mind*, to subordinate revelation to Reason. Hence, as Kroner has remarked, "Divine inspiration seems no longer necessary when reason can provide what, in the biblical view, can be taught only by the prophet" (54). At the end of the *Phenomenology*, Kroner suggests, the supplanting of revelation by reason seems to imply a shift of the center of gravity from God to man.

Bruno Bauer on the "Jewish Question"

Bauer was a leading member of the Left Hegelian circle.[2] His critical analyses of the first three Gospels and of the New Testament in general are still treated with respect by scholars. To understand why the status of Jews in Germany was discussed by Bauer and others, we have to recall that Germany of the 1840s consisted of many autonomous principalities

---

[2] For brief expositions of the ideas of the Left Hegelians, see Irving M. Zeitlin, *The Religious Experience: Classical Philosophical and Social Theories*, Upper Saddle River, NJ: Pearson/Prentice Hall, 2004.

ruled by kings, the landed nobility, and the Church, the people being subjects not citizens. One of the principal preoccupations of the Left Hegelians was, therefore, how to bring about in the Germanies the level of political emancipation that France had achieved.

In *Die Judenfrage* (*The Jewish Question*) (1843), Bauer rejected the demand of German Jews and liberal Germans to grant the Jews civil rights. Jews had been living in the German principalities since the thirteenth century, if not earlier. Because they were not only a conspicuous non-Christian minority, but also despised as the alleged killers of Christ, they were ghettoized and treated by the authorities as a "guest people" residing in Germany on sufferance. As was the case in other European countries from the time of the Middle Ages, the guest status was granted or withdrawn depending on whether the rulers regarded the Jews as economically useful. In the early nineteenth century, the Jews still had no civil rights in the Germanies. They were, for example, excluded from the universities. The few Jews who had gained admission to the universities were, in effect, non-Jews, since their fathers or they themselves had converted to Protestantism. In the German states of the time, being a Christian was a precondition for citizenship and, therefore, for entry into the educational institutions and the liberal professions.

When Bauer rejected granting to the Jews equal civil rights, he grounded his objection in theological arguments, asserting, under Hegelian influence, that Judaism was an insurmountable obstacle to the participation of Jews in the development of modern life. Viewing Judaism as a relic of a bygone era, Bauer held that although Judaism had possessed some validity in the world of the ancient Hebrews, that validity was historically limited and relative, for with the appearance of Jesus of Nazareth and the early Christian community, Judaism was superseded once and for all.

From Bauer's standpoint, contemporary Jews clung stubbornly to their superannuated faith because their "Oriental nature" dictated such an attitude. Following Hegel in that regard, Bauer maintained that the denizens of the Orient had yet to recognize that they were free and gifted with reason. Given, therefore, the Oriental nature of the Jews, they were incapable of participating effectively in the shaping of the modern epoch. They had slavishly adhered to old casuistical doctrines and ritualistic practices, and had failed, consequently, to keep apace of modern, historical developments.

As a materialist, atheist, and critic of religion in general, Bauer insisted that in order for the Jews to become citizens they would first have to become atheists. He proposed this, he said, not out of any anti-Jewish animus, but in the best interest of the Jews. Treating Judaism as an exception to the rule that *all* religions must be subjected to rational criticism would do the Jews more harm than good. Those who wished to spare the

Jews the pains of criticism were the worst enemies of the Jews. No one who had not gone through the fires of rational criticism would be able to enter the new world soon to come.

In Bauer's critique of Judaism, he follows Hegel's theory of four stages of religious development: the Oriental, the Greek, the Roman, and the German-Christian. Bauer accepts the Hegelian proposition that he is living in the German-Christian stage of history; for Bauer, however, this was a transitory stage that would soon be transcended by a higher stage in which religion was left behind altogether. Having, therefore, to address the status of Christianity in this developmental scheme, Bauer posits the appearance of Jesus as a turning point in the world history of religion.

Jesus, Bauer proposes, had identified his consciousness with that of God the Father. The early Christian community went one step farther by identifying itself as an entire united community with God. Theologically, Bauer interprets this as the beginning of the historical process in which a general union of humanity with God would be achieved. Thus, for Bauer, the fundamental difference between Judaism and Christianity was that, in Judaism, the separation of humanity from God was still in effect, insofar as God is conceived as beyond humanity; in contrast, Christianity, in the concept of the Incarnation, has elevated humanity to the level of the Divine. Christianity therefore represents the highest stage in the development of the world religions.

But for Bauer, however great this achievement of raising human consciousness and reducing the degree of separation of humanity from the Divine, it was inadequate, because it remained within the confined illusory framework of religion. The next and purportedly higher stage (the final and fully human stage), to which Bauer eagerly looked forward, would be a totally secularized consciousness – atheism, pure and simple. In Bauer's epoch, as he perceived it, atheism was still struggling for light and supremacy. Only an atheistic consciousness is a free consciousness for Bauer, and only a free consciousness could widen the boundaries of freedom in this world. Europe, Bauer believed, had in fact entered the highest stage in which Europeans would soon recognize the notion of the Divine for what it is – a manifestation of human self-alienation.

It followed, for Bauer, that Judaism stands in the way of this emancipatory process theologically as well as politically. As Judaism represents a throwback to the Oriental stage, Jews must make a dialectical leap into modernity. How? By abandoning their faith. Jews must, in a word, stop being Jews in order to achieve civil emancipation. Christians, in contrast, possessing a less alienated consciousness, need take only a few baby steps in order to enter the modern era.

The German states of the time were, however, Christian, not secular. The equality of opportunity implied by citizenship was not a right in

Germany that had to be granted to non-Christians. Bauer insisted that the gaining of political equality in citizenship was a project of enlightenment. Political equality may be attained only by those who, whether Christians or Jews, are prepared to struggle for a free (i.e., atheistic) consciousness. The followers of both faiths are subjects of a Christian state and therefore not free. As Marx (to whom we shall soon return), in his rather lucid and concise rendering of Bauer's position observed:

> The Christian state, by its very nature, is incapable of emancipating the Jews. But, adds Bauer, the Jew, by his very nature, cannot be emancipated. As long as the state remains Christian, and as long as the Jew remains a Jew, they are equally incapable, the one of conferring emancipation, the other of receiving it.[3]

For Bauer, as for Feuerbach and the other materialists of the Left Hegelian circle, it is owing to the distorted mirror of religious belief that humans diminish their own creative powers by assigning them to a chimerical realm in the heavens. This sad reality is no less evident in Christian states. For there, too, instead of serving humans by granting them true citizenship, the state subjugates them. These critics recognized that this situation has been the case in Germany since the time of Luther who first inspired the desire for freedom in the people and then turned against them, siding with the princes when the people rose up in the revolts of the sixteenth century. So Bauer regards Christianity as an ideology with definite political implications. Christianity has not only undermined self-confidence and discouraged self-mastery, but it has favored the interests of the privileged and powerful against those of the poor and the weak. Originally, Christianity showed promise of becoming a great step forward in human self-understanding and in the expansion of freedom, as in the early Church's institution of social equality and communal property. This promise, however, was never fulfilled. Instead, Bauer avers, from the time of Constantine to his own day, Christianity has served as an ideology in which the quest for freedom is no earthly endeavor. Christianity has failed as an emancipatory project by transferring the hope for salvation to the world beyond. But, though Christianity has failed in this respect, it is just a step away from a liberating, secular consciousness. That appeared to be true for Bauer because he believed that Reason and science were rapidly secularizing the minds

---

[3] Karl Marx, *Early Writings*, transl. and ed. T. B. Bottomore, London: C.A. Watts, 1963, 4. Hereafter, all page references to this work will be cited in parentheses immediately following the quoted passage.

of contemporary European Christians. The rational and moral elements of Christianity would become more and more prominent until they had finally supplanted Christianity as a religion. Judaism, however, was so out of step with the march of history, Bauer concludes, that the Jews should never be granted citizenship in the German states until and unless they willingly make the conscious dialectical leap into atheism.

Marx

Marx agreed with Feuerbach (and Bauer) that criticism of religion as an ideology was necessary before one could proceed to a criticism of society, for religion had throughout history served dominant groups as a primary means of turning away the oppressed and exploited from remedying their circumstances in the present, by offering them the illusory prospect of a heavenly paradise. But in his response to Bauer, we can see how Marx, as early as 1843, was breaking away from the Left Hegelians and developing a theoretical position of his own.

Marx's rejoinder is divided into two parts, the first of which is rigorously argued without any virulent epithets hurled at the Jews. In the second part, however, he attacks the capitalist society of his time, denouncing it as "Jewish" because it is dominated by money, by the callous, cash nexus. In that context he employs, as we shall see, a whole range of vituperative, anti-Jewish rhetoric. His father had converted to Christianity when Karl was seven years of age, which led, somehow, to a form of Jew-hatred rooted in self-hatred.

In Marx's critique he observes that Bauer had considered the "Jewish Question" from only one aspect. For Marx, it was by no means sufficient to ask "who should emancipate?" and "who should be emancipated?" because a third question of moment needed to be addressed: "what kind of emancipation are we talking about?" Marx saw it as an error that Bauer criticized the Christian state, but not the state as such. Bauer had failed to examine the relation of political to human emancipation. Marx therefore asks: for the aim of achieving *political* emancipation must the Jew be required to abandon Judaism, and the Christians compelled to abolish their faith? Marx is thus challenging the notion that, in gaining citizenship, individuals should have to pay the price of giving up their religious beliefs and practices.

In Germany, Marx observes, where the many autonomous principalities are all *Christian* states, none of them is a political state in the constitutional sense in which such a state had already existed in the United States and in France. In the German states, the Jew finds himself in *religious* opposition to the state, which proclaims Christianity as its foundation. In

France, in contrast, which is a *constitutional* state, the Jewish question is a constitutional one: *of the incompleteness of political emancipation.* Marx's meaning here is that in France, despite the Declaration of the Rights of Man and the Code Napoleon's granting of equal rights to all citizens, the Jews were often treated as second-class citizens. Although constitutionally there was no official state religion in France, the vast majority of the citizens were Christian, with the corresponding, historically inherited, anti-Jewish prejudices. There was, therefore, the semblance of a state religion. Hence, the relation of the French state to the Jews retained at the time a form of religious-theological opposition.

It followed for Marx that it was only in America that the so-called Jewish question tended to lose its theological significance. It was quite evident to Marx that where freedom of religion was concerned, the political state appeared in its purest form in America, where the state ceased, constitutionally, to maintain a theological attitude toward the religion of its citizens and adopted a secular attitude.

Marx cites the work of Gustave Beaumont, who had visited America together with his friend, Alexis de Tocqueville. On religion in America, Beaumont observed, "there is not in the United States, either a state religion or a religion declared to be that of a majority, or a predominance of one religion over another. The state remains aloof from all religions." In no state in North America, Beaumont commented, does one find the imposition of a "religious belief or practice as a condition of political rights." On the authority of Beaumont, Tocqueville, and an Englishman, Thomas Hamilton, Marx observed what is still true today: "And North America is pre-eminently the country of religiosity" (Marx, *Early Writings*, 9). Marx thus used the example of America to make a significant point: "If we find in the country that has attained full political emancipation, that religion not only continues to exist, but is *fresh* and *vigorous*, this is proof that the existence of religion is not at all opposed to the perfection of the state" (ibid., 10).

To grasp adequately what Marx is saying here, we have to keep his example of America in mind. How does a state emancipate itself from religion? By liberating itself from the imposition of a *state religion*; by giving official recognition to *no* religion, and by affirming itself purely as a state based on constitutionally determined civil laws granting equal civil rights to all citizens. But in anticipation of his mature social theory, Marx adds that even this high level of political liberty falls short, in his judgment, of the fuller human freedom that he envisioned. In the context of his debate with Bauer, he wants therefore to expose what he regards as the limitations of the existing state, even the most liberal and democratic. Marx again cites Thomas Hamilton who had reported that in several American states property qualifications for electors and representatives were abolished: the people had gained a victory over the property owners and financial wealth. So the mature, radical Marx wants to underscore that, as welcome as such expansions of political democracy are, they fall short of his ideal because what is presupposed in eliminating property qualifications is that private property will remain intact.

In opposition to Bauer, then, and for all of Marx's positing of a communistic ideal, we need to observe that he fully recognized the virtues of political liberty and civil rights, and the highest form in which they expressed themselves in America. (Marx recognized the contradiction of the existence of slavery in a democratic republic; but that contradiction is not directly relevant to the subject of his essay.) Citizenship, Marx had shown Bauer, does not at all require the abolition of religion. Bauer's views had never transcended the standpoint of the Christian state.

But Bauer's views were even more narrow-minded than that, for he had asserted that the Jew is not only unfit for equal civil rights, but unfit as well for human rights – what the French Constitution called the "rights of man," freedom of conscience and opinion. "As long as he remains Jewish," wrote Bauer, "the limited nature which makes him a Jew must prevail over the human nature which should associate him, as a man, with other men; and it will isolate him from everyone who is not a Jew" (Marx, *Early Writings*, 25). This statement of Bauer's is reminiscent of the age-old resentment of the Jews' self-segregation in the diaspora, owing to dietary and other ordinances that made commensalism and connubium so difficult without conversion to Judaism. It is therefore truly noteworthy that Marx responds effectively by stressing that "liberty as a right of man is founded not upon the relations between man and man, but rather upon the *separation of man from man. It is the right of such separation*" (ibid., 25; italics added). In other words, in an open, liberal and democratic society such as America, if citizens wish to live in their own distinctive religious or ethnic communities, that is their right.

Marx's Use of the Terms "Jew" and "Judaism"

Sidney Hook, in his *From Hegel to Marx*, stated that "Although Marx was free of anti-Semitic prejudice he unfortunately was not oversensitive to using the term 'Jew,' often with unsavory adjectives, as an epithet of abuse" (278, fn.2). Hook's statement is too generous, overlooking, as it does, Marx's truly vicious rhetoric where Jews and Judaism are concerned. In part two of his rejoinder to Bauer, Marx asks: what is the secular basis of "Judaism"? And he replies: self-interest, egoism, huckstering, money – capitalism. The essence of the emerging socio-economic system that Marx called "capitalism" was such that human worth was measured by the value of one's money, commodities, and capital. Hence, the sense in which Marx used the terms "Jew" and "Judaism" was this: as capitalism expanded, all civil society was becoming dominated by the so-called "Jewish" *practical* spirit.

Now what is strikingly bizarre about Marx's attributing the capitalist spirit to the Jews is that in his essay he cites – as we have seen – Thomas Hamilton's *Men and Manners in North America* to demonstrate the extent to which Mammon had become the idol of the devout, Protestant New Englander:

> In his view the world is no more than a Stock Exchange, and he is convinced that he has no other destiny here below than to become richer than his neighbor. Trade has seized upon all his thoughts, and he has no other recreation than to exchange objects. When he travels he carries, so to speak, his goods and his counter on his back and talks only of interest and profit. If he loses sight of his own business for an instant it is only in order to pry into the business of his competitors. (Marx, *Early Writings*, 35)

Indeed, as we have seen, Marx also cited Beaumont and the more distinguished Tocqueville who had visited America in the 1830s, and produced soon afterward his classic *Democracy in America*. In that work, Tocqueville also remarked on the connection between religion and commerce in the United States. "Americans," he wrote, "follow their religion from interest." American preachers are always "referring to the earth, and it is only with great difficulty that they can divert their attention from it." Describing their discourses, Tocqueville continues: "It is often difficult to ascertain . . . whether the principal object of religion is to procure eternal felicity in the other world or prosperity in this."[4] America, Tocqueville observed, was uniquely Puritan and bourgeois. He noted frequently the predominantly Puritan background of the independent merchants and entrepreneurs. The values of Puritanism, on the one hand, and of commerce and industry, on the other, appeared to be not only compatible but mutually reinforcing. Although Tocqueville includes other elements that contributed to the pronounced *practical* temperament of Americans, he mentions first their "strictly puritanical origin [and] their exclusively commercial habits" (ibid., 36–7). These people, wrote Tocqueville, spend "every day of the week in making money and Sunday in going to church" (83).

---

[4] *Democracy in America*, vol. 2 (New York: Knopf, 1948), 127.

Weber vs Sombart on the Spirit of Capitalism

What we have here, in Hamilton and Tocqueville, is an anticipation of Max Weber's *The Protestant Ethic and the Spirit of Capitalism*. There he documents the thesis that it was the post-Calvinist, ascetic Protestant denominations such as the Baptists, Quakers, Mennonites, Methodists, and others who, owing to the Puritan idea of the *calling*, and the extraordinary value it assigned to ascetic conduct, profoundly influenced the development of capitalism. For the Puritan, Weber wrote, the pursuit of wealth as an end in itself was highly reprehensible,

> but the attainment of it as the fruit of labor in a calling was a sign of God's blessing. And even more important: the religious valuation of restless, continuous, systematic work in a worldly calling, as the highest means to asceticism, and at the same time the surest and most evident proof of rebirth and genuine faith, must have been the most powerful conceivable lever for the expansion of that attitude toward life which we have here called the spirit of capitalism.[5]

When acquisitive activity was thus positively sanctioned, and a severe limitation was morally imposed upon consumption, there was an unavoidable practical result: capital was accumulated due to the ascetic compulsion to save.

Weber's thesis has stood the test of time, whereas Werner Sombart's has not. The latter's *The Jews and Modern Capitalism* is misleading and wrong with regard to the last two words of Sombart's title. The Jews played a significant role in the commerce and money-lending of the Middle Ages and the later decades of the pre-modern era. But beginning in the seventeenth century and continuing in the eighteenth century, during and after the Industrial Revolution, it was the Puritan entrepreneurs, as Weber has shown, who imparted to early industrial capitalism its dynamic quality. This was the result of the religiously motivated pursuit of their industrial and other business activities in a morally dutiful manner, and their ascetic way of life.

Marx, as we have seen, was aware of Hamilton's and, most likely, of Tocqueville's recognition of Puritanism's affinity for capitalism. The evidence for this is strong. In *Capital* he wrote:

---

[5] Max Weber, *The Protestant Ethic and the Spirit of Capitalism*, transl. Talcott Parsons and introduced by Anthony Giddens, London and New York: Routledge, 1995, 172. For a full exposition of Weber's sociology of religion East and West, see Irving M. Zeitlin, *The Religious Experience: Classical Philosophical and Social Theories*, Upper Saddle River, NJ, Pearson/Prentice Hall, 2004.

For a society based upon the production of commodities, in which the producers in general enter into social relations with one another by treating their products as commodities and values, whereby they reduce their individual private labor to the standard of homogeneous human labor – for such a society, *Christianity* with its cultus of abstract man, more especially in its bourgeois developments, *Protestantism, Deism*, etc. is the most fitting form of religion.[6]

It is clear, then, that the mature Marx was aware of the principal Christian Protestant role in the development of modern capitalism. Given that fact, the conclusion seems to be unavoidable that Marx's equation of capitalism with Judaism, and his anti-Jewish rhetoric more generally, were motivated by his self-consciousness as a Jew, a form of self-hatred.

From his earliest writings and *continuing in his most mature work*, he finds opportunities for gratuitous, anti-Jewish remarks. In the first of his theses on Feuerbach, Marx says that Feuerbach "regards the theoretical attitude as the only genuinely human attitude, while practice is conceived and fixed only in its dirty Jewish manifestation." It is true that this and a few other writings of his youth were abandoned, as he and Engels remarked, to the "gnawing criticism of the mice," and never published in Marx's lifetime. But late in his life he continued to make contemptuous remarks about Jews and Judaism. In *Capital* he wrote: "the capitalist knows that all merchandise . . . is money, internally circumcised Jews" (vol. I, ch. 4). In his correspondence the contempt is shown until his death: "The Jew Steinthal, with the bland smile" (1857); "the cursed Jew of Vienna [Max Friedländer]" (1859); "the author, that pig of a Berlin journalist, is a Jew by the name of Meier" (1860). Leon Poliakov cites even more: Marx's doctor was described as a Jew because he was pressing for payment (1854). If he whom he called a "Jew" happened to be a Jew, it was worse: Bamberger formed part "of the Stock Exchange synagogue of Paris"; Fould was a "Stock Exchange Jew"; Oppenheimer was "the Jew Süss of Egypt." And the contempt for Lasalle, a political rival, brought out the worst quasi-racist remarks: "the shape of his head and his hair show that he was descended from the Negroes"; "he was the most barbarous of all Yids from Poland"; or he was Lazarus the leper who, in his turn, was "the primitive type of Jew" (Poliakov, III, 425f). There is a certain irony in the fact – and perhaps that is what also irritated him – that Marx's friends and disciples drew attention to his Jewishness. His son-in-law, Dr Paul Lafarque, even claimed he could

---

[6] Karl Marx, *Capital*, vol. I (Moscow: Foreign Languages Publishing House, 1954), 79.

discern Jewish "racial" features in the proportions of Marx's body (ibid., III, 426).

Perhaps what is saddest about Marx's Jewish self-loathing and anti-Semitism is that he failed to recognize, or refused to acknowledge, how deeply rooted was his secular eschatology in the visions of the Hebrew prophets of social justice.

19

From Religion to Race

During the long era in which the Jews of Europe had been ghettoized or otherwise segregated from the Christian populace, they were despised for theological reasons and for the economic role into which they had been forced. In the eyes of the Christian onlookers, the Jews were strikingly different in all respects and were, accordingly, objects of contempt or hatred. However, despite their pariah status during that long era, the Jews were nevertheless viewed by their detractors, even the severest of them, as all too human, as possessing all the attributes of human nature. All that was required for the expiation of their sins and for their redemption was to accept Christ.

It is, therefore, an especially interesting fact that it was only after the Jews had been granted emancipation, and were able to mix freely in bourgeois European society, that their status changed qualitatively: from a religiously despised caste to an anthropologically inferior "race." To appreciate how this process of redefining the nature of the Jews emerged, a partial parallel in the history of Afro-Americans might be illuminating.

Afro-American and Jewish Parallels

The enslavement of blacks evolved slowly and gradually in the colonies. Indeed, a few blacks lived in the South many years before chattel slavery emerged as a legal institution. The first black settlers found a niche for themselves that carried with it no racial prejudice. Some owned land, voted, testified in court, and interacted with whites on a more or less equal basis, while others became servants. At first their status was not unlike that of white servants: they gained their freedom after several years of service or with conversion to Christianity. It is true that even at that early stage their servitude was often more severe, with longer and even more indefinite terms. But the greater severity of black servitude merely reflected the fact that, as compared with the white indentured servants, their coming to

America was not a matter of free choice. Nevertheless as Kenneth Stampp has observed, "The Negro and white servants of the 17th century seemed to be remarkably unconcerned about their visible physical differences."[1]

With time, however, clear distinctions between white and black bondsmen did appear. Blacks lacked the protection of the English government; and they had no written indentures defining their rights and limiting their terms of service. Hence, relatively unprotected, they were increasingly subjected to special treatment. In the 1660s, the first legal distinctions between white and black servants were made. New laws were passed stipulating that blacks were to be slaves for life. In the following decades additional laws defined the slaves as property and conferred upon the master considerable power, reinforced by the white governing structure. In time, "Jim Crow" became a synonym for Negro. A great social barrier was erected between whites and blacks. Its purpose was to prevent interracial mixing of any kind and especially intermarriage.

Especially interesting for our purposes, however, is the relatively recent origin of racial segregation. As C. Van Woodward has shown in his highly original book, *The Strange Career of Jim Crow*, such segregation had never existed in the slavery era. It emerged considerably later. So long as blacks were slaves, their social status was clear and unambiguous. Blacks and whites living and working together entailed no threat to the status and power of the whites. But following the Civil War and the Emancipation Proclamation, when the black man became a citizen, a threat to white status and power was recognized. Something had to be done to keep the blacks in their traditionally subordinate place; for now black men had become the rivals of white men occupationally, sexually, and otherwise, thus threatening, in addition, their psychological sense of superiority.

The parallels are clear: so long as the Jews were segregated in ghettos, they constituted no threat to the "host" peoples of Europe. But when the Jews were emancipated and had become citizens with equal rights, a strenuous effort had to be made to keep them in their traditionally subordinate place. In the case of the Jews, however, it was under the influence of the so-called scientific anthropology of the time that they were redefined and turned into a distinct "race."

With the emancipation of European Jews, antipathy toward them became even more marked than before. Such consequences of Enlightenment secularism were unanticipated and disappointing to the Jews. The rationale for hating the Jews was no longer explicitly theological; *but* the new rationale was nonetheless rooted in the fact that the Jews

---

[1] Kenneth Stampp, *The Peculiar Institution*, New York: Vintage Books, 1956, 21–2.

had been, historically, a theologically condemned caste. It was especially those *philosophes* who were more extreme skeptics like Voltaire, or materialists and atheists like Holbach and La Mettrie, who paved the way to the "scientific," "racial" conception of the Jews. These influential thinkers did so by attacking the foundations of the Western table of values; not only Christianity but also its mother, Judaism. Repudiating religion implied that it had to be replaced with a rational, materialistic, scientific approach to all things human. But, as we know, the earliest stages of anthropological thinking were transparently ideological, taking a negative view of all societies except the white ones of Europe.

In nearly all the countries affected by the French Revolution, the liberation of the "pariahs" aroused anxieties and recriminations on the part of the non-Jews. In Germany, for example, the Jews' efforts to assimilate, to cease to be Jews, often had a frightening effect: the more like the Christians they became, the more threatening they appeared to be. Just as the black Americans appeared to have become more threatening and frightening *after* emancipation – especially to the poor whites – so did the emancipated Jews evoke a similar reaction. It was especially their success in the diverse spheres of urban economic life, their notable rise to high positions, that raised the tension and increased the resentment of the Jews' new freedom of opportunity. It was in this historical context that Jewish emancipation itself came under attack. The Jews were not only successful, but were becoming rich and powerful, so powerful that they were planning to rule the planet – alleged, as we shall see, in the forgeries titled *The Protocols of the Elders of Zion*. The reaction to Jewish emancipation gave rise to a pseudo-scientific theory of "Aryanism," and the inequality of the human races, cultures, and languages – all of this to provide a "scientific" rationale for separating the racially superior "Aryans" from all other humans.

Arthur de Gobineau

It was Gobineau who pioneered in advancing racialist, anthropological theories in the guise of science. Rebutting the biblical view that originally there was one human language that became a "babble of tongues" due to divine punishment, Gobineau stated that "we cannot believe for a moment that the Altaic, Aryan and Semitic families were not from the first absolutely foreign to each other."[2] Gobineau rejects the view that the

---

[2] Arthur de Gobineau, *The Inequality of the Human Races*, transl. Adrian Collins, New York: Howard Fertig, 1967, 183. Hereafter, all page references to this work will be cited in parentheses immediately following the quoted passage.

human species started from some one point in its creation of idiom, and insists on many points of departure – so far, nothing necessarily objectionable. But soon we learn that his real aim in this chapter (XV) is not merely to propose that there are distinct languages and language groups, but that "different languages are unequal, and correspond perfectly in relative merit to the races that use them" (182f). The language of a race, Gobineau continues,

> is clearly bound up with its intelligence, and has the power of reflecting its various mental stages . . .
> Where the mental development of a race is faulty or imperfect, the language suffers to the same extent. This is shown by Sanskrit, Greek, and the Semitic group . . . the lack of precision in the Semitic tongues is exactly paralleled by the character of the Semitic peoples. (189)

H. Stewart Chamberlain was a disciple of Gobineau's, at least in the sense of his having been inspired by *The Inequality of the Human Races*. In the year 1900, Chamberlain published *The Foundations of the Nineteenth Century*, elevating "Aryanism" above all other races and devoting more than a hundred pages to the "Aryanism" of Jesus. Chamberlain's book became for Hitler and the Nazis their chief source for "scientific" knowledge about "races." In that light, it is worth noting the irony in the fact that Gobineau himself had neither attacked nor denigrated the Jews from his racialist standpoint. On the contrary, the Jews, he wrote,

> were surrounded by tribes speaking the dialects of a language cognate with their own, and for the most part closely connected with them in race; yet they outdistanced all these tribes. They became warriors, farmers, and traders. Their method of government was extremely complicated; it was a mixture of monarchy and theocracy, of patriarchal and democratic rule (the last being represented by the assemblies and the prophets), all in a curious equilibrium. Under this government they lived through the ages of prosperity and glory, and by a scientific system of emigration they conquered the difficulties . . . [imposed] by the narrow limits of their territory. And what kind of territory was it? Modern travelers know what an amount of organized effort was required from the Israelite farmers, in order to keep up its artificial fertility. Since the chosen race ceased to dwell in the mountains and the plains of Palestine, the well where Jacob's flocks came down to drink has been filled up with sand, Naboth's vineyard has been invaded by the desert, and the bramble flourishes in the place where stood the palace of Ahab. And what did the Jews become, in this miserable corner of the earth? They became a people that succeeded in everything it undertook, a free, strong, and intelligent people, and one which, before it lost, sword in

hand, the name of an independent nation, had given as many learned men to the world as it had merchants. (58–9)

Gobineau's encomium to the Jews does not, of course, change the fact that he had written a four-volume work that today is generally regarded as scientifically wrong. But there is an important difference between Gobineau and Chamberlain. As the Jews are the central subject matter of our inquiry, it is worth noting that although in Gobineau's frequent assertions concerning them he continues to insist that they are a "race," his assertions seem not to be motivated by hate. The Jews, he writes,

have settled in lands with very different climates from that of Palestine, and have given up their ancient mode of life. The Jewish type has, however, remained the same; . . . the warlike Rechoabites of the Arabian desert, the peaceful Portuguese, French, German and Polish Jews – they all look alike . . . the Semitic face looks exactly the same, in its main characteristics, as it appears on the Egyptian paintings of three or four thousand years ago, and more; . . . The identity of the descendant and ancestor does not stop at the features; it continues also in the shape of the limbs and the temperament. (122–3)

Gobineau rejected the principles of the French Revolution and viewed the egalitarian philosophy of the Enlightenment as hopelessly confused and misleading. The idea of the brotherhood of man was a vain and empty dream that never could be realized because it was based on a fallacious belief in the fundamental equality of human beings. Hence, in his introduction of the concept of "race" and his insistence on the inequality of "races," he created a most dangerous myth in addition: the notion of an "Aryan race." The gist of Gobineau's racialist theory can be grasped from the following passage:

Almost the whole of the Continent of Europe is inhabited at the present time [his book was published in 1853] by groups of which the basis is white, but in which the non-Aryan elements are the most numerous. There is no true civilization, amongst the European peoples, where the Aryan branch is not predominant.

. . . no negro race is seen as the initiator of a civilization. Only when it is mixed with some other can it even be initiated into one.

Similarly, no spontaneous civilization is to be found among the yellow races; and when the Aryan blood is exhausted, stagnation supervenes. (212)

Gobineau thus bears direct responsibility for the pernicious views that H. S. Chamberlain carried to an even greater extreme, thus becoming the ideological progenitor of Hitler's *Mein Kampf*. For Chamberlain, every race is destined to realize certain ends. In the case of the predominantly Aryan Germans, the chief end is universal domination, while all other "races" are destined to submit to enslavement by the German masters. Hitler, who, unsurprisingly, was much influenced in his racist thinking by Chamberlain's book, met him in Bayreuth in 1923. The author was greatly taken with the Austrian corporal and wrote him the following:

> You have mighty things to do . . . that in the hour of her deepest need Germany gives birth to a Hitler proves her vitality . . . May God protect you. (William Shirer, *The Rise and Fall of the Third Reich*, 109)

Alexis de Tocqueville, as a personal friend of Gobineau's, carried on a lengthy correspondence with him on the issues raised in the title of his book. Their respective views could not have been more sharply opposed. Indeed, there is, perhaps, no better evidence of Tocqueville's humane outlook than his rejection of racism in his *Democracy in America*, in the chapters on black Americans and the native peoples. For Tocqueville, the so-called "races" are ethnic groups, their differences due to the distinct cultures of which they are the recipients and the political regime to which they are subject. In America, Indians and blacks had been forced into inferior positions, and worse. None of the dehumanizing consequences of slavery had escaped Tocqueville's notice: they were deprived of all "privileges of humanity," of their historic memories, of something as fundamental as the family, and of their languages and customs – without, however, having been allowed any claim to positive, European cultural privileges.

After several years of correspondence with Gobineau, Tocqueville seems to have tired of the debate and of continually rejecting Gobineau's thesis. As a result, finally, Tocqueville wrote Gobineau a letter to the following effect:

> My dear friend: we have for a long time been debating the issues raised in your book. And I have concluded, frankly, that even if your view were scientifically correct, I still would have to reject it because I cannot think of any good that can come of it.

20

From Gobineau and
H. Stewart Chamberlain to Wagner

Gobineau had never concealed the motives prompting him to write his four-volume tract on the so-called inequality of the human races. He wrote at a tumultuous time, during the revolutions of 1848 in France when artisans and laborers were struggling to defend and advance their interests. His friend Tocqueville, in both of his classics – *Democracy in America* and *The Old Regime and the French Revolution* – had documented what he recognized as a historical master trend: a seemingly inexorable movement from aristocracy to democracy. He found the French form of this movement repugnant: the violent, bloody revolution followed by the Napoleonic dictatorship. Tocqueville witnessed the pattern again in 1848 and 1851 with the *coup d'état* of Louis Bonaparte. A major reason for Tocqueville's visit to America was to learn of the conditions that made it possible for democracy to establish itself there without internecine warfare. Although, like Gobineau, Tocqueville had come from an aristocratic background, he found himself able to admire the American form of democracy, with its many manifestations of freedom, and equality of opportunity.

Gobineau, in contrast, had never resigned himself to the master trend that Tocqueville had referred to as "providential." Gobineau looked upon his long essay on the inequality of the human races as a contribution to the great struggle against democracy, equality, and the working-class movements. In his pursuit of this anti-democratic aim, he sought to prove that the human race consists of natural castes in which the inferior must not presume to be equal to the superior.

Ever since their publication, Gobineau's writings had enjoyed a great reputation among those who, out of a vain conceit, were eager to hear his message. Among such individuals was the composer Richard Wagner who rejoiced when he learned of the "scientific" basis for his racist prejudices, encouraging and fortifying him in the production of his virulent and influential racist writings. As we have seen, Gobineau's thesis was taken over entirely and made even more vicious by Wagner's son-in-law,

Houston Stewart Chamberlain, in his *The Foundations of the Nineteenth Century* (1910).

Wagner, as he himself informs us, worked in his youth for the complete political emancipation of the Jews. But then something happened and he made a total reversal. In 1837, as an unknown artist, he formed a relationship with the famous Meyerbeer, 20 years his senior and king, at the time, of European opera. When Wagner left for Paris in 1839 to launch his career, Meyerbeer helped him generously, introducing him to musical circles and lending him money. The young musician accepted it as his entitlement: he could not imagine a better foster-father than a rich and amiable Jewish composer. While Meyerbeer continued to fulfill his role as a gracious patron, his protégé reached the point, somehow, of duplicity. At first, he was not yet openly anti-Semitic, only anti-Meyerbeer, despite his patron's continued work on Wagner's behalf, mounting *Rienzi* in Dresden and *The Flying Dutchman* in Berlin. Wagner thanked him publicly in the first edition of his *Autobiography*, and in a letter of February, 1842: "In all eternity I will never be able to say anything to you but thanks and thanks again" (Poliakov, III, 433). At about the same time, however, he wrote to Schumann that the work of his benefactor was a "spring whose mere smell repels me at a great distance." But he continued nonetheless to enjoy Meyerbeer's hospitality and to accept his services. In fact, since Wagner was always impecunious, he requested and received from his patron financial aid in 1848; but failing eventually in Paris, he returned to Dresden where he directed the opera.

In 1850 he published *Das Judentum in Der Musik*, his most influential book, which he introduces by apologizing for having turned his back on his revolutionary past, on his "aspiration to social liberty." He also comments on his earlier views of Jews:

> Even when we strove for emancipation of the Jews however, we were more the champions of an abstract principle than of a concrete case: just as all our liberalism was a not very lucid mental sport – since we went for freedom of the Folk without knowledge of that Folk itself, nay, with a dislike of any genuine contact with it – so our eagerness to level up the rights of Jews was far more stimulated by a general idea, than by any real sympathy. (Cited in Poliakov, III, 436)

Wagner's new theme is that the Jews dominate a degenerate society, and especially the art of that society:

> We have no need first to substantiate the be-Jewing of modern art; it springs to the eye, and thrusts itself upon the senses . . . But if emancipation from the yoke of Judaism appears to us the greatest of necessities, we must hold

that the most important thing is to prove our forces for the war of liberation. (Ibid.)

The cultural Jew has taken the greatest pains to strip off all the obvious tokens of his lower co-religionists: in many cases he has even held it wise to make a Christian baptism wash away the traces of his origin. This zeal, however, has never gone so far as to let him reap the hoped-for fruits; it has conduced only to his utter isolation, and to making him the most heartless of all human beings; to such a pitch, that we have been bound to lose even our earlier sympathy for the tragic history of his stock. (Ibid., 436–7)

But, as Poliakov remarks, the most treacherous thrusts are aimed at Meyerbeer without ever mentioning his name:

In general, uninspiring, the truly laughable, is the characteristic mark whereby the famed composer shows his Jewhood in his music. From a close survey of the instances adduced above – which we have been able to discover by seeking to justify our indomitable objection to the Jewish nature – a proof emerges for us of the ineptitude of the present musical epoch. (III, 437)

Even Mendelssohn, whom Wagner privately rated highly, had never been able "to call forth in us that deep, that heart-searching effect which we await from Art."

In his *Autobiography*, Wagner alleged that his *Das Judentum in der Musik* provoked a Jewish conspiracy against him, with Meyerbeer at its head. He attributed all the criticism and setbacks he experienced after 1851 to such a conspiracy. It is here, Poliakov observes, that Wagner, in the throes of a persecution mania, has become a "perfect anti-Semite." Liszt, in 1853, described to Princess Wittgenstein their mutual friend's new obsession:

He flung his arms around my neck, then he rolled on the ground, caressing his dog Pepi and talking nonsense to it, in between spitting on the Jews, who are a generic term with him, in a very broad sense. In a word, a grand and grandissimo character, something like Vesuvius. (III, 438–9)

Notwithstanding all this, Wagner preferred Jewish interpreters and orchestral conductors of his music! So much so, that the distinguished Hans von Bülow once humorously exclaimed to a colleague, "why didn't your father and mine have us circumcised at the proper time?" Poliakov provides an interesting discussion of the Jewish interpreters and a fascinating analysis of Wagner's ambivalent relationship with them. Wagner's obsession with the Jews was, however, unflagging to the very end of his life. To the king of Bavaria, Ludwig II, he wrote in 1881:

> I regard the Jewish race as the born enemy of pure humanity and every-thing that is noble in it; it is certain that we Germans will go under before them, and perhaps I am the last German who knows how to stand up as an art-loving man against the Judaism that is already getting control of everything. (III, 447)

Nietzsche, the Jews, and Judaism

It is well known that the young Nietzsche was taken with Wagner and was highly impressed by his artistic talent. Nietzsche, as a philosopher, wrote from an *aesthetic* point of view. Indeed, for him, the aesthetic cri-teria by which he assessed human conduct and creativity far surpassed in importance all other elements, including the moral and ethical. Is it safe, therefore, to assume that in his break with Wagner it was primarily the shortcomings of his art that prompted Nietzsche to separate from him and to declare that "Wagner is a neurosis"?

On balance and in sharp contrast to Wagner, Nietzsche displays a favorable attitude toward the Jews. That is evident in virtually all of his aphorisms concerning the Jews. In *Human, All Too Human*, for example, he averred that Europe owes the Jews gratitude:

> It was Jewish free thinkers, scholars, doctors, who held up the banner of enlightenment and independence of mind in spite of the harshest personal constraints. It is to their efforts that we largely owe the fact that a more natural, more reasonable explanation of the world, at any rate an expla-nation free of myths, was able to regain an upper hand and the chain of civilization that now links us uninterruptedly to the light of Greco-Roman culture. If Christianity did its utmost to Orientalize the West, it is Judaism above all that contributed mainly to Occidentalize it again. Which means, in a sense, to redefine the mission and history of Europe as a perpetuation of Greek history. (*Human, All Too Human*, 475)

But, as Poliakov cogently observes, some of Nietzsche's utterances tend to inflate, in the extreme, both Jewish possibilities and the internal cohe-sion of the Jews. Here is an example:

> It is obvious that the Jews, if they wanted it or were forced to, could right now have control and literally a stranglehold on all of Europe. It is clear, too, that they do not intend to and have no plans of the kind. At

the moment, what they want and wish, even with some insistence, is to be absorbed and dissolved in Europe and by Europe. They are yearning to find a place where they can settle, be acknowledged and respected, and finally to put an end to their nomadic existence as wandering Jews. We ought to take this aspiration into account, this tendency that expresses a certain weakening of their instincts. We ought to favor it. That is why it would be useful and legitimate to expel from the country anti-Semitic loudmouths. (*Beyond Good and Evil*, #251)

And Poliakov comments:

There was perhaps no other human category that Nietzsche despised and loathed so much as the "anti-Semitic loudmouths (among whom his brother-in-law Bernhard Förster occupied a leading place). Nevertheless, he [Nietzsche] fell into a double trap, since he, too, attributed to the Jews almost superhuman powers, and he traced this power to their heredity, to their 'blood." On these points he remained a product of his time and his country. (Poliakov, IV, 10)

There is another important question deserving of discussion in Nietzsche's philosophical outlook where the historical role of the Jews is concerned. *Beyond Good and Evil* is the work in which Nietzsche had first introduced his now famous terms "master morality" and "slave morality," which he elaborated in his *Genealogy of Morals*. These key terms are the "pure" or (in Max Weber's terms "ideal type") conceptual constructs with which Nietzsche seeks to explain how the ideas of "good" and "evil" had first emerged – the origins of morality. Nietzsche proposed that the moral distinction and opposition of values first appeared historically in the political context of the interaction between dominant and dominated groups. As the former becomes aware of how it differs from the latter – slaves and dependents of all kinds – the dominant takes pride in the distinction. When the ruling group determines what is "good," that term refers to its own powerful and exalted status, to its superiority over the servile lower orders who are despised. In this "master morality," the opposition of "good" and "bad" means roughly the same as "noble" and "contemptible."

The dominant, noble man who is, above all, a courageous man of war, feels contempt for the subjugated and servile because they are in his view fearful and cowardly, allowing themselves to be maltreated. The noble type of man, experiencing himself as the creator of values, needs only his own approval and that of his peers. What is harmful to him is itself harmful, and all power-enhancing aspects of his life are honorable. Noble morality is a form of unabashed self-glorification. Life for the noble man is the feeling of the fullness of power, the joy in adventure and high tension, and the awareness of wealth that one can bestow upon one's noble heirs. The noble may also aid those who are lowly and unfortunate, but this is prompted not so much by compassion as by his superabundant power: *noblesse oblige*! In reality, the "master" and "slave" moralities are never found in their "pure," antithetical forms, but are rather mixed. In all cultures one may discern attempts at mediation between the two value-systems, and often an interpenetration of both. The two moralities may even coexist in the same human being, within a single soul, Nietzsche the psychologist avers.

In the *Genealogy*, Nietzsche characterizes the "slave morality" as the product of a long historical process in which the *inversion* of noble values occurred – a consequence of the slaves' resentment of their oppressors. When the suffering, oppressed, and unfree moralize, they express a condemnatory view of the human condition. They view unfavorably the self-glorifying virtues of the powerful, and they are skeptical and suspicious of the so-called "good" that is honored there. The slaves' experience of their oppressors as powerful, dangerous, cruel, and fear-inspiring gives birth to the idea that the oppressors are the embodiment of "evil."

The noble virtues of strength, courage, and hardness emerge of necessity from the life circumstances of the masters, who have to stick together if they want to prevail, which they must do or run the risk of being destroyed, either by hostile neighbors or by their own oppressed multitude. Experience thus teaches the noble warrior caste to which qualities it owes its successes and triumphs, and it is those qualities that are cultivated and regarded as virtues. The noble soul is above all egoistic, holding the conviction that he and his peers are superior, and that those other beings, who are inferior by nature, must subordinate and sacrifice themselves in the interest of the masters. Nietzsche admired not only the historical exemplars of the master morality, but hoped to see its noble qualities in the "higher types" of the future.

This brings us to Nietzsche's conception of the historical role of the Jews. When the highest stratum in a society is the priestly caste, its mode of evaluation can develop into the antithesis of noble values, which is highly probable when the priests and noble warriors stand in zealous opposition to one another and refuse to compromise. Even when the priestly caste had emerged originally from the noble strata, the priestly-noble mode of evaluation, owing to the specialization of the priests in "sacred" functions, soon turns in another direction. As a caste they lose their physical prowess and war skills, thus becoming weak and even powerless. Such priests, for Nietzsche, may become bitter enemies of the powerful whom they oppose precisely because of the priests' powerlessness. For Nietzsche, the Jews are a priestly people par excellence, and he describes in the most dramatic terms their historical role in *inverting* the noble values:

> All that has been done on earth against "the noble," "the powerful," "the masters," "the rulers," is not even worth talking about when compared with what the *Jews* have done against them. The Jews, that most priestly people, who in opposing their enemies and conquerors gained satisfaction only through a radical revaluation of their enemies' values, that is to say, through an act of the *most spiritual revenge* . . . It was the Jews who, with awe-inspiring consistency, dared to invert the aristocratic value-equation (good = noble = powerful = beautiful = happy = beloved of God) and to cling to this inversion with their teeth, the teeth of the most abysmal hatred (the hatred due to impotence), establishing the principle that "the wretched alone are the good; the poor, powerless, lowly alone are the good; the suffering, deprived, sick, ugly, alone are pious, alone are blessed by God – blessedness is for them alone; and you, the powerful and the noble, are, on the contrary, the evil, the cruel, the lustful, the insatiable, the godless to all eternity; and you shall be for all eternity the unblessed, accursed, and damned!" . . . with regard to the tremendous and immeasurably fateful initiative which the Jews have taken, through this most far-reaching of all declarations of war, I recall the proposition I arrived at on an earlier occasion (*Beyond Good and Evil*, 195) – that *the slave revolt in morality* begins with the Jews, a revolt which has a two-thousand-year history behind it and which is no longer so obvious because it has been victorious. (*Genealogy*, I, 7)

How shall we interpret Nietzsche's proposition that it was the Jews who had inverted the noble values and had created the "slave morality"? For Nietzsche, humanity has been engaged in a fearful struggle for thousands of years, a struggle between two opposing value systems: "good and bad" vs "good and evil"; or "Rome against Judea, Judea against Rome"; and no event has been more significant than this deadly confrontation. Rome looked upon the Jew as a dangerous antipode, and rightly so, says Nietzsche, "provided one has a right to regard the future salvation of the human race as contingent upon the unconditional dominance of aristocratic values, Roman values" (*Genealogy*, #16). Which of these, Rome or Judea, has won for the present? The answer for Nietzsche is beyond doubt. Consider, he says, to whom one bows down in Rome itself, and not only in Rome but over half the earth.

There is an ambiguity here. One possible interpretation would be a positive one in which Nietzsche recognizes that even much earlier than Rome – from the time of Moses' and the prophets' repudiation of the values of the Egyptian "house of bondage" – Judaism had developed as a negation and inversion of the oppressors' ideas. For Nietzsche (as for many New Testament scholars), the Jewish negation and inversion would naturally include Jesus' Beatitudes (Matthew 5:3f), for his teachings may be properly viewed as a continuation and accentuation of the inversion process, a rejection, in his case, of the Roman ideals of war, power, and might. Indeed, Nietzsche states that three Jews – Jesus, Peter, and Paul – had proclaimed the counter-values that led to the victory of Judea over Rome.

There is, however, another possible way to interpret Nietzsche's proposition: that he regards the historical role of the Jews negatively. Nietzsche says that Rome looked upon them as "a dangerous antipode," and rightly so, "provided one has a right to regard the future salvation of the human race as contingent upon the unconditional dominance of aristocratic values, Roman values." If, therefore, Nietzsche links the salvation of the human race to Roman values, and those values are "beyond good and evil," it would be difficult to view his proposition concerning the Jews as anything but negative. For if they were the initiators and fosterers of the "slave morality," their role becomes for Nietzsche a "dangerous" one because it tends to preclude the "future salvation of the human race." Nietzsche explicitly employs the word "dangerous":

> The Jews – a people "born of slavery," as Tacitus and the entire ancient world say, "the chosen people among the peoples," as they themselves say and believe – the Jews have accomplished that miraculous feat of an inversion of values, thanks to which life on earth has acquired a new and *dangerous* allurement for a couple of millennia: their prophets have combined "rich," "godless," "evil," "violent," and "sensual" into one and were the first to use the word "world" pejoratively. In this inversion of values (which includes rendering the word "poor" as synonymous with "holy" and "friend") lies the significance of the Jewish people: with them the slave-rebellion in morals begins. (*Beyond Good and Evil*, 195; italics added)

From one angle, then, it seems justifiable to speak of a Nietzschean ambiguity and perhaps even an implicit antipathy, owing to the Jewish role in the inversion process. One can imagine Nietzsche speaking to himself and saying: "As much as I respect the Jews and do not wish to hate or despise them, how can I forgive them for the slave-rebellion in morals?"

On the other hand, maybe ambiguity or ambivalence is closer to the mark than antipathy. Writing from an aesthetic point of view, as noted earlier, and from the standpoint of admiration for what is "noble," Nietzsche wrote:

> In the Jewish "Old Testament," the book of divine justice, there are human beings, things and speeches in so grand a style that the Greek and Indian

literatures have nothing to compare with it. One stands with terror and reverence before these mighty remnants of what humanity once was, and will have sorrowful thoughts about ancient Asia and its protruding little peninsula Europe, which wants in all respects to signify as against Asia the "progress of man" . . . The taste for the Old testament is a touchstone in the consideration of "great" and "small." Perhaps he [The tame, domesticated European"] will find the *New* Testament, the book of grace, rather more after his heart (it is full of the real, tender, musty, fanatic and small-soul smell). To have attached this *New Testament*, a form of rococo of taste in every respect, to the *Old Testament* to create *one* book, as the "Bible," as the Book *par excellence*, that is perhaps the greatest presumption and "sin against the spirit," that literary Europe has on its conscience. (*Beyond Good and Evil*, 52)

And, in the *Genealogy*, Nietzsche says similar things:

I do not like the *"New Testament,"* as should be plain. I find it almost disturbing that in my taste concerning this most highly esteemed and over-rated work, I should stand alone. (The taste of two millennia is against me.) But it can't be helped! "Here I stand, I cannot do otherwise." I have the courage of my bad taste. The *Old* Testament, that is something different: All honor to the Old Testament! There I find great human beings, a heroic land-scape, and something that is rarest in the world, the incomparable naïveté of the *strong heart*; furthermore, I find a people. In the *New* one, in contrast, I find nothing but petty sectarianism, mere rococo of the soul, mere tortu-ous phrases, nooks, queer things, the air of the conventicle, not to forget an occasional whiff of bucolic sweetness, which belongs to the epoch (*and* to the Roman province) and which is not so much Jewish as Hellenistic. (*On the Genealogy of Morals*, III, 22)

We cannot help noting how often Nietzsche speaks of "taste" in those passages. We must, therefore, take him at his word. His preference for the Old Testament appears to be a matter of taste, an aesthetic judgment in which the "noble" elements are the criterion of his preference. He leaves us wondering, however, as to how he would evaluate the "slave morality" of the Hebrew prophets of social justice; how he would compare them evaluatively with his Zarathustra; and which he prefers and why.

Nietzsche's Legacy

Most Nietzsche scholars today would agree that he was neither a racist nor a German nationalist. In his published writings as in his notes he attacks anti-Semitism several times; and, as we have seen, he goes out of his way to praise Jews, Judaism, and the Hebrew Bible. Moreover, we now know how blatant distortions of his work came about. During the last 10 years of Nietzsche's life (1890–1900), the period of his insanity and incapacity, his sister Elizabeth became the executrix of his literary estate. Together with her husband, a notorious Jew-hater named Bernhard Förster, she "edited" and tampered with Nietzsche's writings, interpreting his concept, "will to power," and his conspicuous war rhetoric so as to make him a proto-Nazi theorist highly attractive to Hitler.

And mention of Hitler brings us to the concrete conditions that made it possible for Nazism to sweep Germany with catastrophic consequences – not only for European Jews, but also for the Germans themselves and for all the other peoples of Europe, Asia, and America, who paid a very high human price for Hitlerism.

21

The Rise of Nazism

Nazism emerged in Germany in the aftermath of World War I, following the country's defeat and surrender. In the months prior to the defeat, the German army had suffered several decisive setbacks, which came as a shock to the majority of the people, because the monarchy had misled them into believing that victory was assured. The people at home, war-weary and enduring hunger and privation, now suffered a severe blow to their morale. Food riots and mob violence were daily occurrences, and political street meetings and mass demonstrations became ever more frequent. The Kaiser's regime increasingly lost prestige in the eyes of the people, while authority broke down both at home and at the Front, where soldiers deserted and sailors mutinied. The majority of the people burned with anger and resentment toward the government that had brought so intolerable a situation upon them. The result was that when the defeat finally came in November 1918, the Kaiser was forced to abdicate. The old regime fell, and a republic was proclaimed in its place – the Weimar Republic, so named because the new democratic Constitution was drawn up in the city of Weimar.

Chaos, however, continued to reign in Germany despite the proclamation of the Republic. A major reason for the continuing unrest was that the pillars of the old regime – the army, police, civil bureaucracy – looked upon the Weimar government with contempt. The Republic, from their standpoint, was made up of socialists and other plebeian upstarts who deserved no respect and even less loyalty. The old guard yearned for the restoration of the old order and sought to undermine the Republic by force, from the moment of its birth.

The other major reason for the prevailing violence and anarchy was the conflict between the political parties of the center and left. The Social Democrats favored the Republic and a peaceful, parliamentary evolution toward socialism. In the elections of 1919 to the National Assembly, they received 13,800,000 votes out of 30,000,000 cast, and they won 185 out of 421 seats.[1] They were, therefore, considerably short of a majority. Yet they agreed to govern alone because no other party, whether working class or middle class, would share the burden. Although the two middle-class parties, the Catholic Center and the Democratic Party, professed support for a moderate republic, there was considerable sentiment among them for the restoration of the monarchy.

At the same time there was a deep and growing split in the ranks of the left-wing parties. The Social Democrats were vehemently opposed by the German communists or Spartakists, as they were called. Led by Karl Liebknecht and Rosa Luxemburg, and aided by Soviet Russia, the Spartakists called for an armed insurrection. With the recent Russian Revolution in mind, they turned to the numerous soldiers' and workmen's councils that had sprung up in Germany and called upon them to rise up and to form a dictatorship of the proletariat. Civil war broke out and bloody battles ensued in Berlin, Halle, and several other cities. Soon afterward, the Spartakists were decisively defeated by both regular army units and volunteers who rallied to the support of the republican government.

Moreover, the councils themselves rejected the revolutionary path. At their Berlin Congress of December 16–20, 1918, the delegates voted overwhelmingly in favor of the Republic and the National Assembly. This outcome reflected the mood of the German people of the time. They were bitter toward the old order, but they had no wish to transform the entire structure of society. Nor, certainly, did they want violent insurrection and a prolonged civil war. They longed, rather, for social stability – to get back to work and to live peaceful, normal lives. That was true not only of the large and powerful middle classes but of the majority of workers as well.

Peace, however, was not forthcoming. Instead, the society remained in a state of turmoil, with the supporters and opponents of the Republic constantly at odds. The old guard, the military caste, and all others who had a vested interest in the old regime, did everything they could to discredit and sabotage the new government. The Republic, in contrast, did little to defend itself against the assailants. In fact, the new government continued to employ most of the officials of imperial Germany – the very elements that were most hostile to it. Using those elements to combat the extreme left, the Weimar government found itself largely defenseless against its violent enemies on the right. The latter went so far as to attempt a *coup d'état* in 1920 (the so-called Kapp *Putsch*),

---

[1] In the present discussion I rely heavily on Theodore Abel, *The Nazi Movement: Why Hitler Came to Power*, New York: Atherton Press, 1965 [1938].

resulting in the assassination of several government leaders. Right-wing forces also created all sorts of illegal military organizations with which they harassed and intimidated government and trade-union officials. In sum, the new Republic proved itself incapable of putting an end to the violent conflict and disorganization that the majority of the people found intolerable.

The situation was soon further aggravated by an event that produced a general and profoundly hostile reaction against the Republic.

The Versailles Treaty

In May 1919 the terms of the peace treaty, which the Allies had decided to impose on Germany without negotiation, were published in Berlin. The news came as a staggering blow. Many Germans had come to believe that they were entitled to easy peace terms now that they had rid themselves of the royal family, squashed the communist revolution, and instituted a republican form of government. But instead of easy terms, they were being subjected to conditions they interpreted as "harsh," "unjust," and "intolerable."

If, however, we take a close look at what was to become the Versailles Treaty and compare it with another relevant one – the Treaty of Brest-Litovsk, which Germany had imposed on the Russians only one year earlier – then the terms of the Versailles Treaty appear to be not especially harsh at all. It returned Alsace-Lorraine to France, and Schleswig to Denmark, both of which territories Bismarck had forcefully annexed in the late nineteenth century after defeating those countries in war: the Treaty would have returned to the Poles the area taken by Germany in the partition of Poland in the eighteenth century. The Treaty also provided that some 800 war criminals were to be turned over to the Allies and that the first payment for war reparations, 5 billion dollars in gold marks or in equivalent goods, be paid between 1919 and 1921. Finally, it restricted Germany's army to 100,000 volunteers and prohibited it from having planes or tanks. The navy was also reduced to a token force. It is, therefore, instructive to compare those terms with the conditions imposed on a defeated Russia by the German High Command on March 3, 1918. The Treaty of Brest-Litovsk, writes William L. Shirer,

> deprived Russia of a territory nearly as large as Austria-Hungary and Turkey combined, with 56,000,000 inhabitants, or 32 percent of her whole population; a third of her railway mileage, 73 percent of her total iron ore, 89 percent of her total coal production; and more than 5,000 factories and

industrial plants. Moreover, Russia was obliged to pay Germany an indemnity of six billion marks.[2]

It seems clear, then, that if the Versailles Treaty was "harsh" and "extreme," it was certainly less so than the Treaty which the Germans themselves had imposed on their defeated enemy.

Nevertheless, the terms of the Versailles Treaty were perceived by virtually all segments of German society as a humiliating assault upon the German nation. Opposition to the treaty was nearly unanimous and included not only the pan-German nationalists and reactionaries but the Social Democrats and communists as well. President Ebert and his Social Democratic colleagues consulted the army: could the army resist an Allied attack from the West if the Treaty were rejected? The reply of Field Marshall von Hindenburg and the High Command was in the negative. A resumption of the war, they recognized, would end in the destruction of the German officer corps and, indeed, of Germany itself.

Meanwhile, the Allies, growing impatient, delivered an ultimatum: either the Treaty would be accepted or the armistice would be terminated and the Allied powers would take the steps necessary to enforce the Treaty's terms. Faced with this ultimatum, Ebert once again urgently consulted the High Command. He promised to do his utmost to secure the rejection of the Treaty by the National Assembly if the High Command saw the slightest chance of successful military resistance. The reply he received was the same as before: "Armed resistance is impossible." In light of that reply the National Assembly approved the signing of the Treaty by a large majority and communicated its approval to the French government minutes before the Allied ultimatum expired. Four days later, on June 28, 1919, the peace treaty was signed in the Hall of Mirrors in the palace of Versailles. Ultimately, it was the *army* that had made the final decision to sign. But that fact never became widely known, and the blame was placed squarely upon the *Republic.*

General dissatisfaction with the Republic became evident in the elections of June 6, 1920. The parties that had voted for the treaty – the Social Democrats and the center party – lost a total of 11 million votes, most of which went over to the Nationalists and others who had voted against it. The tide had turned against the Republic, and gathered new momentum from the events of the early 1920s. The mark dropped precipitously from 75 to the dollar in 1921 to 7,000 by the beginning of 1923. Already, in 1922, the German government had requested a moratorium

---

[2] William L. Shirer, *The Rise and Fall of the Third Reich*, New York: Simon and Schuster, 1960, 57.

on reparation payments and received a blunt refusal from the French. When Germany defaulted in the delivery of timber, French forces occupied the Ruhr, thus cutting German industry off from 80 percent of its coal and steel production. The workers of the Ruhr, encouraged and supported by the German government, responded with a general strike, thus further aggravating the state of the German economy. By August 1, 1923, it required 1 million marks to buy a dollar; by November it took 4 billion, and thereafter trillions. German currency had become worthless; the purchasing power of the middle and working classes was destroyed, and their life savings were wiped out. Who was to blame? In the minds of the vast majority of the German people, the answer was clear: the responsibility for the disastrous state of affairs lay squarely with the Republic, for it had surrendered to the enemy and had accepted the intolerable burden of reparations.

The Origins of the Nazi Party

In the general period being reviewed, 1919–23, many political circles had sprung up in Germany. In most cases they consisted of acquaintances who met to express their dissatisfaction with existing conditions. One such circle, made up of a handful of workers, met regularly in a Munich beer hall. Led by a machinist named Anton Drechsler, the circle was the nucleus of what eventually became the National Socialist (i.e., Nazi) Party.

Drechsler had found no ready-made niche for his political views. In 1918 he had written articles for a Munich newspaper, urging workers to support the imperial government and to prosecute the war until victory was achieved. As a worker, he favored the reforms advocated by the Socialists; as an ardent nationalist, however, he opposed the Social Democrats for their internationalism. The aversion for proletarian internationalism was shared by the several other workers who had joined Drechsler. The group soon attracted a few intellectuals, also dedicated to German nationalism. Among them were: Dietrick Eckart, a poet, journalist, and rabid Jew-hater; Alfred Rosenberg, a disciple and enthusiastic supporter of the racist theories of H. Stewart Chamberlain; Count von Bothmer, an advocate of a form of socialism in which the individual is strictly subordinated to the nation; and other men with similar ideas. Drechsler's circle of nationalistic socialists soon came to the attention of the military authorities who eagerly subsidized their nationalistic, propagandistic activities. Adolf Hitler, whose regiment was stationed in Munich at the time, was instructed to contact the circle, which called itself "The German Workers' Party."

Hitler's recollections of his first meeting with the group are given in his book *Mein Kampf* (*My Struggle*). They met in an old dilapidated room in a cheap beer hall. Their discussion struck him as quite boring. At the meeting's end, as Hitler prepared to leave, Drechsler approached him and pressed a pamphlet into his hand, urgently requesting his opinion of it. The following morning Hitler read the slim brochure and, much to his astonishment, found it quite interesting, as it recounted how the author had gone through a welter of Marxian ideas before returning to Nationalism as the only sound outlook. What especially impressed Hitler about Drechsler's story was that it reflected his own experience 12 years earlier. Hitler goes on to relate how he wrestled for days with the question of whether or not to become a member of the group. Like Drechsler, he felt there was no place for him in the major parties; and Drechsler's circle, on the other hand, was unimpressive. Yet, upon reflection, Hitler sensed that precisely this circle might offer a distinct advantage: "It had not yet frozen into an organization."

Hitler then gives us some insight into his motives. He had no credentials with which to impress the leaders of the established conservative and nationalistic parties. But the thought was unbearable that he should remain one of the countless numbers whose lives and deaths went unnoticed. After days of painful indecision, he made up his mind and joined Drechsler's German Workers' Party.

Hitler's entry was a turning point both for him and the group. As a condition for joining the group, he demanded and received full control of its propaganda activities. The right kind of propaganda, he sensed, would lift this insignificant circle out of obscurity. Munich had just experienced the bloodiest social upheaval in its history. It began with the establishment of a communist government and ended, after a period of terrorism, assassinations, and executions, in general disorder. The reaction against communism, together with the treatment accorded Germany by the Allies, led to a powerful revival of nationalist sentiment. As Jews were highly visible among the leaders of the communists and the Republic, anti-Semitism became more widespread. This was the general mood that Hitler exploited effectively. While other agitators attracted only small street audiences, Hitler succeeded by 1921 in recruiting thousands of members to the German Workers' Party, and thousands more to his weekly meetings.

How did he accomplish those results? He did so by employing propaganda techniques that were new in Germany at the time. As he acknowledged in *Mein Kampf*, he imitated the tactics that the Allies had used during the war. He announced his meetings with large glaring placards; he used trucks to distribute the propaganda materials throughout Munich; he made his party immediately recognizable in distinctive uniforms and badges; and he organized dramatic parades and loud street demonstrations. He compelled the opposition to take notice of him and his organization by staging his meetings in Social Democratic strongholds and by disrupting their gatherings by means of heckling and violence. Soon he was able to purchase a daily newspaper and give it his peculiar stamp. Where did the funds come from to pay for Hitler's expanding organizational and promotional activities? Partly from public collections and a few wealthy sympathizers. But the bulk of his funds came from the military authorities, who were interested in the development of a strong nationalist party.

No less important than his propaganda techniques were Hitler's aggressive, intimidating tactics, which appealed especially to many young men who had no better prospects under the circumstances. University students and unemployed young men from middle- and working-class backgrounds became part of his loyal following. Formed into well-disciplined, quasi-military fighting units, their shows of force and actual violence figured more and more prominently in the party's public actions. Those fighting units were the nuclei of what later became Hitler's infamous storm troopers and special guards, the SA and the SS. Soon it was evident to all concerned who the real leader of the party was. Hitler became a favorite, popular orator, as huge crowds eagerly awaited his appearance and gave him long and enthusiastic ovations. It was not long before his followers bestowed upon him the title der Führer, the leader. A veritable Hitler cult developed. He now acquired charisma in the eyes of many, the leader who would save Germany.

By 1923, as noted earlier, German banks were paying 4 billion marks for a dollar and the French army was occupying the Ruhr. The German government now aroused greater animosity than ever for doing nothing in the face of a foreign invasion and a ruinous inflation. Early in the fall of 1923, the several nationalist organizations of Bavaria formed a united front and planned a putsch. Up to that time Hitler had steadfastly avoided cooperation with other groups. All of his energy was devoted to building his own party and his own personal image. But now he succumbed to the pressure and joined the coalition, placing his storm troopers at the disposal of the military. He was appointed leader of the united front and hailed as the German Mussolini. The actions of the front were intended to precipitate a massive nationalist uprising with the support of the military. But the uprising never materialized. On the 8th and 9th of November, Hitler led his troops in a march against the government leaders of Munich and attempted to arrest them. But a volley of bullets by troops loyal to the government brought a quick end to the putsch. Hitler fled but was apprehended, tried, and sentenced to imprisonment.

Although those events were a setback for the movement, Hitler's name now became nationally known. Before the attempted putsch, the German press had practically ignored him and his organization. Afterward, however, the press was compelled to give space to the event and to Hitler's speeches during the trial. He became a national figure overnight. Hitler had learned important lessons from the experience of the abortive putsch. And Theodore Abel has provided cogent insights into Hitler's new attitude:

> Hitler became convinced that his aim could not be realized unless he had the majority of the nation behind him. Consequently he intensified his propaganda, and directed his organization in conformity with legal procedure. Hence the participation of the party in the Reichstag elections and his own candidacy for the presidency. The *Putsch* furthermore convinced Hitler that he could not count on the support of other groups. The policy of no compromise was adopted as a standing principle, and afterwards became the germ of the totalitarian state. (Abel, 70)

After the Putsch

There was another consequence of Hitler's setback at Munich. His imprisonment afforded him the opportunity to pull his ideas together into an integrated ideology. It was during his prison term that he wrote or, more correctly, dictated his autobiography *Mein Kampf* to Rudolf Hess. There Hitler openly formulated and revealed his movement's ideology, strategy, and tactics.

When Hitler was freed from prison in November 1924, he faced a discouraging situation. His erstwhile followers were scattered among other groups, the remains of his party had been badly defeated at the polls, and the nationalist tide had temporarily subsided. He was nevertheless determined to rebuild his organization; and now that he was committed to legal means of struggle, he persuaded the Bavarian authorities of that commitment on his part, and they withdrew the ban on the National Socialist Party. On January 27, 1925, he called a meeting at the Munich beer hall that had been the scene of his previous triumphs. Over 4,000 people showed up to welcome him, most of them his former followers and lieutenants who, in Hitler's absence, had fought among themselves for his crown. But Hitler won them over again and exacted a pledge of exclusive allegiance to him. Thereafter, he was the supreme and unquestioned leader, having lost none of his appeal, apparently, despite the failure of the putsch.

Yet in the new social conditions of the period between 1925 and 1929, Hitler's movement made very little headway; for Germany had now come upon better times, enjoying some material prosperity thanks to enormous American investments. Between 1924 and 1930, the German government borrowed some 7 billion dollars, which was used to pay its reparation debts and to develop a vast system of social services, which evoked admiration throughout the world. State and municipal governments borrowed to finance airfields, theaters, sports stadiums, and public swimming pools. German industry borrowed billions to modernize its productive plant. In 1923, its output had dropped to 55 percent of that in 1913; by 1927, it had risen to 122 percent. By 1928, unemployment for the first time since the war fell below 650,000. Retail sales expanded and real wages rose. Not only the workers but the lower middle classes – millions of small shopkeepers and small-salaried employees – shared in the general prosperity. The Republic now gained prestige in their eyes, and they had little patience for Hitler or any other anti-republican agitator for that matter.

William L. Shirer was an American correspondent stationed in Germany in those years. Describing the mood of the people, he wrote that "A wonderful ferment was working in Germany . . . The old oppressive Prussian spirit seemed to be dead and buried. Most Germans one met – politicians, writers, editors, artists, professors, students, businessmen, labor leaders – struck you as being democratic, liberal, even pacifist" (Shirer, 118). It is not surprising, therefore, that those were very lean years for Hitler and the Nazi movement.

However, the euphoria soon came to a shocking and abrupt end in the Great Crash of 1929. The worldwide economic crisis of unprecedented proportions hit Germany with catastrophic force. Unemployment rose rapidly and attained the staggering total of 5 million. Thousands upon thousands of workers were driven to join the relief rolls; and large numbers of peasants lost their land for defaulting on their mortgage payments. With the drastic reduction in the purchasing power of the masses, small businesses fell by the wayside while the general standard of living in the middle classes sank dramatically. Bitterness mounted steadily, and the government, finding itself powerless in those circumstances, lost the respect it had earlier commanded.

The crisis naturally brought new life to the radical parties of the right and the left, as thousands of new members daily swelled their ranks. The National Socialist and Communist Parties gained most in this period; but the latter was soon outstripped. By 1930, a rising volume of "Heil Hitler" greeted the Nazi parades. But there was also widespread opposition to the Nazis, with the result that violent clashes were common throughout the turbulent period from 1930 to 1932. Street wars were frequently waged between the Nazis on one side, and the pro-Republican, trade union, and communist forces on the other. In time, it became clear that

Table 21.1 Results of election on March 13, 1932

Hindenburg	18,651,497	49.6%
Hitler	11,339,446	30.1%
Thaelmann (communist)	4,983,341	13.2%
Duesterberg (Nationalists)	2,557,729	6.8%

Table 21.2 Results of election on April 10, 1932

Hindenburg	19,359,983	53%
Hitler	13,418,547	36.8%
Thaelmann	3,706,759	10.2%

the odds were overwhelmingly in favor of the Nazis who had become a formidable political-military force capable of fomenting a prolonged and bloody civil war.

From January 1930 to December 1931, the Nazi movement grew from about 400,000 members to well over 800,000. The increased volume of support for the movement became evident in the results of the many local elections of that period. By 1932, Hitler felt strong enough to run for the presidency against Hindenburg, the widely respected, legendary war hero, supported by the conservative anti-Nazi right and the democratic parties as well. Table 21.1 shows the results at the close of the election on March 13, 1932.

The old Hindenburg had defeated the Nazi leader by over 7 million votes; but he fell 0.4 percent short of the required absolute majority. A second election was therefore necessary. Hitler had increased the Nazi vote by almost 5 million since the 1930 elections, but he nevertheless fell far behind Hindenburg. In the second election the Nationalists withdrew Duesterberg from the race, appealing to their followers to vote for Hitler. Table 21.2 shows the results of the second election, on April 10, 1932.

But despite Hitler's electoral defeat, the Nazis held several trump cards: their formidable organization and massive support; their determination to fight to the finish, by violent means when necessary; and the fact that they were the strongest single party in the Reichstag. Hindenburg and his advisers understood all that. After many long conferences and wavering, they decided that Hitler had to be given something in the hope of staving off a *coup d'état* and a long and bloody civil war. Thus, on January 30, 1933, Hitler was appointed Chancellor, that is, Chief Minister of the Reich.

From that strategic vantage point, Hitler was able to aggrandize even more power for himself and his party and to begin the Nazification of

Germany. On the morning of August 2, 1934, Hindenburg died in his 87th year. Some three hours later, it was announced that, in accordance with a law enacted on the *preceding* day, the offices of the chancellor and president had been combined. Adolf Hitler had become the head of state and the commander-in-chief of the armed forces. The title of president was abolished, and Hitler became known as Führer and Reich Chancellor. Hitler had thus established himself as dictator of Germany. With those acts he had, of course, violated the Republic's Constitution, which called for the election of Hindenburg's successor. But the army refrained from interfering and *even swore an oath of allegiance to Hitler personally* to lend his usurpation of power an aura of legitimacy, and Hitler scheduled a plebiscite for August 15. He had somehow managed to prevail upon the deceased president's son, Colonel Oskar von Hindenburg, to broadcast the following message on the eve of the voting: "My father had himself seen in Adolf Hitler his own direct successor as head of the German state, and I am acting according to my father's intention when I call upon all German men and women to vote for the handing over of my father's office to the Fuehrer and Reich Chancellor" (Shirer, 227). Historians are generally agreed, however, that the son's statement was false, and that Hindenburg's last wish was for the restoration of the monarchy. It is almost certain that the portion of Hindenburg's last will and testament conveying that wish was suppressed by the Nazis.

On August 19, 1933, 90 percent of the German voters registered approval of Hitler's usurpation of total power. Now, with total control of the means of violence and coercion in their hands, the Nazis could deal mercilessly with all their opponents, who were thrown into concentration camps, murdered, or exiled. Then, by launching a mammoth rearmaments program, Hitler largely wiped out unemployment by 1936. He thus gained in popularity and retained the support of the privileged classes, as well as of the middle and working classes. The industrialists and financiers enthusiastically supported the profitable business of arms and munitions manufacturing; and the masses were happy to have jobs again even at the cost of their personal freedom and an austere diet – "Guns before butter."

22

The Early Nazi Regime and the Jews as Perceived by Non-Jewish Contemporaries

From the earliest period of the Weimar Republic, as we have seen, there were strong anti-republican elements in Germany who regretted not the war, but only the defeat, and who strove to regain the lost power of Germany so that she might seek and get revenge. Everything such elements resented was skillfully attributed by Hitler to the Republic. However, a more specific enemy was also necessary, and it had to be not only specific, but safe, weak, and vulnerable – sufficiently defenseless to give the Nazis an easy and cheap victory, both propagandistically and materially. When we therefore assess the historical role of an individual in the concrete case of the rise of the Nazi movement, it would be a mistake to underrate the causal weight of Hitler. For it was he who recognized the longstanding pariah status of the Jews in Christian Europe.

In the pre-modern period they were hated, despised, and persecuted primarily for theological reasons; and in the modern period not only for the traditional reasons – though those reasons were definitely implicit, barely beneath the surface – but also for the additional fact that they had become so visibly successful in the urban, middle-class, business, and liberal professions since their civil emancipation.

That Hitler fully recognized the propagandistic value of Jew-hatred in this political context is obvious, regardless of whether he actually believed that "the Jews" were an evil and dangerous menace. His hatred of Jews and his public anti-Jewish utterances were motivated primarily by his political aims. But the intensity of his passion in that regard may also have stemmed from personal experiences. We know, for example, that his mother had died while in the care of a Jewish doctor. There has also been the suggestion – though there is no definite evidence for it – that as an aspiring artist in his youth, he had encounters either with Jewish gallery owners or with art instructors who had treated his artwork condescendingly or worse. One or two of them might even have *laughed* at his artistic pretensions, which would explain why, in a famous speech, he declared gloatingly "we shall see now who will laugh last."

Whatever the reason for Hitler's passionate hatred, it is beyond dispute that he recognized anti-Semitism as a most valuable political weapon. Hermann Rauschning, a late recruit to Nazism who soon repented of having joined it, has left us invaluable insights from actual conversations with Hitler. In one of those conversations, Hitler stated to him:

> My Jews are a valuable hostage given to me by the democracies. Anti-Semitic Propaganda in all countries is an almost indispensable medium for the extension of our political campaign. You will see how little time we shall need in order to upset the ideas and criteria of the whole world, simply and purely by attacking Judaism. It is, beyond question, the most important weapon in my propaganda arsenal.[1]

When Hitler began to wield his "most important weapon" first against the German Jews, they were less than 1 percent of the German population. But, just as in other countries, in Germany the history of the Jews had caused them to concentrate in certain urban occupations. They became prominent in the cultural and professional life of Berlin, and in the commercial business world. The Nazis produced such Berlin statistics as if they were typical of the entire country, trying thus to demonstrate that Germany was dominated by the Jews. But the truth was, rather, that even in Berlin and other large cities, Jews chose certain professions because they were de facto the only ones open to them. They could so rarely become judges that they became solicitors in the legal professions instead. In medicine, they became general practitioners because Jews were, as a rule, excluded from hospitals, universities, and other institutional areas. Moreover, Hitler's propaganda machine so often and consistently used the word "dominant" as a synonym for "prominent," that it was only necessary to show that 10 percent of an occupation consisted of Jews for the profession to appear to be "dominated" by Jews. And for the Nazis it had to be necessarily bad for Germany that the Jews were visible in the medical, legal, and business professions.

Another favorite propaganda ploy was that Germany was being inundated by "foreign Jews" during the period of extreme inflation. But Germany's long tradition of excellent official statistics had in fact shown that the "inundation" amounted to less than one for every thousand of the population, the majority of them poor Jews who had fled from the inhospitable conditions of Poland and other areas of Eastern

---

[1] Hermann Rauschning, *Hitler Speaks*, London: Thornton Butterworth, 1939, 223.

Europe.[2] These Jewish fugitives were even accused of having made huge fortunes at the expense of the German people. And though it was at most an individual or two who was involved in bad scandals at the time, the entire category of "foreign" Jews was condemned, while the primary profiteers of the inflation were the giant industrialists, financiers, and landowners. It was these elements, as James Parkes observed, that

> were able to pay off their debts and mortgages, contracted in pre-1914 marks when they stood at twenty to the pound sterling, when the mark had fallen to one thousand millionth of its value. Others, especially Hugo Stinnes (who was not a Jew), by an ingenious system of borrowing from the State Bank and repaying the loan when the mark had fallen heavily, were able to buy up industries in every field and make enormous profits. (Ibid., 90)

By promising to cleanse the professions of their Jewish elements, Hitler appeared to be opening opportunities for the replacement of the Jews by large numbers of graduates of the universities, technical, and secondary schools, who were unemployed. But the Jews could be used for such concrete propagandistic purposes because of the role of "race" and "soil" in the Nazi *Weltanschuung* or worldview, according to which the Jews were the radically foreign Semitic "other" in contrast to the German, Aryan racial hero. This racial form of Jew-hatred first appeared, as we saw earlier, in the nineteenth and early twentieth centuries with the theories of Gobineau and H. S. Chamberlain. In the latter's *The Foundations of the Nineteenth Century*, he traced, purportedly, the conflict of the Aryan and the Semitic spirit throughout history, flaunting thereby his ignorance in a perverted erudition and failing to understand that "Aryan" and "Semitic" describe families of languages, not peoples.

The views of who was an Aryan "racially" were as diverse in the "racial" school as was the nonsensical nature of the concept of "race" itself. For Chamberlain, Goethe was an example of the purest Aryan. For Lenz, however, of the same school, Goethe was a "Teutonic-Western-Asiatic cross-breed." A third representative of the school was Otto Hauser, who "proved" Goethe's mongrel nature by the "hundreds of quite pitifully bad verses" in Faust. Later in the Nazi era, similar disputes arose about Christianity and Christ himself, some Nazi theologians claiming that Jesus was an Aryan; while to the neo-pagan Nazis, in contrast,

---

[2] See James Parkes, *Antisemitism*, Chicago, IL: Quadrangle Books, 1963, 89. Hereafter, all page references to this book will be cited in parentheses immediately following the quoted passage.

Christianity was the typical Semitic, un-Aryan doctrine which could only undermine the proud Aryan "master morality" by its inculcation of a "slave morality" – an example of the Nazi appropriation of Nietzsche's concepts and rhetoric.

And mention of the "slave morality" provides us with the opportunity to see how the Nazis, even in the earliest phase of their reign, translated the "master morality" into practice. Between 1933 and 1939, all who had known the pre-Nazi conditions agreed that where the Jews were concerned the Nazi propaganda was widely accepted. Every kind of violence and vulgarity was promoted. Force and the threat of force against Jewish men, women, and children were considered to be of great educational value in teaching German youth to despise peace, international cooperation, and Christian morality. The infamous Nazi publication, *Der Stürmer*, issued an illustrated book for children that opened with the medieval statement that the father of the Jews is the devil, and inculcating throughout the idea that it is noble to fight against the Jewish people and their children. The schools reinforced this notion of how the racially superior noble masters should behave toward the racially inferior Jewish children. Teachers insulted Jewish children in their classes and suppressed all signs of sympathy on the part of the other children. James Parkes, reflecting on the prevailing conditions, calls attention to the material-economic incentives behind the Nazi policy:

> Anti-Semitism was thus woven into every strand of the thought and activity of Hitler's Germany; it was also interwoven into the whole of her economic life. The capital stolen from her half-million Jews was extremely useful to the treasury; the threat of confiscation, deflation or violence provided endless opportunities of blackmail not only to individual Nazi officials, but even to the German government in its foreign commercial relations. And, of course, dispossessing Jews provided a quantity of houses, profitable businesses, furniture, jewelry, *objets d'art* and jobs to Hitler's followers . . . The tragic evidence is that, though a minority was horrified and ashamed, anti-Semitic prejudice had so hypnotized the bulk of the German people that they accepted, against the evidence of their own eyes, the pseudo-scientific and statistical expositions of their government, and of every Nazi speaker on the subject. (Parkes, 95)

Parkes also cites an Australian professor, Stephen Roberts, who related his own experience in 1937:

> Worst of all, worse even than individual suffering of today amongst the Jews, is the creation of a national mentality bred on such hate as that which the German feels for the Jews. "The other nations are not yet awake," a

university professor said to me, "and the time will come when the world will be grateful to us for upholding civilization against the Jews." I showed him my Australian passport with the name of a Jewish governor-general on the front cover, Isaac Isaacs, and told him of the other Jewish commander-in-chief, Monash, who first broke through the Hindenburg Line; and his only retort was that such a degradation of a fine community only proved the truth of his contention!

The most tragic thought of all is that Germany is behind Hitler in his campaign against *Rassenschande* or race-defilement. I spoke about it to peasants, and great industrialists, army officers, and factory laborers; and all approved of it, although a few regretted the tone of *Der Stürmer*. (That there is some opposition, however, is evident from the numerous attacks in Party papers on "Jew-lackeys," that is, Aryans who disapprove of brutality towards Jews.) When a nation can willingly concur in a pogrom against half a million Jews – when it sees nothing tragic in the starving of little children and the holding of them up to execration in kindergartens – when it sees nothing funny in the official decree of the town of Königsdorf that "cows purchased either directly or indirectly from Jews are not allowed to be served by the communal bull," then it reaches the point where its institutions are utterly incomprehensible to us.[3]

No sooner had Hitler usurped power in January 1933 by means of the plebiscite, and become the Führer of Germany, than "spontaneous" outbursts followed all over the country against Jews. Jewish judges, lawyers, teachers, doctors, shops, and businesses were attacked; everywhere Hitler's brown shirts, the private army of the Nazis, played a key role in those attacks. In April, the first law regulating the Civil Service was enacted, compelling the vast mass of German government employees of every kind to produce evidence of the religion of their parents and grandparents, and to prove their "Aryan" status. To the chagrin of the Nazi Party, which had been ceaselessly proclaiming that under the Weimar Republic the entire state apparatus was in the hands of foreign Jews, it became evident that the law affected 25,000 Jewish families out of at least 1,000,000 families of officials. Then, in 1934, Jews were disallowed the honor of pursuing a military career and fighting for Germany. Instead, they were conscripted as a labor force. At the same time all Jewish names were erased from the war memorials of World War I. All Jewish lawyers were denied the right to practice law. By 1938, Jews were prohibited from employing an "Aryan" lawyer, as were "Aryans"

---

[3] S. H. Roberts, *The House That Hitler Built*, Methuen, 1937, 266; cited in Parkes, 95.

from employing a Jewish lawyer. The same policy was applied to doctors.

Following the Nuremberg Rally of September 1935, new racial laws protecting "German blood and honor" were passed, forbidding all marriages between Aryans and non-Aryans. Meanwhile, the picketing of Jewish-owned shops became a commonplace event, followed by laws compelling Jewish businesses to take Aryan partners who soon ousted the Jew with impunity. All of this was, of course, accompanied by deliberately orchestrated violence against the Jews, culminating in the Kristallnacht pogrom of 1938, when all over the Reich Jews were beaten, their synagogues burned, and their shops destroyed. What led up to this event was the new Nazi decree expelling East European Jews from Germany. Thousands were rounded up and forced across the frontier at Zbonszyn, a border post on the line from Berlin to Warsaw. But the Polish authorities, unprepared for such a huge influx of immigrants, refused them refuge in Poland, with the result that they were left stranded to die of starvation or cold. One of these forlorn Jewish couples, named Grünspan, had a son who was so outraged by the German expulsion and its consequences that he took it upon himself to enter the German embassy in Paris, and shoot and kill an embassy official, Ernst vom Rath. Hitler, on the Nazi principle of collective responsibility, declared all of Germany's surviving Jews as guilty of the crime. A fine of many millions of marks was imposed on what remained of Jewish property, and the carefully organized "spontaneous" anger of the people was allowed a night of unbridled violence and pillage against the hapless victims.

When Hitler annexed Austria in the spring of 1938, the fate of the Austrian Jews and, later in the year, of the Czechoslovakian Jews, was quite the same as that of the German Jews. Then with the outbreak of war in 1939, and the conquest of almost all of Europe in 1940, some 9 million Jews were placed in the hands of the Nazis and, of the 9 million, two thirds were eventually annihilated. The process by which the Nazi regime accomplished this is a subject that has been given careful and detailed analysis by outstanding scholars.

But before we turn to that subject, it is desirable to shed some light on the aftermath of World War I and the conditions that made Nazism and other totalitarian regimes possible.

World War I, the Collapse of the Old Regimes, and the Rise of Totalitarianism

The world war, with its four terrible years of carnage, had horrified human beings everywhere. In Europe, the determination to prevent the repetition of any such disaster was a principal cause of the peace movement that led to the drafting of the Covenant for a League of Nations. Closely associated with the ideal of putting an end to war was the belief in democracy as the best way of life, an ideal which Woodrow Wilson in his Fourteen Points had made a paramount war aim of the Allied powers. The link between democracy and the movement for peace was based on the assumed fact that the mass of the population had borne the brunt of every great war, and especially in the destructive struggle of 1914–18. It seemed logical, therefore, that if the masses controlled international policy they would be steadfast in refusing to fight again. The liberal democracies believed that humans were rational, at least in the sense of following a program of simple self-interest. Common self-interest among democratic states would therefore lead to permanent peace.

Proponents of this view argued that all that was necessary to end the reign of violence between states was to establish some machinery for international government. There must be international courts, the argument went, to settle disputes between states, and there must be legislative bodies to substitute political debate for warfare as an instrument of international policy. What such proponents had overlooked in the aftermath of World War I, and once again after World War II, was the valid, trans-historical insight of Thomas Hobbes: all states claim sovereignty for themselves and remain in the posture of armed gladiators toward one another. For Hobbes, there is only one *sine qua non* for peace, and that is a "common power." That is true within states and would have to be true for international peace. So long as no such common power or Leviathan exists in the international arena, there can be no international peace. And the evidence of historical experience strongly suggests that no such power can ever be established in the international arena as a whole. Hence, as Hobbes would have predicted, the nations entering the League made no substantial surrender of their sovereignty, and the peace machinery lacked any real coercive power. When, therefore, the major interests of a great power conflicted with the demands of the League, self-interest impelled the state to ignore its League obligations and consider only its own interests. In each of the successive crises of European diplomacy after 1930, that is precisely what happened.

There is an additional proposition which seems to be valid as applied to the political consequences of World War I: it led to the destruction of the old regimes of Europe and to the emergence of new regimes which were in all respects worse than the old – worse in that they were totalitarian and genocidal. As bad as the monarchs of the old regimes might have been, they were never as murderous as were the rulers of the new regimes – rulers who appear in virtually all cases to be depraved beings from the abyss of human degeneracy. The monarchs of the old regimes oppressed and exploited their own peoples, and persecuted and expelled their "guest peoples," but the thought of exterminating an entire people never, apparently, crossed their minds. But when we reflect on the regimes of Hitler, Stalin, Mao, Pol Pot, and others, we readily recognize policies that were the product of a depraved and degenerate "beyond good and evil" ideology.

As our main subject is Hitler's policies, we shall restrict ourselves to his totalitarian, genocidal regime. One of the first objects of the Nazis was, as we have seen, to consolidate their control of the government. This required the rule of only one party, the National Socialists. The parties of the left were dissolved as traitorous, their leaders were either thrown out of office or murdered, and their party funds confiscated. Those of the center and right assented, more or less voluntarily, to their own dissolution while their members were attached to the Nazi organizations. The formation of any new political parties was treason.

Another chief feature of totalitarianism was the complete centralization of power. In Germany, the various states were deprived of their sovereignty as their powers were transferred to the central government. State legislatures lost their legislative functions and state governors were appointed by and made accountable to Hitler alone. The entire Civil Service was likewise placed under the control of the Führer. Similarly, all municipal officials and councils were subordinated to the central regime. All branches of economic life were coordinated so as to make all agencies work for the interests of the state as defined by the Nazi Party. Germany had already been highly organized in cartels for industrialists, chambers of commerce, associations of physicians, lawyers, teachers, trade unions, and peasant organizations. All that was necessary, then, to obtain centralized state control, was to install Nazi officials as heads of all these organizations. Of all the German economic groups, labor was placed under the strictest control. The Social Democratic and Catholic trade unions were dissolved, while collective bargaining and strikes were forbidden.

In addition to the coordination of political and economic institutions, the Nazis placed under central control all cultural and religious associations. This meant central control of schools, artistic and literary production, and the churches. All Germans were to subscribe to the Nazi ideology as propagated by the Ministry of Propaganda headed by Paul Joseph Goebels. Freedom of speech and the press was abolished, and a rigid censorship was installed. The entire educational system was brought under Nazi control. In the schools, Nazi ideology was imposed so that even scientific subjects had to be taught from the Nazi point of view, which held that every people or "race" sees nature in its own way and must therefore construct its own sciences; from which it followed, for example, that Einstein's theory of relativity must be rejected because he was a Jew.

The chief victims of the policy of "cultural coordination" were the German Jews. Hatred of Jews, as we have seen, was an essential element of the Nazi program, rationalized by the Nazi racial theories according to which the Jews were a non-assimilatable Eastern race with characteristics diametrically opposed to the creative Nordics. The Nazi opposition to all forms of internationalism meant that the Jews were to be blamed for the sins of both international finance and the international communist movement. In addition to all the other official attacks upon the Jews we have reviewed, a new citizen law of 1935 declared that all persons with more than two Jewish grandparents were no longer German citizens, but only subjects, while the status of "hybrids" was strictly regulated with the aim of assimilating persons with no more than 25 percent of so-called Jewish blood, and excluding all others from the German community. The Nazi policies toward the Jews in this period, together with the unofficial brutalities, led to the emigration of large numbers, which was permitted only if they left all their property behind.

More on Nazi Ideology, Internal Factions, and Foreign Policy Aims

The Nazi Party had recruited followers of every shade of opinion: racial fanatics, German nationalists, economic radicals, and plain adventurers. Former conservatives, especially from the Junker class, wanted no thoroughgoing economic change; but at the other extreme were those who proposed to seize the large estates and put into effect at least some of the socialism implied in the party name. Apparently Ernst Röhm, the early chief of Hitler's storm troopers, assumed leadership of those in the party who took seriously the socialism part of the Nazi program. Röhm may even have planned to overthrow Hitler. Whether or not that was Röhm's intention, Hitler was able to strike first and, at the end of June 1934, carried out a purge in which a number of leaders were seized and murdered without a trial, among them Röhm himself, the former chancellor Schleicher, and Klausner, leader of the Catholic action group. The bloody purge may have alienated some elements of the German populace, but it further consolidated Hitler's control over the whole state apparatus, and even over public opinion. For, as we have seen, when President Hindenburg died, the presidency and chancellorship were combined into one office and appropriated by Hitler, a move endorsed by a plebiscite in which 88 percent of the voters had cast ballots approving Hitler's action.

It is most likely that for the majority of Germans it was Hitler's success in international affairs that won them over to the Nazi regime. Given the high pitch of German nationalism at that historical moment, it was undoubtedly his reoccupation of the Rhineland, the regaining of the Saar, and the bold rearmament of Germany that removed some of the resentment caused by the Versailles Treaty. The annexation of Austria and the Sudeten Germans of Czechoslovakia, which accorded with the notion of unifying all Germans into one nation, certainly added to the widespread intoxication with the Führer. Moreover, in internal affairs, the new regime's success in virtually eliminating unemployment during the years of the worldwide Great Depression naturally met with approval – though it was achieved mainly through concentration upon armament production, which lowered living standards.

In Hitler's *Mein Kampf* and Alfred Rosenberg's *The Myth of the Twentieth Century*, one finds the application of H. S. Chamberlain's racial theories and the exaltation of the Aryan race. Other Northern peoples are described as carriers of cultures but not creators; they may serve the cause of creating the civilization of the *Herrenvolk* only under German leadership. But the Near Eastern race, represented especially by the Jews, is defined as the foe of all Aryan values, standing for the domination of matter over spirit. For Alfred Rosenberg, it was the influence of this Near Eastern people that was uppermost in the creation of Christianity. Furthermore, the Enlightenment's exaltation of Reason must also be rejected. The true Aryan "thinks with his blood; intuition is a more reliable guide to fundamental truths than reason." This emphasis on German "blood" resonated so well with the traditional German submission to temporal authority that it made easier the German people's acceptance of the Nazi "leadership principle."

The "leader" is the one who embodies the mystic intuition of the whole people; the people wills its own good and demands the subjugation of all individual wills to the general will. This mystic will is expressed not through democratic forms as in Rousseau, but through the leader, the fountainhead of the totalitarian state. There thus arises a new ethics: obedience to the will of the leader and the willingness to sacrifice oneself for the good of the whole. A corollary of this Nazi doctrine was the right of a "superior" people to dominate and rule those who are inferior. In *Mein Kampf*, Hitler expressly designated Central and Eastern Europe as the natural field for German expansion. There the German people would find its *Lebensraum*. The Nazis had thus abandoned and repudiated all traditional moral scruples in molding the German people into a powerful and soulless instrument of military aggression, conquest, and mass murder.

The war that Hitler first declared against the Jews soon engulfed all of Europe, Asia, and Africa through the Rome-Berlin-Tokyo axis. The occupation of Czechoslovakia in March 1939, in violation of the German pledge at Munich, had already convinced the British and French governments that counter-action was unavoidable. They now warned Hitler that further aggression would be met with force. But at this stage it proved impossible to check Nazi German power with mere words. The whole Nazi program was constructed on the principle of dynamic expansion and conquest, with each phase of an advance becoming the basis for a new advance, and culminating in the Nazi German domination of the European continent. Hitler had grown contemptuous of democratic warnings and was determined not only to consolidate past victories, but to continue the program of conquest. The evidence seems to be indisputable that Britain and France had been so often defeated, in the diplomatic duels between 1933 and 1939, that Hitler was persuaded of the infallibility of his methods: the "degenerate democracies" lacked the will to resist German expansion by force.

The Turning Point: The Attack on Poland

The Nazis had two grievances against Poland, which had existed since Versailles. First, the city of Danzig, 96 percent German in population, had been taken from Germany and made a "free city" under League supervision but united with Poland in a customs union. Second, the province of Pomorze had also been taken from Germany and incorporated in the new Polish state to provide it with a "corridor" to the sea. The corridor separated East Prussia from the rest of Germany; and for realistic observers, it was a near certainty that Hitler would redress the situation at the earliest opportunity. At first, however, he not only made no move against Poland, but even signed a 10-year non-aggression pact with the Warsaw government. At the time of the Munich pact, Poland even cooperated with Germany in the dismemberment of Czechoslovakia.

Polish illusions were, however, abruptly shattered in the summer of 1939 when Hitler launched his campaign for the recovery of Danzig and demanded the return of the corridor. In this crisis Britain and France declared support for Polish resistance. But the democracies pursued a policy that was doomed to failure: they tried to persuade Poland and Germany to settle their dispute peaceably, while at the same time warning Germany again that aggression against Poland would lead to a general war. The warnings went unheeded, of course, and on August 25, 1939, the world was shocked to learn of the Hitler-Stalin, non-aggression pact, a frightening event to the democracies because it now appeared that Germany need not fear the prospect of fighting a two-front war.

On September 1, 1939, Germany invaded Poland, and two days later Britain and France declared war upon Germany. Thus began World War II, and the consequent destruction of Europe. In 1933, Germany was a defeated and practically disarmed state without allies and without real international, political influence. By 1939, Hitler's Reich had become the colossus and terror of Europe. By the annexation of Austria, Czechoslovakia, and (thanks to the Hitler-Stalin pact) Memel, a port-city of the USSR in West Lithuania on the Baltic, the territorial holdings of the Third Reich became more extensive than those of the German Empire in 1914. The Reich had the largest army in Europe outside Russia, and had military alliances or "friendly understandings" with Italy, Russia, Hungary, Poland, Denmark, Lithuania, Spain, and Japan. In addition, Germany exercised extensive influence in the affairs of Romania, Yugoslavia, Bulgaria, and the Scandinavian states!

If we place ourselves in that historical context and ask how such a world crisis came about, the answer lies in the contrasting ideologies and outlooks of the Axis powers and those of the democracies. Nazi Germany, like fascist Italy and Japan, glorified war as a normal instrument of statecraft and even as the ideal condition of society. In their foreign policies they repeatedly threatened violence or war, and acted upon that threat to attain their objectives. The peoples of Britain and France, in contrast, who only 20 years earlier had lived through a war they regarded as the most horrible of all social catastrophes, shuddered at the prospect of another such bloodletting ordeal. The statesmen of the democracies were hampered in every crisis before 1939 by the knowledge that no will to war existed among their peoples, and that they, the statesmen, could make no move that might entail the danger of war.

Moreover, the political leaders of the democracies recognized just how formidable was the Nazi war machine in which the army was completely subservient. A close identity existed between the ruling party and the military caste. The officer corps, as we noted earlier, had sworn *personal* allegiance to Hitler. The close identity between the army and the party was the result of a deliberate Nazi policy, in which any real autonomy on the part of the military was destroyed. Officers of the old army caste who attempted to differ with the tenets of Hitler's foreign policy were eliminated. Hence, by 1938, the Nazi foreign office was able to back up its constant threat of war with a powerful war machine that had become an utterly subservient organization fully under the control of Hitler.

It seems clear in retrospect that German rearmament and aggression had, to some extent, taken Britain and France by surprise, owing to their miscalculation of the Nazi's real and ultimate aims. Britain, in particular, had adopted a policy of appeasement, acting on the mistaken assumption that Germany would become satiated and moderate with a few diplomatic victories. When, however, it became evident by 1938 that the Nazi appetite for conquest was insatiable, the democracies were caught completely off-guard. For by that time Hitler, at Munich, was able to force them to capitulate as they recognized he had temporarily gained the upper hand with his gigantic air fleet and fully armed ground forces. The appeasement policy did permit Germany to rearm, to carry through a series of audacious aggressions, and, finally, to plunge Europe and the world into a new catastrophe that came to be called "World War II."

The preceding historical sketch gives us some idea of what was transpiring at that time on center stage: the Nazi conquest of Europe and, with the invasion of the Soviet Union in 1941, the planned enslavement of the "lower" Slavic peoples. But, offstage, the Nazi war against the Jews was also set in motion – "offstage" because it received precious little attention outside of Germany.

The Nazi perpetration of genocide requires an understanding of the unique method employed, and its roots in Nazi and German ideology. And a good way to begin to convey the uniqueness of the method is to listen to Max Weber on the subject of modern "bureaucracy."

24

Max Weber on Bureaucracy and its Relevance for an Analysis of the *Shoah* (Holocaust)

Paramount in Weber's *Verstehensoziologie* (Interpretive Sociology) is the proposition that understanding others requires a method by which to grasp the motives and meanings of human actions – bearing in mind that meanings and motives are themselves causal components of action. In his typology of action, the first two types are directly relevant to the Nazi program for the extermination of an entire people. The first he calls *Zweckrationalität*, "goal rational" action. This is a cold rationality in the formal, technical, instrumental sense. The primary aim of such rationality is to find the most efficient and least costly means of attaining a given end. The second type Weber calls *Wertrationalität*, "value-rational" action. In one form of this type the individual has an overwhelming commitment to certain ultimate worldly ends, which he pursues unrelentingly without regard for the cost (human or material) that such a single-minded pursuit entails. Such conduct can take the form of exceedingly zealous actions, and even irrational fanaticism. Weber's conception of bureaucracy, as a "pure type," embraces both the "goal rational" and the "value rational" types of action.

Bureaucracy

For Weber, growing bureaucratization was one more powerful manifestation of the general "rationalization process" in modern Western industrial society. Conceived as a pure type, the modern bureaucratic organization has several distinctive characteristics. A "bureau," or "office," is an official jurisdictional area regulated by definite administrative rules. The typical bureaucrat's responsibilities are regarded as duties which he is qualified to carry out owing to specialized training. Bureaus are arranged in a hierarchy, a system of superordinate and subordinate offices. The underlying administrative rules of this type of organization are *general*, compelling the official to regulate matters abstractly, to treat people outside the organization as members of categories. The bureaucratic official fulfills his tasks in a dutiful manner and owes his allegiance to the office. He obeys orders and follows the rules not as a personal servant of his superior, but as an incumbent of office who is dedicated to the organization's mission. The increasing expansion of bureaucracy in modern society may be accounted for by the nature and growth of administrative tasks. In Weber's words:

> The decisive reason for the advance of bureaucratic organization has always been its purely *technical* superiority over any other form of organization. The fully developed bureaucratic apparatus compares with other organizations exactly as does the machine with the non-mechanical modes of production. *Precision, speed, unambiguity, knowledge of the files, continuity . . . strict subordination, reduction of friction and of material and personal costs – these are raised to the optimum point in the strictly bureaucratic administration, and especially in its monocratic form.*[1]

As Weber emphasizes, however, both in the private and state spheres, it is not merely considerations of efficiency but also of *power* that have accounted for growing bureaucratization. The bureaucratic tendency has been promoted by power politics, warfare, the creation of large standing armies, and by the immense budgets required for such purposes. Once bureaucratic structures are established, they are practically indestructible, Weber avers, because a state bureaucracy is a power instrument of the first order for those who occupy its command posts. It makes possible the domination and control of large numbers of people, both inside and outside the organization. The individual bureaucrat is chained to his specialized activity and is only a small cog in the total operation. His entire mind and body have been trained for obedience, and those who rule such organizations expect compliance as a matter of course. The vested power interests, and the widespread social control that the bureaucratic organization makes possible, also make the dismantling of bureaucracies extraordinarily difficult. Indeed, state bureaucracies are rarely, if ever, dismantled; they are merely taken over. The bureaucratic state apparatus, Weber observes, can be "made to work for *anybody* who knows how to gain control over it. A rationally ordered officialdom *continues to function smoothly after the enemy has occupied*

---

[1] Max Weber, *Economy and Society*, ed. Guenther Roth and Claus Wittich, 3 vols, New York: Bedminster Press, 1968, vol. III, 973, italics added. Hereafter, all page references to this work will be cited in parentheses immediately following the quoted passage.

the territory; he merely needs to change the top officials" (989; italics added).

Weber viewed the bureaucratization of modern society with apprehension. The immense concentration of power in fewer and fewer hands was bound to endanger liberal-democratic institutions and to diminish individual freedoms. For Weber, bureaucratic "discipline is nothing but the consistently rationalized, methodically prepared and *exact execution of the received order,* in which all personal criticism is unconditionally suspended and the action is unswervingly and exclusively set for carrying out the command" (1149; italics added).

German Ideology and Bureaucracy

Weber goes farther and passes judgment on the German variant of the bureaucratic phenomenon. Reflecting on Bismarck's legacy and its influence on the modern, political structure of Germany, Weber wrote in 1917:

> Bismarck left behind as a political heritage a nation without any political education, far below the level which, in this respect, it had reached twenty years earlier. Above all he left behind a nation without any political will, accustomed to allow the great statesmen at its head to look after its policy for it. Moreover, as a consequence of his misuse of the monarchy as a cover for his own interests in the struggle of political parties, he left a nation accustomed to submit, under the label of constitutional monarchy, to anything which was decided for it, without criticizing the political qualifications of those who now occupied Bismarck's empty place and who with incredible ingenuousness now took the reins of power into their hands.[2]

And J. P. Mayer remarks that Weber "never lacked the courage to say what he felt needed saying. Under the regime of the unknown corporal [Hitler], if he had experienced it, Max Weber would have died in a concentration camp" (ibid.).

J. P. Mayer also adds that the political docility of the German nation was formed by two conditions long before Bismarck. The first condition was:

---

[2] Cited in J. P. Mayer, *Max Weber and German Politics*, London: Faber and Faber, 1944, 78. Hereafter, all page references to this work will be cited in parentheses immediately following the quoted passage.

German Protestantism . . . while Luther directed the German individual soul to its mystical depth, he accepted "order" and "authority" with regard to the worldly state. Personal religiosity and state were thus fundamentally separated. Once the religious soul was assured of its intimate mystical union with its God, the individual could submit to the State, convinced that the sphere of the state could never interfere with his "real" depth. So the "free Christian" easily became the slave of the state. The Prussian state was predominantly Protestant. Church and Army concluded an alliance which explains, at least historically, what has been termed here political docility. (78–9)

Citing the work of Otto Hintze, *Die Hohenzollern und ihr Werk* (1916), Mayer avers:

All able-bodied men in Germany for more than a hundred years went through the "educational" machinery of the German Army; here, too, blind belief in "order" and "authority" were the guiding norms. They permeated the whole of German society. It has been said that the discipline of the German working-class organizations was a reflection of army discipline. The German workers obeyed their leaders, perhaps to a large extent against their better judgment, until their final doom was inevitable. (79)

Weber fully recognized that a docile submission to authority was a salient German characteristic; he recognized, too, that bureaucracy in Germany was a potentially dangerous instrument of tyranny. Given this danger, how did Weber propose to minimize the likelihood of the German bureaucracy's becoming a highly effective instrument in the hands of a tyrant?

It seems to be beyond dispute that for Weber the answer lay in the concept of "charisma." When the routine forms of social life prove to be inadequate for mastering a growing condition of distress, conflict, and suffering, Weber proposed charisma as a counterbalance to bureaucracy. He borrowed the term from Rudolf Sohm, the Church historian and jurist. As H. H. Gerth and C. Wright Mills observed, Weber used the term "to characterize self-appointed leaders who are followed by those who are in distress and who need to follow the leader because they believe him to be extraordinarily qualified."[3] It is a "gift of grace" (*Gnadengabe*), Weber believed, for a people or a nation to have a great, charismatic political leader. When used in a strictly technical-analytical manner,

---

[3] *From Max Weber: Essays in Sociology*, transl. and ed.,with an Introduction by H. H. Gerth and C. Wright Mills, London: Routledge & Kegan Paul, 1948, 52.

Weber's concept of charisma is supposed to be value-free. It has been applied to the founders of the world religions, and to historical figures such as Napoleon and Hitler.

Weber's Serious Error

Weber's theoretical ideas on charismatic leadership crystallized in the course of his reflections on post-war Germany and the embattled Weimar Republic. In the debates of 1919–20 on the new Constitution, Weber vigorously supported provisions for a popularly elected president. Describing Weber's attitude in this regard, Wolfgang J. Mommsen writes:

> by virtue of his direct links with the will of the masses the *Reich präsident* was to be an opening for the rise of political leaders over and above party machines and parliaments. In this way Weber hoped to assist a "leader democracy" to come to the fore in Germany, in which charismatically quali- fied politicians with a sense of foresight but also with a sense of proportion are at the helm, instead of a "leaderless" democracy of professional politi- cians without a calling.[4]

Like Nietzsche, and most likely under his influence, Weber assigned considerable weight to the role of the extraordinary individual in history. Only such individuals could make history by setting new goals and thus imparting new energy to the people. There was, however, no Nietzschean contempt for the masses here. "In contrast to Nietzsche's ethic of the master," writes Mommsen, "which culminated in the outright rejection of all democratic politics, Weber adhered to the fundamental principles of liberalism which hold sacrosanct the dignity of the individual and aspire to see society organized in such a way that all individuals may preserve a maximum of free initiative" (27). It was on the basis of such principles, and certainly not in opposition to them, that Weber formu- lated his ideas on charismatic leadership. What Weimar Germany needed in particular, Weber believed, were leaders of quality who could persuade the masses to voluntarily follow them. For Weber, great leaders emerged in response to an inner "calling"; they lived *for* politics, not off politics. In the competition of such leaders for mass followings, however, Weber

---

[4] *The Political and Social Theory of Max Weber*, Cambridge: University of Chicago Press/Polity, 1989, 22. Hereafter cited in parentheses immediately following the quoted passage.

approved of demagogy and emotional appeals designed to bind the masses to the leader.

A careful examination of Weber's writings reveals that he viewed charismatic leadership in a purely positive light. He was blind, somehow, to the anti-democratic and tyrannical potential of charismatic leadership. Only by keeping the charismatic principle alive could the world (Germany!) be saved from the mediocrity accompanying the inexorable advance of bureaucracy. Not too long after he died, however, the charismatic and bureaucratic principles were fused, in his homeland, in a *horrendous synthesis*. In that light, Weber's view of personal, *political* charisma, insofar as it was for him a purely positive phenomenon, was a serious error. Where Weimar Germany is concerned, it is easy to see why Weber discerned the need for strong liberal-democratic leadership. But it is difficult to understand why he failed to anticipate an anti-liberal fusion of the charismatic and bureaucratic principles, for he fully recognized the political immaturity and weakness of the German middle classes. Given their economic power and interests, they should have supported the strengthening of the Republic and its Constitution. Instead, however, they sought the protection of the old-regime elements against the working classes. The source of Weber's error, Mommsen proposes, was Weber's notion that the unrestrained will of the masses and their demands for equality were by far the greatest threat to the foundations of freedom in the Western world. Mommsen writes:

> By contrast, he [Weber] regarded as comparatively negligible the danger that the rule of the *Führer*, legitimized through a personal plebiscite, could turn into a dictatorial (or even fascist) regime, even though Weber himself had pointed out that in general "leader democracies" were characterized by a highly emotional type of devotion to and trust in the leader, and this accounted for a tendency to follow as a leader the type of individual who is most unusual, who promises the most or who employs the most effective propaganda measures. (34)

Under modern conditions, Weber proposed, a "leader democracy" requires a bureaucratic, administrative apparatus as well as a bureaucratic party organization. Their role is to serve as "obedient servants," ensuring that the leader's decisions are effectively carried out. Here, again, it is remarkable that the dangers and risks Weber perceived in this connection were the gradual undermining of the leader's charisma by the bureaucrats. The opposite danger, that the leader would succeed in wielding the entire state and party apparatus as an instrument of cold-blooded tyranny, Weber failed altogether to foresee. So, although Weber had never intended his theory of the charismatic political leader to be construed in an anti-democratic manner, his theory nevertheless lent itself to such an interpretation, for it gave pre-eminence to the political leader as opposed to the citizenry. Moreover, if one compares Weber with Robert Michels, a Weber disciple, one sees that Weber misinterpreted the relevant evidence. Michels decried the oligarchial tendency in democratic organizations in which leaders employed the administrative apparatus to preserve their own status and interests. The leaders of the German Social-Democratic Party, for example, behaved in a manner reminiscent of the Sun King, each thinking of himself: *Le parti c'est moi!* As Mommsen reminds us, however, Weber

> drew very different conclusions from the evidence of an increasing bureau-cratization within modern parties. Not only did he consider the trend towards "plebiscitarian democracy," which inevitably involved a sub-stantial enhancement of the role of political leaders at the expense of the "ruled," to be irreversible; he saw it also as a *positive* development, in that it served as a counterweight to the bureaucratization of the apparatuses of power. (100)

However, to support his contention that Weber's conception could be misconstrued even by a careful and sophisticated thinker, Mommsen cites the fact that

> Michels justified his decision to support Mussolini and the Italian fascist *Führerstaat* by express reference to Max Weber. Among other things, Michels was able to invoke Weber's explicit claim that the emotional attachment of the broad masses to the leader constitutes the specific characteristic of charismatic authority, and that the leader determines the content of policy on his own ultimate authority alone, while the assent of the supporters resides purely in their trust in the leader's charismatic lead-ership-qualities as such, rather than in their concurrence with the particular objectives he lays down. (102)

In this frank examination of Weber's theory of charismatic political leadership we see that he had failed to anticipate what I have called the "horrendous fusion of the charismatic and bureaucratic principles," which characterized Hitler's Nazi regime, and which made possible the destruction of the European Jews.

25

Charisma, Bureaucracy, and the "Final Solution"

Raul Hilberg's *The Destruction of the European Jews*

Hilberg began the research for this classic study soon after World War II and the perpetration of the mass murder of Europe's Jews. In the preceding chapter we considered the chief characteristics of bureaucracy as defined by Max Weber. It is therefore fitting for us to rely on Hilberg's pioneering analysis of the *Shoah* (the Hebrew word for the catastrophe that has come to be called the Holocaust), since his primary aim was to explore the bureaucratic instrument of destruction. As he proceeded in his analysis, he came to recognize that he was studying an administrative process "carried out by bureaucrats in a network of offices spanning a continent."[1] Gaining an understanding of the components of the bureaucratic apparatus became the principal task of Hilberg's lifework. In order to explain how the destruction process was carried out, he had to examine the roles of the main historical actors – the perpetrators, the victims, and the bystanders.

To appreciate the complexity and challenging nature of Hilberg's task, we have to remember that the planning of the *Shoah*, and the putting of it into practice, was from start to finish kept as secret as possible. No document stated explicitly the Nazi aim of annihilating a whole people. All available Nazi German documents relevant directly or indirectly to the *Shoah*, employed euphemisms, the real meaning of which the office holders in the bureaucratic hierarchy clearly understood. The term "final solution" itself serves as a primary example of an apparently innocuous phrase whose dreadful meaning soon came to be grasped even by the passive bystanders.

---

[1] Raul Hilberg, *The Destruction of the European Jews,* 3 vols, revised and definitive edn, New York: Holmes and Meier, 1985, ix. Hereafter, all page references to these volumes will be cited in parentheses immediately following the quoted passage.

The planning and implementing of the systematic annihilation of the Jews transpired between 1933 and 1945. It was an unprecedented event, an administrative process during which between 5 and 6 million men, women, and children were murdered in the short space of a few years. The fact that the plan for the *Shoah* and its actual perpetration were unprecedented helps explain why acts of armed resistance and opposition were desperate acts of last resort. For armed opposition to persecution and pogroms were almost absent from Jewish exilic history. The Jewish war against the Roman Empire that began in 66 CE and ended in 70 with the destruction of the Second Temple, and the later revolt of bar Kochba in *c.*135, are the last times we hear of major armed revolts. But the Jews at that time were still envisioning an independent Judea and still living in compact communities in the Eastern Mediterranean region, where such communities could render occasional support for the revolt. During the Middle Ages, however, the scattered Jewish communities of medieval Europe no longer contemplated armed resistance, and, instead, placed themselves under the protection of the rulers.

The Jews, as a "guest" people in the Christian countries of Europe, migrated chiefly as a response to two causes: expulsion and vanishing or declining opportunities by which to make a living. They rarely ran from a pogrom, a massacre organized or provoked by the regime, or a spontaneous outburst of the oppressed populace against the Jews for being apparent accomplices of the regime. The Jewish tendency had been not to run, but to survive under anti-Jewish regimes. For historical experience had taught the Jews that pogroms are temporary phenomena; they blow over and "normal" conditions, however oppressive, return. It should therefore be not surprising, given the unprecedented nature of the organized and unrelenting Nazi violence against the Jews, that at first they attempted to live with Hitler. They simply could not believe that the Nazi pogroms, too, would not cease. That was the main reason for the failure to escape while there was still time – refusing to believe the worst until the killers were already upon them. If we add the strikingly high degree of cultural assimilation and intermarriage of German Jews, it helps us understand why the Jewish leadership thought that compliance would somehow serve as an effective survival strategy. But, of course, the results of the compliance policy were catastrophic. The German Jews failed to recognize in time that for Hitler the destruction of the Jews overrode all other economic and military considerations. In contrast to all preceding pogroms, this one would continue until much of the "final solution" was realized. The German Nazi bureaucratic machine operated with accelerating speed and ever-widening destructive effect until the European Jews were destroyed.

The Administration of the Destructive Process

The process began with the task of definition. In 1933, the rate of inter-marriage between German Jews and Germans was most probably higher than in any other European country. The Jews had become, officially, almost completely emancipated and highly integrated into German society – at least in its everyday economic life, if not in its after-work, inter-ethnic social life. Defining who was a Jew with the aim of severing Jews from Germans was, therefore, an extraordinarily complex process. Hence, the early stage entailed definition, expropriation, and forced emigration; the later stage (1941–5) was an administratively continuous process that became more and more extreme. The bureaucrats sought ways of removing formal, procedural requirements that they found to be restraints on their actions. This bureaucratic striving for more efficiency and quicker results proceeded under the imposed requirement of strict secrecy. Increasingly, written documents, public pronouncements, and lawmaking, were abandoned and superseded by unpublished written directives and broad authorization to subordinates; and, eventually, by oral directives and by implicit understandings among officials that required no explicit orders. Consequently, as Hilberg writes:

> There was hardly an agency, an office, or an organization that did not at one time or another have an interest in anti-Jewish measures. If we were to enumerate the public and private agencies that may be called the "German government" and those agencies that may be called the "machinery of destruction," we would discover that we are dealing with identical offices. (I, 55)

The role of each hierarchy can be assessed along jurisdictional lines. The civil servants of the ministerial bureaucracy were the chief implementers of the anti-Jewish decrees of the early stages of the destructive process. It was they who wrote the decrees and regulations defining the concept of "Jew" – the regulations which provided for the expropriation of Jewish property and the ghettoization of the German Jews. But the same civil service played a large role in the actual destructive stage: the Foreign Office negotiated with Axis states for the deportation of Jews to killing centers; the German railways attended to the transport of the victims; the police fused with the Nazi Party's SS, engaged in the killing operations. The army, after the outbreak of war, and owing to its control of vast territories in Eastern and Western Europe, participated in the killing of Jews by special mobile units and the transport of Jews to the death camps. The big industrial and financial corporations fulfilled a major role in the expropriations, in the forced labor system, and even in the gassing of the victims. The party dealt with the delicate questions of German-Jewish relations – half-Jews, Jews in mixed marriages – and pressed for drastic action. The SS, the military arm of the party, amalgamated with the Interior Ministry's police to carry out the killing operations. Hence, the civil service, the army, the industrial and financial corporations, the police, and the party were the component elements of the far-flung administrative apparatus that carried out the destruction of the Jews. Each component fulfilled a specific function in the process, and each found the means of carrying out its task. In a word, the instrument of destruction was the *existing* German bureaucracy, so that no special agency and no special budget were necessary for the fulfillment of Hitler's mission.

If we return for a moment to the Nazi effort at determining who was a Jew and who an "Aryan," Hilberg shows that it was no easy task. The decrees of April 1933 stated that officials of *non-Aryan descent* were to be retired, the italicized phrase referring to any person who had a Jewish parent or grandparent, or was presumed to be Jewish if he or she belonged to the Jewish religion. The ministry had divided the populace into two categories: "Aryans," people with no Jewish ancestors (of pure "German blood"), and "non-Aryans," Jewish or Christian persons who had at least one Jewish parent or grandparent. What is especially interesting about this categorization is that it challenges a prevalent notion that the Nazi definition of Jewishness was based on *racial* criteria. But, as Hilberg emphasizes, the sole criterion for distinguishing "Aryan" from "non-Aryan" was religion, not the religion of the individual in question, but the religion of his ancestors. The Nazis were interested not in the "Jewish nose," but in eliminating the "Jewish influence." Even after the Nuremberg Nazi Party rally, when Hitler, on September 13, 1935, ordered a written decree to protect German blood and honor, the criteria remained unchanged. The non-Aryans were: *Mischlinge* of the second degree – persons descended from one Jewish grandparent; *Mischlinge* of the first degree – persons descended from two Jewish grandparents, but not belonging to the Jewish *religion* and not married to a Jewish person on September 15, 1935. Jews, however, were "persons descended from two Jewish grandparents belonging to the Jewish religion or married to a Jewish person on September 15, 1935, and persons descended from three or four Jewish grandparents (Hilberg, I, 80).

Before the bureaucratic machine had set in motion the actual process of annihilation, it turned its attention to the expropriation of Jewish property. Increasingly, Jewish families found themselves impoverished. The assault upon the Jews was general, affecting them in all walks of life. They were deprived of their professions, their enterprises, their savings, their wages, their claims upon food and shelter, and their personal belongings – including, at the end, the gold in their teeth and women's hair. Expropriation, then, after definition, was the second phase on the way to destruction. The third phase was the concentration, first of the German Jews and then of the Jews of the conquered territories.

The Reich-Protektorat Area

It was the German bureaucracy that planned and implemented the isolation of the Jews from the surrounding German population. It was a form of ghettoization, but without the walls of the later ghettos set up in Poland and Russia. Nevertheless, the Jewish communities formed under Nazi coercion in the cities of the Reich and the Bohemian-Moravian Protektorat had several characteristics of a ghetto, reflected in the five stages of the coercive process: (1) the severance of all social contact between Jews and Germans; (2) the restriction of places of residence; (3) the strict regulation of movement; (4) the imposition of measures for the identification of Jews; and (5) the introduction of a Jewish administrative role.

It was Heydrich who late in 1938 first proposed a direct marking of the Jews by means of "an insignia." But Hitler opposed the scheme at the time for some unknown reason – perhaps on aesthetic grounds. His opposition applied to the Reich-Protektorat area, so the marking of the Jews was first introduced in Poland, where it was assumed that Hitler's opposition was not in effect. In August 1941 the Propaganda Ministry at its own initiative approached Hitler to change his mind, and he agreed. A decree dated September 1, 1941 was issued, requiring Jews six years or over to appear in public only when wearing the Jewish star. Soon after this decree, the Security Policy extended the marking to residences. In 1942 the Jews were ordered to paste the star on their doors, in black print on white paper. The whole identification system, as Hilberg shows, greatly strengthened the powers of the police by making the enforcement of the decrees easier, and by enabling them to arrest any Jew anywhere at any time. Perhaps the worst consequence of the identification scheme was the paralyzing effect it had on its victims. It caused the Jews to be even more submissive than before. The wearer of the star felt as though all eyes were fixed upon him, as if "the whole population had become a police force, watching him and guiding his actions" (I, 179–80).

The Creation of a Centralized Authority in Ghettoized Jewish Communities

As Hilberg convincingly observes, the German Jews had themselves taken a fateful step in creating an administrative mechanism by means of which the Germans exercised a stranglehold on the Jewish population. Before 1933, the Jewish community organization was still decentralized, each city with a Jewish population having responsibility for the operation of Jewish schools, synagogues, hospitals, orphanages, and welfare activities. But during the days of the Weimar Republic, and reflecting the general political trend in Germany, Jewish leaders prepared plans for a central Jewish organization; and by the spring of 1933 a rudimentary central Jewish organization had been formed.

When, in that year, Jewish leadership, including the famous Leo Baeck, was confronted by the Nazi take-over, the leadership sought first an "open debate" with the Nazis on the subject of anti-Semitism and the Jewish future in Germany. The Jewish leaders expressed dismay at the Nazi boycott, and called attention to the 12,000 Jewish dead of World War I. The leaders of the now centralized Jewish community sought interviews with Hitler and other high-ranking Nazi officials, but only one materialized with Göring on March 25, 1933. After that, Jewish leaders were forced to deal with Nazi officials of lower and lower rank, until they were appealing to SS captains. But in 1933 such an outcome could not be foreseen. Leo Baeck recognized the powerlessness of the centralized agency and resigned from it after a few months.

It is understandable, then, why the *initial* policy of the Jewish leadership was based on the hope that the Nazis would moderate their anti-Jewish course. But by 1935, if not earlier, it had become clear that no moderation was to be expected. With the events of Kristallnacht and the aftermath in 1938, the Reichsvertretung (the centralized Jewish organization) had all but lost its representational character, and had become a federation for administrative purposes. The Jewish leadership decided that all those in the Old Reich who were Jews by religion should have to belong to this federation (Reichsverband). And by February 1939 this new, all-inclusive organization (Gesamtorganisation) acquired yet another name, the Reichsvereinigung. It is at this point that the last critical change occurred. On July 4, 1939, the last-named organization was taken over lock, stock, and barrel by the Security Police, who were empowered to assign additional tasks to it. Thus the centralized Jewish organization had inadvertently become an auxiliary instrument for the annihilation of the Jews.

What is truly remarkable about this phenomenon is the fact that the Germans had neither created this auxiliary instrument nor appointed its leaders, Rabbi Leo Baeck, Dr Otto Hirsch, and Direktor Heinrich Stahl. Equally remarkable was the diligence with which these leaders assisted the Germans in operations that had become lethal. The pattern of compliance began by reporting deaths, births, and other demographic data to the Reich security main office and by conveying German regulations in the publication *Jüdisches Nachrichtenblatt* to the Jewish populace. The pattern continued with the creation of special bank accounts accessible to the Gestapo, and with the concentration of Jews in designated apartment houses. And toward the end of the compliance pattern, the leadership consented to the provision of charts, maps, lists, space, supplies, and personnel in the preparations for deportation!

We have already touched upon the question of why the idea of resistance, in some form or other, seems never to have crossed the minds of the Jewish leadership. Armed resistance was out of the question for an unarmed populace with no recent military traditions of self-defense, especially since such traditions appeared to be totally unnecessary in the relatively civilized conditions of pre-Nazi Germany. Decades after the *Shoah*, some individuals have asked this counter-factual question: what if, after Kristallnacht and perhaps even later, the Jews had either spontaneously or under leadership expressed some form of non-violent resistance? The short answer is that the question itself is anachronistic, given the absence of any such tradition among the Jews or among any other European people, for that matter. On the question of resistance, it is perhaps relevant to cite the massacre in the Katyn Forest of many thousand members of the Polish officer corps and intelligentsia by another totalitarian power, the Soviet Union under Stalin. Many of those victims were armed, but that did not matter in the face of a decisively superior force. When a state has a monopoly on the most effective means of violence, resistance is almost impossible.

The German army, with its decisively superior forces, moved into Poland in September 1939, with terrible consequences for the Poles and the Jews, but especially for the latter. But it was there, as we shall see, where the Jews did finally take up arms under the most disadvantaged circumstances.

The Polish Jews under the Nazis

In Poland, the destruction process was well under way at the concentration stage when the German army moved into that country in September 1939. The Nazi bureaucratic machine moved faster in Poland where the Germans looked upon the East Europeans as subhuman and the East European Jews as even lower. This meant that in Poland no thought or care had to be given, as it had in Germany, to couples in mixed marriages or to the disruption of German-Jewish business relationships. Moreover, the exceptionally large Jewish population in Poland prompted greater destructive efficiency on the part of the executioners, with 10 percent of the Polish population being Jewish. Out of 33,000,000 million people

3,300,000 were Jews. Following the Stalin-Hitler pact, when the USSR and Germany divided Poland, 2,000,000 of those Jews suddenly found themselves under German domination. In Warsaw alone there were about 400,000 Jews, almost as many as had lived in Germany in 1933 and more than had remained in the entire Reich-Protektorat area at the end of 1939. The weight of such numbers posed different problems for the planners of the extermination of the Jews, and gave rise to different solutions. The initial governing authority was the army and the armed SS (*Waffen*-SS), the Nazi Party military formations that fought as integral units of the armed forces.

In September 1939, under orders from Security Police Chief Heydrich, the decision was made to clear German-speaking areas of Jews; to remove them from the Polish countryside, and to concentrate them in ghettos in the major cities. The Jews were to be ejected from Danzig, West Prussia, Poznan, and Eastern Upper Selesia, and to be shoved into the interior of Poland, a territory later known as the "Generalgouvernement." Once concentrated there, the Jews were to be further concentrated in cities located at railroad junctions or at least along a railroad.

Heydrich's orders stipulated, in addition, that a council of Jewish elders consisting of rabbis and influential individuals be set up in each Jewish community. The councils were to be held fully responsible for the exact execution of all Nazi instructions. Each council was to carry out a census of the Jews in its area and would be made responsible for the evacuation of the Jews from the countryside to the concentration points, for the maintenance of the Jews during transport, and for housing them upon arrival. The army, wanting no role in executing this plan, avoided, for the time being, dirtying its hands with this business. Ghettoization therefore became the responsibility of the Security Police Administration, which established several Jewish councils simply by identifying a Jewish leader and ordering him to form a *Judenrat*.

By December 1, the trains began to roll into the area of the General Government. Not only Jews and Poles from the conquered territories, but also Jews and Gypsies from the Reich were dispatched to the Generalgouvernement, the head governor of which was Hans Frank who ruled with an iron hand, zealously guarding his vast jurisdiction, but fighting a desperate battle with elements in Berlin who wanted to reduce his power or rob him of it altogether. There were therefore definite exceptions to his power, the first of which being the army, over which Frank had no authority. The second exception was the railway administration that had gained considerable autonomy and a crucial role in concentrating and deporting the victims. The third exception to Frank's authority was the combined force of the SS and the police, the domain of Heinrich Himmler, whose enormous power rested on his independence of any hierarchy, and his strategic position between two hierarchies: the ministe-rial bureaucracies and the party. His independence derived from the fact that he received most of his funds from the Finance Ministry and that he recruited most of his men from the party. Both fiscally and in its person-nel, the SS and police were, therefore, a civil service-party amalgamation.

Thus, Frank and Himmler were enemies from the very beginning, and it should come as no surprise that the conflict between them found its first target in the Jews; for Himmler's apparatus claimed primary author-ity in Jewish matters throughout Poland, where the destruction process began in its concentration stage. As noted earlier, Security Police Chief Heydrich issued his ghettoization order on September 21, 1939, *before* the civil administration had had a chance to organize itself for its role. This meant that in "Jewish affairs" Himmler was not only independ-ent of, but ahead of, Frank. These two men were the key leaders of the destruction process in Poland; for, as enemies and rivals, they competed in ruthlessness. Far from benefiting the Jews, the Frank–Himmler rivalry accelerated their destruction.

The ghettoization and dense concentration of the Jews in close quar-ters led to a typhus epidemic. Himmler could see no valid objection to the overstuffing of Jewish quarters. For Frank, however, the ceaseless stream of victims meant the plan to send many more thousands of Jews and Poles into the Generalgouvernement was out of the question simply because of space considerations, especially since the army was expropri-ating large tracts of land for maneuvers. On July 12, 1940, he informed his subordinates that the Führer himself had decided that no more trans-ports of Jews would be sent into the Generalgouvernement. Instead, all the Jews in the Reich, the Protektorat, *and* the Generalgouvernement were to be sent as soon as possible to an African or American colony. The general thinking, Frank said, centered on Madagascar, which France was to cede to Germany for that purpose. But Frank's assumption that he had prevailed was premature. There was no peace treaty with France and no African island for the Jews. Frank was stuck with his Jews, so he again protested that it was utterly impossible to receive such masses of Poles and Jews; there simply was no space for them. At this point, however, Hitler expressed his indifference to the population density of the Generalgouvernement, which, as far as he was concerned, was a "huge Polish labor camp" (Hilberg, I, 211).

The Jewish Councils (Judenräte)

Hilberg recognized that the "most important concentration measure prior to the formation of the ghettos was the establishment of the Jewish councils" (I, 216). A Generalgouvernement decree of November 28, 1939, required every Jewish community with a population of up to 10,000 to elect a Judenrat of 12 members, and every community exceeding 10,000 to choose 24. In Poland, as in the Reich, the Judenräte consisted of pre-war Jewish leaders. The members of these new councils naturally felt the anxieties associated with the magnitude of the responsibilities foisted upon them. Hilberg relates the recollection of one veteran Jewish member of the Warsaw Judenrat: when Adam Czerniakow, the leader of the council (a chemical engineer by training), met with several new appointees in his office, he showed them where he was keeping a key to the drawer of his desk in which he had placed a bottle with 24 cyanide pills.

In an earlier discussion, we attempted to explain the compliance of these councils by stressing the unprecedented and therefore unanticipated nature of the genocidal threat they faced. On the basis of Jewish historical experience, they believed and hoped that the murderous hostility of the Nazis was a temporary phenomenon. It, too, would pass. If we pose another counter-factual question, and think away the highly centralized organization of the Jewish communities in the Reich, and then in Poland – that is, think away the councils – that would have meant that the Jews would have had to fend for themselves when faced with the diverse Nazi threats. Doubtless, many would have perished in such circumstances. But it is a near certainty that far fewer would have died.

This is a highly plausible scenario in light of the facilitating role the councils played in identifying and concentrating the Jews. The councils transmitted German directives and orders to the Jewish populace and employed Jewish police to cooperate in enforcing the Nazi will. On the one hand, the councils made desperate attempts to alleviate the suffering and to stop the mass dying in the ghettos. On the other hand, and at the same time, the councils complied automatically with German demands and invoked German authority to exact the community's obedience and submission. The members of the Judenräte were held personally responsible for the execution of all the Security Police's demands. The Jewish leaders' understandable fear of the German overlords was such that the Nazi officers had merely to express their wishes. A few of the Jewish leaders felt an almost irresistible urge to emulate their German masters, while the majority complied in recognition of their powerlessness and in the hope of minimizing suffering and death.

The earliest ghettos appeared in the incorporated territories in the winter of 1939–40, and the first major ghetto was formed in the city of Lodz in April 1940. The Warsaw ghetto was established in October of that year. In August 1941, the Generalgouvernement acquired Galicia, an area the German army had wrested from Soviet occupation. The Galician capital, Lwow (Lemberg), became, in December 1941, the site of the third largest ghetto. For the Lodz ghetto the Security Police chose a slum area for its site, an area that had already contained 62,000 Jews and into which another 100,000 Jews had to be moved. The preparations for this plan had to be kept secret, and the moving of the Jews was to be sudden and precise. The point of the secrecy was to ensure the hurried abandonment of Jewish property, which could then be conveniently confiscated. After the movements had been completed, the Germans threw a fence around the ghetto. The Nazi in charge of the whole operation was Regierungs Präsident Uebelhoer who, of course, looked upon the creation of the ghetto as a transitional measure – a transition not to emigration, but to annihilation. The inmates of the Lodz ghetto either died there or were deported to a killing center.

Forming ghettos was not an easy undertaking from the start. In the case of Warsaw, the process took a year, beginning early in November 1939 when the military commander imposed a "quarantine" on the old part of the city, inhabited largely by Jews. Gouverneur Fischer of the Warsaw district proposed that the Warsaw Jews, whose number he estimated at 300,000, be incarcerated in a ghetto, and Frank gave his consent. The location of the ghetto for so large a population was an early issue. The first idea was to locate the ghetto on the eastern bank of the Vistula River, but it was turned down when it became known that 80 percent of Warsaw's artisans were Jews and that, as they were indispensable, it made no economic sense to wall them in. But in due course economic considerations were ignored, the Warsaw ghetto was enclosed by walls, and the policy of enclosing ghettos and cutting off all contact with the outside world was followed throughout the Generalgouvernement. In town after town, officials followed the same three-stage process. They selected the location for the ghetto, issued secret orders for the quick and sudden movement of the victims, and sealed off the ghetto upon its completion.

Owing to the high proportion of skilled Jewish workers, the ghettos became, ironically, an integral part of the German war economy. The entire Jewish populace was divided into occupational categories, carpenters in one section, tailors in another, and so forth. No manufacture requiring secrecy was allowed, and labor-intensive projects were favored. Typical ghetto production consisted of uniforms, ammunition boxes, leather and wooden shoes, metal gadgets and metal finishing work, brushes, brooms, baskets, and other such goods, the chief "customers" for which were the armed forces, the SS, and the police. The Germans came to depend on the output of the Jewish labor force. Frank himself acknowledged this dependence in the following remarks he added to his speech in a secret conference:

As for the rest, the Jews in the Generalgouvernement are not always decrepit creatures but a necessary skilled-labor component of the total structure of Polish life . . . we can teach the Poles neither the energy nor the ability to take the place of the Jews. That is why we are forced to permit these skilled Jewish laborers to continue in their work.

And Hilberg comments: "Indeed, the Jews had a powerful motivation to labor diligently. In their indispensability they saw their chance for survival" (I, 259).

Nazi Food Controls

But the indispensability of the Jewish skilled workers was temporary, as the Nazi chiefs knew and as the Jews themselves suspected. The survival of the ghetto population depended upon the supply of food and fuel. By decreasing and choking off the food supply, the Germans turned the ghettos into death traps. The Gestapo often complained to the other Nazi chiefs of the ghettos that they were receiving too much food and that the existing allocations were unjustified. In response, the Nazi chiefs would point to the raging epidemic, and to the collapse of workers who produced war material for the German army. The chiefs warned that even the existing food supply to the ghetto could no longer guarantee the continuation of production.

The consequences of the drastic reduction in deliveries of food, coal, and soap to the ghettos were rampant sickness and death. Typhus was virtually confined to the Jews, the causes being insufficient coal and soap, excessive room density leading to the multiplication of lice, and the lack of food lowering resistance to disease. In the situation of the Warsaw ghetto, fairly typical of the other ghettos, epidemics started in the synagogues and in other public buildings housing thousands of homeless people. In winter, the sewage pipes froze, the toilets could no longer be used, and human excrement was dumped together with garbage into the streets. Although typhus was the leading ghetto disease, tuberculosis in the fall and influenza in the winter were not far behind. As ghetto hunger went unchecked, and diseases spread, the mortality rate rose dramatically. A common sight in every ghetto was that of corpses lying on the sidewalk, covered with newspapers, pending the arrival of cemetery carts. For the Nazis this was an "aesthetic" problem. "The bodies," said Gouverneur Fischer to Czerniakow, "were creating a bad impression" (I, 268). For the German decision-makers, the death rate was in any case too slow. They sought and found a means of accelerating the destruction process.

Mobile Killing Operations

Defining, expropriating, and concentrating the Jews in ghettos were the first three steps taken by the Nazi bureaucracy toward the "final solution" of the so-called "Jewish problem." The euphemism "final solution" meant literally putting an end to Jewish existence in Europe.

The annihilation began in two major operations, the first of which was launched on June 22, 1941, with the invasion of the USSR. Together with the German army, small units of the SS and police entered Soviet territory with the aim of murdering all Jewish inhabitants wherever they were found. Soon after this operation began, a second followed in which the Jewish populations of Central, Western, and Southeastern Europe were transplanted to camps equipped with gassing installations. In the occupied areas of the USSR, the killers moved to the victims; outside of this arena, the victims were brought to the killers.

We know that the German invasion of the USSR had taken the Soviet government by surprise. Evidently, Stalin took seriously the non-aggression pact he had made with Hitler in 1939, refusing therefore to believe the invasion had taken place even after his generals had informed him of the fact. And it is true that the Germans did nothing to alert the Soviet government to any such imminent event. The absence of any alert meant that there were no effective defense measures in the frontline areas. This fact, and the special arrangement of the killing units with the German army, made it quite easy for the cowardly mobile units to go about their special business of murdering the unarmed Jewish civilian populace. In effect, the army provided cover for the mobile killers, for they did their dirty work in conquered territory.

The so-called Einsatzgruppen were the first mobile killing units. In March 1941, there was an agreement between the army and the RSHA[2] outlining the terms under which the Einsatzgruppen could operate in the USSR. The crucial sentence in the draft of the accord provided that "within the framework of their instructions and upon their own responsibility, the SonderKommandos [the mobile SS killers] are entitled to carry out executive measures against the civilian population" (I, 285). The army was to control the movements of the mobile units, and was to furnish the Einsatzgruppen with quarters, gasoline, food rations, and radio communications. More, according to the agreement of the army and the RSHA, the Einsatzgruppen were to be permitted to operate not only in army rear areas, but also in the corps areas right on the front line. This concession, as Hilberg observes, "was of great importance to the

---

[2] *Reichssicherheithauptamt* (principal service for the security of the Reich).

Einsatzgruppen, for the victims were to be caught as quickly as possible. They were to be given no warning and no chance to escape" (I, 286).

Who were these men of the Einsatzgruppen? Hilberg shows that the great majority were professional men. They included a physician (Weinmann), a professional opera singer (Klingelhöfer), and a larger number of lawyers. Hilberg writes:

> These men were in no sense hoodlums, delinquents, common criminals or sex maniacs. Most were intellectuals . . . [T]here is no indication that any of them sought an assignment to a commando. All we know is that they brought to their new task all the skills and training that they were capable of contributing. These men, in short, became efficient killers. (I, 289)

All this suggests that the army, though it claimed adherence to noble warrior values, was directly complicit in the mass killings of unarmed civilians. It suggests, too, that the party, through Hitler and Himmler, dictated policy to the army, which either could not or would not refuse complicity in the dirty work. The army allowed itself to provide cover for each of the Einsatzgruppen. Einsatzgruppe A was assigned to Army Group North; Einsatzgruppe B was detailed to Army Group Center; Einsatzgruppe C moved into the sector of Army Group South; and Einsatzgruppe D was attached to the Eleventh Army, in the extreme south.

When these mobile killing units crossed the border into the USSR, 5 million Jews were living under the Soviet flag. The majority of them were concentrated in the western parts of the country. Four million lived in territories overrun by the German army. Hilberg provides the size of the Jewish population for about 35 key cities, and the percentage of the total population that the Jews comprised. These data show that the geographic distribution of Soviet Jewry largely determined the strategy of the mobile killing units, their aim being to reach as many cities as fast as possible. The killing units moved closely on the heels of the advancing armies, trapping the large Jewish population before they had a chance to discover their fate. That was the reason for the RSHA's insistence on the right to send its mobile units to the front lines. The protective role of the army and the cowardice of the mobile killers is demonstrated by the fact that occasionally they found themselves in the middle of heavy fighting. "Einsatzkommando 12," Hilberg writes, "moving on the coastline east of Odessa to perform mass shootings of the Jews, was surprised by a Soviet landing party of 2,500 men and fled hurriedly under fire" (I, 293).

A few more words need to be said about the army's cooperation with the Einsatzgruppen that far exceeded the minimal support functions of the original agreement with the RSHA. The cooperation was all the more remarkable because the Security Police had expected only grudging acquiescence in the killing operations. Instead, the commanders of the Einsatzgruppen were pleased to see the army going out of its way not only to turn over Jews to the mobile killers, but also to participate in the killing operations, and to shoot Jewish hostages for alleged attacks on the occupation forces. The army sought to justify its actions on the pretext that the Jews were a bunch of Bolsheviks who supported the partisan war behind the German lines. The army generals had become so impatient for action that they virtually pushed the Einsatzgruppen into killing operations. This conduct on the part of the German officer corps, drawn from the ranks of the aristocracy, should not be altogether surprising; for they betrayed their noble-warrior ethos as soon as they swore personal allegiance to the "unknown corporal," and continued to defer to him in all matters.

The Role of the Other Ethnic Groups

In Hilberg's examination of the roles of the Hungarians, Romanians, Ukrainians, and Slavs in the destruction process, he found that the scarce references to the Hungarians show them to have been uncooperative with the Germans. In Zithomir, the Hungarian army stopped an action by police against the Jews. And Einsatzgruppe D reported that it had cleared a territory of Jews *except* for a small area occupied by Hungarian forces. The Romanian attitude, however, was one of sharp contrast. Romanian forces on the march repeatedly invaded Jewish quarters and killed Jews. Indeed, soon the mobile killings had become an operation of SS, police, and Romanian and German military units.

Hilberg proposes that much depended on the attitude of the civilian population among whom the Jews lived. He addresses the question of how the Slavs would react to the sudden annihilation of an entire people living in their midst. Would they hide the Jews or turn them over to the German occupation forces? Would they resist the killers or join in the killings? From the standpoint of the Einsatzgruppen commanders, these were important questions. The attitude of the Slavs seems to have been passive and inert. They felt no special affection for the Jews, and insofar as they felt any impulse to help the Jews, clearly they would have feared reprisals from the Germans.

One tactic of the Einsatzgruppen was to try to incite pogroms against the Jews, and to make them appear spontaneous. They had some success in the Baltic area, yet even there a commander remarked, "to our surprise, it was not easy at first to set in motion an extensive pogrom against the Jews." In fact, as Hilberg notes, no truly spontaneous pogroms, free from Einsatzgruppen influence, took place. All outbreaks were either organized or inspired by the mobile killers. All pogroms were implemented soon after the arrival of the killing units; the outbreaks were not self-perpetuating. Nor did new ones occur after the killers left and things had settled down.

Definition of "Jew" Again, and Himmler

The mobile killing units had no use for definitions. To them it made no difference whether the victims were half-Jews or quarter-Jews. Anyone who lived in the Jewish communities, who answered to the name "Jew," or was denounced as a Jew, was killed as a Jew. But the military and civilian bureaucrats and the police imported into the occupied territories the Nuremberg definition (three Jewish grandparents plus the Jewish religion or a Jewish marital partner), for the purpose of marking, identifying, concentrating, and ghettoizing the Jews. The definition, found only in secret directives with controlled distribution, met with no protests from the SS or the police. In the beginning of 1942, however, the Ministry for Eastern Occupied Territories decided to issue a definition more appropriate for the Eastern area than the Nuremberg decree. The new definition was broader: any person was to be considered Jewish if he belonged to the Jewish religion or had a parent who belonged to the Jewish religion. A declaration that the father or mother was Jewish was to be entirely sufficient. When Himmler heard about the definition-making, he wrote the following letter to the chief of the SS-Main Office, Obergruppenführer Berger:

> I request urgently that no ordinance be issued about the concept of "Jew." With all these foolish definitions we are only tying our hands. The occupied eastern territories will be cleared of Jews. The implementation of this very hard order has been placed on my shoulders by the Führer. No one can release me from this responsibility in any case. So I forbid all interferences. (Hilberg, I, 368)

And Hilberg comments: "no one could interfere with Himmler now, for the second sweep [of mobile killings] had begun, leaving in its wake the demolished ghettos of the occupied East" (ibid.). The second sweep began in the Baltic area in the fall of 1941 and spread through the rest of the occupied territory during the following year. The killing machinery of the second sweep was larger and more elaborate than the first. Himmler's forces were now joined by army personnel in mobile and local operations designed for the total annihilation of the remaining Jews of the Soviet Union. As the Red Army advanced westward, Himmler ordered the destruction of all the grave sites so as to leave not a single trace of the massive and deliberate destruction of human life.

Himmler and all the direct and indirect participants in the destruction process obeyed Hitler as if he were God. When, in the nineteenth century, Nietzsche proclaimed that God is dead, he never could have anticipated the apotheosis of an individual like Hitler. The campaign to annihilate the Jews originated with Hitler, who recognized the pariah status of the Jews in Western Christendom, and the political usefulness of this traditional scapegoat. But there was also a personal, vengeful motive in Hitler's depraved mind. In a speech he delivered in January 1939, he revealed the personal source of his hatred for the Jews, though he couched it in imaginary and preposterous allegations:

> In my life, I have often been a prophet, *and most of the time I have been laughed at.* During the period of my struggle for power, it was in the first instance *the Jewish people that received with laughter my prophecies that some day I would take over the leadership of the state and thereby of the whole people, and that I would among other things solve also the Jewish problem. I believe that in the meantime that hyenous laughter of the Jews of Germany has been smothered in their throats.* I want to be a prophet once more: If international-finance Jewry inside and outside of Europe should succeed once more in plunging nations into another world war, the consequences will not be the Bolshevization of the earth and thereby the victory of Jewry, but the annihilation [*Vernichtung*] of the Jewish race in Europe. (Hilberg II, 393; italics added)

No one likes being laughed at; and it appears that for this self-styled "prophet" the laughter of the Jews had provoked an obsessive, unceasing murderous hatred. This speech is quite similar to the political testament Hitler dictated in his own bunker in the early morning hours of April 29, 1945, just before he put an end to his life. In this testament the Jews remain his *idée fixe* as he again accuses the Jews of having caused the war that he himself had provoked with such catastrophic consequences for all peoples, including the German people. For this "unknown corporal," who had become the pompous, arrogant, genocidal dictator of Germany, his own role in causing World War II remained, apparently, hidden from him in an unbelievable form of self-deceit; it was either that or a deliberate attempt to continue to deceive those who were already inclined to be thus deceived. Hitler, at the very end of his life, dictated this exercise in self-deceit or big-lie deceit, concerning his legacy:

It is untrue that I or anyone else in Germany wanted the war in 1939. It was desired and instigated exclusively by those international statesmen who were either of Jewish descent or worked for Jewish interests. I have made too many offers for the control and limitation of armaments – which posterity will not for all time be able to disregard – for the responsibility for the outbreak of this war to be laid on me. I have, further, never wished that after the first fatal war a second against England, or even America, should break out. Centuries will pass away, but out of the ruins of our towns and monuments the hatred against those finally responsible, whom we have to thank for everything, international Jewry and its helpers, will grow.

I also made it quite plain that if the nations of Europe were once more to be regarded as mere chattel to be bought and sold by these international conspirators in money and finance, then that race, Jewry, which is the real criminal of this murderous struggle, will be saddled with the responsibility. Furthermore, I left no one in doubt that this time not only would millions of children of Europe's Aryan peoples die of hunger, not only would millions of grown men suffer death, and not only would hundreds of thousands of women and children be burned and bombed to death in the cities – but also the real criminal would have to atone for his guilt, even if by more human [sic] means.

After six years of war, which in spite of all setbacks will go down one day in history as the most glorious and valiant demonstration of a nation's life purpose, I cannot forsake the city which is the capital of this Reich. As the forces are too small to make any further stand against the enemy attack at this place, and our resistance is gradually being weakened by men who are as deluded as they are lacking in initiative, I should like, by remaining in this town, to share my fate with those millions of others, who have also taken it upon themselves to do so. Moreover, I do not wish to fall into the hands of an enemy who requires a new spectacle organized by the Jews for the amusement of their hysterical masses.

I have decided therefore to remain in Berlin and there of my own free will to choose death at the moment when I believe the position of the Führer and Chancellor itself can no longer be held. (cited in Hilberg, III, 989)

Ian Kershaw's Recent Re-examination of the Issues

In his study, titled *Hitler, the Germans and the Final Solution*, Ian Kershaw reviews the latest research on the subject, giving special attention to the literature published after Raul Hilberg's monumental work. Kershaw's review tends to support the proposition that Hitler might never have given an explicit order for the "Final Solution." But, of course, he had no need to give such an order, since his speeches were tantamount to such an order. We have already examined the significance of his 1939 speech in which he "prophesied" the destruction of a multitude of Jews. He made a similar "prophecy" in the remarks he addressed to his party leaders in the Reich Chancellery on December 12, 1941. We learn from Goebels' diary the gist of what Hitler had said. "With regard to the Jewish Question," Goebels wrote, "the Führer is determined to make a clean sweep. He prophesied that if they brought about another world war, they would experience their annihilation. This was no empty talk. The world war is here. The annihilation of the Jews must be the necessary consequence."[3] Four days later, on December 16, Hans Frank, Governor-General of Poland, speaking to his own circle, repeated Hitler's "prophecy" almost verbatim: "What is to happen to the Jews?" he asked rhetorically. "Do you believe they'll be accommodated in village settlements in the *Ostland*? They said to us in Berlin: why are you giving us all this trouble? . . . Liquidate them yourselves! We must destroy the Jews wherever we find them." But *how* this was to be accomplished he did not as yet know. His estimate of the number of Jews in his domain was 3.5 million. "We can't shoot these 3.5 million Jews," he mused, "can't poison them, but we must be able to take steps leading somehow to a success in extermination" (ibid.). Clearly, Frank's remarks preceded the extermination program. Neither he nor his subordinates needed an explicit order from Hitler.

Several weeks later at the Wannsee Conference on January 20, 1942, Frank's right-hand man, Josef Bühler, asked whether steps could be taken immediately in his area. Evidently, the answer was in the affirmative, since by the spring of 1942 a comprehensive extermination program was set in motion, extending from certain districts to the whole of the Generalgouvernement as trainloads of Jews were transported to the newly erected camps of Belzec, Sobibor, and, somewhat later, Treblinka. Ten days after the Wannsee Conference, on January 30, 1942, speaking at the Sportpalast, Hitler again invoked his "prophecy" of 1939, assuring his listeners that the war would end with the annihilation of Jewry. Goebels again wrote in his diary (end of March 1942), "the Führer is the unswerving champion and spokesman of a radical solution." In the spring and summer of 1942 the deportations to the death camps in Poland – now including the largest of all, Auschwitz-Birkenau – were extended to the whole of the Generalgouvernement and to Slovakia and the occupied countries of Western Europe. And Kershaw cogently remarks:

---

[3] Ian Kershaw, *Hitler, the Germans, and the Final Solution*, New Haven, CT, and London: Yale University Press, 2008, 107. Hereafter, all page references to this work will be cited in parentheses immediately following the quoted passage.

previous important decisions concerning the "solution of the Jewish Question," such as the introduction of the yellow star or the deportation of the Reich Jews, had required Hitler's authorization. It is unimaginable that it was not again sought and given for the massive extension of the killing program. (Ibid.)

According to post-war testimony of his former personal adjutant, Otto Günsche, and his manservant, Heinz Linge, Hitler showed a direct interest in the development of gas chambers. Given the Nazi determination to shroud the destruction of the Jews in secrecy and to avoid explicit statements in documents, there is no reason to doubt that Hitler gave verbal consent to the accelerated extermination and stood behind every major decision of Himmler's and his underlings. In any case, all that was necessary for the bureaucracy to get the "message" and attend to the "details" was the "charismatic leader's" spewing of hatred of the Jews unceasingly. Without Hitler, Kershaw concludes, "the creation of a program to bring about the physical extermination of the Jews of Europe is unimaginable" (111).

26

Leon Poliakov's Complementary Analysis of the *Shoah*

From both Hilberg and Poliakov we learn that the annihilation of the Jews was ordered in 1941, at the moment when it had become clear that Hitler's dreams of 1939–40 would not materialize. The war he had started as a blitzkrieg would be prolonged. Speedy new victories were out of the question; chances of a compromise peace with Britain had vanished; and the invasion of Russia with an army in its summer uniforms was not turning out well.

Hence, it quite accorded with the mental attitude of the Führer and his circle to make the German people accomplices in the perpetration of an unprecedented collective crime. The point was to involve the people in an undertaking from which there was no turning back. Poliakov cites a passage from Goebels' diary, dated March 2, 1943, that has the ring of desperation:

> We are so entangled in the Jewish question that henceforth it is impossible to retreat. All the better. A movement and a people that have burned their bridges behind them, fight with a great deal more energy – experience shows it – than those who are still able to retreat.[1]

The phrase "final solution" first appeared in 1938 and changed its meaning in the proceeding contexts. At first it was applied to the project for total emigration – the so-called Madagascar plan. From the end of 1941 on, however, it indicated annihilation. This is evident, as we have seen, from the fact that with the invasion of Russia, the Jews of

---

[1] Leon Poliakov, *Harvest of Hate: The Nazi Program for the Destruction of the Jews of Europe* (originally published as *Bréviare de la haine*, Paris: Calmann-Lévy, 1951. First English edition published in New York by Syracuse University Press, 1954). Foreword by Reinhold Niebuhr. The quote is from 110 of the English edition. Hereafter, all page references to this work will be cited in parentheses immediately following the quoted passage.

the invaded territories were systematically murdered by the mobile SS detachments, the Einsatzgruppen, who followed behind the armies. Jews were executed on the spot, the technique being simply a matter of shooting people and dumping them into common graves.

That was the nature of the first stage, a prelude to a more sophisticated method of murdering a large number of human beings. Beginning in the spring of 1942, many of the death camps (Belzec, Treblinka, Sobibor) began to operate in Poland, destroying thousands of victims every day. The assassination of Heydrich in May 1942 had the effect of accelerating the mass deportation from Warsaw. Adolf Eichmann, the chief cog in the bureaucratic structure, extended his network throughout Europe. Poland, the "trashcan of Europe" in Nazi terminology, was the place of execution, the site where the gas chambers and crematories were constructed. Striving for new and improved methods for the killing of multitudes, "Cyclone B" – an insecticide with a prussic acid base – soon replaced carbon monoxide at Auschwitz. There seems to have been a third stage in October 1942, with a new and final intensification of operations. At the end of September, von Ribbentrop instructed all the German diplomatic services "to speed up as much as possible the deportation of all Jews from Europe." Everywhere German diplomats assisted Eichmann. His boss, Himmler, ordered the setting aside of all economic considerations, and replaced with Polish Aryans the remaining Jewish specialists in German industries.

The extent to which the Jews were a personal obsession for Hitler is evident in the fact that a few weeks later he ordered Himmler to put the extermination program into high gear. It appears that every Allied act that threatened to thwart Nazi plans prompted Hitler to order the acceleration of the destruction process. Poliakov cites the words of Himmler in a conversation with Dr Felix Kersten. In answer to the Allied landing in North Africa, the "Führer ordered intensified action against the Jews still in our power" (116). Indeed, the Führer asked for a statistical report on the progress of the mass murder, and had the satisfaction of learning that "since 1933, i.e., during the first decade of National Socialism, European Judaism decreased by almost one half" (ibid).

Hitler's Euthanasia Program

The "German technical genius for efficiency" is something of a cliché, and yet the phrase is a quite apt description of the rationalized industry of death that the Germans had set up within a few months. In 1939, it became known in Germany and beyond that effective and discreet methods of extermination were first perfected by German doctors and scientists for application in Hitler's euthanasia program. The methods of putting to death the so-called mentally ill were, in due course, applied on a large industrial scale by Himmler's SS as the most efficient way to dispose of Europe's Jews. It is significant that the decree activating the euthanasia program is dated September 1, 1939, the day on which war was declared. Hitler took the precaution of trying to keep the program secret, and it was never officially promulgated. The chief administrators were well-known German scientists who participated with enthusiasm, estimating at 1 million the number of Germans whom it would be desirable to excise from the German populace. The program, as a state matter, commenced and proceeded without informing or consulting either the prospective victims or their families. The method the doctors and scientists devised was asphyxiation by carbon-monoxide gas. The installations constructed with that aim in view were euthanasia stations, each consisting of a hermetically sealed room camouflaged as a shower with pipes connected to cylinders of the gas. From January 1940 to August 1941, when the euthanasia program was stopped, 70,273 mental patients were so treated.

In its operations, the program came directly under the Führer's personal authority and was not officially connected with Himmler's RSHA. But Poliakov regards it as no accident that the euthanasia stations were established near large concentration camps, for it is a fact that from the summer of 1940 on, the chiefs of the camps made periodic selections of candidates for euthanasia from among the camp prisoners. And they were picked not on the basis of their poor mental condition, but rather for the political reasons of their original arrests. Despite the attempt to keep the program secret, its existence became known. Families suspected something terribly wrong when they received death notices, and told their friends. Moreover, the collective transfer of "patients" from the asylums to "observation" facilities, and from there to the euthanasia stations, could not go unnoticed. Soon the truth became known and spread all over Germany.

The expression of popular outrage made it easier for the Catholic and Protestant Churches to take a firm stand. The Nazis tried to change the Churches' attitude, but to no avail. Popular opposition grew and Hitler had to back down, ordering, in August 1941, that the program be discontinued. *This was the one and only time* that the German people had effectively set limits to Hitler's power. He could often whip up popular emotions with his rhetoric, leading them in dangerous paths, but in this case the horrors of the program were such that it elicited from the people a nearly unanimous opposition to the Führer's will. Horrors perpetrated by the Hitler regime on Germans was one thing, but perpetrated on Jews and other "subhumans" was quite another. The euthanasia program was, in effect, a dress rehearsal for the implementation of the "final solution."

The first death camp, Chelmno, near Lodz, began operations in the annexed territory in December 1941, with a maximum rate of a thousand executions a day. But Chelmno had not as yet constructed permanent gas chambers; it possessed only a large garage with several "gas trucks." In March 1942 the completion of the Belzec camp, with a daily rate of several thousand executions, made a real start on the destruction of the Jews. The Maidenek camp, near Lublin, was a "delayed extermination camp" – the victims were either worked to death or, if they survived, gassed to death. A Polish government commission concluded that at Maidenek over 200,000 Jews and non-Jews died during 1943–4. And the inquiries of the Polish Commission for war crimes have established that the total number of victims at Belzec was close to 600,000; 250,000 at Sobibor, more than 700,000 at Treblinka, and more than 300,000 at Chelmno. More than 90 percent were Polish Jews.

Auschwitz

Rudolf-Franz-Ferdinand Hoess, the son of a tradesman, member of the party from 1922, and a member of the SS "Death's Head Division" from 1934, advanced rapidly up the ladder of the SS administration of the concentration camps. In 1940, Hoess became the head of the new camp built a few kilometers from the little town of Auschwitz (in Polish, Oswiecim) in Upper Silesia, an area which Poland and Germany had fought over, and which with Poland's defeat was annexed by the Third Reich.

The abundance of manpower attracted German industries to the site, where I.G. Farben and the Hermann Goering works began building factories near the camp in the spring of 1941. Among the principals in the extermination program, Hoess was the only one captured and tried by the Allies. In the course of his trial he made lengthy depositions, which may be summed up succinctly: Himmler had called him to Berlin in June 1941, informing him that Hitler had given orders to proceed with the "solution of the Jewish question in Europe." Auschwitz, situated as it was near the junction of four railroads, lent itself to the task of wholesale extermination. That was the reason for the choice of Auschwitz, and Himmler ordered Hoess to start preparations immediately.

Hoess' statement, together with the rest of his testimony, was substantiated by an Inquiry Commission set up by the Polish government after the war. It fell to Hoess to devise the most efficient means of extermination. The idea was simple: all kinds of vermin, bedbugs, and the like infested the old Auschwitz barracks, and conventional methods were employed for getting rid of them. Working for the *Wehrmacht* at that time was the Testa Company that supplied a gas with a prussic acid base, patented as "Cyclone B." As a stock of it was on hand, it required little imagination to hit upon the idea of using this gas on human beings. It somehow followed logically from Hitler's curses and the threats uttered by Goebels. Poliakov cites Hitler's remarks in *Mein Kampf*:

if at the beginning of, or during the war [World War I] 12,000 or 15,000 of these Jewish corrupters of the people had been plunged into an asphyxiating gas ... the sacrifice of millions of soldiers would not have been in vain. (199)

And Goebels:

It is true that the Jew is human, but the flea is also a living being, not too pleasant a one ... Our duty towards ourselves and our conscience consists in making the flea harmless. The same is true of the Jews. (Poliakov, 199–200)

The capacity of the earliest permanent installations for the gassing of victims was small; and as there was no crematory, the bodies were burned in the open. The earliest victims in 1941 appear to have been Russian prisoners of war, 70,000 approximately. It was not until the summer of 1942 that the mass murder of the Jews began. By then Auschwitz had undergone major changes, having become a "concentration-camp" city with a population of at least 150,000, guarded by more than 3,000 SS men. The guarded were not only the prospective victims of the gas chambers, but also the many thousands of deported slave laborers. Tens of thousands of prisoners, Jews and non-Jews, worked in the I.G. Farben factories, producing artificial rubber and synthetic gasoline. Other prisoners toiled in the Krupp armament works, in the coalmines of the Upper Silesian basin, in diverse secondary factories, or in the many farms and the SS experimental stations. The selections took place upon the arrival of the victims, and the majority were sent immediately to an anonymous death; the others joined the ranks of the slaves and were tattooed with a number. The average life expectancy for them was no more than three months.

In time, the two original gas chambers proved to be inadequate, and four new ones were built. The contractors who were awarded the work wanted to bring under one roof the two phases of the operation, asphyxiation and incineration. At the beginning of 1943, crematories II and III were dedicated in the presence of "very important persons" from Berlin; 8,000 Jews from Cracow, the capital of the Generalgouvernement and the residence of Hans Frank, were the first victims of the new crematory techniques. The four crematories contained 41 ovens, with a total capacity of 12,000 bodies every 24 hours. By 1944, even the four crematories proved to be inadequate and the ovens had deteriorated, so the attendants resorted to huge funeral pyres in the open. This was the time, a night in August 1944, when 4,000 Gypsies were gassed, the last survivors of

Auschwitz's Gypsy population – the only example of a total and mass extermination of non-Jews. After some 30 months of operation, the Auschwitz balance sheet showed close to 2 million exterminations, to which must be added the deaths of some 300,000 numbered prisoners, most of them Jews.

Poliakov provides the gory details of how selections were made for annihilation. The men and women who could walk proceeded to the gas chambers on foot; the old and sick were transported in trucks. There they were told by the SS man that they were going to shower and be disinfected. Then they were led to "dressing rooms," where numbered hooks lined the walls, and the guide advised them not to forget their numbers. To strengthen the deception, bars of gritty soap were distributed. In most cases the deception worked. The gas chambers into which they were led even had simulated shower heads. An SS man, wearing a gas mask, dropped the required number of cans of Cyclone B gas (from 5 to 7 kilos for every 1,500 persons) through the small windows on the roof that had been constructed for that purpose. The asphyxiation lasted three to ten minutes, depending on resistance and "atmospheric conditions" – the gas worked more rapidly in warm and dry weather. A half-hour later, the members of the "Sonderkommando" opened the doors and transported the bodies to the ovens – after cutting off the women's hair and removing all gold teeth, rings, and earrings. Incineration took a half-hour, four or five bodies incinerated at a time in each oven. At first, the ashes were simply dumped into ditches; later, the ashes were loaded on to trucks and emptied into the nearby Vistula. As the make-believe showers and bars of soap served their purpose, the victims recognized their fate only at the last moment. Hoess, in his complacent discussion of these matters in his depositions, insisted on "this advance" made over Treblinka: "The Treblinka victims almost always knew they were going to be exterminated, while at Auschwitz we joked with them, made them believe that they were going to have a delousing treatment" (cited in Poliakov, 205–6).

Poliakov adds a few words about Auschwitz's innovation: Cyclone B. The Testa Company's books recorded the delivery of more than 27,000 kilos of Cyclone B to the SS camp administration during the years 1942–3, of which more than 20 thousand were for the Auschwitz camp alone. The gross profit from this delivery was 32,000 Reichmarks in 1942, and 128,000 Reichmarks in 1943.

The "Death's Head" Formations (SS Totenkopf)

Trained in 1933 to guard, degrade, and torture the "subhumans" and enemies of the regime, the chief function of these "specialized troops" was to crush the slightest tendency toward resistance in the inmates of the camps. The Death's Heads' one and only method was the infliction of a variety of cruel and refined suffering. Owing to the "refined" and "efficient" methods employed, only a few dozen officials participated directly in the extermination process. The Sonderkommandos, consisting of prisoners, served the crematories. A few SS men and doctors constituted the German personnel. "It was indeed," as Poliakov observes, "a factory working with great efficiency on the assembly-line principle." That is why Hoess could state: "I have never personally killed or struck anybody" (209).

Back to the Question of a Distinctive German National Character

Poliakov cites the testimony of Dr Gilbert, the Nuremberg prison psychiatrist, who questioned Hoess several times in his cell, and could only get the following out of him: "You can be sure that it was not always a pleasure to see those mountains of corpses and to smell the continual burning – But Himmler had ordered it and had even explained the necessity, and I really never gave much thought to whether it was wrong. It just seemed a necessity." Hoess showed not the slightest sign of remorse. When pressed further by Dr Gilbert, Hoess replied: "The thought of refusing an order just didn't enter one's head, regardless of what kind of order it was . . . Guess you cannot understand our world. – I naturally had to obey orders and I must now stand to take the consequences" (211).

But if a few dozen Germans – hundreds at the most – were directly involved in the last agony of the Jews in the gas chambers, those

who witnessed their long Calvary were numbered in the hundreds of thousands. The SS formations stationed in the camps; the German workers, Army units, and officials at the numerous yards and factories where the Jewish slaves were used, whom they passed by daily; the railway men handling the innumerable transports of deportees all over Germany, which they saw coming back empty, if they were not loaded with used clothing which was distributed to the needy [Germans] by all the welfare offices in the country. This is a very incomplete list of those who can properly be called eye witnesses. As for the rest of the Germans, the press and radio of the Reich undertook to inform them more and more openly of what was going on. The time for vague and prophetic imprecations by Hitler had passed. The language now sharpens and it is the past tense that is employed. "The Jewish population of Poland has been neutralized, and the same may be said right now for Hungary. By this action five million Jews have been eliminated in these two countries," a Danzig newspaper wrote in May 1944. And the next day Goebels' *Der Angriff* published under the byline of Ley: "Judea must perish that mankind be saved." The extermination policy thus became a matter of common knowledge, and enough information filtered through a thousand channels for the location of the murder camps and the methods of execution to become notorious. (Poliakov, 211–12)

But one must ask whether there were extenuating circumstances that ought to be taken into account before we judge the German people of the time. In the historically specific conditions of totalitarian Germany, we have, perhaps, to ask whether organized resistance to Hitler's regime was possible. Decent individuals and small groups of conscience who wish to resist in such circumstances must themselves be prepared to die and also to place their loved ones in extreme jeopardy. Although it is most probably true that the majority of Germans knew what was being perpetrated, the question remains: what could they have done about it? What might they have done to prevent or to put a stop to it? Poliakov addresses this question.

A significant number of Germans were in fact prepared to die and to place their loved ones in serious jeopardy. They not only rendered secret help to the Jews in distress, but dedicated their lives to resisting Nazism. Poliakov cites the dean of the Church of Saint Hedwige in Berlin, Canon Lichtenberg who was imprisoned in October 1941 for his pro-Jewish sermons and public protests. At his own request, the Gestapo transferred him to the Lodz ghetto, and he died at Dachau in 1943. There was the anonymous German doctor who voluntarily followed his Jewish wife to the Warsaw ghetto, where he was killed in the uprising of April 1943. There must have been hundreds and perhaps thousands of such cases when we remember that there were several thousand German Jews with false papers who found secret shelter in Nazi Germany. And it is a significant and relevant fact that in the last Reichstag elections of 1933, 55 percent of the German electorate voted against Hitler.

We cannot, of course, know with certainty how the majority of people in other states might have behaved in circumstances similar to those in Nazi Germany – although we do have comparative evidence from the other totalitarian regimes of the twentieth century, where there was also precious little resistance. Can we nevertheless speak of a specifically German mode of thinking and conduct? As we saw in an earlier discussion of the German national character from the time of Luther, obedience to temporal authority became an increasingly paramount principle. Philosophers, journalists, and teachers exalted the Prussian ideal of inflexible hardness and blind obedience until Hegel himself deified the

Prussian state. By the late nineteenth century, pan-German agitation had reached a peak in Germany, creating fertile ideological soil for Hitler's National Socialism.

It was partly as a reaction to Napoleon's defeat of Prussia that German nationalism emerged. In the succeeding decades, however, German nationalism increasingly began to proclaim the superiority of the German "race," urging Germany on to new and joyous wars. In that sense, the ground had been prepared for the Nazi catastrophe and for the apotheosis of a Führer. In Poliakov's words: "when the Führer, before marching the Nazi legions off to conquer the world, carefully trained them to be hard, cruel and violent men, to stamp all pity from their hearts, to silence their *conscience* – that 'Jewish invention' – he merely gave life and form to a vague ancestral dream" (285).

Significant Political Differences Between Eastern and Western Europe

When we review the experience of the Jews in the countries under Nazi occupation, a political factor becomes salient in distinguishing Eastern from Western Europe. Countries like Poland, Ukraine, and Romania were ruled between the two world wars by autocratic regimes. In those countries, speaking generally, there was either complete apathy where the fate of the Jews was concerned, or complicity in determining their fate. In addition to the autocratic nature of the regimes, it was the long tradition of violent anti-Semitism – a view of the "guest people" as being not only "strangers" religiously and culturally, but also better off materially. In contrast to the peasants, the Jews were primarily an urban people engaged in the trades and in commerce.

Popular reaction to Nazi occupation in West European countries was quite different. Historically, the Jews were viewed as a pariah people in those countries too, despised and ghettoized. But by the time of the rise of Nazism, countries like France – an important test case – had a long tradition of liberal democracy and the rule of law. More, the democratic-egalitarian ethos had instilled in the French *conscience* (embracing in English the meanings of both consciousness and conscience) a fundamental principle of justice: that the weak must be protected and defended against the strong. Hence, the Jews fared better wherever there was a long and profound tradition of decency and compassion for the underdog in the populace; and wherever the political officials and Church leaders courageously led the populace in resisting the Nazis and rescuing Jews. Poliakov recognizes the validity of that proposition. It can be seen clearly, he writes, that the little pacific peoples with their old democratic traditions were the ones that reacted with the most firmness and unanimity. In the Netherlands, in February 1941, the first deportations caused such an uproar that a general strike of several days' duration, something inconceivable under the Nazi boot, broke out spontaneously. In Denmark the deportations were blocked by the active cooperation of the whole population; the Germans did not dare impose the yellow star on the Jews because of the attitude of King Christian X. (Remember, too, that in tiny, far-off Bulgaria, great popular demonstrations took place at the time of the deportations, to the cry of "we want the Jews back"). (293)

The Role of the Christian Churches

It was St Augustine who introduced the doctrine that the Jewish people must be preserved as living evidence of the price paid for not accepting Christ. Their humbled and abased status was to be a living testimony to the truth of the Christian faith. As we reflect on the long history of the Church since his time, we see that with notable exceptions the Church adhered to his doctrine while at the same time sanctioning the persecution and humiliation of the Jews. The Church and the Catholic princes often opposed the massacre of the Jews in the name of Christian charity, but their theology accepted and justified the oppressed condition of the Jews. The Lateran Council of 1215 decreed that the Jews must wear a badge, long before the Nazis imposed the yellow star on their Jewish victims. As Poliakov cogently observes, these two attitudes – striving to humiliate the Jews while preaching the inviolability of their lives – proved impossible to reconcile during centuries of recurrent massacres.

But Poliakov hastens to add that the Church's humanitarian efforts in the face of Hitler's genocidal program should never be forgotten. Slovakia, for example, was the first satellite country completely subjugated by the Nazis; and yet, thanks to the leadership of the clergy under the influence of the Holy See, the Germans encountered a strong enough resistance to force them to interrupt their plans for the "final solution." In Poland, there was a similar stand taken by the Vatican – for the ideas privately developed by Monseigneur Szepticki, Metropolitan of the Uniate Catholic Church of Galicia – according to which the "extermination of the Jews was inadmissible." A witness to this confidential conversation quickly informed the Germans about it, adding: "He [the Metropolitan] is expressing the same thoughts as the French, Belgian, and Dutch bishops, as if they had all received the same instructions from the Vatican" (295).

However, the clergy of the countries of Eastern Europe were, as a rule, less bold in their defiance of the Nazis than the West European clergy. In

France, for example, a series of pamphlets called *Temoignage Chretien* (*Christian Witness*) clandestinely continued the tradition of Charles Péguy: barring the way to racist contagion under the slogan "France, take care lest you lose your souls." Poliakov describes this as one of the finest pages of the French Resistance.

Poliakov also recognizes that the Vatican had to carry on its humanitarian activities in a cautious and quiet way, fearing a Nazi retaliatory assault upon the Church's extensive interests – which may account for the Pope's failure to issue that public condemnation that the victims of Nazism looked forward to so ardently.

With regard to the Pope's reluctance to make condemnatory, public utterances, Poliakov cites a Catholic writer, Jacques Maudale, who proposed that "it is almost impossible for the Pope to express an opinion unless he is forced to it by a kind of great movement of opinion arising in the masses and communicating itself to the priests from the faithful." And Poliakov comments on the implications of this assessment: if the Pope made no move, he perhaps did not feel sure of this "great movement of opinion arising in the masses." But then it would follow from this – and this is the gravest aspect of the matter – that the Vatican's silence only reflected the deep feeling of the Catholic masses of Europe. Here, one has reason to believe, is an essential element in the background of the causes that led on to genocide, its last necessary condition. Does not the catechism teach tens of millions of modern children that the Jews were the murderers of Jesus and therefore condemned until the Last Judgment? (299).

Postscript

Timothy Snyder's *Bloodlands: Europe Between Hitler and Stalin*[2] appeared after I had completed my discussion of the *Shoah*. Snyder's work is a masterful re-examination of the horrific subject matter we have just reviewed. His study, based as it is on more recently available materials than were available to Hilberg and Poliakov, yields new insights derived from his systematic attention to the roles of both of the most murderous European tyrants of the twentieth century. By 1933, the year Hitler came to power, Stalin was deliberately starving Soviet Ukraine, resulting in the death of more than 3,000,000 people. Seven hundred thousand more innocents were the victims of Stalin's Great Terror of 1937–8. When Hitler betrayed Stalin, the Germans starved to death 4,000,000 Soviet citizens. Later, the

---

[2] New York: Basic Books, 2010.

Germans gassed or shot more than 5,000,000 Jews. Between the Nazi and Soviet regimes, then, some 14,000,000 people were murdered – not a single one of them an armed soldier on active duty.

What amounts to a new emphasis, in Snyder's book, is that the 14,000,000 were all victims of a Soviet or Nazi killing policy, a consequence of an *interaction* between the Soviet Union and Nazi Germany. A quarter of them were killed before World War II even began. A further 200,000 died between 1939 and 1941, while Hitler and Stalin were carving up Europe as *allies* – in accordance with the terms of the Stalin-Hitler pact. As Snyder observes, German policies of mass killing came to rival Soviet ones between 1939 and 1941 "after Stalin allowed Hitler to begin a war" (xi). Both regimes shot Polish citizens in the tens of thousands. Then the worst of the killing began when Hitler betrayed Stalin and the German forces crossed into the recently enlarged Soviet Union in June 1941 – recently enlarged owing to the terms of the Stalin-Hitler pact.

Snyder thus gives the attention it deserves to the consequences of the pact, to Hitler's betrayal and to Stalin's stubborn refusal to believe in the betrayal even after his officer corps had repeatedly informed him of the German advance. Snyder writes:

> In Soviet Ukraine, Soviet Belarus, and the Leningrad district, lands where the Stalinist regime had starved and shot some 4,000,000 people in the previous eight years, German forces managed to starve and shoot even more in half the time. Right after the invasion began, the Wehrmacht began to starve its Soviet prisoners, and special task forces called Einsatzgruppen began to shoot political enemies and Jews. (xi)

In Stalin's Great Terror of 1937–8, nearly 700,000 Soviet citizens were shot. The 200,000 or so Poles killed by the Germans and the Soviets "during their joint occupation of Poland were shot. The more than 300,000 Belarusians and the comparable number of Poles executed in German 'reprisals' were shot. The Jews killed in the Holocaust were about as likely to be shot as to be gassed" (xiv). As Snyder perceptively notes, "no matter which technology was used, the killing was *personal*. People who starved were observed, often from watchtowers, by those who denied them food. People who were shot were seen through the sights of rifles at very close range, or held by two men while a third placed a pistol at the base of the skull" (xv; italics added).

Finally, because these chapters are focused on the Jewish experience in the "Bloodlands," I need to conclude this precis with a most dramatic statistic: "On any given day in the second half of 1941, the Germans shot more Jews than had been killed by pogroms in the entire history of the Russian Empire" (227).

27

The Battle of the Warsaw Ghetto

In chapter 28, we will explore the religious and historical origins of the Zionist idea, and the modern political movement that emerged out of that idea. Here, however, we need to say a few words about that movement because it inspired armed Jewish resistance to the Nazis.

Ever since World War I,[1] Poland had been the principal training ground for Jewish youth who regarded themselves as pioneers or *chalutzim*, in Hebrew. These young people looked forward to creating a Jewish homeland in Palestine based on Jewish agricultural and industrial labor. They believed that the most appropriate social form by which to accomplish their mission was the kibbutz, a democratic-egalitarian, agricultural commune. The main mission of these young pioneers in the diaspora was to educate and recruit as many other young people as possible and give them the preparatory agricultural and artisanal training. In anticipation of forming kibbutzim (Heb. plural) in Palestine, they created them in Warsaw and in other cities of Poland, and it was those kibbutzim that became the clandestine cells of Jewish-organized resistance.

It was, however, not only these young labor-Zionists but also two other groups that led a secret existence in the Warsaw ghetto, publishing pamphlets and newspapers and plotting armed resistance. The first of these was the *Bund*, the Jewish Socialist Party of Eastern Europe that opposed Zionism. The second group was the Communist Party, which also opposed Zionism. The old ideological differences between the three political organizations continued to make themselves felt. When the *chalutzim* proposed to the others that they put aside their differences and unite for the ultimate resistance – after the start of deportations in June 1942 – the other organizations replied that in their judgment the time

---

[1] In the present discussion I rely on Leon Poliakov, *Harvest of Hate: The Nazi Program for the Destruction of the Jews of Europe*, New York: Syracuse University Press, 1954, ch. 9.

had not yet come. The *chalutzim* then tried to organize their own combat group, whose arms consisted, at the time, of one handgun. However, a few weeks after the Zionist initiative, other clandestine groups joined them, forming a coordinating committee with members of all political factions and establishing contact with the Polish resistance, the essential condition for acquiring arms and ammunition. Elected as head of this combat organization was Mordecai Anielewicz, a 24-year-old Zionist.

The ghetto population, owing to the deportations, had already been reduced by nine tenths, numbering only about 40,000 persons. But they included a large proportion of young, able-bodied workers. In the fall of 1942, when the Germans ravaged the ghettos in Poland one after another, the underground combat group engaged in intense, secret work. The German authorities had ordered anti-aircraft shelters to be constructed in the city, which gave the ghetto population the opportunity to dig a network of camouflaged hiding places with false entrances deep under the earth. Some of these hiding places were quite elaborate, with baths, toilets, space for lodging entire families, ammunition depots, and food supplies in anticipation of a long siege. This underground became the main base for the Jewish combat group, whose principal task was the procurement of arms, which could come only from outside, the "Aryan" part of Warsaw. After 1942, the Polish Communist Party turned over a few revolvers and grenades, but the "Armia Krajowa," the central organization of Polish resistance, refused to provide any form of assistance. The Jewish combat group had, therefore, to purchase a few additional handguns, rifles, and several pounds of dynamite from German or Italian deserters. One has to imagine the endless, dangerous obstacles that had to be overcome in order to smuggle into the closely guarded ghetto even a single weapon. The stratagem employed was to recruit young girls of "Aryan" appearance – blonde hair and blue eyes. Several hundred Jewish fighters trained secretly with their meager supply of weapons in the network of shelters. Despite its small numbers and few weapons, the Jewish combat group became a power in the ghetto, soon replacing the Jewish Council.

For the SS, the central concern was security, as Warsaw was a way station of prime importance for the Eastern Front. Disturbances in the ghetto, if they spread to other parts of the city, might threaten the *Wehrmacht's* supply lines. But the SS, especially at the beginning, never imagining that the Jews would put up a serious fight, used a simple police operation in emptying the ghetto in January 1943. To their surprise, the opposition they encountered forced them to call a halt to the deportations. For the first time, German units entering the ghetto were temporarily repulsed by salvos of shots.

As Poliakov observes, although the first clash between the Jews and the Germans brought no long-range, strategic gains for the Jews, it certainly fired up the zeal of the young Jewish fighters. Moreover, the clash prompted the "Armia Krajowa," the Polish resistance, to provide the Jews, on February 2, 1943, with more arms – 50 handguns, 50 grenades, and 5 kilos of explosives. In addition, WRN, an underground, Polish socialist organization, made possible the purchase of 2,000 liters of gasoline, a supply of potassium chloride, and other materials for making primitive explosives. All this, together with the German postponement of deportations, enabled the Jewish combat group to make further preparations. They organized themselves in 22 groups, each consisting of 30 men who were assigned to a certain sector or block. The Jewish fighters had no illusions about the outcome, but it was an integral element of their *chalutz* ideology that they must fight to the death to save their Jewish honor.

On April 19, 1943, General Jürgen Stroop launched the final operation against the ghetto, with more than 2,000 elite troops and a detachment of engineers, tanks, and light artillery. Opposing him were several hundred men armed with revolvers and grenades. As Stroop's forces entered the ghetto at dawn, they were greeted by a sustained fusillade. Some German soldiers fell and two tanks were set on fire. The SS began assaulting the Jewish strongholds one by one, but the defenders managed to escape over rooftops or through the cellars to other strong points. In many places the Germans were forced to retreat, though they had employed artillery and flame-throwers from the very first day. Neither the first nor the second day yielded decisive results for the Germans. When Stroop, who had counted on finishing the action in three days at most, failed, he was roundly reprimanded by Himmler, who ordered the "complete destruction by fire of the blocks of Jewish houses, including those attached to the armament factories." For Himmler, acting on the orders of the Führer, the destruction of the Jews took precedence over everything else – even at the cost of reduced armaments production and the interests of the corporate slave-traders, who now recognized that Himmler's decree had put an end to the extraordinary profits derived from the ghetto's slave-laborers.

Stroop observed that the Jewish fighters preferred the flames to falling into the Germans' hands. He noted, in addition, that the women in the combat groups were armed just as the men. But the new tactic, of setting aflame and demolishing the buildings, enabled the Germans to carry off more than 20,000 unarmed workers who were sent to Trawniki, where they were murdered the following November.

Faced with the new German tactic, the Jewish fighters went completely underground; and though their shelters were crammed with women and children, the defenders continued to offer savage resistance. The Germans resorted to mechanical drills, dynamite, and gas shells that replaced the artillery and tanks. They flooded the sewers, unleashed police dogs, and tortured the prisoners to reveal the principal shelters. The conditions of horror to which the defenders were subjected come through in Stroop's report:

The best and only way to wipe out the Jews is by fire. These creatures understand that they have only two possibilities: to hide as long as they can, or to come out trying to kill or wound the largest possible number of soldiers and Waffen SS men. (Cited in Poliakov, *Harvest of Hate*, 235)

On May 8, the headquarter-shelter of the Jewish combat group was discovered, and most of the defenders, including Anielewicz, took their own lives. On May 16, Stroop dynamited the big synagogue, one of the few buildings that still remained standing, and declared the major operations over. The battle had lasted four weeks, during which the Jewish group tied down more than 2,000 picked German soldiers, and the German war industry lost one of its most important supply centers in the East. The concern that the ghetto revolt caused in the highest Nazi circles may be sensed in Goebels' personal diary, May 1, 1943:

the extremely bitter fighting at Warsaw between our police forces and the *Wehrmacht* itself and the rebellious Jews should be noted. The Jews have succeeded in making the ghetto into a kind of fortified position.

Fierce fighting is in progress and the Jewish high command even publishes daily communiqués. This joke isn't going to last long. But one sees what the Jews can do when they are armed. (Poliakov, *Harvest of Hate*, 236)

The great majority of the Jewish defenders died in battle. Dozens, at most, escaped through the sewers and joined the partisan groups. A few other groups survived weeks and even months, leading a ghost-like life in the ruins, eluding the German patrols by continually changing their hiding places and feeding themselves from the caches the fire and dynamite had not destroyed. Some held out until the fall of 1943, miraculously finding refuge on the "Aryan" side and living through the war. Jewish resistance in the other ghettos followed the main patterns of the Warsaw ghetto.

A Reflection on Jewish Resistance

The uprisings in the Warsaw, Lodz, and other ghettos, together with the evidence we have for Jewish resistance in Western Europe, help us to understand the conditions that made resistance possible. Poliakov cites David Knout's *La Résistance juive*, showing that in France the proportion of Jews in all echelons of the resistance organizations varied between 15 and 30 percent. "Just as in France," writes Poliakov, "*and wherever circumstances elsewhere made it possible*, in Holland, Belgium, and in Italy, the Jews played an essential and sometimes preponderant role in the resistance movements" (244; italics added).

And one may add this hypothesis: had the Jews of Germany early recognized the fundamental difference between the Nazi assault upon them, and all previous assaults in history, it is highly probable that a significant resistance movement would have emerged in Hitler's Germany as well.

28

Zionism, Israel, and the Palestinians

The roots of the Zionist idea can be traced to the Hebrew prophets of social justice and to the promise that the people would be restored to their homeland. First, the Assyrians conquered the Northern kingdom of Israel; not long afterwards, the Babylonians conquered Judea, destroyed the First Temple, and created the earliest Jewish diaspora. Then and there, under the prophetic influence, the hope and expectation emerged that the exiled community would cleanse itself morally so that it might return to Zion and enjoy the divine reward of peace and mutual respect among the nations.

The modern Zionist idea, though rooted in the ancient messianic hopes, was a rather secular phenomenon, a response to a deep disappointment: the Enlightenment of the eighteenth and nineteenth centuries in Europe had failed to deliver on its promises. Neither the French Revolution, with the Declaration of the Rights of Man, nor the Code Napoleon had succeeded in excising from the general West European consciousness the age-old pariah status of the Jews. The hatred and persecution of Jews in Eastern Europe, periodically taking the form of pogroms, was not surprising to Theodor Herzl and the other early promulgators of the modern Zionist idea; but it was a disappointing surprise to witness in a country like France, home of the Declaration of the Rights of Man, that the Jews, no matter how loyal and patriotic, remained objects of contempt and scapegoats.

On October 15, 1894, Captain Alfred Dreyfus, a French Jew attached to the General Staff, was arrested on the charge of having given staff secrets to the German government. Condemned by a court martial for high treason, he was sentenced to life imprisonment in a fortress. On January 15, 1895, he was publicly degraded on the Champ de Mars in Paris; he vehemently protested his innocence, crying out: "Long live France! Long live the army!" But the mob shouted "Death to the traitor!" This was a cabal contrived by the clerical-royalist enemies of the Third Republic, in league with certain generals of the army. In publications like *La France Juive*, they inveighed against the Republic, alleging it was under Jewish domination. From 1892 on, Drumont, a notorious Jew-hater, published a sheet insinuating that Jewish army officers were guilty of treasonous acts. The charge against Dreyfus was based on a copy of a certain secret document alleged to be in his handwriting. Thanks to the investigation of Scheurer-Kestner and Colonel Picquart, it was brought to light in 1897 that the document was in reality the work of Esterhazy, a major in the French army and a spy in the pay of Germany. Dreyfus had meanwhile been transferred to Devil's Island near the Guiana coast, where he was subjected to conditions intended to break down his spirit and elicit from him a confession of guilt.

It was then that the novelist Émile Zola arraigned the enemies of justice in an open letter addressed to the president of the Republic, which became famous through the repeated phrase "J'accuse!" More and more French citizens became convinced of Dreyfus' innocence, and soon France was divided into two camps, Dreyfusard and anti-Dreyfusard. A Colonel Henry of the General Staff produced new forgeries in the attempt to fasten the guilt upon the now-hated Jewish captain. But the colonel, too, was soon exposed, and he took his own life (1898). And yet all sorts of obstacles were placed in the way of reopening the case, the government fearing to break with the clerical-royalist nationalists. After the death of President Faure (1898), a new ministry was formed and Dreyfus was brought back and retried. Once again he was condemned by the Council of War at Rennes, but President Loubet granted a pardon. In the year 1900, the Court of Cassation quashed the earlier verdict and pronounced Dreyfus innocent.

Theodor Herzl

The Dreyfus case is relevant to the birth-hour of Zionism. Herzl was at the time residing in Paris as permanent correspondent of a Vienna daily, the *Neue Freie Presse*. He was little concerned with either Jewish matters or Judaism; but he attended the sessions of the court when Dreyfus was first tried, and witnessed the degradation of the Jewish captain. It seemed to Herzl that France had revoked the principles of her Great Revolution and her Constitution. He felt keenly the blow struck at the whole Jewish people in the person of one Jew. Witnessing this event was a life-altering experience for Herzl, for he now became greatly concerned with Jewish matters, and the so-called "Jewish Question," which for him was prima-rily a political and national one. The Jews, he reasoned, were a nation, and yet they differed from all other nations in possessing no land of their own. Other nations also have their diasporas, but the majority of their peoples live in their national homelands. From this simple but inspired premise, he drew the obvious inference that the Jews must form a state of their own.

While still in Paris, he wrote his *Judenstaat* (*Jews' State*). He had not as yet learned, however, that other Jewish thinkers, notably Moses Hess and Leo Pinsker, had preceded him in proposing the establishment of a Jewish state. For Herzl, however, at this stage of his thinking, the aim was to let the Jews be granted sovereignty over some area of the earth – Argentina or Palestine – sufficient for their just national needs – and then they would take care of themselves. Herzl regarded this project as urgent, since he had given up on the Enlightenment idea that, as Reason widens its boundaries, Jew-hatred will pass away.

It was natural for Herzl and other Jewish thinkers to conceive of a *national* solution to the plight of the Jews. By the time Herzl had written his pamphlet, nationalism had become the most powerful ideology of the nineteenth century, and had produced the unified nation-states of Germany and Italy. And nationalist ideology remained strong in the twentieth century, gaining momentum among colonial peoples, such as the Arabs. It is, therefore, a tragic fact that Arab nationalism and Jewish nationalism emerged at about the same time, and that the goal of one could not be attained without bringing it into mortal conflict with the other.

The Historical Jewish Presence in the Arab World

Even after the Roman destruction of the Second Temple in 70 CE, throughout the periods of the Islamic imperial hegemony and the later Ottoman Empire, there was no time during which a small Jewish community did not exist in Palestine – varying between 5 and 10 percent of the total population. But the vast majority of the inhabitants, since the Arab conquests in the seventh and eighth centuries, were Arabs, Muslim, and Christian. Before the birth of Zionism, the Jewish minority in Palestine consisted mainly of pious, orthodox Jews who, from religious motives, wished to live and die in the Holy Land. In the 1880s, however, a new phenomenon appeared, following an outbreak of violent anti-Semitism in Russia, prompting many Russian Jews to flee to Palestine. There, they established agricultural settlements and though they themselves worked the land, they also employed Arab peasants. But the Jews of that period made no political claim to the land and submitted willingly to Ottoman rule. Nevertheless, even in that period the size and prosperity of the settlements had already begun to arouse concern among Arab national leaders.

After World War I, Zionism had become a significant political movement among the Jews of Britain and America. Distinguished Jews, pleading the cause of the movement in the press and among the members of the two governments, called for a Jewish national home. The call was designed to appeal to liberals as a humanitarian measure that would go far in solving the "Jewish problem." The Zionist argument included the proposition that, given the relative economic backwardness of the Arabs, a Jewish homeland in Palestine would serve to modernize the Middle East. It would also lend support to British imperial interests in the region. To pious Christians, it might even serve as a sign of the fulfillment of the word of God.

Enter Chaim Weizmann, a Jewish scientist whose chemical researches had aided the Allied war effort, and who was able, therefore, to make the Zionist appeal to Lord Balfour and Lloyd George. Churchill and Woodrow Wilson were also won over to the Zionist cause. And it would be fair to say – as both Arab and Jewish scholars have observed – that none of those well-known statesmen had given much serious thought to the existence and rights of the Arabs of Palestine. The outcome of the Zionist appeal was an official statement by the British government that came to be called the "Balfour Declaration":

> H.M. Government view with favour the establishment in Palestine of a national home for the Jewish people, and will use their best endeavours to facilitate this object, it being clearly understood that nothing shall be done to prejudice the civil and religious rights of other non-Jewish communities in Palestine, or the rights and political status enjoyed by Jews in any other country.

Arab scholars and political leaders were, of course, opposed to the Declaration, and especially offended by the clause "non-Jewish communities" with which to refer to 90 percent of the population of the country.

The Peace Conference of 1919

The Conference dispatched the King-Crane Commission to Syria and Palestine to ascertain the wishes of the Arabs concerning their destiny under the League of Nations mandatory system, which was to be a substitute for colonialism. President Wilson's Fourteen Points had included the principle that the Allied powers should not acquire any new colonies, or annex any of the countries of the liberated peoples. In an attempt to reconcile this principle with the Sykes-Picot Agreement, Class "A" mandates were to be created by the League of Nations, to determine how the provinces of the former Ottoman Empire would be governed by the mandatory powers. Wilson invited Lloyd George and Clemenceau to join him in sending an Allied commission to Syria and Palestine to learn the wishes of the people. The British and French leaders declined the invitation, but Wilson dispatched an all-American Commission, consisting of two distinguished and impartial individuals: Dr Henry King and Mr Charles Crane, both members of the American Peace delegation and of the Peace Conference's Mandate Commission. Among their other proposals, they recommended "serious modification of the extreme Zionist program for Palestine of unlimited immigration of Jews, looking forward to making Palestine distinctly a Jewish state."[1]

But the Peace Conference took no notice of this report. Instead, the Supreme Allied Conference, meeting at San Remo in 1920, made a series of decisions that completely disregarded the wishes of the Arabs and the recommendations of the King-Crane Commission. Britain received a mandate for Palestine, with the obligation to establish in it the Jewish national home promised in the Balfour Declaration. This decision together with the others taken at San Remo – the breaking up of geographical Syria into Palestine, Lebanon, and a reduced Syria, with France receiving a mandate for Lebanon and Syria – produced a shockingly disappointed and violent psychological reaction among the Arabs, who felt they had been betrayed, their wishes cynically set aside in the interests of the rival imperialistic policies of Britain and France.

The stage was thus set for a long and bitter conflict between Arabs on the one side, and the British, French, and Zionists on the other. France's part in the struggle came to an end in 1945, with the full realization of Syrian and Lebanese independence. Britain withdrew from Palestine in 1948, by giving up her mandate there and subsequently also in Iraq. Jordan was detached from Palestine in 1922 and placed under the Emir – later King Abdullah. Thus the era of Anglo–Arab conflict had pretty much come to an end. However, the conflict between the Arabs and the Zionists had not only continued but intensified, becoming more and more deadly.

These facts prompted some Jewish thinkers to reassess the Zionist project. For the establishment of a Jewish state in Israel was supposed to go far in reducing anti-Semitism and solving the so-called "Jewish question" in a peaceful, civilized manner. Instead, the creation in 1948 of a Jewish state in the heart of the Arab world provoked several wars –

---

[1] Walter Laqueur, *A History of Zionism*, New York: Holt, Rinehart and Winston, 1972, 451. Hereafter, all page references to this work will be cited in parentheses immediately following the quoted passage.

in 1956, 1967, and 1973; and in the decades following those wars it has become clear that for certain political, Muslim spokesmen, the very existence of Israel is a shocking encroachment on what should be, according to a version of Islamic doctrine, an exclusively Islamic domain. Indeed, from that standpoint, all geographical areas that had once been subject to Muslim imperial rule remain forever sacred to Islam.

"The Unseen Question"

This is the title of chapter 5 of Walter Laqueur's masterful history of the Zionist movement. We have seen that Zionism, as a national movement, emerged at about the same time as Arab nationalism. The clash between them became increasingly evident in Palestine with the bloody riots of May 1, 1921, which followed the violent confrontations in Jerusalem and the attacks in Galilee the previous year. These events shocked and confused many of the Zionists, who became aware for the first time of the danger of a major conflict between the two peoples. Arab spokesmen asserted that Zionist ignorance and recalcitrance were to blame, because at the time of the Balfour Declaration the Muslims had been favorably inclined toward the Jews, but had found among them no willingness to compromise. As a result, the Muslims made common cause with Christian Arab leaders against the "Zionist peril." As Laqueur remarks, whatever the cause of the 1921 riots, the political question of how to relate to the Arabs became more frequent in the Zionist congresses. Yet 15 years later, when the "Arab question" had become the most urgent issue in Zionist politics, Jewish critics argued once again that the movement was paying the price for having so long ignored Arab interests and national aspirations. The Zionists, the critics claimed, had conducted themselves as if Palestine was an empty land. "Herzl visits Palestine but seems to find nobody there but his fellow Jews; Arabs apparently vanish before him as in their own Arabian nights" (210).

Similarly, in Weizmann's speech of 1931, there was hardly a word about the Arabs. It is true that the Zionists paid little attention to the first signs of the Arab national movement, and few anticipated a clash of national interests. They did, however, know that several hundred thousand Arabs lived in the country; but the Russian Zionists were nevertheless confident that Jews and Arabs could live together. They had the notion that if a hundred thousand Jewish families were to settle in the country over a period of 20 years, the Jews and Arabs would no longer be strangers to one another. The famous Zionist theorist, Ahad Ha'am, came to Palestine in 1891, and reported that the Arabs, especially the town-dwellers, were quite aware of "Jewish activities and desires, but pretended not to notice them so long as they seemed to constitute no real danger. But if one day the Jews were to become stronger and threaten Arab predominance, they [the Arabs] would hardly take this quietly" (ibid.).

In Herzl's utopian view, substantial Jewish immigration to Palestine would be a blessing for the Arabs. When Ahad Ha'am asked how millions of Jews could live in a country which barely provided a poor living for a few hundred thousand Arabs, Max Nordau replied that he and Herzl were thinking of modern methods of cultivation which would make mass settlement possible without any need to displace the Arabs.

The total population of Palestine before World War I was almost 700,000. Between 1882 and 1914, more than 100,000 Jews had entered Palestine, but half of them did not stay. In 1905, Jerusalem was the largest city in the country. Of its total population of 60,000, 40,000 were Jews, and the rest Muslim and Christian Arabs. The majority of the Jews belonged to the pre-immigration community, either uninterested in Zionism or actually opposed to it because of its secularism. They were the pious men and women who depended on the alms donated by their co-religionists abroad. The Zionist immigrants numbered no more than 40,000 in 1914, of whom one third lived in agricultural settlements. While Arab spokesmen protested against Jewish immigration, Jewish observers noted that the annual natural increase of the Arab population was about as large as the total number of Jews who had settled with so much effort and sacrifice on the land over a period of 40 years. Some leading Zionists recognized that the insufficient attention to the Arabs in the early days was a most fateful mistake of Zionist policy. This was the view of Dr Auerbach, who added, however, that he was not at all certain that more attention would have solved the problem, for "the Arabs are hostile and will always be hostile," even if the Jews were to become paragons of modesty and self-denial.

It is often argued by Zionists that the early immigrant Jews had purchased the land and therefore possessed it legally. But the land was most often sold by absentee landlords. The land of the early Jewish settlements had formerly belonged to Arab villagers who were heavily in debt and therefore forced to sell. Naturally, there was bitterness against the newcomers, with occasional armed attacks, "and the situation was aggravated by the refusal of the Jewish settlers to share the pasture land with the Arabs as had been the custom before" (214).

Before the fall of the Sultan in 1908, Arab nationalism had no organized political expression, since no political activity was permitted within the Ottoman Empire. But when the Young Turks overthrew the Sultan, the pent up Arab nationalism burst forth with radical demands unheard of before. With this national upsurge, the struggle against Zionism became a central element in Palestinian Arab policy, calling on the Arabs not to sell any more land to the Jews and demanding a total cessation of Jewish immigration.

As Laqueur remarks, the question of how to establish friendly relations with the Arabs was easier to pose than to answer. There had been a few lonely, warning voices. Yitzhak Epstein, a teacher and agriculturist, had said in a closed meeting at the time of the Seventh Zionist Congress (1905) that the Arab question was the most important of all the problems facing Zionism, and that Zionism should enter into an alliance with the Arabs. Epstein reminded his audience that in not a few cases Arab and Druze smallholders had lost their livelihood as a result of Zionist land purchases. The purchases were legal, but the political and moral aspects meant that the settlers had a clear moral obligation to the *fellaheen*. He strongly insisted that only such land should be bought that others were not already cultivating. The mistake made by the Zionists from the very beginning was in talking to the British and Ottoman governments but not to the Arab people, the inhabitants of the land.

Morally sensitive settlers did in fact try to carry out some of Epstein's urgent proposals: they drained swamps and irrigated desert lands. They were profoundly influenced by Tolstoy and the Jewish thinker A. D. Gordon, believing that only a return to the soil and productive labor would redeem the Jewish people. When they arrived in Palestine, they discovered that the great majority of those employed in the existing Jewish settlements were Arabs. For the followers of A. D. Gordon, this was a cancer on the body politic of the *Yishuv*, the Jewish community. It had never been the aim of Zionism, they reminded all who would listen, to create a class of landowners in Palestine whose vineyards, orchards, and orange groves were attended by Arab plantation laborers.

The early Zionists were all basically pacifists. The idea that it might be impossible to establish a state without bloodshed seems never to have entered their heads. They failed to grasp fully the long-term implications of an unavoidable clash between two national movements. The list of Arab grievances was a long one. There were complaints, for example, that the Zionists displaced Arab workers at the ports of Jaffa and Haifa, and from the orange groves; that the Jewish trade unions followed a policy of Jewish labor only. Arab wages in Palestine were two or three times higher than in Syria and Iraq; but the Palestinian Arab workers compared their income and standard of living not with those of their compatriots in other countries, but with the higher wages paid to Jewish workers. Drawing attention in 1924 to the discrepancy in wages and working hours between Arab and Jewish workers, Ben Gurion declared: "Together we shall rise or go under." But Jewish employers were faced with a "damned if you do, damned if you don't" situation. If they refused to employ Arabs, they were charged with chauvinism; but if they employed Arabs, they were accused of exploiting cheap labor. When the *Histadrut*, the federation of Jewish trade unions, attempted to organize Arab labor, it was attacked for interfering in Arab politics. When the same federation refrained from doing so, it was charged with willfully neglecting the interests of the Arab worker.

However, more important than these economic issues, especially for the Arab intelligentsia, was the absence of any political role for the Arabs. There was an insistent demand on their part for representative government. But on this issue the Zionist movement was quite unwilling to compromise, for it would have meant the cessation of immigration and settlement. According to the official Zionist formula of the 1920s, Palestine belonged on the one hand to the Arabs living there, and on the other to the entire Jewish people, not merely to the portion of it resident in Palestine. Even left-wing Zionists adhered to that view. From a socialist standpoint, some argued, the Jews had a good claim: the right of the only landless people of the earth, the right of the dispossessed masses. What the Zionists of the time consistently failed to understand was that Arab nationalism overrode class interests. Yes, there were conflicting class interests between *effendis* and *fellaheen*, but there was also a stronger feeling of national solidarity.

After World War I, an organization emerged within the Zionist movement called *Brit Shalom* (League for Peace). Its principal idea was that Palestine should be neither a Jewish nor an Arab state, but rather a binational state in which both peoples should enjoy equal civil, political, and social rights. But this idea never acquired a mass following, and the political impact of the organization remained negligible. A major reason for its failure to become a mass movement among the Jews was the absence of any political force in the Arab camp willing to cooperate on the basis of the minimal conditions outlined by the leaders of the *Brit Shalom*. Even the Zionist "hawks" had come to recognize the inexorability of Arab nationalism. When King (then Emir) Abdulla in 1922 was said to be willing to accept the Balfour Declaration under Arab leadership, even Vladimir Jabotinsky, spiritual leader of the right-wing Revisionists, was in favor of taking up the suggestion.

The year 1929 brought with it a worsening of Arab–Jewish relations in Palestine, the dispute arising about the respective rights of Jews and Arabs at the Wailing Wall, a quarrel by no means new. On the Day of Atonement, in 1925, Jewish worshipers brought in seats and benches for the old and infirm, but the police removed the new accommodations in the middle of the service. The Jews protested strongly, but similar scenes occurred again on the Day of Atonement in 1928, the Arabs complaining that the Jews had attached a screen to the pavement adjoining the wall to divide the men from the women. Once again, on Arab insistence, the police removed the screen, to the great indignation of the Jews who claimed the Wailing Wall was holy to no one but themselves. But the Arabs categorically refused to allow the Jews to alter the status quo. Several months later the Arabs began building on and around the wall in such a way as to cause great commotion among sections of the Jewish populace. Jabotinsky's Revisionists staged a demonstration, protesting what they described as an unprecedented and unspeakable injustice. "The wall is ours" became the slogan. A few hundred young Jews marched to the wall, raised the blue and white flag, kept a two-minute silence, sang *Hatikva* (the Jewish national anthem), and dispersed. On August 15, 2,000 Arabs staged a counter-demonstration, and, on August 23, widespread violence broke out which lasted a week. In Hebron 60 Jews were killed, in Safed 45 were killed and wounded. These riots of 1929, Laqueur proposes, marked a turning point in Arab–Jewish relations. What was new in these riots was the extremism of the propaganda on both sides. Laqueur's analysis could hardly be more lucid:

> Among the Jews the main outcry came not from those directly affected, the orthodox and ultra-orthodox Jews, who had always shown great circumspection in their relations with the Arabs, but from the Revisionists for whom the wall was a national rather than a religious symbol. The Revisionist stand on the Arab question lacked neither logic nor consistency. Jabotinsky had early on reached the conclusion that Zionism did not make sense without a Jewish majority in Palestine, for the real cause of anti-Semitism was that Jews were everywhere a minority . . . But the Arabs loved their country as much as the Jews did. Instinctively they understood Zionist aspirations very well, and their decision to resist them was only natural . . . There was no misunderstanding between Jews and Arabs but a natural conflict. (256–7)

Continuing his superb analysis of the Revisionist ideology, Laqueur writes:

> Zionism, Jabotinsky argued, was either *ab initio* moral or immoral. If the basic principle was moral, it was bound to remain so even if some people opposed it. There were no empty spaces in the world. The Jews would have encountered the opposition of a native population even in Uganda. Jabotinsky denounced the "cannibalist ethics" of the anti-Zionists. How could anyone, on the basis of moral criteria, deny the validity of the Zionist claim, given that the Arabs had so much land and the Jews none at all . . . He thought that it was impossible to expel the Arabs, and that Palestine would always remain a multinational state. The weakest part of Jabotinsky's

doctrine was no doubt his assumption that Zionism was bound to remain unassailable whatever the means applied. In their transfer to Palestine, Jabotinsky's views lost much of their sophistication and moderation, and served as the ideological justification for primitive and chauvinistic slogans which helped to poison Arab–Jewish relations during the 1930s and 1940s. (257)

Arab Rebellion

The third and most prolonged wave of attacks began in April 1936, lasting with brief interruptions for three years, and ending in the summer of 1939. It required a major military effort on the part of the mandatory powers to defeat the armed gangs, which had established their rule in various parts of the country. With Hitler's rise to power, the number of immigrants increased steadily – 30,000 in 1933; 42,000 in 1934; and 61,000 in 1935. By the mid-1930s, the Jews constituted 30 percent of Palestine's total population. The Arabs looked upon the international situation as an opportune time for their nationalist demands. The Berlin–Rome axis had brought about a shift in the balance of power. British influence seemed on the decline, with Iraq's independence in 1932–3, and with the Arab movement for independence having made substantial progress in Egypt and Syria as well. The Palestinian Arab leaders most likely concluded that this was the right moment for the achievement of their own demands: the establishment of an Arab government, and the immediate prohibition of Jewish immigration and land sales. The armed revolt was not successful and independence was not attained. But, as Laqueur observes, "it was not a total failure either, for Jewish immigration and land purchases were severely curtailed, and the [British] White Paper of 1939 envisaged the virtual repudiation of the Balfour Declaration" (261).

Confronted by Arab guerrilla warfare, the Yishuv (the civic Jewish community) had to decide how to react. At first, it was official Zionist policy to refrain from retaliation (*havlaga*), and even Jabotinsky's paramilitary group adhered to the policy. But when the Arab revolt reached its more intense stage in 1937–8, the policy of non-retaliation was discontinued by both the Hagana, which opted for selective retaliation, and the Revisionist organization, IZL (Irgun Zevai Léumi), which was more intent upon shows of force wherever possible. But another consequence of the Arab revolt was a new awakening, among some Zionist leaders, to the fact that the yearning for independence among the Arabs of Palestine was no merely sectarian phenomenon; it had become a serious political movement. Moshe Sharett (then Shertok), for example, noted in his diary that the participation of young Arab women in the movement proved that it was revolutionary in character, and that the Arab intelligentsia supported the "gangs" in the same way that the Jews sympathized with the Hagana.

The communist line at the time was that Jews should join the revolutionary movement wherever they lived; and, when the world revolution occurred, it would eradicate anti-Semitism and solve the "Jewish problem" once and for all. But the socialist Zionist groups, such as Hashomer Hatzair (the Young Guard) and Poale Zion (the Workers of Zion), came to recognize, as had the Brit Shalom, that without mutual accommodation between Arabs and Jews, the Yishuv, the fledgling civil community of the Jews in Palestine, would have to live in a condition of permanent warfare with its neighbors. What these socialist Zionists failed to realize, however, was that from the Arab standpoint the Zionist left was part of the enemy camp just as much as Ben Gurion and Jabotinsky. For the Arabs, the Jews' insistence on further immigration was an unacceptable evil; and, insofar as the Zionist left supported unlimited immigration, its socialist program was irrelevant.

During World War II, the establishment of a Jewish state became the official aim of the Zionist movement, and the notion of a "partition plan" emerged, according to which Palestine would be divided into two states, Arab and Jewish side by side. But Hashomer Hatzair, favoring a bi-national state, objected on the same ground as did Judah Magnes of *Brit Shalom*: "Satisfactory national boundaries, if the object is to promote peace, cannot be drawn. Wherever you draw those boundaries, you create an irredenta on either side of the border. An irredenta almost invariably leads to war." Magnes continued to maintain, as did Hashomer Hatzair even in the 1950s, that a bi-national state was, in the long run, not only the ideal but the sole practical solution. But when precious few Arab leaders, whom you could barely count on the fingers of one hand, gave serious attention to the idea of a bi-national state – on the principle of no domination of one nation over the other – those leaders were assassinated. The growing recognition, on the part of the Zionists, of the irreconcilability of the two nationalisms led them to argue – during and after the *Shoah* – that their own case was the stronger.

Laqueur published his extraordinarily insightful history of Zionism in 1972, just before the Yom Kippur War. His thesis concerning the basic cause of the Arab–Jewish conflict needs to be carefully pondered if there is to be a realistic possibility of reconciliation between Israel and the Palestinians. In order to move toward such reconciliation, one has to recognize that Arab intransigence was a natural reaction of a people unwilling to share its country with another; viewed from the Arab standpoint, Zionism was an aggressive movement, an invasion in the form of immigration. In the clash of Arab and Jewish nationalisms, both movements, as we have seen, feared becoming national minorities in a situation in which the national majority might become politically dominant.

If, therefore, peace is ever to be achieved between Israel and the Palestinians, the unassailable logic of our analysis requires a political solution that enables both peoples to be majorities in their respective states. A two-state solution appears, therefore, to be the most just. Is it also realistic and realizable? The answer must be in the affirmative to avoid the mutually undesirable consequences of failure.

Works Cited

Abel, Theodore, *The Nazi Movement: Why Hitler Came to Power* (New York: Atherton Press, 1965).

Ahmad, Barakat, *Muhammad and the Jews: A Re-examination* (New Delhi: Vikas, 1979).

Amor, Meir, "State Persecution and Vulnerability: A Comparative Historical Analysis of Violent Ethnocentrism" (PhD diss., University of Toronto, 1999).

Ando, Clifford, *Times Literary Supplement*, 5427 (April 6, 2007).

Arendt, Hannah, *The Origins of Totalitarianism* (San Diego, CA: A Harvest Book, Harcourt, Inc., 1976).

Arendt, Hannah, *The Jewish Writings*, ed. Jerome Kohn and Ron H. Feldman (New York: Shocken Books, 2007).

Baer, Yitzhak, *A History of the Jews in Christian Spain*, transl. from the Hebrew by Louis Schoffman (Philadelphia, PA: Jewish Publication Society of America, 1961).

Bainton, Roland, *Here I Stand: A Life of Martin Luther* (Nashville, TN: Abingdon Press, 1950).

Bammel, Ernst (ed.), *The Trial of Jesus* (London: SCM Press, 1970).

Baron, Salo Wittmayer, *A Social and Religious History of the Jews* (New York: Columbia University Press, 1952–83).

Biale, David (ed.), *Cultures of the Jews*, 2 vols (New York: Schocken Books, 2002).

Bossenbrook, William J. et al., *Development of Contemporary Civilization* (Boston, MA: D.C. Heath and Company, 1940).

Boyarin, Jonathan and Daniel, *Powers of Diaspora* (Minneapolis, MN: University of Minnesota Press, 2002).

Castro, Americo, *The Structure of Spanish History*, transl. Edmund L. King (Princeton, NJ: Princeton University Press, 1954).

Clifford, James, *Routes: Travel and Translation in the Late Twentieth Century* (Cambridge, MA: Harvard University Press, 1997).

Cohen, Jeremy and Moshe Rosman, *Rethinking European Jewish History* (Portland, OR: Littman Library of Jewish Civilization, 2009).

Cohen, Robin, *Global Diasporas: An Introduction* (London: Routledge, 2008).

Dubnov (also transliterated as Dubnow), Simon, *History of the Jews: From the Beginning to Early Christianity*, 2 vols, transl. from Russian by Moshe Spiegel (New York: Thomas Yoseloff, 1967).

Dubnow (also transliterated as Dubnov), Simon M., *History of the Jews in Poland and Russia*, transl. from Russian by I. Friedlaender (Philadelphia, PA: Jewish Publication Society of America, 1918).

Dubnow (also transliterated as Dubnov), Hebrew text, *Toledot Ha-Hasidut, the History of Hasidism* (Tel Aviv: Devir Publishing Company Ltd, 1966).

Dufoix, Stéphane, *Diasporas*, transl. William Rodarmor with a Foreword by Roger Waldinger (Berkeley, CA, and London: University of California Press, 2008).

Engels, Frederick, *The Peasant War in Germany* (Moscow: Foreign Languages Publishing House, 1956).

Gilroy, Paul, *The Black Atlantic: Modernity and Double Consciousness* (Cambridge, MA: Harvard University Press, 1993).

Gobineau, Arthur de, *The Inequality of the Human Races*, transl. Adrian Collins (New York: Howard Fertig, 1967).

Goodman, Martin, *Rome and Jerusalem* (New York: Alfred A. Knopf, 2007).

Graetz, Heinrich, *History of the Jews*, 6 vols (Philadephia, PA: Jewish Publication Society of America, 1939).

Hamilton, Edith, *Mythology* (New York and Toronto: Mentor Books, 1940).

Hegel, G. W. F., *Early Theological Writings*, transl. T. M. Knox, with an introduction and fragments transl. by Richard Kroner (Chicago, IL: University of Chicago Press, 1948).

Hegel, G. W. F., *Three Essays, 1793–1795*, ed. and transl. with an Introduction and notes by Peter Fuss and John Dobbins (Notre Dame, IN: University of Notre Dame Press, 1984).

Hegel, G. W. F., *Phenomenology of Spirit*, transl. J. L. H. Thomas, from M. J. Inwood, ed., *Hegel: Selections*, The Great Philosophers series, ed. Paul Edwards (New York: Macmillan, 1989).

Herzberg, Arthur, *The French Enlightenment and the Jews* (New York: Columbia University Press, 1968).

Hilberg, Raul, *The Destruction of the European Jews*, 3 vols, revised, definitive edn (New York: Holmes and Meier, 1985).

Josephus, *The Jewish War*, transl. with an Introduction by G. A. Williamson (New York: Penguin Books, 1959).

Josephus, 9 vols., including *The Life; Against Apion; The Jewish War; and Jewish Antiquities*, Loeb Classical Library, transl. H. St J. Thackeray (Cambridge, MA.: Harvard University Press, 1976).

Kaufmann, Yehezkel, *The Religion of Israel*, trans. and abridged by Moshe Greenberg (Chicago, IL: University of Chicago Press, 1969).

Kershaw, Ian, *Hitler, the Germans, and the Final Solution* (New Haven, CT, and London: Yale University Press, 2008).

Kramnick, Isaac, *The Portable Enlightenment Reader* (New York: Penguin Books, 1995).

Laqueur, Walter, *A History of Zionism* (New York: Holt, Rinehart and Winston, 1972).

McCullough, W. Stewart, *The History and Literature of the Palestinian Jews from Cyrus to Herod, 550BC to 4BC* (Toronto: University of Toronto Press, 1975).

Machiavelli, *The Prince*, transl. with an Introduction by George Bull (London: Penguin, 1961).

Margolis, Max L. and Alexander Marx, *A History of the Jewish People* (Philadelphia, PA: Jewish Publication Society of America, 1941).

Marx, Karl, *Capital*, vol. I (Moscow: Foreign Languages Publishing House, 1954).

Marx, Karl, *Early Writings*, transl. and ed. T. B. Bottomore (London: C.A. Watts, 1963).

Mayer, J. P., *Max Weber and German Politics* (London: Faber and Faber, 1944).

Michels, Robert, *Political Parties* (New York: Dover Publications, 1959).

Millar, Fergus, *The Roman Near East, 31BC–AD337* (Cambridge, MA, and London: Harvard University Press, 1993).

Mommsen, Wolfgang J., *The Political and Social Theory of Max Weber* (Chicago, IL: University of Chicago Press, 1989).

Montagu, Ashley, *Man's Most Dangerous Myth: The Fallacy of Race* (London: Oxford University Press, 5th edn, revised and enlarged, 1974).

Nicholls, William, *Christian Antisemitism: A History of Hate* (Northvale, NJ: Jason Aronson, Inc., 1995).

Nietzsche, Friedrich, *Beyond Good and Evil*, transl. Walter Kaufmann (New York: Vintage Books, 1966).

Nietzsche, Friedrich, *On the Genealogy of Morals*, ed. with Commentary by Walter Kaufmann (New York: Vintage, 1969).

Parkes, James, *Antisemitism* (Chicago, IL: Quadrangle Books, 1963).

Plato, *Plato: The Collected Dialogues, Including the Letters*, ed. Edith Hamilton and Huntington Cairns, with Introduction and prefatory notes, Bollingen Series LXXI, 13th edn (Princeton, NJ: Princeton University Press, 1987).

Poliakov, Leon, *Harvest of Hate: The Nazi Program for the Destruction of the Jews of Europe*, revsd and expanded edn, foreword by Reinhold Niebuhr (Syracuse, NY: Syracuse University Press, 1954).

Poliakov, Leon, *The History of Anti-Semitism*, trans. Miriam Kochan, 4 vols (Philadelphia, PA: University of Pennsylvania Press, 1975).

Rauschning, Hermann, *Hitler Speaks* (London: Thornton Butterworth, 1939).

Roberts, S. H., *The House That Hitler Built* (London: Methuen, 1937).

Roland, Christopher, *Christian Origins* (London: SPCK, 1985).

Rosman, Moshe, *How Jewish is Jewish History?* (Portland, OR: Littman Library of Jewish Civilization, 2007).

Rousseau, Jean-Jacques, *Émile* (Paris: Gallimard, 1969).

Ruether, Rosemary Radford, *Faith and Fratricide: The Theological Roots of Anti-Semitism* (New York: The Seabury Press, 1974).

Scholem, Gershom G., *Major Trends in Jewish Mysticism* (New York: Schocken Books, 1941).

Scholem, Gershom, *Sabbatai Sevi: The Mystical Messiah*, transl. R. J. Zwi Werblowsky (Princeton, NJ: Princeton University Press, Bollingen Series XCIII, 1973).

Schürer, Emil, *The History of the Jewish People in the Age of Jesus Christ*, revsd and ed. Geza Vermes, Fergus Millar, and Matthew Black, 3 vols (Edinburgh: T.&T. Clark Ltd., 1973).

Shirer, William L., *The Rise and Fall of the Third Reich* (New York: Simon and Schuster, 1960).

Snyder, Timothy, *Bloodlands: Europe Between Hitler and Stalin* (New York: Basic Books, 2010).

Sombart, Werner, *The Jews and Modern Capitalism*, transl. from German by M. Epstein (New York: Collier Books, 1951).

Stampp, Kenneth, *The Peculiar Institution* (New York: Vintage Books, 1956).

Steindorff, George, and Keith C. Steele, *When Egypt Ruled the East* (Chicago, IL: University of Chicago Press, 1971).

Stonequist, Everett W., *The Marginal Man* (New York: Chas. Scribner's Sons, 1937).

Tocqueville, Alexis de, *Democracy in America* (New York: Knopf, 1948).

Vermes, Geza, *The Passion* (New York: Penguin Books, 2005).

Weber, Max, *From Max Weber: Essays in Sociology*, transl. and ed. with an Introduction by H. H. Gerth and C. Wright Mills (London: Routledge & Kegan Paul, 1948).

Weber, Max, *The Methodology of the Social Sciences*, transl. and ed. Edward A. Shils and Henry A. Finch (Glencoe, IL: Free Press, 1949).

Weber, Max, *Ancient Judaism*, transl. and ed. H. H. Gerth and Don Martindale (New York: Free Press, 1952).

Weber, Max, *General Economic History*, transl. Frank H. Knight (New York: Collier Books, 1961).

Weber, Max, *The Sociology of Religion*, transl. Ephraim Fischoff (Boston, MA: Beacon Press, 1964).

Weber, Max, *Economy and Society*, ed. Guenther Roth and Claus Wittich, 3 vols (New York: Bedminster Press, 1968).

Weber, Max, *The Agrarian Sociology of Ancient Civilizaitons*, transl. R. I. Frank (London: NLB, 1976).

Weber, Max, *The Protestant Ethic and the Spirit of Capitalism*, transl. Talcott Parsons and Introduction by Anthony Giddens (London and New York: Routledge, 1995).

Winter, Paul, *On the Trial of Jesus*, 2nd edn, revsd and ed. by T. A. Burkill and Geza Vermes (Berlin and New York: Walter De Gruyter, 1974).

Zeitlin, Irving M., *Liberty, Equality and Revolution in Alexis de Tocqueville* (Boston, MA: Little Brown and Company, 1971).

Zeitlin, Irving M., *Ancient Judaism* (Cambridge: Polity, 1984).

Zeitlin, Irving M., *Jesus and the Judaism of His Time* (Cambridge: Polity, 1988).

Zeitlin, Irving M., *Nietzsche: A Re-Examination* (Cambridge: Polity, 1994).

Zeitlin, Irving M., *The Religious Experience: Classical Philosophical and Social Theories* (Upper Saddle River, NJ: Pearson/Prentice Hall, 2004).

Index

Aaron of Karlin 111
Abdullah, Emir (later King) 267, 271
Abel, Theodore 202
Abraham 45, 57
Abraham Ibn Ezra 128–9
Abydos, Sabbatai Zevi in 94–5
Adorno, T. 24
Africa
  and the black diaspora 8, 9, 24
  "out of Africa" hypothesis 11
  pan-Africanism 25
Afro-Americans 7, 8, 9–10
  black culture and Jews 25
  black settlers and white servants
    179–80
  parallels with the Jews 179–81
  and racialist theories 184
  segregation and "Jim Crow" laws 8,
    180
  slaves 8, 10, 17, 18–25
Agrippa I 73
Ahad Ha'am 268–9
Ahaz, Israelite King 42, 56
Ahijah of Shilo 109
Ahmad, Barakat 114
Alexander the Great 64
Alexander II, Pope 115
Alexander VII, Pope 119–20
Alexandria 4, 67–9, 73
Alfonso, bishop of Aragon 121
Alfonso XI, King of Spain 116
Algazi, Solomon 94
*American Encyclopaedia of the Social
  Sciences* 10
American history
  ethnic immigration and diasporas 7–8

American Philosophical Society 142
American Pragmatism 2–3
Ammon 51
Ammonites 57
Amos, Prophet 41–2, 43, 45, 46, 164
Anatoth 60
Andalusia
  conversos and the Inquisition 120,
    132
  expulsion of Jews from 132
Ando, Clifford 80, 81–2
Anielewicz, Mordecai 259, 261
anti-Semitism
  and Chamberlain 182, 185–6, 208
  and the concept of diaspora 24, 25
  and the Enlightenment 140
  in France 263–4
  and Gobineau 181–4, 185–6, 208
  and Hitler 206–11, 242–3
  and Israel 267–8
  and Jewish emancipation 179, 180–1
  and the Jews as Christ-killers 4,
    256
  and the Jews as a "race" 179
  and Marx 177–8
  and Nazi Germany 200, 206–11, 214,
    231, 254
  and Nietzsche 194–5
  "pariah" status of European Jews
    68–9, 179, 206, 242, 263
  and Polish Jews 84–6
  in the Roman Empire 70–1, 72–3,
    80–2
  and Spanish Jews 122–8, 130, 131–2
  and Voltaire 144–6
  and Wagner 185–8

Antigonus, Hasmonean King 69
Antioch 66, 69, 73
Antiochus Epiphanus 35, 65
Antiochus IV 65–6
Apion 30–1, 73
Apollonius Molon of Rodos 71
Arabs
　Arab nationalism and Zionism 265,
　　268–75
　Arab rebellion (1936–9) 273–4
　early Jewish settlers in the Arab world
　　265–8
　and the Palestine Peace Conference
　　(1919) 266–8
Aragon
　conversos and the Inquisition 116,
　　117, 119–20, 121–2
　expulsion of Jews from 134
　massacres of Jews in 124–5
Aramaic language 62, 65, 68
Arbues, Pedro 121
Aristotle 127
Armenians 5, 6, 10, 12
"Armia Krajowa" (Polish resistance
　movement) 259, 260
Arsakid, Parthian monarch 69
Aryanism
　Chamberlain's racialist theory 182–4,
　　208
　and Gobineau's racialist theory
　　183–4
　and Jewish emancipation 181
　Nazi definitions of "Jews" and
　　"Aryans" 229
　and Nazi Germany 208–11, 215–16
Ashkenazic Jews 5, 28, 102
Asia Minor 64, 68, 69, 71, 74–5
Assyrian exile 57–8, 60
Assyrians 41, 42, 43, 45, 50–1, 56, 165,
　263
astronomy and the Enlightenment 138,
　140
atheism
　and the Enlightenment 137, 146
　Jews accused of 30, 73
　and Left Hegelians 169–70
Athens 70, 80
Auerbach, Dr 269
Augustine, St 114, 255
Augustus, Roman Emperor 67, 71, 75
Auschwitz-Birkenau 244, 247, 249–51

Austerlitz, battle of 152
Austria 152
　Nazi annexation of 211, 215, 217
Averroes 127–8
Avignon 151

Baal-Shem-Tob ("the Besht") 105–9,
　111, 136
Babylonia 4, 41, 42, 45, 48, 50–6, 165,
　263
　Jewish culture in 69–70
Babylonian exiles 54–5, 57–8, 59, 60, 61
　and Ezekiel 60–1
　and the proto-synagogue 48–9, 62
Baden 152, 153
Baeck, Rabbi Leo 231
Baer of Mezherich 109, 111
Baer, Yitzhak 116, 126, 127–8, 130, 133,
　134, 135
Bainton, Roland 154, 155, 156–7,
　159–60
Balfour Declaration 266, 267, 268, 271,
　273
Baltic states
　and Nazi Germany 240–1
Barcelona 115, 122, 126
Baron, Salo W. 30
Baruch 51, 56
Bauer, Bruno 167, 168–72, 174
Bauman, Zygmunt 25
Bavaria 152
Beaumont, Gustave 173, 175
Belgium 5, 262
Belzec death camp 249
Ben Gurion, David 270, 274
Benjamin, W. 24
Benveniste, Hayim 93
"the Besht" (Israel, Baal-Shem-Tob)
　105–9, 111, 136
Biale, David
　Cultures of the Jews: A New History
　　29, 33–5
the Bible
　and English Deism 139–41
　on polytheism 36
　see also New Testament; Old
　　Testament (Hebrew Bible)
Bismarck, Otto von 221
black Americans *see* Afro-Americans
Black Plague 84
Black Sea 72

Blyden 24–5
Boleslav V, King of Poland 83
Bonaparte, Louis (Napoleon III) 185
Bothmer, Count von 199
Boyarin, Jonathan and Daniel
    "Diaspora: Generation and the
    Ground of Jewish Identity" 26–7,
    28
    Powers of Diaspora 13–18, 23
Brit Shalom movement 271, 274
Britain
    diasporas 5
    the Enlightenment in 137, 138–41
    and Nazi Germany 216, 217, 218
    and Palestine 266, 267, 273
Bühler, Josef 244
Bukhara 114
Bulgaria 12
    and Nazi Germany 217, 255
Bülow, Hans von 187
Bundschuh movement in Germany 155
bureaucracy 218, 219–25
    characteristics of 219–20
    and charismatic leadership 222–5
    and the destruction of European Jews
    226–45
    and German ideology 221–3
    state bureaucracies 220–1
Burgos 123–4, 126
Burke, Edmund 161

Cadiz 120
Caesarea 78–9
Canaan 40, 45, 57, 59
capitalism
    and the Enlightenment 137
    and Left Hegelians 168
    Marx on 172, 175–6
Cardoso, Abraham Michael 95
Caribbean diaspora 5, 6
Carmichael, Joel
    The Shaping of the Arabs 114
Casimir the Great, King of Poland 83
Casimir IV, King of Poland 83
Castile 116, 117, 123–4
    Kabbalism in 128
    massacres of Jews in 123–4
Catalonia 115, 124, 125–6
    Kabbalism in 90
Catholic Church
    and the Enlightenment 140, 142

and the French Revolution 150
in Germany 152
and Luther 155–6, 158–9
and Nazi Germany 256
in Poland 83, 86–7
and the Spanish Inquisition 117–22
Chamberlain, H. Stewart 199, 215
    *The Foundations of the Nineteenth
    Century* 182, 185–6, 208
charismatic leadership 222–5
Chelbi, Raphael Joseph 92
Chelmno death camp 248–9
children and Nazi propaganda 209
Chinatowns 10
Chmelnitzky Uprising (1648–1649)
    87–9, 98, 99, 102
Christianity
    and Afro-Americans 179
    and anti-Semitism 4
    Arab Christians in Palestine 265, 268,
    269
    Armenians 12
    and Ashkenazic Jews 28
    bodily resurrection concept 61
    Christian churches and the *Shoah*
    248, 254, 255–6
    doctrine of Incarnation 162, 170
    and the Enlightenment 136, 138–41,
    143
    and German Jews 168, 170–2, 172–3
    Greek Orthodox Church 86, 87–8
    and Hegelian evolutionary theory
    163
    and Islam 114
    and Jewish emancipation 181
    and the Jews as a "pariah people" 49
    Luther on the Jews and 158–60
    and Nazi Germany 208–9
    and Polish Jews 83–4
    and the Roman Empire 78, 80, 81–2
    and the soul 47
    and Spanish *conversos* 117–26, 127,
    131–2, 134
    and Spanish Jews 115–17, 130
    see also Catholic Church;
        Protestantism
Churchill, Winston 266
Cicero 70–1
    Pro Flacco 144
circumcision 65, 75, 81
citizenship and German Jews 170–4

Claudius, Roman Emperor 73, 75
Clemenceau, Georges 267
Clifford, James
  Routes: Travel and Translation in the Late Twentieth Century 26–8
Cohen, Jacob Joseph 109–10
Cohen, Jeremy and Rosman, Moshe
  Rethinking European Jewish History 34
Cohen, Nehemiah 94–5
Cohen, Robert
  Global Diasporas 4–8
collective memories/myths 6
commensalism 59
communism
  German communists 196, 198, 200, 203
  Polish Communist Party 258, 259
  and Zionism 274
Confederation of the Rhine 152–3
Confucianism 37
connubiam 59
Constantine 171
Constantinople
  and the Sabbatian movement 94, 98, 101
conversos in Spain 117–26, 127, 131–2, 134
Corinth 70
Cossacks 87, 88, 88–9, 101
the Covenant xi–xii, 39–40, 112, 163
Covey, Edward 19–20
Crane, Charles 267
Crimea 72
  Tatars 87–8, 89, 100–1
"Critical Philosophy" 113
the Crusades 4, 88, 115, 155
cultural diasporas 6
cultural hybridism 29
cultural power of Jewish diasporas 13–18, 27
culture of the Jews 33–5
Cyrenaica (Tripoli) 68, 69
Cyrus, Persian King 58
Czechoslovakia
  and Nazi Germany 211, 215, 216, 217
Czerniakow, Adam 235, 237

Damascus 69, 75
Daniel 61

Danzig 216, 217, 233
Daphna (Taphnis) 56
David, King 42, 43, 49
Declaration of the Rights of Man and of Citizens 150–1, 173, 174, 263
Deism 139–41, 146
democracy
  and bureaucracy 221
  and charismatic leadership 224–5
  and the League of Nations 212
  Tocqueville on American democracy 185
  see also liberalism/liberal democracy
Denmark 217, 255
Descartes, R. 138
Dewey, John 2
diaspora, concept of xii, 1–28
  black diasporas 8, 9–10, 17, 18–25
  cultural power of the Jewish diaspora 13–18
  Dufoix's history of 8, 9–13
  global diasporas 4–8
  Irish diaspora 7–8
  and other ethnic groups 3, 5–6
  Weber on concepts and the ideal type 1–3
Diderot, Denis 150
dietary laws 69
Dostoevsky, F. 146
Douglass, Frederick 19–20, 23
Drechsler, Anton 199, 200
Dreyfus case 263–4
Du Bois, W. E. 20, 24–5
Dubnov, Simon 11, 29, 30, 69
  on Hasidism 111
  on the messianic vision 77
  on Polish Jews 88, 89, 105, 113
  on Roman Jews 71, 75
  on the Sabbatian movement 100–3
Dufoix, Stéphane
  Diasporas 8, 9–13
Durkheim, Émile 13

Eastern European Jews
  and the Christian Churches 255–6
  and the concept of diaspora 5, 15
  and Kabbalistic teachings 136
  and Nazi Germany 211, 232, 254
  and slave-morality strategy 15
  and Zionism 258
  see also Polish Jews

Ebert, Friedrich 198
Eckart, Dietrich 199
Edomites 57
education
  in Rousseau's *Émile* 146–7
Egypt
  Alexandria 4, 67–9, 73
  and ancient Judaism 39, 41, 42
  and Babylonia 50, 53, 54
  exodus from 60
  and Hebrew prophets 41, 43, 45
  Hellenistic culture in 64, 65
  Jewish communities 67–8, 72
  the Jews and Egyptian bondage 14,
    15, 40, 164, 191
  Judean emigration to 55–6
  Ptolemic kingdom 64, 65, 67
  Roman sovereignty 67–8
Eichmann, Adolf 247
Elijah, Prophet 109
Elijah of Vilna (the Gaon) 112
Engels, Friedrich 156, 158, 177
England, expulsion of Jews from 116,
  134
English Deism 139–41, 146
English Revolution 136
the Enlightenment 103, 112–13,
  136–51
  and English Deism 138–41, 146
  and the French *philosophes* 137–8,
    142–50, 160, 181
  in Germany 137, 154, 160–1
  and Jewish emancipation 180–1
  and racialist conceptions of the Jews
    183
  and Zionism 263, 265
Ephesus 69
Epstein, Yitzak 270
Essenes 30
ethical core of Judaism 76–7
ethnic cleansing 7
ethnic groups
  and the concept of diaspora 3, 5–6
euthanasia, Nazi program of 247–9
existentialism 167
the Exodus
  and black slave identity 24
  and the Hebrew prophets 45
Ezekiel, Prophet 41, 42, 44, 52, 53, 58,
  60–1
Ezra 59, 61, 62, 65

feminization thesis
  and Jewish diasporic tactics 16–17,
    18, 23
Ferdinand and Isabella of Spain
  117–18, 119, 121–2
  and the conquest of Granada 132–3
festivals, Jewish
  and Babylonian exiles 60
  Hegel on 162
  Spanish Jews and *conversos* 131
Feuerbach, Ludwig 167, 171, 172,
  177
Fichte, J. G. 153
Fischer, Gouverneur of the Warsaw
  ghetto 236, 237
formal-technical rationality 25
Förster, Bernhard 194
France
  Avignon 151
  Christian clergy and the Jews 255,
    256
  Code Napoleon 263
  Declaration of the Rights of Man
    and of Citizens 150–1, 173, 174,
    263
  diasporas 5
  Dreyfus case 263–4
  expulsion of Jews from 134
  Herzl and the "Jewish Question"
    264–5
  Jewish emancipation 150–1
  and Left Hegelians in Germany 169,
    172, 173
  and Nazi Germany 216, 217, 218,
    254
  and Palestine 267
  Paris Commune 151
  philosophes 137–8, 142–50, 160,
    181
  Resistance 256, 261–2
Frank, Hans 233–4, 236–7, 244
Frankfurt school 24
Frankism 104–5, 112
Franklin, Benjamin 142
French Revolution (1789) 136, 137,
  150, 161, 166
  and Jewish emancipation 181
  and racialist conceptions of the Jews
    183
  Tocqueville's views on the 185
  and Zionism 263

Galicia 235–6, 255
Galileo 138
The Galut
  and Kabbalism in Spain 129
Garvey, Marcus 8, 9
Gaza, Sabbatai Zevi in 93
Gedaliah 55, 56
gender
  feminization and Jewish diasporic
    tactics 16–17, 18, 23
  masculinity and black slaves 20–1,
    22, 23
German Jews 4, 5, 32–3
  cultural assimilation and
    intermarriage 227
  emancipation of 169–74, 181
  expulsion of 134
  Luther's attitude to 158–60
  and Nazi Germany 206–11, 227,
    228–32, 253, 262
Germany 151, 152–65
  army 197, 198, 205, 222
  Bundschuh movement 155
  and charismatic leadership 223–4,
    225
  communists 196, 198, 200, 203
  the Enlightenment in 137, 154,
    160–1
  German ideology and bureaucracy
    221–3
  and the Great Depression (1929) 203,
    215
  guest status of Jews in 169
  Kapp *Putsch* 196–7
  and Left Hegelians 166–78
  legal and administrative reforms 155
  Luther and Lutheranism 154–60,
    161, 168, 171, 253
  and the Napoleonic Wars 152–4, 161
  national character 252–4
  nationalism 152, 153–4
  navy 197
  peasant uprisings 154–7
  and political docility 222
  Prussia 152, 153–4, 161, 165
  Rhineland Jews 4, 5
  and Rousseau 160–1
  Social Democrats 158, 195–6, 198,
    199, 201, 225
  Sturm und Drang movement 160
  Versailles Treaty (1919) 197–9, 215

war reparations 197, 198–9
  see also Hegel, G. W. F.; Nazi
    Germany; Weimar Republic
Gerona, Kabbalism in 90
Gershon Kutover 105
Gerth, H. H. 222
ghettoized communities
  in Nazi Germany 230–2
  in Poland 233–7
  Warsaw ghetto 235, 236, 253, 258–62
Gilroy, Paul
  The Black Atlantic 18–25, 26
global diasporas 4–8
goal-rational action, Weber on 219
Gobineau, Arthur de 208
  The Inequality of the Human Race
    181–4, 185–6
God
  Covenant with the Jews xi–xii, 39–40,
    112, 163
  and Hasidism 107–8
  Hebrew name for (Yahweh) 53, 59,
    92
  and the Hebrew prophets 41, 42,
    43–4, 45–6, 47, 48, 56
  Jewish concept of (formless, invisible
    and incorporeal) 30, 38, 73, 163
  and monotheism 38, 39–40, 59
  Rousseau on 147–8, 149–50
Goebbels, Joseph 214, 244, 246, 250,
  253, 261
Goethe, Johann von 167, 208
Goitein, S. D. 27, 28
Goodman, Martin
  Rome and Jerusalem 80, 81–2
Gordon, A. D. 270
Göring, Hermann 231
Graetz, Heinrich 29–30, 100–1
Granada 132–3
Greece
  and the concept of diaspora 6, 10
  deities 31–2, 37, 74
  Greco-Roman culture and Voltaire
    144–6
  Hellenistic culture 64–6, 67–8
  Jewish communities 4, 70, 72, 75
  Jewish and Greek cultural interaction
    34
Greek language 34, 65
Greek Orthodox Church 86, 87–8
Günsche, Otto 245

Gypsies
  and the Nazi death camps 250–1

Hadrian, Emperor 81
Hamilton, Thomas 173–4, 176
  Men and Manners in North America
  175
Hananiah, Prophet 44
Hashomer Hatzair (the Young Guard)
  274
the Hasideans
  and Hellenized Jews 65–6
Hasidism 103, 104–13, 136
  and Mitnagdim 136
  and Rabbinism 111, 112–13
  and "the Besht" 105–9, 111, 136
  and Tzaddikism 108, 109–11
Hasmonean Wars 70
Hausser, Otto 208
Hebrew Bible *see* Old Testament
  (Hebrew Bible)
Hebrew language 34, 62, 68
Hebrew prophets xii, 40–9
  and Babylonia 41, 42, 45, 48, 50–1,
  50–6, 57, 58
  as political demagogues 41–2
  social class background 42–3
  of social justice xii, 15, 45–9, 71, 76,
  112, 136, 164, 178, 193, 263
Hegel, G. W. F. 24, 160–5, 166
  on Jews and Judaism 162–5
  and Kierkegaard 167
  Phenomenology of Mind 168
  Phenomenology of Spirit 18–20
  Philosophy of History 162–3
  Philosophy of Right 167
  and the Prussian state 161, 165,
  166–7, 168, 253
  and Reason 161
  theory of four stages of religious
  development 170
  see also Left Hegelians
Hellenistic culture 64–6, 67–8, 69,
  69–70
Herod 67
Herzberg, Arthur 144–5, 146
Herzl, Theodore 263, 264–5, 268, 269
  Judenstaat (Jews' State) 265
Hesiod
  Theogony 37
Hess, Moses 265

Hess, Rudolf 202
Heydrich, Reinhard 230, 233, 234, 247
Hezekiah 42
Hilberg, Raul
  Destruction of the European Jews
  226–7, 228, 230–1, 237, 238–9, 240,
  241, 246
Hillel school of Judaism 30, 69–70
Himmler, Heinrich 233–4, 241–2, 245,
  247, 248, 249, 252
  and the Warsaw ghetto 260
Hindenburg, Oskar von 205
Hindenburg, Paul von 198, 204, 205,
  215
Hinduism 37
Hintze, Otto
  Die Hohenzollern und ihr Werk 222
Hirsch, Dr Otto 231
Hitler, Adolf 199–205, 213
  and anti-Semitism 206–11, 242–3
  and the army 205, 217–18
  Chamberlain and Aryanism 182, 184
  and charismatic leadership 224, 225
  cult of 201
  euthanasia program 247–9
  and the "Final Solution" 242–5, 246,
  247
  and the Generalgouvernement 234
  and German Jews 227, 230
  and the Holocaust 229
  invasion of Poland 216–18
  and Jewish emigration to Palestine
  273
  Mein Kampf 184, 200, 202, 215, 250
  Munich beer hall putsch (1923)
  201–2
  and Nazi propaganda 200–1
  and Nietzsche 194
  and the origins of the Nazi Party
  199–202
  programme of conquest 216
  and racial laws 210–11
  rise to power 202–5, 210, 215
  and Stalin 256–7
  totalitarian regime 213–14
  and the Warsaw ghetto battle 260
  and Weber 221
  see also Nazi Germany
Hobbes, Thomas 14, 24, 212–13
Hoess, Rudolf-Franz-Ferdinand 249,
  251, 252

Holbach, Baron d' 136, 141–2, 150, 181
Holland (Netherlands) 255, 262
and the Sabbatian movement 98, 102
Holocaust see Shoah (Holocaust)
Holy Roman Empire 152
homelands 6
Homer 37, 145
Hook, Sidney
From Hegel to Marx 174
Hophrah, Pharaoh (Apris) 55
Horace 75
Horkheimer, M. 24
Hosea, Prophet 41, 44, 46, 92
Hourwitz, Zalkind 151
human rights 174
human sacrifice and the Assyrians 42, 56
humanism 26
Hungary
and Nazi Germany 217, 240, 252–3
hunter-gatherers 11

ideal types
and the concept of diaspora 2–3, 13
imperial diasporas 6
Incarnation, Christian doctrine of 162, 170
Indian diaspora 5, 6
the Inquisition
and the French philosophes 142
and Spanish Jews 117–22, 131, 134–5
Iraq 267
Irish immigration to the United States 7–8
Isabella and Ferdinand of Spain 117–18, 119, 121–2, 132
and the conquest of Granada 132–3
Isaiah, Prophet 41, 42, 44, 46, 164
Islam
and Israel 268
Jewish diasporas 4–5
and Jews in Spain 114–15, 116, 132
in Palestine 265, 268, 269
and Sabbatai Zevi 94–5
Israel
establishment of a Jewish state 267–8, 274–5
Northern kingdom of 40–1, 50, 57, 59, 60, 263
Israel (Baal-Shem-Tob, "the Besht") 105–9, 111, 136

Israel, Jonathan
European Jewry in the Age of Mercantilism 33
Italy
fascist 225
Jewish communities 70–1, 75
Jewish resistance in 262
and Nazi Germany 217
and the Sabbatian movement 98, 102
IZL (Irgun Zevai Léumi) 273

Jabotinsky, Vladimir 271, 272, 273, 274
James, William 2
Jameson, Frederic 24
Japan 217
Jason, high priest 35, 65, 66
Jehoiachim, Judean King 50, 51
Jehoiachin, Judean King 51–2
Jerboam II, Israelite King 41
Jeremiah, Prophet 41, 42, 44, 164
and Babylonian rule in Jerusalem 51, 52–3, 54
in Egypt 56
and the prophetic ethic 46
social background 43
Jericho 60
Jerome, St 139
Jerusalem
Assyrian siege of 42, 50–1
Babylonian rule in 50, 51–5
and the Crusaders 4
destruction of the First Temple 48, 53–5, 60
the diaspora and the Temple 62, 68, 70, 80
Hellenized Jews in 65, 66
Jewish revolt and the destruction of the Second Temple 4, 49, 80, 81, 227, 265
Jews, Arabs and the Wailing Wall 271–2
and the Persian supremacy 58–9
Roman conquest of 70
and Sabbatai Zevi 93
second Jewish revolt (132–135 ce) 79, 81
and syncretism in Jewish history 35
and Zionist immigrants 269
see also Judea

Jesus of Nazareth 18, 78
  Bauer on 169, 170
  Beatitudes 192
  and the Jews as Christ-killers 4, 256
  and Nazi propaganda 208–9
Jewish emancipation
  and anti-Semitism 179, 180–1
  and Aryanism 181
  Bauer on 169–72
  in France 150–1
  in Germany 169–74, 181
  Marx on 172–4
Jewish Question 24, 174
  and Left Hegelians 168–74
  and Zionism 264–5
Johanan ben Kareath 55–6
John Casimir, King of Poland 88
John I, King of Castile 123, 126–7
Joiakim, Israelite King 41
Jordan 267
Josephus 79
  Against Apion 30–2, 71, 73, 74
  Jewish War 78
Judah Ibn Verga 132
Judea
  Babylonian conquest of 41, 50–6
  and Babylonian exiles 61
  and the Hebrew prophets 40–9
  Jewish revolt (66–70 ce) 4, 49, 78–9, 80, 81
  Nietzsche on Roman values and 191, 192
  and the Persian Empire 58–9, 64
  Pompey's invasion of 67
  Roman rule in 32, 49, 71, 76–7, 78–82
  and the synagogue 60
  and Zionism 263
  see also Jerusalem
Judenräte (Jewish Councils) in Poland 234–7
Julius Caesar 66, 67, 68, 69, 71

Kabbalism 90–1, 113, 136
  and Hasidism 105–9
  and the Sabbatian movement 92–6, 99, 100, 102–3
  and Spanish Jews 90, 128–30
  and *Zohar (The Book of Splendour)* 90–1, 93, 96, 102–3, 128, 130
Kafka, F. 24

Kant, Emmanuel 11, 113, 157
Kaufmann, Yehezkel 36
Kepler, Johann 138
Kershaw, Ian
  Hitler, the Germans and the Final Solution 243–5
Kersten, Dr Felix 247
Khazars 5
kibbutzim 258
Kierkegaard, Søren 167
King, Dr Henry 267
Kishivev pogroms (1903) 10
Knout, David
  La Résistance juive 261–2
Koestler, Arthur 5
Kroner, Richard 166–7, 168

La Mettrie, Julien Offray de 181
  Man a Machine 142
labour diasporas 6
Lacan, Jacques 16
Lafarque, Dr Paul 177–8
language, Gobineau on race and 182
Lapapa, Aaron 93
Laqueur, Walter 268, 270, 272, 273, 274–5
Lateran Council (1215) 255
the Law *see* Torah (Jewish Law)
League of Nations 212–13, 216
  and Palestine 266–7
Lee, Rose Hum 10
Left Hegelians 166–78
  Bauer 167, 168–72, 174
  members of the group 167
  see also Marx, Karl
legal profession
  and German Jews 207, 210–11
Leghorn 98
Leibniz, G. 138
Levi, Primo 25
Levinas, Emmanuel 25
liberalism/liberal democracy
  and bureaucracy 221
  and charismatic leadership 223, 224
  in France 254
Lichtenberg, Canon 253
Liebknecht, Karl 196
Linge, Heinz 245
Liszt, Franz 187
Lithuania
  and Nazi Germany 217

Lithuanian Jews 32–3, 83, 85, 88
  and Hasidism 109, 111
  and Talmudic scholasticism 105
Lloyd George, David 266, 267
local studies 29
Locke, John 142
Lodz ghetto 235, 236, 253, 261
Ludwig II, King of Bavaria 188
Lukács, Georg 24
Luria, Isaac
  and Kabbalism 90–1, 92, 99
  secret writings of (Ari) 100, 105
Luther, Martin/Lutheranism 154–60,
  161, 253
  attitude towards the Jews 158–60
  and Left Hegelians 168, 171
  and the peasant uprisings 154–7
Luxemburg, Rosa 196
Lwow (Lemberg) ghetto 236
Lybia (Cyrenaica) 68, 72

Machiavelli, N.
  The Prince 17
McNeil, William 11
Madagascar plan 234, 246
Madrid 123
Magnes, Judas 274
Maidenek death camp 249
Maimon, Solomon 113
Maimonides 113, 127, 128–9
Majorca 122, 126
Manasseh, Israelite King 42, 43, 56
Mao Zedong 213
Mark Antony 67, 69
Martinez, Ferdinand 131
Martinez, Ferrant, archdeacon of Ecija
  122–3
Marx, Karl 158, 161, 167, 172–8
  and anti-Semitism 177–8
  Capital 176–7
Masada 78
masculinity and black slaves 20–1, 22,
  23
master morality 18, 189–90
  and Nazi Germany 209
materialism
  and the Enlightenment 137, 146
  and Left Hegelians 167
Maudale, Jacques 256
Mayer, J. P. 221–2
Mead, George Herbert 2

the Medes 50
medical profession
  and German Jews 207, 211
Mendel of Vitepsk 111
Mendelssohn, Felix 187
Mendelssohn, Moses 112, 113
Menelaus, high priest 35, 65
Merlot, Abbé 151
Mesopotamia 68
the Messiah 76–7, 90, 91
  and Hasidism 108
  and Hegel 162
  and the Sabbatian movement 91,
    93–4, 99, 104, 136
Meyerbeer, Giacomo 186, 187
Micah, Prophet 41, 42–3, 46
Michels, Robert 158, 225
Miczynski, Sebastian
  Mirror of the Polish Crown 85
Middle Ages
  and the Enlightenment 137
middle classes
  and the Enlightenment 150, 154
  and Polish Jews 83, 84
  and the rise of Nazism 196, 199, 203,
    205
migration
  reasons for Jews migrating 227
  voluntary and involuntary 6–7, 7–8
Millar, Fergus 78, 79
Mitnagdim 136
Mizpah 55, 56
Moab/Moabites 51, 57
modernity
  and anti-Semitism 24
  and slavery 20
moira (fate)
  and polytheism 36–7
Mommsen, Wolfgang J. 223, 224, 225
monotheism 35–6, 38, 39–40, 59, 74–5
  and Kabbalism 129
Montesquieu, M. de 136, 141, 150
  The Spirit of the Laws 142–3
Moroccan Jews
  and the Sabbatian movement 98
Morrison, Toni
  Beloved 25
Moses 34, 39, 57
  and the Israelites' covenant with God
    xi–xii, 39, 40
  and the Law (Torah) 31

and the prophets 45
Rousseau on 149–50
Moses de Leon 130
Munich Agreement (1938) 216, 218
Mussolini, Benito 225

Nabupolasser, King of Babylonia 50
Nachmanides
commentary on the Pentateuch
128–9
Napoleon Bonaparte 223
Napoleonic Wars 15, 150
and Germany 152–4, 161, 166
Nathan of Gaza 93, 95
national consciousness
and Roman Jews 74, 79
nationalism
Arab 265, 268–73, 274–5
and diaspora ideology 26
German 152, 153–4
Hegel on Judaism and 164–5
see also Zionism
natural disasters 7
Nazarenes 139
Nazi Germany 194, 213–18
and anti-Semitism 200, 206–11, 214,
231
army 217–18, 232, 238–40
and Aryanism 208–11, 215–16, 229
attack on Poland (1939) 216–18
attitude of Jews to 227
and the battle of the Warsaw ghetto
258–62
Chamberlain and Aryanism 182
and charismatic leadership 224–5
and Christianity 208–9
destruction of European Jews
226–45
educational system 214
emigration of Jews from 214
and German Jews 206–11, 227,
228–32, 253, 262
and the German national character
252–4
Jewish resistance to 258–62
Kristallnacht pogrom (1938) 211,
231, 232
origins of 199–202
racial laws 210–11, 214
rise to power 202–5
and socialism 214–15

and the Soviet Union 217, 218, 233,
238, 256–7
territorial holdings 217
totalitarian regime 213–16
and unemployment 215
and World War II 211, 217–18
see also Hitler, Adolf; Shoah
(Holocaust)
Nebuchadnezzar, King of Babylonia
50, 51, 52, 56
conquest of Jerusalem and exile
policy 53–5, 58
Nebuzaradan, Babylonian commander
54–5, 56
Nehemiah 59, 61
Nero, Roman Emperor 75
Netherlands see Holland (Netherlands)
New Testament
on the Jewish diaspora 72
on Jewish proselytism 74, 76
Nietzsche on the 193
Newton, Isaac 138, 139, 140, 147
Nietzsche, F. 188–94
and anti-Semitism 193–4
Beyond Good and Evil 15, 189, 191,
192
on the historical role of the Jews
190–4
Human, All Too Human 188
on the Jews as a priestly people
14–15, 190–1
and Nazi Germany 209
On the Genealogy of Morals 15, 70–1,
189–90, 191
on the slave-morality of the Jews
14–16, 17, 70–1, 189–90, 191–2
and Wagner 188
and Weber 223
noble-warrior values 14–18
and Nazi Germany 240
Nietzsche on 14–15, 189–90, 191,
192–3
Socrates on 17–18
Nordau, Max 269
North Africa 114

Old Testament (Hebrew Bible) 136
and the concept of diaspora 9
on the Covenant xi–xii
and Hegel 164–5
and Jewish culture 34

Old Testament (Hebrew Bible) (*cont.*)
  and the Law 31
  Nietzsche on the 192–3
  and Rousseau 147
  the *Septuagint* (Greek translation) 4,
    9, 65
  and the soul 46–7
Onias III, Syrian King 35, 66
"Oriental" nature of Judaism
  Bauer on 169, 170
  Hegel on 162, 164–5
Ottoman Empire 5
  and Armenians 12
  and Palestine 265, 267, 269, 270
  and Sabbatai Zevi 94–5
  see also Turkey
Ovid
  Art of Love 75

Paine, Thomas
  The Age of Reason 142
Palestine 258, 265–75
  Arab labour in 270–1
  Arab nationalism and Zionism 265,
    268–73
  Arab rebellion (1936–9) 273–4
  and Babylonia 56
  and the Balfour Declaration 266,
    267, 268, 271, 273
  early Jewish settlers 265–6, 269
  Peace Conference (1919) 266–8
  and the Romans 49, 79, 80
  Yishuv (civic Jewish community)
    273, 274
  Zionist land purchases 269, 270
  see also Zionism
papacy
  and Luther 159
  and the Spanish Inquisition 117–18,
    119–20, 121, 122
Paris Commune 151
Park, Robert 10–11
Parkes, James 208, 209–10
Paul the Apostle 70, 72, 75, 81
Pavluk (Cossack leader) 87
peasants, German 153
  uprisings 154–7
Péguy, Charles 256
Peirce, Charles Sanders 2
Persian Empire 49, 58–63, 64
  Jewish communities 61–2

phallus/penis distinction
  and Jewish diasporic strategies 16,
    17, 23
Pharisaic Revolution 30, 61, 76–7, 90,
  113
Philistines 49, 57
Phillipi 70
Philo Judaeus of Alexandria 67, 68,
  69–70
  Delegation to Gaius (Caligula) 72
philosophes 137–8, 142–50, 160
  and the racial conception of the Jews
    181
Phoenician alphabet
  and Aramaic 62
Pinheiro, Moses 93, 95
Pinsker, Leo 265
Plato 127
Poale Zion (the Workers of Zion) 274
pogroms 7, 263
  Jewish attitudes to 227
  Kishivev (1903) 10
  Kristallnacht (1938) 211, 231, 232
  and Polish Jews 86
Pol Pot 213
Poland
  Armenians in 12
  "Armia Krajowa" (Polish resistance
    movement) 259, 260
  Communist Party 258, 259
  death camps 244, 247, 248–52
  Galicia 235–6, 255
  Generalgouvernement 233–7, 244
  and Nazi Germany 217, 254
  Nazi invasion of (1939) 216–18
  Polish "corridor" 216–17
  and the Treaty of Brest-Litovsk 19
  Warsaw ghetto 235, 236, 253,
    258–62
  see also Polish Jews
Poliakov, Leon 83, 85, 101, 140–1
  on the battle of the Warsaw ghetto
    259–60, 261–2
  on Hegel 162
  on Marx 177
  on Nietzsche 188, 189
  on Rousseau 149
  on the *Shoah* (Holocaust) 246–57
  on Voltaire 144
  on Wagner 186, 187–8
Polish Commission for war crimes 249

Polish Jews 32–3, 83–9
  charters granted to 83
  and the Chmelnitzsky Uprising
    (1648–1649) 86–9, 98, 99, 102
  and the Enlightenment 112
  expulsions 83
  and Frankism 104–5
  ghettoization of 233–7
  and Hasidism 109, 110
  Jewish Councils (Judenräte) 234–7
  and the *kahal* 84–5
  labor force 236–7
  and Nazi Germany 207–8, 232–7,
    252
  numbers of 233
  occupations of 84
  and the Sabbatian movement 92, 94,
    97, 98–9, 100, 102–3, 104
  and "the Besht" 105–9
  and Yiddish 84
  youth resistance (*chalutzim*) 258–9
  see also Warsaw
Polish–Turkish War (1672) 103
polytheism 35–8, 39, 48
  and Kabbalism 129
  and Roman Jews 74
Pompey 70
Portugal 134–5, 151
postmodernism
  and the concept of diaspora 11
power
  cultural power of Jewish diasporas
    13–18
prayer
  Romans and the Jews at prayer 74
  sacrificial offerings replaced by 60
priestly people, Nietzsche on the Jews as
  a 190–1
Primo, Samuel 93–4
prooftexting 90, 113
prophets *see* Hebrew prophets
proselytism in Judaism 74–7
Protestantism
  and the Enlightenment 137, 154
  and German ideology 222
  and Jews in Germany 169
  and Left Hegelians 168
  Lutheranism 154–60, 161, 222
  in the United States 175
The Protocols of the Elders of Zion
  181

Prussia 152, 153–4, 161, 165
  Hegel and the Prussian state 161,
    165, 166–7, 168, 253–4
  Protestantism and political docility
    222
Ptolemy Philadelphus 4
Puritanism and capitalism 175, 176–7

Rabbinism 111, 112–13
racial segregation
  "Jim Crow" laws and black
    Americans 8, 180
racialist conception of the Jews 179,
  180, 181–4
  Chamberlain 182, 183–4, 215
  Gobineau 181–4
  and Nazi Germany 208–11, 215
  Tocqueville's rejection of 184
Ramah 60
Rath, Ernst von 211
Rauschning, Hermann 207
religious experience and Jewish history
  29–38
religious toleration
  and the Enlightenment 142–3, 150
  the Renaissance
  and the Enlightenment 150
resurrection, belief in 61, 90
Rhineland Jews 4, 5
Ribbentrop, Joachim von 247
Rivkin, Ellis
  The Shaping of a Jewish History 114
Roberts, Stephen 209–10
Röhm, Ernst 214–15
Roman, Charles Victor
  American Civilization and the Negro
    9–10
Roman Empire 64, 72–7
  and the concept of diaspora 10, 16
  and Egypt 67–9
  and Jewish religious experience 32
  Jewish revolt against Rome 4, 49, 78,
    227, 265
  and the Jews in exile 49
  the Near East 78–82
  Nietzsche on Roman values 191–2
  Roman Jews 70–1, 79–82
Roman law in Germany 155
Romania
  and Nazi Germany 217, 240, 254
Romantic movement 146, 161

Rosenberg, Alfred 199
  The Myth of the Twentienth Century
  215
Rosman, Moshe 29–30
  on European Jewish history
  32–5
Rousseau, Jean-Jacques 146–50,
  216
  Émile 146–7
  on Judaism and the Jews 148–50
  Social Contract 160–1
Russia
  and the Khazars 5
  Kishivev pogroms(1903) 10
  and the Treaty of Brest-Litovsk
  197–8
  see also Soviet Union
Russian Jews
  and Hasidism 111
  Zionists 265, 268
Russian serfs in the Ukraine 86–7
Ruthenia (Lvov) 85

Sabbatai Raphael 95
Sabbath observance 31, 60, 69
  Hegel on 162
  and Roman Jews 71, 73, 75
  and Sabbatai Zevi 94
Sabbatian movement 89, 90–103, 112,
  113, 136
  and Frankism 104–5
  and Islam 94–5
  life of Sabbatai Zevi 91–6
  Scholem's study of 89, 91, 97–103
sacrificial offerings
  human sacrifice and the Assyrians
  42, 56
  replaced by prayer 60
Sadduccees 30
Safran, William 5
Salonika 98, 103
Samaria 57–8
Saragossa 126, 134
Sargon 58
Sasportas, Jacob 93
Saxony 153
Scandinavian state
  and Nazi Germany 217
Scholem, Gershom 130
  and the Sabbatian movement 89, 91,
  97–103

science
  and the Enlightenment 137, 138
  and German Protestantism 154
secularism
  and Jewish emancipation 180–1
  and Left Hegelians 167
segregation
  and the Babylonian exiles 48–9
  "Jim Crow" laws and black
  Americans 8, 180
Seleucid Empire 69
Seneca 75
the Septuagint 4, 9, 65
serfdom
  abolition of in Prussia 153
  Russian serfs in the Ukraine 86–7
Seville
  conversos and the Inquisition 118–19,
  120, 123
  expulsion of Jews from 132
  massacres of Jews in 123, 126
Shammai school of Judaism 30
Sharett, Moshe (then Shertok) 273–4
Shirer, William L.
  The Rise and Fall of the Third Reich
  184, 197–8, 203
Shoah (Holocaust) 25, 226–57
  and the bureaucratic apparatus
  226–45
  and Christian churches 248, 254,
  255–6
  death camps 228, 247, 248–52
  and the euthanasia program 247–9
  expropriation of Jewish property
  229–30
  gas chambers/crematoria 250–1
  and German Jews 228–32
  and the German national character
  252–4
  and the Germany army 228,
  238–40
  ghetto diseases 237
  ghettoized communities 230–2,
  233–7, 253, 258–62
  and Hitler 242–5, 246, 247–9
  Jewish community leaders (*Judenräte*)
  231–2, 234–7
  marking of the Jews (Jewish star)
  230, 255
  mobile killing units (*Einsatzgruppen*)
  228, 238–42, 247, 257

and Nazi definition of Jews 229, 241–2
and Polish Jews 207–8, 232–7, 252–3
political differences between Eastern and Western Europe 254–5
the Reicht-Protektorat Area 230, 233, 234
and resistance 232, 235, 253
and the Soviet Union 238–40, 242
and the SS ("Death's Head") formations 251–2
and the term "final solution" 226, 238, 246
and total emigration (the Madagascar plan) 234, 246
and Zionism 274
Silverman 16
Simmel, Georg 11
Sixtus IV, Pope 117–18, 119–20
Skarga, Peter
Lives of the Saints 85–6
slave-morality of the Jews 15–16, 17–18, 70–1
and Nazi Germany 209
in Nietzsche 14–15, 17, 70–1, 189–90, 191–2
slavery
black slaves in America 8, 10, 17, 18–25
Jewish slaves in Rome 70
the Jews and Egyptian bondage 14, 15, 40, 164
Slavs 240
Slovakia 244
Smyrna
and the Sabbatian movement 93, 94, 100
Snyder, Timothy
Bloodlands: Europe Between Hitler and Stalin 256–7
social class
and Arab nationalism 271
and conversos in Spain 127
and the Enlightenment 150
and Kabbalism in Spain 129–30
and Polish Jews 83, 84, 85
and Prussia 153
and the rise of Nazism 196, 199, 203, 205
and the Sabbatian movement 98

social evolutionism
Hegel's theories of 163
social justice
and Kabbalism 129–30
see also Hebrew prophets
socialism
and Nazi Germany 214–15
Socratic inversion
of noble-warrior values 17–18
Sohm, Rudolf 222
Solomon, King 43
Sombart, Werner
The Jews and Modern Capitalism 176
Sophocles
Oedipus Rex 37
the soul
and the Hebrew prophets 46–7
Southeast Asia 5
Soviet Union
and German Communism 196
Katyn Forest massacre of Polish officers 232
and Nazi Germany 217, 218, 233, 238, 256–7
and Poland 233
Spain and Nazi Germany 217
Spanish Jews 114–35
and anti-Semitism 122–8, 130, 131–2
aristocracy 130
and Christianity 115–16
and conversos (new Christians) 117–26, 127, 131–2, 134
expulsion from Spain 132–5
and the Inquisition 117–22, 131, 134, 134–5
and Islam 114–15, 116
and Kabbalism 90, 128–30
and the laws on money-lending 116–17
pogroms (1391) 122–6
and the Reconquest 115, 132–3
Spinoza, B. 93, 138
Stäel, Madame de 157–8
Stahl, Heinrich 231
Stalin, Joseph 213, 217, 232, 238
Great Terror (1937–8) 256, 257
and Hitler 256–7
Stampp, Kenneth 21–2, 22–3, 180
state sovereignty
and the League of Nations 212–13

statelessness
    and the power of Jewish diasporas 14
Stiles, Ezra 142
Stirner, Max 167
Strabo, Greek geographer 67
Strauss, David Friedrich 167
Stroop, General Jürgen 260, 261
synagogues
    Babylonian exiles and the
        proto-synagogue 48–9, 62
    established as an institution 60, 62–3
    and the first-century diaspora 72
syncretism
    Hellenistic culture 64–6, 67–8, 69–70
    in Jewish history 34–5
Syria 50–1, 53, 68, 69, 74
    Antioch 66, 69, 73
    Damascus 69, 75
    and Hellenistic culture 65–6
    and the King-Crane Commission
        266–7
    Voltaire on 144
Szepticki, Monsignor 255

Tagenbund (Prussian secret society) 153
Talleyrand, Bishop 151
the Talmud 90, 136
    Talmudic learning and Hasidism 106,
        107, 112
Taoism 37
Taphnis (Daphna) 56
Tarragona 124
Tatars 87–8, 89, 100–1
taxes
    Jerusalem Temple tax 70, 80
    and Polish Jews 84–5
Tertullian 80
Thackeray, H. St John 30
the Crimea 72
Thessalonica 70
tikkun, concept of 90–1
Titus 4, 32, 49, 73, 81
Tocqueville, Alexis de 7, 173, 176
    Democracy in America 175, 184, 185
    and Gobineau's racialist theory 184,
        185
    The Old Regime and the French
        Revolution 185
Toland, John 139–40
    Reasons for Naturalizing the Jews in
        Great Britain and Ireland 140

Toledo 122, 123, 126, 132
Tolstoy, Leo 270
Torah (Jewish Law)
    as the Constitution of the Jews 59
    and Josephus on Jewish religious
        experience 31, 32
    and the Pharisees 76
    and the prophets 46, 48
    and Sabbatai 92
    and the synagogue 62
Torah-teachers (proto-rabbis) 62–3
Torquemada, Thomas de 119, 120, 121,
        122, 132
totalitarianism
    and Nazi Germany 213–16
trade
    diasporas 6
    and Jewish communities in the
        Persian Empire 61–2
transnationalism
    and the concept of diaspora 11
    transnational communities and
        diasporas 3
Treblinka death camp 249, 251
Trotsky, L. 14
Turkey
    expelled Spanish Jews in 135
    Polish–Turkish War (1672) 103
    religious toleration in 143
    and the Sabbatian movement 93–4,
        98, 99, 100, 101, 102, 103
    see also Ottoman Empire
Turner, Nat 21, 22
Tzaddikism 108, 109–11

Uebelhoer, Regierungs Präsident 236
Ukraine
    Armenians in 12
    and the Chmelnitzsky Uprising
        (1648–1649) 86–8
    Cossacks 87
    and Nazi Germany 254, 257
    and the Sabbatian movement 101
United States
    American Indians 7
    Civil War and slave emancipation
        180
    and the concept of diaspora 10–11
    Irish immigrants 7–8
    and the Jewish question 173–4
    Protestantism and capitalism 175

race riots (St Louis, 1917) 10
Tocqueville on racial inequalities and
democracy 184, 185
see also Afro-Americans

Valencia 121, 124, 125
Valerius Flaccus 70
value-rational action, Weber on 219
Versailles Treaty (1919) 197–9, 215
Vesey, Denmark 21, 22
Vespasian, Roman general 4, 32, 49,
78–9
victim diasporas 6
Vienna, Congress of 151
Volhynia 85
Volk concept in Germany 161
Voltaire 140, 143–6, 150, 181
Correspondence 144
Lettres de Memmius à Ciceron 144
Sermon du Rabbin Akib 143

Wagner, Richard 158–8
Autobiography 186
Das Judentum in Der Musik 186–7
The Flying Dutchman 186
and Nietzsche 188
Rienzi 186
"wandering Jew" image 4
Wannsee Conference (1942) 244
Warburton, William 140
Warsaw
ghetto 235, 236, 253, 258–62
Jews in 233
Judenrat 235
Weber, Max 14, 24, 36, 59, 112, 163
Ancient Judaism xii, 39–49
on bureaucracy 218, 219–25
on charismatic leadership 222–5
on concepts and ideal types 1, 2–3,
13
on goal-rational and value-rational
action 219
on Hellenized Jews 65
*The Protestant Ethic and the Spirit of
Capitalism* 176
Weimar Republic 195–7, 198–9, 202–5,
206, 210
and charismatic leadership 223–4
and Jewish community leaders 231
Weinreich, Max 28
Weizmann, Chaim 266, 268

Western Europe, Nazi occupation in
254–5
Westphalia 152
Whiston, William
*Essay Towards Restoring the True
Text of the Old Testament* 140
Wilhelm II, German Kaiser 195
Wilson, Woodrow 212, 266, 267
Wittgenstein, Ludwig 8, 12, 13
women
in the battle of the Warsaw ghetto
260
black slaves 20, 21–2
and first-century Judaism 75
Woodward, C. Van
The Strange Career of Jim Crow 180
Woolsten, Pastor 140–1
World War I
and Armenians 12
Jewish dead of 231
and Nazi anti-Semitism 210
political consequences of 212–14
post-war Zionism 266
and the rise of Nazism 195
World War II
battle of the Warsaw ghetto 258–62
and Hitler 242–3
and Nazi Germany 211, 217–18
and Zionism 274
Wright Mills, C. 222
Würtemberg 152, 153

Yemen 114
Yiddish 5, 84
Yohanan ben Zakkai 18
Yom Kippur War 274
Yugoslavia and Nazi Germany 217

Zacuto, Moses 93
Zalman of Ladi 111
Zalman Shneorsohn 111
Zaporozhian Cossacks 87
Zealots 30
Zedekiah, Judean King 52, 54
Zephaniah, Prophet 42, 53
Zerubabel 61
Zeus (Greek deity) 35, 37, 74
Zionism 26, 258–9, 263–75
and the Arab–Jewish conflict 273–5
and the black diaspora 8, 9, 24
Brit Shalom movement 271, 274

Zionism (*cont.*)
   and the Enlightenment 263, 265
   gender and Zionist ideology 16
   and the Hebrew prophets 263
   and Luther 159
   and the prophets of social justice
     263

   socialist groups 274
   Zionist settlers in Palestine 268–73
   see also Palestine
Zohar (The Book of Splendour) 90–1,
   93, 96, 102–3, 128, 130
Zola, Émile 264
Zoroastrianism 38